Sir Hans Singer

Sir Hans Singer

The Life and Work of a Development Economist

D. John Shaw

Foreword by Richard Jolly

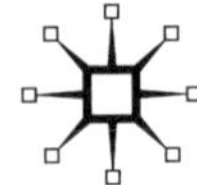

First published 2002 by
PALGRAVE MACMILLAN
Houndmills, Basingstoke, Hampshire RG21 6XS and
175 Fifth Avenue, New York, N. Y. 10010
Companies and representatives throughout the world

PALGRAVE MACMILLAN is the global academic imprint of the Palgrave
Macmillan division of St. Martin's Press, LLC and of Palgrave Macmillan Ltd.
Macmillan® is a registered trademark in the United States, United
Kingdom and other countries. Palgrave is a registered trademark in the
European Union and other countries.

ISBN 0–333–71130–0

This book is printed on paper suitable for recycling and made from fully
managed and sustained forest sources.

A catalogue record for this book is available from the British Library.

Library of Congress Cataloging-in-Publication Data
Shaw, D. John.
    Sir Hans Singer: the life and work of a development economist/
    D. John Shaw; foreword by Richard Jolly.
       p. cm.
    Includes bibliographical references and index.
    ISBN 0–333–71130–0 (cloth)
       1. Singer, Hans Wolfgang, 1910– 2. Economists–Great Britain–Biography.
    3. Development economics. I. Title.
    HB103.S56 S5 2002
    330'.92–dc21
    [B]   2002020728

10 9 8 7 6 5 4 3 2 1
11 10 09 08 07 06 05 04 03 02

Printed and bound in Great Britain by
Antony Rowe Ltd, Chippenham and Eastbourne

To the memory of
Ilse Plaut Singer,
wife, companion and
support of Hans Singer for 67 years

Contents

List of Illustrations

Lists of Tables and Figures

Tables

Figure

Foreword

Development economics, in many ways, is a subject of the last half-century. Though with roots deep in the classics of the last 200 years, notably of Adam Smith, Ricardo, Marx and John Stuart Mill, the burgeoning of ideas and writings on the development problems of the developing countries is a post-Second World War phenomenon. Beginning with the United Nations in the late 1940s, accelerating with a spate of articles and books in the 1950s and 1960s, development economics has maintained a momentum of writing and research, teaching and policy-making, which continues strongly today.

Of course, there have been fluctuations and waverings along the way. In the 1970s, some talked and wrote about the 'death' of development economics. In the 1980s, in the heyday of Thatcher–Reaganism, there was a neoclassical backlash arguing that economics as a science was universal – and any suggestion that a separate economics of development was needed to treat the problems of the poorer countries was plainly misguided. But the century ended with development economics an active field, especially in the Third World, Europe, and the international agencies.

Hans Singer has been a pioneer and leading contributor to development economics over the whole of this period, and indeed for a decade before and in the early years of the new century. His intellectual teachers were the greatest – Schumpeter in Bonn when Hans was an undergraduate followed by Keynes in Cambridge for his doctoral studies. After this, Hans worked on a study of unemployment in Britain undertaken by William Temple, then Archbishop of York, later of Canterbury. He lived with unemployed families in different towns of the depressed areas of Britain, consciously chosen to give him, and his other colleagues, a closer understanding of the human challenges of poverty and unemployment. These early experiences – including those of being a refugee from Hitler's Germany – laid intellectual foundations of the very highest quality and, equally important, lit a flame of passion and commitment against injustice and poverty, which has stayed with him throughout his life.

Hans' partnership with Ilse Plaut Singer over 67 years ensured that the flame of this commitment burned strongly. Married in 1934 in a ceremony taking only three days to organize, Hans and Ilse left

Germany in the darkening, early days of Hitler to move to the freedom of Cambridge, and later Manchester and Glasgow. In 1947, they moved to New York and 22 years later to Ovingdean in Sussex, England. Ilse was the one of the partnership who established the strongest links with these communities outside the intense and somewhat rarefied international atmosphere of development work. Hans never lost his intensely human touch – but it was Ilse who set it in the broader context of home, community and local politics, including feminist commitments.

As this intellectual biography makes clear, Hans Singer's output over his life has been prodigious – in articles and books, policy papers and memoranda, as well as in teaching and interaction with literally hundreds of professional colleagues and students. When proposing a toast on Hans' 75th birthday in 1985, I jokingly referred to the occasion as a 'mid-career' celebration. Little did I realize that in the decade and a half which followed, Hans would produce well over a hundred publications, making my speech less a jocular remark and more of a prediction.

There are several distinctive features of Hans' work. It is analytical but accessible, eschewing the mathematics, and even mathematical pyrotechnics, which characterize much economics of the last 40 years. It focuses on real life issues and reaches conclusions for policy – skilfully maintaining a balance between the particulars of the issue under review and the need to relate to broader issues of development policy and strategy. It has been consistently progressive without falling into the traps of fashion, ideology or political correctness. If there is one line where Hans' commitments have never wavered, it is to internationalism and the United Nations.

This has not been without its costs to Hans' influence on the wider economics profession of colleagues and students. For those in development economics and development studies, Hans Singer is a household name. But to the economics profession at large, Hans is a development specialist, whose work is known primarily for his pioneering contribution to the formulation of the Prebisch–Singer thesis (which, as John Shaw points out, in the light of recent research should really be known as the Singer–Prebisch thesis). But Hans' myriad of other contributions, including the ones of the last decade, are not widely recognized among the general economics profession. 'Not mainstream and thus not important', many would probably reply.

This is, in the view of those of us in development studies, a mistaken and most unfortunate attitude. In the globalizing world of the last quarter-century, issues of the developing countries are not only central to the concerns of 85 per cent of humanity. They are of central importance to the interests and well-being of the 15 per cent of the world's population living in the so-called 'developed' countries. It is a measure of the utterly short-sighted nature of much rich-country thinking that one had to wait for a massive rise in oil prices, as in the 1970s, or a collapse of the financial system, as in South-East Asia in the later 1990s, before the West woke up to the links between its own prosperity and Third World prosperity, development and stability.

Hans has never suffered from these delusions. For over 50 years, from the early days in the United Nations to his recent writings in the Institute of Development Studies, he has held a truly global view of the world economy. But more than this, Hans' view is people-centred. Economies exist for people – and economic performance is to be judged by how well, or how badly, each economy serves its people. This means taking account of the well-being of the whole population, young and old, the employed and unemployed, and those outside the labour force. It also means taking account of the international links between economies and how these affect people in other countries, especially how the rich economies of the world impact on people in the poorer countries.

On all of these matters, Hans has been endlessly creative in exploring the implications for policy. His mission has always been to understand the world in order to change it. It would be impossible to count the ideas and proposals put forward by him in his writings and speeches and through his interactions with colleagues and students. One of his endearing characteristics, often noted by friends and enemies alike, is Hans' indefatigable persistence in exploring new ways to tackle new and old problems. In the difficult and often exasperating world of development, many give up in despair or cynicism in their thirties or forties, some last to their fifties and sixties. Hans is still going strong – now in his nineties.

But to what effect? Many will ask this – as many have done about international policy and efforts ever since the United Nations was founded in 1945 and, indeed, before. An objective assessment is both more difficult and more subtle than many observers recognize. The test of any person engaged in making recommendations for policy is rarely decided by trying to give a simple answer to 'whether the recommendation was adopted and implemented or not'. Seldom is it possible to give a clear answer to such a question – and even if the answer is 'yes', further questions must be posed. Was the policy implemented as intended? What was the result – and was this result good or bad? Had circumstances changed, requiring modifications of the original policy, and had this been foreseen? And so on, and on and on.

In the United Nations Intellectual Project, which aims to analyze the evolution of key ideas and concepts about economic and social development within the United Nations system – in which Hans Singer figures prominently – we have been faced with a need to assess whether the ideas of the United Nations have on the whole made a positive impact or not. To do this, we have identified four ways in which ideas can have an impact on events by:

- influencing the ways issues and situations are perceived;
- defining an agenda for action;
- helping to build new alliances for change, which can serve to mobilize interest and action; and
- becoming institutionalized into some existing or new organization, which helps take the idea forward into action.

By all four of these more subtle tests, Hans' ideas and thinking have had considerable impact. The Singer–Prebisch thesis has changed for ever the way trade between the rich and the poor, the strong and the weak, is viewed and analyzed. Many disagreed, and for a substantial period of time econometricians declared the thesis not proven. But as John Shaw makes clear, current opinion now accepts the thesis as revealing a long-run trend. But this is not the point I want to make here. Ever since the thesis was first propounded in 1948, it has entered the literature of analysis and policy as a matter of necessary debate.

Hans has also made many contributions to agendas for policy and action. The study on unemployment in Britain in the 1930s, *Men Without Work*, underlined the need to pay attention to the impact of unemployment on a person's dignity and morale. His work in the United Nations on attempts to set up a Special United Nations Fund for Economic Development (SUNFED) in the 1950s placed on the agenda for action a long list of issues, some taken up later, as with the creation of the International Development Association (IDA), the soft-financing window of the World Bank. His work on savings and investment, on fungibility, on child nutrition and education, on food aid, on employment and technology in developing countries, on equity and redistribution – all these and dozens more have helped to define and enrich policy agendas in developing countries and in international agencies and organizations. Indeed, in drafting the *Proposals for Action* for the first United Nations Development Decade of the 1960s, Hans very specifically helped define an agenda for national and international action. The same could be said of the *Sussex Manifesto* on science and technology for developing countries, although this never achieved the formal recognition of the UN Development Decade.

Because of Hans Singer's clear style of communication and persistent relevance, his works have served to make an impact by the third criterion – serving as a focus around which interests could be mobilized. His work in mapping out approaches for people-focused development has been drawn upon by governments and NGOs as well as by international agencies to explore new ways forward. His work on employment and technology has probably been even more important than his theoretical work on trade.

By the fourth criterion, ideas gain influence by becoming embedded in new institutions, the creation of the United Nations Conference on Trade and Development (UNCTAD) is probably the clearest example – though even to say this is to recognize that UNCTAD had several parents and many midwives. If one has to identify a single parent, it would surely be Raul Prebisch. But Hans is also an intellectual co-parent. The problems of unequal trade relationships between developed and developing countries are embodied in the very foundations of UNCTAD, one of the most Third World oriented agencies of the UN system.

For other institutions also, Hans has played a formative role: in defining the rationale and roles of the UN World Food Programme; for UNICEF; the need and agenda for United Nations development research for social development, embodied in the UN Research Institute for Social Development (UNRISD); of industrial strategy embodied in the United Nations Industrial Development Organization (UNIDO); in supporting the enlargement of United Nations technical assistance leading to the UN Expanded Programme for Technical Assistance (EPTA) and subsequently to the UN Special Fund and the founding of the United Nations Development Programme (UNDP). In these ways, Hans Singer has helped to lay the institutional foundations of key elements of the United Nations system.

Hans has thus made an extraordinary impact on development thinking and practice, judged by all four avenues of influence.

John Shaw has performed a great service by documenting the record of these achievements in detail, with particular attention to Hans Singer's writings and intellectual contributions over the whole of his life. It is an extraordinary story and John Shaw brings out well the details and the particular features, Hans' special attributes as well as the twists of fate which set the stage for his exceptional contributions. But the story is one of seizing opportunities, rather than of preordained destiny. To this reader, and to many others who have know Hans well, it is his continuing commitment, his seemingly unlimited energy, and his indefatigable persistence, which has turned opportunity into achievement, made possible by the 67 years of partnership with his wife, Ilse.

Hans has never been one to make claims on his own behalf. His style and bearing is modest, and has always been. He has always had time, and made time, for students just as he has always been available for academic colleagues with some new matter to discuss, and for heads of UN agencies with yet another request for help. He has worn his achievements and successes, his honorary degrees and other awards, and his knighthood, with modesty and gentleness.

I recall in a hotel room in Kenya years ago, the difficulty with which the cleaning lady tried to take her leave. Hans thanked her and nodded politely after the room was cleaned. She smiled and nodded politely in return. But as Hans would not avert his gaze, so she also felt she could not avert hers. She had not had the usual dismissive signal to depart. The gentle standoff continued for a minute or two, until it was clear that the cleaning-lady must herself make the first move if any one was to depart. Hans' modest demeanour was, in a sense, her empowerment.

The United Nations system from the beginning has been built on the rights and dignity of every person – and on actions, political, economic, social and culture, to make this a reality in every part of the world. Hans Singer has contributed mightily to the achievement of this vision and, in his own way, demonstrated how it can be achieved.

RICHARD JOLLY
Honorary Professor of the
Institute of Development Studies at the
University of Sussex, UK,
and
Co-Director of the United Nations
Intellectual History Project,
City University, New York,
USA

Preface

I first met Hans Singer in Khartoum, Sudan, in 1963. At the time, I was teaching at the University of Khartoum. He was United Nations Special Adviser to the Executive Secretary of the then recently formed UN Economic Commission for Africa and was assisting the Government of Sudan with its first ten-year development plan. I subsequently became associated with the UN World Food Programme (WFP) in Rome, Italy, which continued for over 30 years. Hans Singer played a leading role both at the United Nations in New York and at the Food and Agriculture Organization of the United Nations (FAO) in Rome in the creation and continuation of WFP. Thus began a glorious friendship which has endured to the present time.

Over the past almost 40 years, Hans Singer has constantly encouraged me in my work. We have collaborated in a number of joint ventures and publications. I helped to organize and publish a *Festschrift* on the occasion of his 75th birthday and took part in, and contributed to, another *Festschrift* ten years later. Over time, I got to know the remarkable story of Hans Singer's development as a development economist, and the incredible amount of work he has produced not only for a better understanding of the difficulties of developing countries but also in seeking solution to their problems. It seemed to me that his life and experience deserved to be told. It has been both a privilege and a pleasure to write his biography. I hope that it will provide inspiration to future generations of development economists.

This is a selective, rather than comprehensive, intellectual biography. To cover all his work adequately would have required much more than one volume. I have endeavoured to show how Hans Singer's thought on, and understanding of, development issues evolved over the years. In order to do this, I have stayed close to the language he has used in his publications to portray both his sense of meaning and to convey his lucid and easy style and clarity of concepts. I have actually quoted his precise words in many places to give these effects. It is important that the reader observe the dates of publication of his works so that his views are placed in the context of the time in which they were made. A thematic rather than strict chronological approach has been followed within three broad time periods: the early years up to 1947, when he took up service in the United Nations; the years he spent in the UN up to his retirement in 1969; and the subsequent years up to the beginning of the new millennium.

I have also recognized the role that Hans Singer's wife, Ilse, played in providing the support and companionship, and domestic stability and contentment, that enabled him to devote entirely his considerable intellectual and academic ability and interests for the benefit of the developing countries and people. This biography is dedicated to her memory.

The terms 'underdeveloped' and 'developing' countries are used interchangeably throughout the text.

I should stress that although I have had the complete support and co-operation of Hans Singer, and many others, in writing this biography, this is my own personal account and assessment of his work and contribution to the field of development economics, which does not necessarily represent his or their views.

D. John Shaw

Acknowledgements

Writing this biography has involved the help of many people and institutions. Without their co-operation, it would not have been possible to have given all the details contained in this account. In many ways, this book is the outcome of their generosity of time, support and co-operation. I hope that I have adequately conveyed my sense of indebtedness to them and that they feel that the final product repays with gratitude all the assistance they gave me.

I begin my debts of gratitude with Hans Singer himself. He made available to me all his papers and publications, responded to my many questions, and read and commented in detail on the draft instalments of this biography as I produced them. I would also like to express my special appreciation to Richard Jolly not only for writing the *Foreword* to this biography but also for reading and commenting on the entire draft manuscript and for making available to me the transcripts of his interviews with Hans Singer for the United Nations Intellectual History Project, of which he is a co-director. Simon Maxwell also read the entire draft manuscript and provided perceptive comments. Both have known and worked closely with Hans Singer over many years and this biography has benefited considerably from their views and comments. The late Sir Alec Cairncross stimulated me throughout the writing of the biography, gave me his account of the time he spent with Hans Singer during their PhD studies together at Cambridge University, and made available to me the prolific correspondence that Hans Singer had with him during the period 1935 to 1951, which he had kept with care. David Sapsford read and commented on the material I have written on the Prebisch–Singer thesis, gave me an account of his own work on the subject, and provided copies of his papers. John Toye sent me the manuscript of the paper he produced with his son Richard on the origins of the Prebisch–Singer thesis as well as his comments on the section of the biography on that subject. Louis Emmerij gave me his personal account of Hans Singer's work for the ILO World Employment Programme and the Kenya employment mission in 1971/2, and of the award of Honorary Fellow to Hans Singer at the Institute of Social Studies in The Hague, The Netherlands, in 1977, of which he was Rector at the time. Wolfgang Stolper, Paul Streeten, Rameshwar Tandon, and the Director and Fellowship of the Institute of

Development Studies at the University of Sussex, United Kingdom gave me their encouragement. Hans Ulrich Esslinger and Neelamber Hatti shared with me their biographical accounts of Hans Singer's work. And Margaretta Jolly provided me with a transcript of the interviews she had with Ilse Singer in September 1997.

For their help and co-operation in guiding me through a vast amount of historical and archival material, I would like to record my sincere appreciation to: Mary Hall, former archivist and staff of the FAO Archives in Rome, Italy; Dr Marilla Bliss Guptil and staff of the United Nations Archives and Records Centre in New York; the Librarian and staff of the British Library of Development Studies, and of the University Library, at the University of Sussex, United Kingdom; Dr Mark Nicholls of the Department of Manuscripts and University Archives, Cambridge University Library; and Jacqueline Cox, Modern Archivist, King's College, Cambridge University.

Finally, I owe a special debt of gratitude to the outstanding and dedicated secretaries who have worked with Hans Singer since his arrival at the Institute of Developmental Studies in 1969: Judy Barrow, Margot Cameron, Kim Collins, Julia Cross, Caroline Pybus and the late Joyce Stacey. They were particularly helpful in compiling Hans Singer's academic honours, career and the list of his publications that appear in the appendix to this biography.

I alone am responsible for any shortcomings or errors that may be contained in this biography.

D. John Shaw

List of Abbreviations

ADB	African Development Bank
BBC	British Broadcasting Corporation
CCFF	Compensatory and Contingency Financing Facility (IMF)
CDF	Capital Development Fund (UN)
CFF	Compensatory Financing Facility (IMF)
ECA	Economic Commission for Africa (UN)
ECE	Economic Commission for Europe (UN)
ECLA	Economic Commission for Latin America (UN)
ECOSOC	Economic and Social Council (UN)
EOI	Export-oriented industrialization
EPTA	Expanded Program of Technical Assistance (UN)
ESCAP	Economic Commission for Asia and the Pacific (UN)
FAO	Food and Agriculture Organization of the United Nations
G7	Group of seven leading industrial countries (Canada, France, Germany, Italy, Japan, United Kingdom, United States)
GATT	General Agreement on Tariffs and Trade
GDP	Gross Domestic Product
GNP	Gross National Product
HIPC	Heavily indebted poor countries
IBRD	International Bank for Reconstruction and Development
ICOR	Incremental capital/output ratio
IDA	International Development Association (World Bank)
IDB	Inter-American Development Bank
IDS	Institute of Development Studies at the University of Sussex, UK
IEFR	International Emergency Food Reserve
IFC	International Finance Corporation (World Bank)
ILO	International Labour Organization
IMF	International Monetary Fund
IRA	Immediate response account (of the IEFR)
ISI	Import-substituting industrialization
ITO	International Trade Organization
LDC	Least-developed countries
NIEO	New international economic order
ODA	Official development assistance

OECD	Organisation for Economic Co-operation and Development
OPEC	Organization of Petroleum Exporting Countries
OPEX	UN programme for the provision of operational and executive personnel
R & D	Research and development
SDR	Special drawing rights (IMF)
SIDA	Swedish International Development Authority
SUNFED	Special United Nations Fund for Economic Development
TCDC	Technical co-operation among developing countries
UN	United Nations
UNCTAD	United Nations Conference on Trade and Development
UNDEA	United Nations Department of Economic Affairs
UNDP	United Nations Development Programme
UNEDA	United Nations Economic Development Administration
UNEP	United Nations Environment Programme
UNESCO	United Nations Educational, Scientific and Cultural Organization
UNICEF	United Nations Children's Fund
UNIDO	United Nations Industrial Organization
UNITAR	United Nations Institute for Training and Research
UNRISD	United Nations Research Institute for Social Development
UNRRA	United Nations Relief and Rehabilitation Agency
UNSF	United Nations Special Fund
UNTAB	United Nations Technical Assistance Board
USAID	United States Agency for International Development
WEP	World Employment Programme (ILO)
WFP	World Food Programme
WHO	World Health Organization
WTO	World Trade Organization

Part I

The Early Years (1910–47)

'	'Each is given a bag of tools
	A shapeless mass, a book of rules
	And each must make ere life is flown
	A stumbling block or a stepping stone.'

(Anon)

1
Growing Up in the Rhineland, Germany

Hans Wolfgang Singer was born on 29 November 1910 in Elberfeld in the Rhineland of Germany, which is now part of the town of Wuppertal. He was brought up as a member of a minority within a minority within a minority – in a Jewish community, within a Protestant enclave, in a largely Roman Catholic population. Identifying with groups that were oppressed or discriminated against, and with 'under-dog' minorities, was strongly impressed and bred into him by early experience.[1]

Singer was born into a strongly assimilated, largely secular, middle-class Jewish family. His father, Heinrich, a doctor, was a German patriot who voted for the liberal central party, the equivalent of the Liberal Democrats in the United Kingdom. His mother, Antonia, was a house-wife in the old style whose main interest was to look after the family. Singer had two younger brothers. One was two years his junior, with whom he never had a very close relation. He eventually became an industrial chemist and emigrated to Brazil when Hitler came to power. The other was born mentally handicapped and died at an early age.

Singer's early education was in the strictly classical tradition at the all-boys local gymnasium with nine years of Latin and six years of Greek, little mathematics, and history lessons that stopped at 1871. He grew up in a world of 'lost causes'. When he was eight, Germany had lost the First World War, and his father, who had served in the German army as a doctor, came back from the front with his health ruined. The part of Germany in which he lived was demilitarized and occupied by allied troops. One part of the Rhineland was in the British zone and the other in the French zone. Singer lived just inside the latter, but close to the former, in a kind of 'no-man's land'. Between the impressionable ages of thirteen and twenty, he experienced the great inflation of 1923 and the great depression of 1930–31 when everything around him seemed to crumble.

Two personalities in particular helped to form his outlook on life. One was his father who was extremely busy and hard-worked. He had a large practice and was always available for sick people. They could call him at any hour. He often treated the poor without charge. The second influence was the local rabbi, Dr Norden. He was a highly respected member of the local society, the model of a humane man. The instruction he gave was not so much about the Jewish religion as about ethics, moral values and civic responsibility. He was highly unorthodox and like most in the small Jewish community was fully assimilated into German society. Where Singer was brought up, most of the Jewish community had originally come from Spain. His mother's family ancestors had lived in the lower Rhineland for centuries. As a result, Singer was raised in a very liberal Jewish environment. The two reminders that he was Jewish were: the high Jewish holidays off from school, when he went to the synagogue; and the religious instruction he received from Dr Norden. Up to 1929, when he went to university, he never recalled any form of anti-Semitism.

Singer's father wanted him to follow in his footsteps and study medicine. But the inflation and depression of the 1920s and 1930s turned the attention of the schoolboy and young student to the study of economic and social problems and institutions. His already inquisitive mind led him to try to understand what had caused these economic catastrophes, and what might be done to overcome them. He got much of his economic news and ideas from the *Manchester Guardian Weekly*, which he read avidly with a largely self-taught English. In this way, he read about a certain 'Mr Keynes', who became an heroic figure because of his criticism of the war reparations imposed on Germany after the First World War by the Treaty of Versailles. At the time, there was never any hint that one day Singer would leave Germany and study under Keynes. Members of his community were very loyal Germans, and the idea that Hitler might take over did not occur until several years later.

2
Bonn University: The Influence of Schumpeter and Spiethoff

Singer enrolled at Bonn University in 1929 at the age of nineteen originally with the intention, encouraged by his father, to study medicine. He actually attended some lectures in the medical faculty until someone drew his attention to Joseph Schumpeter, the professor of economics, and said that he must hear him. He had not registered with the economics faculty but smuggled himself in as a member of the audience. It was a decisive moment. Schumpeter was a brilliant and stimulating lecturer. Singer came under his spell and immediately wanted to study economics. Schumpeter introduced a new world in economics and general thinking. He was the very antithesis of the traditional remote and austere German professor in every detail – dress, language, lecturing style, relations with students, conduct of examinations – and deliberately so. He opened doors to Walras and Pareto, to Anglo-Saxon economics, to sociology, quantitative methods and econometrics, to the history of economic thought, and to inter-disciplinary thinking. Above all, there was his admired masterpiece written long before at the early age of 28, his *Theory of Economic Development*, the textbook of the day, in which the dynamic, innovating entrepreneur was depicted as 'the linchpin of the capitalist system, responsible not just for technical progress but the very existence of a positive rate of profit in capital' (Blaug, 1986; Schumpeter, 1912, 1926, 1934).[2]

Singer was fortunate not only in finding Schumpeter an inspiring teacher but also in the exceptional circumstance that made him much more accessible to a young student than would normally have been the case, especially in the German university system which lacked the touch of college life and the tutorial system that he was later to find at Cambridge University. Schumpeter was a lonely man. He had lost a personal fortune, had failed in political life and as Austrian finance minister, and had been passed over in the election to the prestigious chair of economics at Berlin University. His adored wife had died before he went to Bonn and he was out of tune with the stiff German university tradition. For him, contact with a select group of students, which included Singer, in whom he sensed a response and a hope for the future, was a natural outlet. It was a mutual attraction, and it led to a kind of relationship unheard of in German universities.

Later, Singer realized more clearly than at the time how deeply relevant much of Schumpeter's teaching was to the development of poor countries and people. He singled out two particular themes from Schumpeter's *Theory of Economic Development*, which were to influence his own work at the United Nations and later in the Institute of Development Studies at the University of Sussex in the United Kingdom. He confessed that it took him many years of work in development studies before he came back to their full implications which now seem to him to be among the keys to an understanding of the problems of development of poor countries. First, the great importance of technology, innovation, access to innovation, and the ability and the means of linking innovation with the production process in the form of new products or processes or the development of new markets. Second, the emphasis placed on the fact that development represents a disruption of familiar and traditional processes of stationary circulation, arousing resistance and hurting established interests. As Schumpeter put it, 'By development we shall understand only such changes in economic life as are not forced upon it from without but arise by its own initiative, from within.' For Singer, this brought shades, in more modern parlance, of 'self-reliance', 'self-sustaining growth', 'dependency', 'backwash effects', and the like.[3]

The second dominant influence on Singer at Bonn University was Arthur Spiethoff, whom he described as 'the embodiment of Teutonic academic punctiliousness', the chronicler in minute detail of the history of trade cycles, and the pupil and admirer of Schmoller and his 'institutionalism'. Spiethoff perfectly complemented the broad macro-economic themes he learnt from Schumputer. From him, Singer learned to pay attention to detail, to take an interest in history (later to emerge in his interest in historical series, land values, unemployment and terms of trade), and to study institutions (leading to later interests in the working of international organizations and the role of the economist as adviser to governments in developing countries). After Singer received his diploma in political economy in 1931, he started work on

1.   Farewell party to Schumpeter at Bonn University in 1932 before taking up a professorship in economics at Harvard University in the United States (*Courtesy of Hans Singer*)

a PhD dissertation under Schumpeter's guidance, which was related to his theory of economic development. However, Schumpeter left Bonn in 1932 to take up a chair in economics at Harvard University in the United States (where he was to remain until his death in 1950). Spiethoff, who was head of department, became his supervisor.

Singer enjoyed a good relationship with Spiethoff, whose main interest was in trade cycles, and as part of that interest, cycles in the building industry. Under his influence, Singer started work on a dissertation on urban housing and urban land values (which he was later to complete at Cambridge University). Spiethoff gave Singer his first job as a research assistant. He also helped Spiethoff in editing the conference proceedings of the *Verein für Sozialpolitik* (the German equivalent of the Royal Economic Society in the United Kingdom), when he learnt how to sort out and present opposing views and to make a coherent report out of often fragmentary and incoherent discussion. This skill later stood him in good stead for his work in the United Nations.[4] Singer's PhD subject also merged into subsequent work on development problems, 'since the process of development is also a process of urbanization', and was to have a major influence on the initial assignment of his position and work in the United Nations (see later). Even more significant, Spiethoff, although a right-wing nationalist, probably saved Singer's life on more than one occasion by not permitting the Nazi detachments to enter the premises of the economics faculty at Bonn University to collect their 'opponents'.

Apart from Schumpeter and Spiethoff, Singer recognized that he also owed much to a selected group of outstanding fellow students, an 'inner circle' whom Schumpeter chose to talk to separately outside his lectures at his villa by the Rhine. From them, he learned his first 'real economics' and, beyond that, attitudes to life and the issues of the day. August Loesch, who was intellectually and morally inspiring, became famous as a location theorist,[5] and died a staunch anti-Nazi as a member of the religious (Protestant) resistance movement, having ignored all prospects of a prosperous career under the Nazis because he refused to take the oath of allegiance to the Fuhrer. Wolfgang Stolper, who emigrated to the United States, became a well-known collaborator of Paul Samuelson, professor of economics at the University of Michigan, and the biographer of Schumpeter (Stolper, 1994). Stolper recalled an incident which showed Singer's early interest in equipment to assist him in his econometric study of long-term historical data series (Stolper, in Sapsford and Chen, 1998a, p. 522). Spiethoff had bought a calculator, a big, noisy mechanical contraption which could just about do the four basic mathematical operations. The students were enthusiastic about this modern marvel, none more so that Singer, who demonstrated how simple it had now become to multiply 2×2!

Singer felt that he was fortunate to become a member of a group of contemporaries who had a great deal in common, many of whom became close and lifelong friends. In the days before Hitler, the group dominated the economics faculty's *Fachschaft* (faculty association) intellectually and, to some extent, also organizationally in a liberal and anti-Nazi direction. They were all loyal Germans and the idea that Hitler might take over did not occur to them. They were all staunch anti-Nazis, liberals and social democrats. Singer attributed his shortsightedness to the growing dangers of Nazism to the fact that he grew up in the somewhat sheltered and tolerant environment in the Rhineland. Since everybody was in a religious minority, it did not matter so much to which minority you belonged. He carried with him liberal values, a desire to understand the economic and social forces shaping the lives of common people, and a sense of identification with struggling and handicapped countries, groups of people and minorities.

But this safe and secure academic world was to be shattered when the Nazis came to power. Stolper recalls how vicious attacks were directed at Singer and how he, and members of his student group, met them head on (Stolper, in Sapsford and Chen, 1998a, p. 522). On one occasion, someone had written anti-Semitic remarks directed at Singer on the faculty bulletin board. Singer wrote beside the remarks, 'Will whoever wrote this at least sign his name, or else he is not only a swine but a coward', or words to that effect. With the help of a graphologist, the offender was identified and was expelled by the student Nazi sympathizers not for writing the remarks, but for having denied doing so.

In the nick of time, Singer managed to join Wolfgang Stolper in Switzerland in 1933 where Stolper was staying with his Swiss fiancée, who later became his wife. From there, then 22, Singer went to Istanbul, Turkey with the idea of opening an academic bookshop in partnership with Stolper's older brother. At the time, Kemal Pasha (Ataturk) was promoting his objective of modernizing and westernizing Turkey, which included plans for advancing Turkish universities along western lines. Asylum was offered to a number of well-established refugee scholars from Germany. Although Singer did not fit into that category, he harboured the hope of continuing his academic work under Wilhelm Ropke (an important figure in the development of social market economics who eventually ended his academic life at the University of Geneva in Switzerland). Singer had met Ropke in Germany who also became an academic refugee in Turkey. His intention was to work as a research assistant and finish his PhD dissertation.

Neither his hopes of establishing a bookshop nor of academic work advanced very far. Out of the blue, he received a letter from Richard (later Lord) Kahn informing him that he had been proposed for a scholarship in King's College at Cambridge University and inviting him to Cambridge for an interview. This was to have a dramatic effect on his future career. The letter mentioned that Singer had been recommended to Keynes by Schumpeter and as a result he stood a good chance of getting a scholarship. The mention of Keynes in Kahn's letter was the first intimation that Singer might actually have a chance of learning at the feet of the great economist whom had read about in his youth. Schumpeter, in his informal evening seminars in his villa by the Rhine, had impressed upon his students the importance of Keynes' monetary writings. Keynes was also immensely popular because of his book on German reparation problems following the First World War in which he had demonstrated that the punitive reparations demanded in the Treaty of Versailles could not be paid (Keynes, 1919).

Schumpeter therefore played a crucial role in the furtherance of Hans Singer's academic career. Singer had written to him on his departure from Germany asking for his help.[6] An opportunity came when the faculty of economics at Cambridge University decided to make a grant available from its reserve fund to help two German refugee students. Schumpeter wrote to Keynes recommending Singer. Austin Robinson, who was secretary of a small committee consisting of Pigou, Keynes and Clapham which interviewed the candidates, recalls that Singer was selected from a 'large number of others and saw much of him when he first arrived in Cambridge. How greatly he has justified our expectations!' (Robinson, 1976, p. 181). The interview was somewhat perfunctory. It was evident that Schumpeter's recommendation was instrumental in the decision to award Singer a two-year scholarship of 150 pounds sterling a year, plus meals in college, which was increased to 200 pounds in the second year.

On the strength of the scholarship, Singer returned briefly to Germany, and in the space of three days, and at the risk of being apprehended, married Ilse Lina Plaut in her home town of Hildesheim and left immediately for Cambridge. Hans had met Ilse at Bonn University where she studied medicine, and was engaged to her before he left for Istanbul. Despite being born into a wealthy family less than a year after Singer – her father was a banker – Ilse developed strong socialist and feminist principles from an early age and a deep concern for the underprivileged. Her subsequent life proved the old adage that 'behind every great man stands a largely unrecognized, but equally remarkable, woman'. She was not able to pursue a career in medicine. Instead, for the next 67 years, she was to dedicate herself to being a constant support and companion to Singer, to bringing up their two sons, but at the same time to engage in many voluntary activities on behalf of oppressed and disadvantaged people, especially women and children, until her death on 3 March 2001. She was more than a housewife and in many ways she practised what Singer 'preached' in his work and publications.[7]

Singer paid tribute to Turkey for its friendly and welcoming attitude towards the academic refugees from Nazi Germany, which probably saved many lives. He was certainly happy to be given such ready asylum even though he was still a graduate student and too young to make a contribution to modernizing Turkish universities in the western tradition.

2.   Wedding of Hans Singer and Ilse Lina Plaut in Hildesheim, Germany, on 24 March 1934 (*Courtesy of Hans Singer*)

3
Keynes and the Cambridge Economics School

As Alec (later Sir Alec) Cairncross, a fellow postgraduate student who became a close life-long friend of Singer, later recalled, Cambridge was unfamiliar territory to which it took some time to get accustomed (Cairncross, in Sapsford and Chen, 1998a, p. 12). The Singers' social life was restricted by their limited financial means reduced further by the fact that they had to rent furnished accommodation. They soon made friends from among university colleagues and the increasing number of refugees who had come to Cambridge. Singer took dinner twice or three times a week in college and immersed himself in his studies, ever conscious of the limited time he had to complete his PhD studies, and of taking full advantage of the wealth of outstanding talent which surrounded him. Up to 1935, the Singers and other refugees regarded their status as temporary and lived in the hope that Hitler would soon be overthrown. Up to that time, Singer harboured the idea of returning to Bonn after he had completed his PhD studies and taking up a university appointment. Thereafter, they realized that Nazism had become widespread and deep-rooted and return to Germany could not be contemplated in the near future. By that time, they were beginning to feel at home in the new surroundings.

In his first days, Singer was a little concerned to see a newspaper billboard which proclaimed 'Australia collapses'. He was much more deeply concerned when a day or two later the billboard read 'England collapses'. In his ignorance of test match cricket, he wondered if he had been a little rash to forsake the relative safety of Istanbul for the instability of England. Singer had also to conform to the routine and ritual of college life. On entering college, the porter would address him with the standard greeting, 'Nice day today!', if the weather was fine, to which Singer had to reply, 'Indeed!'. If the weather was not so good, the porter would say, 'Nasty day today!', to which Singer would reply, 'Rather!'. He had also to brush up his spoken and written English. For this he was fortunate to have the guidance of John Cairncross, the younger brother of Alec, who was also studying at Cambridge at the time. To Singer, his Scottish accent was infinitely more understandable than the tortured diction of the students from public schools. (There was no hint at the time that John Cairncross was to become the 'fifth man' and long sought Soviet agent (Cairncross, 1998).) He quickly developed an easy and lucid style, which became the hallmark of his subsequent writings.

The Germanic academic traits that Singer brought with him from Bonn were, however, fortified further by the unique atmosphere he found at Cambridge, with its reputation for 'thoroughness, accuracy and theoretical expertise' (Cairncross, 1993, p. 15). He was admitted to King's College at the height of the Keynesian consensus in 1934 to complete his PhD work on urban land values. Keynes was at work on his masterpiece, *The General Theory of Employment, Interest and Money* (Keynes, 1936). As Keynes put it, the new book switched attention to the *causes* and employment effects of changes in the level of output and, for the first time, provided a theory of demand and supply for output as a whole. The work became 'the bible of the economics profession and the politicians they advised' (Skidelsky, 1996, p. 70).

Singer found a similar collegiate spirit at Cambridge to that which he had enjoyed in Bonn, and a paradise after Hitler's Germany.[8] As he described it, 'Cambridge was the centre of the universe, King's College was the centre of Cambridge, and Keynes was the centre of King's College' (Singer, 1997e, p. 20). Around Keynes there was a much-envied 'inner circle' with direct access to Keynes, and with whom Keynes exchanged early ideas and drafts for his *General Theory*. Singer included Colin Clark, Maurice Dobb, Claude Guillebaud, James Meade, Richard Kahn, Dennis Robertson, Austin and Joan Robinson, Gerald Shove and Piero Sraffa in the inner circle, and exclaimed 'With such teachers, one would have had to be hopeless indeed *not* to have learned' (original emphasis) (Singer, 1992j, p. 6). Then there was an 'outer circle' of eager and talented graduate students and selected undergraduates including David Bensusan-Butt, Bob Bryce, David Champernowne, Alec Cairncross, V. K. R. V. Rao, Brian Reddaway and Lorie Tarshis, to which Singer was admitted.

Singer had the good fortune to be enrolled in King's College. Richard Kahn played a prominent role in helping him to get through the early days, guiding his first reading and discussions toward an understanding of economics at the level, and of the kind, practised in Cambridge in

general, and the emerging new economics of the *General Theory* in particular. He considered himself fortunate to have as his guide the discoverer
of the 'multiplier', and one who was so closely in touch with the germi-
nation of Keynesian thinking.

Singer had hoped that Keynes would be his supervisor since he was
in Keynes' college and Keynes had agreed. But in the summer of 1934,
not only was Keynes bound up with the writing of *The General Theory*,
and numerous other demands on his time, but he fell ill and requested
Colin Clark to be Singer's supervisor. Singer acknowledged the role
that Colin Clark played as the supervisor of his work on his PhD thesis.
Through him, he was able to learn the 'tricks' of national income
accounting against an understanding of the Keynesian model on
which it was based. It was mainly through Colin Clark that he maintained an interest in statistics and statistical techniques, which was
vital for his PhD work on urban land values, subsequent analysis of
employment statistics, and a later interest in development models,
starting from the Harrod–Domar model. Keynes often asked about the
progress of Singer's doctoral dissertation and was invariably kind and
patient in answering questions. His discussion and acceptance of
Singer's early notes and later Singer's articles for *The Economic Journal*
(of which Keynes was editor) were also a great encouragement. Singer
still remembers vividly the mental block he had to overcome when
addressing him not as 'Professor or Dr Keynes', but as plain 'Mr Keynes'.
Coming from the hierarchical structure of German academic life, this
was difficult to reconcile with Keynes' eminence, but was somewhat
reminiscent of the attitude of Schumpeter.

Singer also came to know something about Keynes' humorous side.
He remembered Keynes coming down to breakfast chortling over the
answer he proposed to send to those who kept thrusting their books on
him for review: 'Mr Keynes thanks Mr X for sending him his book and
will lose no time in reading it' (Cairncross, 1998, p. 50).

Singer also acknowledged his debt to his fellow students for helping
him to be quickly assimilated into the Cambridge environment despite
his initial disadvantages of background and language. They listened
eagerly to Keynes' lectures in Mill Lane, by the river, in Cambridge,
and to his trial runs of successive drafts of the chapters of *The General
Theory*. They keenly discussed his lectures among themselves and with
members of Keynes' inner circle. They also eagerly followed the
progress of the writing of *The General Theory* through the conduits of
Richard Kahn and David Bensusan-Butt, a research assistant of Keynes,
who were best informed on the latest developments.

Peter Drucker who, like Singer, also attended seminars of both Schumpeter and Keynes, had a different view of Keynes' lectures (*Financial Times*, 1999). He regarded both masters as 'miserable teacher: though Schumpeter was very good in small seminars'. The Keynes seminar had about 30 people and was a 'theatrical production'. Keynes would lecture for about 20 minutes, pointing to a formula on an enormous blackboard. Then he would exit and in would come Richard Kahn who would wipe the blackboard clean and without saying a word would write equations for about 25 minutes and then exit. Keynes would then re-enter the room and lecture on the new equations in turn. Drucker said that the students had a theory that they were the same person: 'one talked, the other scribbled'.

Singer observed that Keynes was a 'passionate and habitual conversationalist' (Jöhr and Singer, 1955, p. 93; see also Harrod, 1951). For him, conversation and discussion were ways of achieving that 'amalgam of logic and intuition and the wide knowledge of facts, most of which are not precise', which he considered the prerequisite for judging economic problems. On reflection, Singer noted that conversation and discussion served a number of functions. They avoided overlooking any important points of view. They provided an opportunity for testing the correctness of criteria. They provided information about the existing situation and 'gave a living content to the bareness of statistical data'. And they enabled him to estimate correctly the indirect effects of the measures he was contemplating. Singer was to carry the benefits of conversation and discussion with him to his work at the United Nations.

Although direct contact with Keynes was limited, Singer was admitted into the Political Economy Club, which met in Keynes' rooms in King's College. He recalls that Richard Kahn went around the assembled graduate students with slips of paper. If a numbered slip was drawn, students had to speak in the discussion on the subject of the day, in the order of the numbers drawn, in the presence of Keynes. Singer had two vivid memories of these meetings. One was the mixture of fear and hope of drawing a number: fear of having nothing to say and making a fool of oneself; and the hope of saying something that drew Keynes' attention and support in his summing up. The second memory was that speakers had to stand in front of a roaring fire so that when he subsequently thought of the club, he still had a burning sensation on the relevant parts of his anatomy.

Another regular meeting was the Oxford–Cambridge–London School of Economics seminars, which rotated among the three locations and

3.   Sir Alec Cairncross and Sir Hans Singer at the Conference held at the Grillhof Conference Centre, Vill, Innsbruck, Austria to celebrate the latter's 85th birthday, 5 May 1996 (*Professor David Sapsford*)

were held over weekends. Lively debates were held among graduate students and young faculty members of the three universities. Singer recalls, for example, the occasion when the Polish economist Michal Kalecki and Tjalling Koopmans came to blows physically over, of all things, the definition of 'liquidity preference'. The participants took their discussions very seriously.

Singer had two other PhD student colleagues in economics with whom he established life-long friendships. One was Alec Cairncross. He became Professor of Applied Economics at Glasgow University, economic adviser to the OECD, director of the Economic Section of the Treasury and head of the Government Economic Service during the British Labour government administration of Harold Wilson, master of St. Peter's College, Oxford University and chancellor of Glasgow University. The other was V. K. R. V. ('Alphabet') Rao. He became a leading Indian economist, founder and director of the New Delhi Institute of Economic Growth, vice-chancellor of Delhi University, a minister in India's federal government, and founder of the Economic and Social Research Institute in Bangalore. Colin Clark was supervisor of the PhD work of both Rao and Singer, who discussed their work together. This was one of the earliest occasions when Singer thought about the problems of developing countries. Rao's dissertation was on *The National Income of British India, 1931–32*. His and Singer's dissertations were approved on the same day. Singer took his degree on 13 November 1936 and Rao on 12 March 1937, both by proxy, only the third and fourth candidates to be awarded a PhD in economics from Cambridge University (after George Jones and Alec Cairncross).[9] Later, Singer was to visit India on a number of occasions and lectured at the Delhi School of Economics.

Singer's dissertation, entitled *Materials for the Study of Urban Ground Rent*, established that for the period 1845 to 1913 the two dominant factors in the accumulation of urban ground rents were: the progress of urbanization; and the increase in incomes (Cambridge University Dissertations, 1936–37, pp. 69–70; see also Singer, 1942a). A statistical regularity was described, and an index of urbanization derived from it, which allowed measurement and inter-temporal and inter-local comparisons of the state of urbanization. Schwabe's Law, on the relationship between income and expenditure on house rents, was analyzed and shown to be formally correct, but concealed the real connection and gave rise to various errors.

The accumulation of urban ground rents from 1845 to 1913 was statistically determined and an index of house rents constructed.

Fluctuations in the rate of accumulation of urban ground rents were attributed to changes in building costs rather than to changes in house rents. The application of the statistical method devised for this purpose to the post-First World War situation led to the interesting result that, to a large extent, current land values were based on expectations of rising rents, falling building costs, or building subsidies. One of these three factors would have to happen if the permanent renewal of existing building was to be secured.

The theory that urban ground rents were to be explained by causes operating through the demand for house-room was considered and rejected. This theory drew a sharp theoretical distinction between agricultural and urban ground rents but minimized the social and economic effects of the latter. The significance of the transference of income involved in the payment of urban ground rent was stressed. However, the conclusion was drawn from a calculation of income elasticity of the demand for house-room that, for the abolition of overcrowding, more would be needed than mere elimination of urban ground rents. Although Singer's formidable statistical and analytical work was never published, a synopsis of its findings was produced in an article in 1942 (Singer, 1942a) and Colin Clark summarized its results in his *National Income and Outlay* (published by Macmillan, 1937) and his *Conditions of Economic Progress* (Macmillan, 1940).

Schumpeter visited Cambridge several times during Singer's period of study there. It was a great disappointment to Singer to find that the two great beacons in his academic development as an economist did not get on well together. Both initially respected each other's work but after *The General Theory* was published, and many of Schumpeter's followers became Keynesians, and when Keynes became successful in other fields where Schumpeter had dismally failed, Schumpeter turned against Keynes and even accused him of being a warmonger and of trying to influence President Roosevelt to enter the Second World War on the British side. As a result, Schumpeter was suspected of being a German agent and became an isolated figure at Harvard. Schumpeter was scathing about the Anglo-Saxon tradition of not properly distinguishing between interest and profit, and investment and enterprise, and for concentrating on the conditions of static equilibrium rather than the forces of innovation. He had little sympathy, therefore, with Keynes' methods (Skidelsky, 1992, p. 704).

When asked what he had learned from Keynes that he was to apply directly to his later work in development economics, Singer once replied 'everything'. More analytically, however, Singer identified six key elements (Singer, 1976a, pp. 8–10):

- The macroeconomic framework, the interlinking of consumption/ savings/investment and public/private sector accounts, the importance of thinking in real terms as well as appreciating the monetary factors involved. It was difficult to see how to sort out the problems of development policy without such a framework as a starting point.
- There were also the Keynesian values. Singer felt these were nowhere better expressed than in Keynes' essay on *Economic Possibilities for Our Grandchildren*, though also inherent in his *The General Theory* and *The Means of Prosperity*. The real resources of a country were its people. The purpose of economic policy and analysis should be to prevent the waste and dissipation of human resources.
- Keynes was the admired example of a man combining a supreme standard of intellect and theory with involvement in the problems of the day.
- Then there was the Keynesian belief that we are in control of our own destiny, and that by social and economic planning, socially agreed objectives can be achieved.
- In a more technical sense, Keynesian demand analysis had a great deal of application to the situations of developing countries.
- Much of the emphasis placed in development strategies on the reduction of poverty by means of the creation of productive employment was based on the Keynesian model in which fuller employment and economic growth are complementary instead of trade-offs.

Subsequently, perhaps more than any other person, Singer was to advocate the value of the Keynesian consensus in solving the problems of developing countries in a number of papers that appeared over many years (e.g. Singer 1984c, 1992j, 1998c).

4
Early Employment and Experience

The Pilgrim Trust unemployment enquiry (1936–38)

Singer's first employment after Cambridge was to have a profound and lasting effect on his later work and career. In 1936, the influential Pilgrim Trust in the United Kingdom embarked upon a major enquiry into high and protracted unemployment that existed in the depressed areas of Britain. The study was conducted under the supervision of a high-level committee with William Temple (then the Archbishop of York, later Archbishop of Canterbury) as chairman and Sir William (later Lord) Beveridge (the author of the famous 'Beveridge Plan' of 1942 on social welfare – see below) as its main adviser. Both men were to have a strong influence on Singer's future thinking in addition to the circles of teachers and friends he had enjoyed in Bonn and Cambridge.

A detailed investigation into the causes and effects of unemployment was to be conducted on the basis of a sample survey in various parts of the country. Two researchers had already been recruited to carry out the survey – Walter Oakeshott (a master at Winchester College, a leading English public school, and subsequently Rector of Lincoln College, and vice-chancellor, of Oxford University) and David Owen (secretary of the civics section of Political and Economic Planning (PEP) in London, who subsequently became the first head of the UN Economic Affairs Department and later co-administrator of UNDP). A third member of the team was required, particularly to link the findings of the survey with macroeconomic policies and also to act as the statistician and data analyst of the group. Singer was recommended from Cambridge, presumably by Keynes who had developed a special interest in the problem of unemployment as a central part of his economic thinking.

Dr Wagner, a psychologist who had taken part in the survey of unemployment carried out in Marienthal in Austria, [10] was also engaged for the enquiry, as was Eleanora Iredale, the secretary to Archbishop Temple's unemployment committee and initiator of all the enquiry's activities, who devoted special attention to that part of the enquiry which related to women. A distinctive feature of the enquiry was that although the members of the team were specialists in their own subject, the whole team shared fully the work of drafting the report.

Singer was apprehensive at first. This was a new world to him. He had great difficulty in understanding the language and dialects of the unemployed people he lived with. He was puzzled, for example, when they referred to the staff of the Unemployment Assistance Board, the body responsible for means-tested payments to the long-term unemployed, as 'buggers', and called for a translation from his co-workers. He was also worried whether being a foreigner would work against him. But he found exactly the opposite. It actually helped because nobody suspected him of being a spy for the Unemployed Assistance Board, and confided in him without fear. It was always possible that the team would be treated as informers and that if they observed that someone was making some income on the side, they would be denounced to officials. The team was therefore very careful to establish its completely non-official credentials, which was easier to do in Singer's case.

The survey had particular characteristics which were to make a strong impression on a young economist starting out on his professional career. It was to be an inter-disciplinary study, which provided the sharpest possible reminder that economics was a social science affecting the lives of people in a direct and profound way. Far from being a desk study, the team was to immerse itself in the lives of the unemployed by living with them in the poor areas of the country, tracing back their life histories, trying to understand their concerns, and thinking about answers to their problems. Its was to be a team effort. By living together, and continuously exchanging ideas and impressions, they learned from each other in a way that only those who have taken part in such projects can realize. (This experience was to repeat itself many times later in Singer's work at the United Nations and in the joint projects with friends and colleagues in the Institute of Development Studies at the University of Sussex in the United Kingdom.) Finally, it was not an academic study but was to lead to practical results, which was assured by the influential committee to whom the team reported.

The report that was produced remains one of the best of its kind (Oakeshott, Owen and Singer, 1938a). In his *Introduction* to the report, Archbishop Temple recalled that in 1933, when unemployment in Britain was still at its worst, he had invited a group of people to consult with him about the problem. The committee which he formed became convinced that there was need for a thorough investigation into the effects of unemployment and the real needs of the unemployed, beginning with an account of the unemployed themselves. At the suggestion of Sir William Beveridge, the investigation focused on the effects of what was called 'long employment', i.e., unemployment continued for more than one year, a new problem on an unprecedented scale which involved not only an economic burden for the country but a real danger of moral decay. Archbishop Temple found 'Much of (the report) was novel, even to those expert in the subject. And it is a genuinely human document, which being readable as well as scientific, may well win the attention of a large public.'

Since the First World War, unemployment had been 'one of the greatest social problems' of Britain. But little was known in detail of the poverty and distress it caused. A sample survey technique was adopted involving about a thousand long-term unemployed, interviewed in their homes, in six depressed areas of the country. The selection of those included in the survey was taken at random from the live register of the Unemployment Assistance Board, the body responsible for the maintenance of the long-term unemployed. In November 1936, when the sample enquiry was undertaken, a cycle of three years of growing depression, followed by four years of recovery, had just been completed and 27 out of 100 people were still unemployed. The burden fell not only on the unemployed themselves but also on their wives, whose burden was perhaps the heaviest of all, and young children.

For the first time, the report produced a detailed statistical account of the dimensions of, and local differences in, long-term unemployed, based mainly on the work of Singer, for which he was awarded the Frances Wood Memorial Prize of the Royal Statistical Society (Singer, 1938b-f). By its terms of reference, the enquiry was directed to consider the effects of unemployment on those most affected, including its economic, physical, psychological and moral effects. The report examined various aspects of long-term unemployment including the cycle of working-class economic life. It measured the income of the long-term unemployed; analyzed the types of households affected and the performance of housekeeping on very low incomes; the effects of unemployment on household income and the resultant economies and debts; on living conditions, the physical environment and employability; and on health standards. In an interim paper of the enquiry on unemployment and health, Singer found that the effects of unemployment were traceable 'only in a comparatively slight degree' in the figures of infantile mortality, diphtheria, and various other diseases, but the connection was clear in the case of maternal child-birth mortality not only because of the effects of nervous strain and malnutrition but also of economies in the public medical services (Singer, 1938f). Even so, the instinct to shield children in the worst-affected households remained. The team justified the length to which it treated these various dimensions of poverty in that it provided material background against which all the dimensions and difficulties of unemployment could be gauged. This was done by actually visiting the homes of the long-term unemployed. To meet the unemployed themselves was to be aware of depression, apathy, physical deterioration, and other things. But it was only by contact with them in their houses that the full dimensions of the poverty associated with unemployment could be realized.

The wide scope of the enquiry also included the psychological and moral problems of unemployment, including the willingness of the unemployed to work and the effects on independence and respectability. Well ahead of its time, it also dealt in detail with the effects of unemployment on women. The problem of women was recognized as being more complicated than that of men. A woman, whether employed or unemployed, had to try to fulfil not just one role but three. She had to be mother, wife and breadwinner at the same time, and often played a key role in coping with the effects of unemployment on the household as a whole. The report ended with an analysis of the roles of the social service movement, the voluntary agencies and social clubs, in coping with the problems of unemployment. The survey showed that these services were often underfunded, and that the main direction of their work would have to be in the hands of bodies well acquainted with the conditions of their regions. The survey of the work done by voluntary agencies for the unemployed ended by raising the question as to whether this system could become the foundation for a new approach, through which people could find opportunities to develop new interests and friendships. Unemployment had shown the need for such a system.

When Walter (by then Sir Walter) Oakeshott died in 1987, for his memorial service Singer chose selected passages from the chapter on 'Moral Problems' of *Men without Work*. He said:

It looks as though some new principle will have to be put into operation whereby a man is offered the chance to give as well as to receive. Within two years of writing this, the war called upon these men to give. We can best honour Walter Oakeshott's memory by striving for a society in which all have a chance to give as well as to receive. My enduring memory is how again and again, first in discussing our impressions and notes from our interviews, and then in writing our report, he lifted our eyes from the collections and tabulations to the meaning and significance of what we had found – a real problem of waste: of material, potentially good which was rotting for lack of use.

Unemployment and the unemployed (1940)

By the time the results of the enquiry were published in 1938, war was brewing again, rearmament had become an accepted policy, the worst of the economic depression was over, and unemployment was beginning to fall. But Singer was to reveal a foresight, which was to be repeated later in his career. He had been deeply impressed by his experience in working on the unemployment enquiry and maintained his interest in the subject of unemployment and the unemployed. Although the results of the Pilgrim Trust enquiry had been summarized in *Men without Work*, a wealth of impressions and material had been left behind, which Singer used to produce articles for the *Review of Economic Studies* and another book, completed before the outbreak of the Second World War but published during the war in 1940, on *Unemployment and the Unemployed* (Singer, 1938j, 1938k, 1940a). While the war temporarily eclipsed the 'grave social problem' of unemployment, Singer warned that it was likely to return again. He recalled that the problem of heavy unemployment between 1920 and 1939 originated in the economic collapse terminating a hectic post-First World War boom. Singer reasoned that it was not too early to think about the best ways of handling the problem before it returned again. The policy evolved in the previous twenty years embodied experience from which to learn and to avoid the mistakes of the past. The object of his book was to review this experience and the issues involved. He gave an almost clinical examination and explanation of the causes and various stages and conditions of unemployment. All this was to stand him in good stead for his later work on developing countries at the United Nations and later in the Institute of Development Studies (IDS).

At the time of writing the book (March 1939), there were still two million people unemployed in the United Kingdom. Singer noted that few ordinary people could comprehend that figure (adding, somewhat knowingly, that statisticians 'could not imagine any figure lower than one million'). This represented one out of every seven working persons in the country. Singer distinguished between what he called the 'standing army' and the 'stage army' of the unemployed. The former were the long-term unemployed who were permanently out of work. The latter were employed for short periods in between long periods of unemployment. They had no certainty that they would get a job, whether the new job would be in their own trade, what working conditions or wages would be, where the employment would be, and what the working hours would be. It was this element of fear and uncertainty which was one of the main dangers of unemployment. It was perhaps more pronounced among the temporary than the permanently unemployed 'who had got used to expecting nothing'. Only small 'sheltered corners' of the labour market were free from fear of unemployment and insecurity. The highest degree of skill was no protection as it could soon become obsolete.

Singer then set about explaining, in the simplest language, what had been the past attempts to bring unemployment down to an 'irreducible minimum'. One policy was to reduce the number of people competing for jobs by, for example, encouraging early retirement, pensioning people off at an early age in the depressed areas, and taking jobs away from women, immigrants and minority groups. This was not a cure but an alleviation of unemployment, 'a reduction in unemployment statistics'. The danger of this policy was that it was so popular yet, in reality, represented a 'policy of despair' that nothing could be done to solve the problem.

Another policy he characterized as the 'treasury view', which in essence was that the number of jobs going was fixed by the extent to which employers found it worthwhile to offer jobs. The 'treasury view' had two schools: those who believed that nothing could be done; and those who felt that unemployment could be reduced by making it easy, tempting and worthwhile for private enterprise to create a large number of jobs on its own so that no vain attempt needed to be made to increase the number employed artificially.

The main means of tempting private enterprise to do so was to give free and easy access to the capital they needed to create new jobs in what was known as a 'policy of cheap money'. This policy had been used successfully in the fight out of the great depression of the 1930s up to a certain point. It was not difficult to see what that point was. Cheap money increased the number of jobs in occupations requiring the acquisition of additional 'capital' (i.e., machines and material) by the employer, and particularly where the outlay of capital came all at once, and not gradually over the course of time by the additional jobs themselves as, for example, in the building industry where the capital cost of building houses had to be found at once before work could start. Afterwards, relatively little capital was required for maintenance work.

The building boom of the 1930s had gone a long way towards dealing with the unemployment problem. But there were two snags. First, cheap money favoured the 'once and for all' type of employment and therefore tended to bring about a precarious, unreliable and unstable improvement in employment. Secondly, it made it easy and cheap only for those employers who needed new capital for expansion and the erection of new plant. It did not encourage those employers whose problem was to set some of the idle old capital to work in providing new jobs. This was the situation in those trades where employment was slack and demand had fallen off, leaving much of the existing capital idle, as in the depressed 'heavy' industries such as coal-mining, ship-building, iron and steel making, and the textile industry. Thus, while the policy of 'cheap money' helped the growth of those trades which were already growing, it did little to avert or mitigate decline in those industries which were decaying. While unemployment was diminished, therefore, that process was unequally distributed, leading to the creation of what came to be known as 'depressed areas'.

Singer set out to dispel the idea that there was 'a fixed pool of jobs' and replace it with the notion that jobs may be sufficient but that people could not gain access to them. Machinery was necessary to bring people and jobs together. He identified five barriers to bringing this about, based on the results of the Pilgrim Trust unemployment enquiry. The first barrier was that of *distance*. People were located in places where jobs were not available, and vice versa. The second barrier was lack of *skills*. The majority of the unemployed belonged to two classes of workers: unskilled labourer; and workers highly skilled in only doing certain types of work. The greatest demand was for semi-skilled workers who, above all, were 'machine minded', particularly in the new light industries. The barriers of distance and skills came together to create the problem of the depressed areas. The third barrier, or what Singer called the 'centre of breakdown', was that of *age*. The proportion of jobs for young people was much higher than the proportion of young people wanting jobs. Some of the difficulties in getting the family man and older men into work arose because the family allowance system did not work upward from the standard wage of the family man but downward from the standard wage for the young man. Apart from the question of wages was that of efficiency. Many employers assumed that young men were more mechanically minded and better able to cope with mechanical work, which was not always the case. The fourth barrier was that of *gender*. The bulk of unemployment consisted of men, whereas a large proportion of new jobs were for females and younger people based on lower wages. In that sense, the fourth barrier was one of wages rather than gender. The final barrier was *trade*. Between the two world wars, Britain was faced, for the first time, with the problem that particularly important trades, which had formerly been the pillars of the economic structure, were on the decline. New jobs were being created in trades to which people did not belong, and people were attached to trades in which no jobs were going. The most important thing to be done about unemployment, therefore, was to remove these barriers between people and jobs.

Singer described in detail the nature of these barriers in the depressed areas of Britain, and how to remove them.[11] He pointed out that depressed areas had existed before the First World War. Four factors had 'solved' the problem in the past. (a) The unemployed had taken up other trades which were very similar in nature to the old trade but had not been affected by the same decline. (b) Some reduced their customary standard of living and accepted work as unskilled labourers elsewhere. (c) For others there was actual starvation and a removal to workhouses. And (d) there was large-scale emigration overseas. These four 'remedies' were no longer available; other solutions had to be found. Two policies had been applied simultaneously: getting people to where the jobs were; and taking jobs to the people. But Singer showed that both involved some contradictions, required complicated machinery, and were often not much better than doing nothing at all. He also exploded the myth that the unemployed were a homogeneous group, identifying no less than sixteen different 'unemployments', which he classified into four groups: temporary unemployment caused by an interruption in the normal production process, as, for example, when there was a temporary scarcity of raw materials; temporary unemployment caused by seasonal slackness in the production process; longer-term unemployment caused by technological change; and unemployment caused by artificial restrictions in production with the purpose of keeping prices up through creating artificial scarcities.

Singer was at pains to point out the differences among unemployed people, that they did not live in isolation, and that the policy of providing 'maintenance' for them was distinctly different from looking after their 'welfare'. He went further to assert the importance of the non-economic effects of unemployment – that work meant often more than just providing a living, and gave people a status in their communities and a sense of dignity, and the most satisfactory, or only, means of self-expression. Any policy that was devised for the unemployed should take account of these differences, and of the non-economic as well as the economic effects of unemployment bound up in a social welfare, as opposed to a maintenance, approach to their problems. This was particularly important for the young unemployed and what he referred to as 'the thorny problem of compulsion'.

University of Manchester (1938–44)

Singer's first academic post was as a research assistant at the Economic Research Section, later assistant lecturer in the Faculty of Economics, of the University of Manchester in England. Keynes and Singer's work on the unemployment enquiry were influential in his appointment. Professor John Jewkes was the dominant figure in the research section and Professor (later Sir) John Hicks, after the death of Professor Daniels, was head of the economics faculty. Academic leadership was much disrupted by the threat, and then the outbreak, of the Second World War. Jewkes and others were called away to work on government projects in London. Singer, who switched from the research section to the faculty of economics and worked under Hicks, was left to handle much of the undergraduate teaching in applied economics, statistics and domestic problems, including a course on wartime planning. He also found time to take an active part in the economic courses of the Workers Education Association (WEA) outside the university in the Greater Manchester areas. At the same time, Ilse, his wife, was engaged in refugee work, interviewing women for domestic service.

While at Manchester, Singer also repaid his debt and appreciation for his earlier reliance on the *Manchester Guardian Weekly* as a source of information during his school days in Germany by providing material regularly to A. P. Wadsworth, the editor of the newspaper, particularly on the German war economy, and was already showing signs of his prolific output that was to continue both in and outside the academic world. Sir Alec Cairncross recalled that 'The very facility of his writing has irked some economists, one of whom described him unkindly ... as "the Edgar Wallace of modern economics"', Edgar Wallace being a prolific writer of detective stories at the time (Cairncross and Puri, 1975, p. ix). Apart from continuing his work on unemployment (described above) and on social welfare (see below), he wrote on prices and the trade cycle, price dispersions in periods of change, and the inflexibility of the price system (Singer, 1938h, 1938i, 1939).

Internment (1940)

His interests and work were suddenly interrupted when to his surprise and anguish he, along with others of 'alien origin', were subjected to a brief period of internment in 1940. He and his wife had applied for United Kingdom citizenship in 1938 as soon as the five-year waiting period after his arrival at Cambridge was over. In support of their applications, he had given the names of Keynes, Beveridge, Archbishop Temple, and the vice-chancellor of Manchester University, Sir John Sebastian Bach Stopford. He suspected that this might be 'overkill' when their applications were not processed before war was declared. Britain's isolation after May 1940, and each German success, brought an increase in the number of 'alien' subjects to internment as the British authorities successively tightened up their regulations and as new countries, including Italy, entered the war on the German side. The number of internees increased to about 65,000. The government proposed to intern them on the Isle of Man and then send them to the Dominions as shipping space became available. 'Valuable' aliens were, however, allowed to remain in England with limited freedom of movement.

Despite the appeal of the vice-chancellor of Manchester University, and the remonstrations of his wife, Singer was interned in an isolated camp in Huyton, Cheshire, in the United Kingdom. He had no idea of how long he would be interned or whether it would last for the duration of the war. As it happened, it was to last for only about six weeks and took place during the university vacation so that he did not miss a day of work. A number of other economists were also interned, notably Edward Rosenhaum, Erwin Rothbarth, Piero Sraffa and Paul Streeten.

Keynes also intervened with all possible authorities from the Home Secretary downward to obtain their release for normal teaching and research duties. Singer advised Keynes to build his case entirely on 'national interest' and that 'distinction, loyalty, anti-nazism don't count, only usefulness'. Singer was offered a job at the BBC (the British Broadcasting Corporation). He told them that he probably would be unable to accept but if they really wanted him they should help to get him naturalized and he would be prepared to join and 'sweep the floors', adding that 'maybe it would have made a difference because it shows utility'.[12] Keynes argued that there were likely to be more enemy sympathizers in Whitehall than among those detained. In the end, Keynes was successful, but he worried about the 'thousands of more obscure people who cannot be dealt with in this way', and regarded the whole affair as 'the most disgraceful and humiliating thing which has happened for a long time ... If there are any Nazi sympathizers at large in this country look for them in the War Office and our secret services' (Moggridge, 1992, p. 636; Skidelsky, 2000, p. 78). The Archbishop of York, Dr Temple, also wrote 'as strongly as he could' to the Home Office to prevent Singer's detention.[13] Singer even contemplated army service to avoid internment but his lack of British nationality prevented him, as it did from securing other permanent employment.

It was a frustrating time but he kept his spirits up, and his sense of humour. In a letter to Alec Cairncross in 1942, well after his internment was over, he wrote: 'Well maybe they'll open a University of Madagascar after the war. Sounds quite nice for an obituary notice in the E.J. [*Economic Journal*] "held the chair in Diego Suarez for over thirty years showing himself fully worthy of the high traditions of this institution".'[14] He wrote in his son's alphabet book 'H is for Huyton and daddy is there, but to be at home he would vastly prefer'. In characteristic fashion, Singer spent his period of internment giving lectures to his fellow inmates on various aspects of the economic problems of the day. The Singer family eventually obtained naturalization after the war on 28 June 1946. In typically bureaucratic fashion, the official document wrote that in the case of their sons, as they were born in Britain, they were 'neither in need of, nor indeed capable of, naturalization'.

The German war economy (1940–44)

On his release, Singer was designated a 'friendly enemy alien' 'by the British Home Office and resumed work at the University of Manchester. At the request of Keynes, who with Austin Robinson was editor of the journal, Singer produced a series of twelve articles on the German war economy, which were published in consecutive issues of *The Economic Journal* during the height of the war (Singer, 1940–44). He undertook this work with the support of a grant from the National Institute of Economic and Social Research. Of the highest interest, these articles covered a wide range of issues concerning the German war economy, including: general planning and organization; organization of supplies; labour supply; wage policy; price control; restriction of investment and consumption; war finance, substitution production and materials; and monetary policy, which he contrasted with the respective developments and data in Great Britain. He estimated, for example, that German real wages were 57 per cent of UK wages in April 1943. Singer's articles were largely based on German economic periodicals, including the official *Vierjahresplan* and the unofficial *Deutsche Volkswirt*, supplemented by other material. The Ministry of Economic Warfare gave him access to, or sent him, material on Germany that reached Britain through neutral countries. The ministry also asked him to interview businessmen from neutral countries who had visited Germany and had acquired some knowledge of German war production.

One of his articles referred to the proclamation by Walter Funk, Hitler's Minister of Economics and President of the Reichbank, in 1940, at the height of Nazi power, of a 'new order' under which Europe with its colonies would be unified under German leadership (Singer, 1995h, p. 17). Claude Guillebaud had also referred to this announcement in his paper on 'Hitler's New Economic Order for Europe' in *The Economic Journal* in December 1940 (pp. 447–60), based on an address he had given to the Royal Institute of International Affairs at Chatham House, London on 3 September 1940. This was treated as a big propaganda item by the Nazis. The British Minister of Information, Harold Nicholson, worried about its potential disruptive effect on allied countries. He asked Keynes to prepare a radio broadcast to counteract and discredit the proposal. Keynes felt that a more effective counter-move would be to prepare a valid counter-proposal rather than attack Funk's 'fraudulent offer', as he called it. This was to lead to the formulation of Keynes' proposals for a new world economic system that were eventually presented at the Bretton Woods conference in 1944 (see later).

Singer's account of the measures taken in Germany on war-time rationing (cf. Singer, 1940–44, I and II) set a new direction in the British debate on the subject. Richard Kahn, who was working as temporary administrator in the Board of Trade in London, took note of the German points rationing system described by Singer and proposed a similar system based on Singer's article. Under this system, consumers were issued with a specific number of coupons, valued at a number of points, which could be spent within a limited period on items from a group of rationed goods. Within each group, the items had a points value and customers had to surrender both coupons and money for their purchase. Goods covered by the rationing system could be purchased only if the customers had the required number of points (Booth, 1985, pp. 297–8). This system allowed the proper planning and regulation of supply and demand for consumer goods.

Singer also produced papers on various aspect of the German war economy for other academic journals including what he called 'some disguised blessings of the war', and the sources of finance for the German war economy (Singer, 1941b, 1942b, 1943d). In his work on standardized accounting in Germany, he showed how disastrously German industry had exaggerated profit during the inflation that followed the First World War (Singer, 1943a).

The social welfare state (1943)

Drawing on his earlier experience on the unemployment enquiry and his subsequent writings on that subject, and fully imbibed of the Keynesian spirit, Singer took up another subject that was to underpin his own personal philosophy. In 1942, at the height of war and with remarkable foresight, Sir William Beveridge produced his far-reaching report on *Social Insurance and Allied Services* (Beveridge, 1942). This, together with his *Full Employment in a Free Society*, which he produced in 1944, formed the blueprint for Britain's welfare state. Singer, who was already an admirer of Beveridge through his contacts with him during the unemployment enquiry, wrote in support of Beveridge's proposals (Singer, 1943b, 1943c).

Like Singer, Beveridge had witnessed poverty at first hand. After graduating from university, Beveridge had worked at Toynbee Hall, a university foundation in London's East End. Beveridge was shocked by what he saw. As with Singer, this experience was to have a lasting influence. His academic career was interspersed with public service. In the Second World War, already in his sixties, he was given the job of co-ordinating government social services. This was his opportunity to try to improve the lot of the poor, and he seized it by producing a report that was to 'change the face of Britain'. Beveridge declared war on the five evils of 'Want, Disease, Ignorance, Squalor and Idleness' (original capitalization). He mapped out a scheme for children's allowances, a comprehensive health service, and the maintenance of employment that he felt would be a new 'way of life, not only for Britain but for the whole civilized world'. In his introduction to the report, Beveridge stated that 'a revolutionary moment in the world's history is a time for revolutions, not for patching'.

Beveridge's legacy should be understood in the context of his time (Timmins, 1996). Britain had in recent memory passed through two wars (the Boer War and the First World War) that had revealed that large swathes of its population were, literally, unfit to fight. Beveridge's report was produced in the backwash of the searing mass unemployment of the 1930s, in the middle of another war, when already the focus was on reconstruction, the British people felt growing admiration for the stand of the Russian communists against Hitler, and war service was radicalizing millions of soldiers.

Singer joined the fray when questions were raised as to how affordable Beveridge's vision of the welfare state would be. There could be no question that any improved provision for persons in special need (such as the unemployed, old-age pensioners, the ill, widows and large families) was a 'good thing'. But how much improvement could be afforded, and at what point did the price of any further improvement begin to be excessive? Singer addressed these questions by subjecting the Beveridge plan to the approach and thoroughness of a student of Keynes, and answered the rhetorical question 'Can we afford 'Beveridge'?' with the rhetorical reply 'Can we afford not to afford it?'. (Singer was to use the same approach as the theme of the last chapter of the mission report on employment in Kenya, entitled 'The Cost of Inaction', in 1972 (see below).)

Singer confronted the argument that the quantitative aspects of the Beveridge plan were not worth discussing because it was a good thing 'regardless of its cost'. He identified four senses in which the money cost of the scheme was meaningless, and that the real value of money was what mattered:

- First, money was itself meaningless except as a 'ticket' for goods and services. Everything that people enjoyed must come out of the production or import of tangible goods or actual services. The distribution of money may become useless in alleviating want if: the production or import of useful goods stopped; extra money was unspendable; or its purchasing power was whittled down by excessive inflation.
- Secondly, Singer pointed out that the real cost of any economic policy lay not in money but in the goods and services which have been diverted from other purposes in pursuance of the specific economic action decided upon, i.e., in their 'opportunity cost'.
- Thirdly, the money which figured in the national budget as the cost of the Beveridge plan was largely meaningless as a measure of its true cost.
- And, finally, the absolute money figures given for executing the plan were quite meaningless unless they were related to some more meaningful concept.

What mattered was the relation between the money figure for the plan and that final fund from which all claims had ultimately to be satisfied, i.e., the national output (and excess imports, if any). Singer concluded that a proper assessment of the cost of the Beveridge plan was necessary for forming an opinion as to its practicability. The idea that money was only 'redistributed' by the plan and therefore 'not lost' could be misleading. It was true that money was circulated and not lost but the same was not true of the physical goods which money sets in motion.

Singer went on to examine: the proposed items of expenditures under the Beveridge plan; whether the projected post-war national income of Britain would be sufficient to meet those expenditures; the budgetary aspects of the plan, distinguishing between taxation and contributions; and the effects of the plan on exports. He also responded to the criticisms that the plan focused too much on distribution and not enough on production, and that it 'committed the future'. He reminded the reader that any redistribution which increased the utility of what is produced by directing it into more urgent channels was a contribution to national production. He considered that in an era of mass unemployment, there was a tendency to think too much of the quantity of output and not enough of its quality. The much-discussed assumption of full employment in the Beveridge plan ought perhaps to be reinterpreted in this qualitative rather than quantitative sense. Not employment for its own sake, but for the satisfaction of the basic needs of the broad masses of the people. That was what the Beveridge plan partly assumed and partly would help to promote by dispensation of a steady stream of purchasing power through the channels of a unified social service system. As to the criticism of 'committing the future', that would clearly be the negation of any conscious economic planning and action – 'that we should refrain from doing certain things for fear of committing the future is an absurd request, incapable of fulfilment'. Later, Singer was to recall that 'a partisan to the social welfare state was attracted by the thought and possibility of a global welfare state represented by the United Nations in the hopeful first days of naive utopianism' (Singer, 1984c, p. 276).

Ministry of Town and Country Planning, London (1945–46)

In the first national election in the United Kingdom after the Second World War, the Labour Party won with a manifesto that included the nationalization of the development rights in urban land. Keynes, recalling Singer's PhD work at Cambridge on urban land values, recommended him for a post in the Ministry of Town and Country Planning, where he was involved in the calculation of proper compensation for urban land owners. This brief experience was to play an important part in the direction and development of his career as a development economist in the United Nations. While in London, he also did some work with the newly-established United Nation Relief and Rehabilitation Agency (UNRRA). At one point he had also been drawn into the preparatory work for the Bretton Woods conference that was going on in the UK Treasury. He also met David Owen, who by then was adviser to Sir Stafford Cripps in whose department the preparatory work on the United Nations fell. Owen had returned from the San Francisco conference that established the United Nations to London as deputy executive officer of the UN Preparatory Commission. It was at Church House in London that the first steps were made toward the organization of the UN. Singer discussed developments briefly with him but none of this provided an inkling of his future career.

University of Glasgow (1946–47)

Singer had been appointed to a lectureship in economics at Glasgow University towards the end of the Second World War but was given leave of absence to undertake work at the Ministry of Town and Country Planning. He looked forward to renewing his association with Alec (later Sir Alec) Cairncross and David Owen, who had also been appointed to lectureships in the Economics Faculty at Glasgow University, and to continuing his interests in problems of unemployment, social welfare and regional disparities in Great Britain. He became involved, with C. E. V. Leser, in a study of differentials in development indicators between England and Scotland, which was subsequently published, and also read as a paper to the Royal Statistical Society, in 1950 (Singer and Leser, 1948b). Singer recalled later that this work on depressed areas and unemployment was a forerunner to his work on developing countries. He had already been forced to think about 'vicious circles' and 'poverty traps' (Singer, 1992d, p. 7).

But another twist of fate was to redirect Singer's career as a development economist, this time with international dimensions. David Owen had been appointed to head the Department of Economic Affairs at the newly created United Nations at Lake Success in the United States.[15] He wrote to the principal of Glasgow University, Sir Hector Hetherington, asking whether either Alec Cairncross or Hans Singer could be seconded for two years to help him establish the new department. Cairncross was not available at the time (being deeply involved in the problems of

German post-war settlement, and his wife was expecting their first child). So, somewhat reluctantly, as he was looking forward to settling down to an academic life in Glasgow and regarded a move to the UN as a 'step down', and on Sir Hector's insistence, Singer was released, provisionally on a two-year assignment that was to last 22 years.

As Singer explained, 'there was always continuity, and my life was intertwined with that of friends, but always there was also accident and coincidence', corresponding to two different versions of history: one, 'the gradual unfolding of an influential, innate meaning'; and the other of history as 'just one damn thing after another' (Singer, 1976a, p. 13; 1992d, p. 609).

Part II

Service in the United Nations (1947–69)

'Hans is a rare being, an economist of world repute, a departmental draftsman of prodigious productivity, an inexhaustible fountain of stimulating ideas for almost all occasions (providing that economic development or the welfare of children are somehow involved) and a living proof that an international civil servant can play a creative role in the great task of changing the policies of nations.'

(David Owen, on Hans Singer's retirement from the United Nations in 1969)

5
Initiation: A Case of Mistaken Identity

Singer recounted how the twists of fate went further, and how a person born and brought up in an industrial country, trained as an economist under Schumpeter and Keynes, who had studied the problems of a developed country, and never set foot in a developing country, came henceforth to be absorbed by the concerns of the Third World (Singer, 1976a, pp. 3–4; 1984c, pp. 275–9). He described two scenarios, one logical, the other fortuitous, that led him to leave the mainstream and join the then tiny band of 'development economists'.

From his first student days in Bonn, Singer had been brought up on a diet of economic development by his mentor, Schumpeter. Through him, a lasting interest in problems of technical innovation and progress as well as in long-run economics was kindled. This interest was further fuelled at Cambridge. In some sense, Keynes was the real creator of development economics insofar as he broke with 'mono-economics', the view that economics consisted of a body of universal truth applicable to all countries and in all conditions (Hirschman, 1981). Keynes showed that, on the contrary, the rules of the game applicable to a condition of unemployment were not the same as those of classical economics. It was a natural step to apply this view to countries at different stages of development. As a student of Keynes during the formative years of *The General Theory*, Singer was 'intellectually pre-conditioned' to think in terms of different rules of the game applying to developing countries and the idea of 'nonorthodox' policies in relation to them. He recalled that the analogy between the existence of unemployment in an industrial country and the existence of surplus labour in a developing country was carried a 'decisive step further' by Arthur Lewis in his path-breaking paper on economic development with unlimited supplies of labour (Lewis, 1954). Through his work on the Pilgrim Trust unemployment enquiry, Singer became 'greatly interested' in the problems of depressed areas – somewhat like 'developing countries' within the United Kingdom – and, by extension, through the influence of Beveridge, with the development of a social welfare state immediately after the Second World War.

But there was also a fortuitous scenario, a 'misunderstanding' due to what Singer described as a 'linguistic difference' between the American and English usage of the term 'country planning'. When Singer arrived at the United Nations in early 1947, David Owen was away on duty. He was welcomed by Owen's deputy, David Weintraub, who did not know Singer or his previous work. Weintraub explained the various activities that were already going on in the UN Economic Affairs Department, and introduced the staff undertaking them, a number of whom were already well known to Singer. The department was still in a fledgling state with only a small staff carrying out loosely connected assignments. The statistician Harry Campion, Singer's old friend and colleague from his Manchester days, was there, engaged in extending the Keynesian national income framework on an international scale as a UN-sponsored national system of accounts. Folke Hilgerdt was doing his fascinating studies on networks for world trade. Michal Kalecki was working on inflationary and deflationary tendencies, the forerunner of the UN *World Economic Survey*. Weintraub also mentioned that there was a small section dealing with the problems of 'underdeveloped' countries, as they were then called ('developing countries' in today's parlance).

When Singer said that he would like to work with any of his former colleagues on the problems they were tackling, and not on the problems of developing countries, Weintraub was distinctly unhappy as that was precisely the section that he hoped Singer would join. When Singer expressed his surprise, Weintraub retorted 'but you are a planning expert'. The confusion had arisen because Weintraub had noticed from Singer's *curriculum vitae* that he had worked at the Ministry of Town and Country Planning in London. To an American, 'country planning' meant national planning. Singer did not want to disappoint Weintraub, and in any case he considered that everything would be provisional until David Owen came back, so he accepted an assignment to work on underdeveloped countries. But there was 'nothing more permanent than the temporary', and for the next 22 years Singer was to grapple with the problem of developing countries that was decided by the interest in urban land values kindled by Spiethoff, Keynes' memory of a Cambridge PhD thesis when a post in the Ministry of Town and Country Planning came to be filled, David Owen's absence, and the subtle difference between American and English linguistic concepts. Such were the twists of fate that led to the path that Singer was to take during his long and distinguished career as a development economist in the Department of Economic Affairs of the United Nations.

David Weintraub had not exaggerated when he said there was a 'small development section' in the UN Economics Affairs Department. It consisted of only three people, including Singer. By the time he left over two decades later, there were many more staff dealing with the problems of developing countries. In reality, his original assignment was anything but restrictive. The UN secretariat was 'a hothouse for ideas and early development economists' (Emmerij *et al.*, 2001, p. 27). By contrast, economics as taught in the 1940s was not about development but focused on microeconomics, with Keynesian analysis of unemployment the exciting frontier for both analysis and policy to prevent its resurgence in the post-war world (Hall, 1989). Paul Samuelson's first edition of his classic introductory textbook, *Economics*, published in 1948, 'contained less than three sentences on development' (Kapur *et al.*, 1997, p. 67).

Singer had 'the feeling of being at the centre of things, very privileged to be there. After all, the UN was the home of mankind. It was then at the centre of international organizations, the Bank and the Fund were very much on the periphery in those days' (Emmerij *et al.*, 2001, p. 27). These were indeed the halcyon days of the United Nations. The *Charter of the United Nations*, which had been signed on 26 June 1945 in San Franciso at the conclusion of the United Nations Conference on International Organization, came into force on 24 October 1945. Article 55 of Chapter IX the *Charter*, on 'International Economic and Social Co-operation', stated:

With a view to the creation of conditions of stability and well-being which are necessary for peaceful and friendly relations among nations based on respect for the principle of equal rights and self-determination of peoples, the United Nations shall promote:
a. higher standards of living , full employment, and conditions of economic and social progress and development;
b. solutions of international economic, social, health, and related problems, and international cultural and educational co-operation; and
c. universal respect for, and observance of, human rights, and fundamental freedoms for all without distinction as to race, sex, language, or religion.

The *Universal Declaration of Human Rights*, adopted by the UN General Assembly on 10 December 1948, proclaimed (in Article 25) that:

> Everyone has the right to a standard of living adequate for the health and well-being of himself and of his family, including food, clothing, housing and medical care and the necessary social services, and the right to security in the event of unemployment, sickness, disability, widowhood, old age or other lack of livelihood in circumstances beyond his control.

There was an ethical commitment and acceptance that the purpose was to contribute to a world of greater economic and social justice with less poverty, and that work for the UN was a service to the larger community of states and people in addition to being professional work (Emmerij *et al.*, 2001, p. 29). Seminal reports were produced on various aspects of the problems of development by teams of prominent economists from different parts of the world, with the support of the UN secretariat. The economists included some of the leaders in their profession who subsequently were awarded the Nobel Prize in economics, including Arthur Lewis, Gunnar Myrdal and Theodor W. Schultz.

It was against this background that Singer took up his work at the United Nations. On reflection, Singer saw several connecting strands between the new problems that he now had an opportunity to study and his earlier interests. His fertile mind and fondness for grappling with practical issues and current problems, combined with the fact that the new department he had joined was not rigidly structured but consisted more of a small group of individuals pursuing their chosen subjects, meant that Singer was able to take up a wide range of assignments with equal effectiveness. He was also driven by the desire to learn as much as possible about the problems of developing countries at first hand. He confessed to a distinct feeling of inferiority in discussions with friends and colleagues from developing countries, like V. K. R. V. Rao. He felt this inferiority complex could only be overcome by immersing himself in Third World issues as quickly as possible and by experiencing them at first hand, as he had done in the study of unemployment in the depressed areas of the United Kingdom.

During his service in the UN, Singer served in a number of posts, including: chief of the Development Section, and special adviser to the under-secretary, in the UN Department of Economic and Social Affairs; director of the Economic Division of the United Nations Industrial Development Organization; associate director of the United Nations

Research Institute for Social Development; chairperson, secretary or member of a number of UN preparatory committees; senior UN interregional adviser on development planning; and leader of many UN missions to, and adviser to governments in, developing countries during the formative years of the UN.

Singer's pioneering work came to the fore. His incisive, analytical mind, coupled with a deep and abiding concern for the well-being of poor people in developing countries, resulted in a number of significant initiatives the benefits of which were to have their impact to this day. Time and again the visions of Schumpeter and Keynes were to shine through in his work. He never minded having his work set out for him by the need to prepare UN reports in response to resolutions of UN bodies, or having to write field reports, or go on missions in response to requests from various countries. His workload was phenomenal, generated by the principle that 'work gravitates to he who works'. As we shall see, he was to write prolifically, mostly as anonymous contributions to official UN publications. His ideas and thinking underpinned many UN initiatives.

Shortly after arriving at the United Nations, Singer paid his respects to Schumpeter at Harvard University. When Singer told him that his work at the UN was to be on the problems of developing countries, Schumpeter's surprising response was 'But I thought you were an economist – isn't this more a matter for anthropologists, sociologists, geographers, etc.?'. And this from the author of the *Theory of Economic Development*. Singer recalled that he felt very discouraged at the time. Two years later, when Schumpeter heard him present his paper on what came to be known as the 'terms of trade controversy', Singer was more encouraged by his remark that 'there were interesting economic problems there after all'. Singer was to realize more and more the wisdom of Schumpeter's remark, which he took as a reminder of the non-economic and inter-disciplinary dimensions of the development process. Even without Schumpeter's warning, this was subsequently borne upon him by extensive work in developing countries, and through contacts with national aid organizations, UN delegates and others.

Initially, Singer was to find life in the United States as puzzling as he had found it at first in Cambridge. He had practically to learn a new language. When, for example, he went in search of accommodation, he saw a sign across the street that read 'flats fixed'. Thinking that this was an advertisement for apartments, he crossed the road only to find that it was a car repairs workshop.

6
The Economist as Adviser in an International Organization

Some five years after taking up his appointment at the United Nations, Singer gave a fascinating insight into the views he had formed of the role of an economist as an adviser in an international organization, which could be seen in the work he performed. The 'accident' by which this happened is interesting. Singer wrote a review of a book by W. A. Jöhr, a professor at the Technical University in St. Gallen, Switzerland on *Die Beurteilung konkreter wirschaftspolitischer Probleme* ('The Judgement of Concrete Problems in Economic Policy'), which appeared in the June 1952 number of *The Economic Journal* (pp. 385–7). Singer considered the book, which he described as being about the techniques of applied economics, as 'a gem' and of 'intriguing interest' as an introduction to the techniques and dangers of elucidating problems of economic policy for the economist acting in an advisory capacity to a national government on particular measures of economic policy. At the same time, having his own work in mind, he found it deficient in that it failed to deal with the problems and difficulties which confronted economists working in large international organizations.

Singer noted that interesting points on ethics emerged from Jöhr's book. For example, Jöhr declared that it would be unethical for a British 'neo-liberal' to advise a Labour government about nationalization measures but that it would not be unethical for an American economist, who was a socialist, to work out measures for the improvement of the capitalist system in the United States. The reason given for this distiction was that private enterprise in the United Kingdom was a real possibility, whereas socialism in the United States was 'merely an academic hypothesis'.

Austin Robinson, joint editor (with Roy Harrod) of the *The Economic Journal* at the time, having read the review, suggested that

Jöhr and Singer join forces to produce a book on *The Role of the Economist as Official Adviser* in which Jöhr's work would be expanded and supplemented by contributions from Singer on the specific functions and working experience of economists engaged in the research staff of international organizations. Robinson even interested a publisher for their work. Since Jöhr's original book had been carefully planned, it was agreed that Singer would provide a running commentary on Jöhr's expanded and updated treatment. The book was published in 1955 (Jöhr and Singer, 1955a). In his Foreword to the book, Austin Robinson wrote: 'One reader at least has greatly enjoyed the modest wisdom of this small book, and has wished that he might have read it all sixteen years ago before embarking on some of the tasks that Professor Jöhr and Dr Singer would have helped him so greatly discharge.'

The authors made their position known from the outset. For them, 'Economists engaged in basic research have been well described as the tool-makers, and those concerned with the problems of economic policy as the tool-users.' This metaphor made it clear that those engaged in basic research should no more lose sight of the problems of economic policy 'than the manufacturers of machine tools should lose sight of their tools of production engineering'.

Problems of economic policy contained, 'like every practical problem', three constituent elements: the aim; the situation; and what action has to be taken. All three elements were of importance in the economic research work carried out in international organizations. The objective was often represented by the provisions of the UN Charter or the terms of agreement of international agencies, and also by the texts of the resolutions of councils, conferences or meetings. A good deal of the research consisted in analyzing existing situations or measures from this particular point of view. An existing situation was the starting point, particularly in the case of period reports, which formed a considerable part of the work on international secretariats. All three elements were also important for the development programmes of under-developed countries.

Compared with economists working for national governments, those engaged in international organizations were in a 'somewhat peculiar position'. They would not be able to convince their employers of the rightness of their own value judgements. They would be working as members of a team drawn from different countries, presenting different backgrounds and divergent value judgements. Their work would be anonymous. And the research work carried out was expected to be purely technical in nature: they were not supposed to express any aims and value judgements except those of the charter or other basic instruments of their organization. This special situation was full of 'novel problems', complicated further by the fact that the origin of research frequently lay in resolutions of councils or conferences, which themselves reflected compromises, and the value judgements they contained were not clear or homogeneous. Quite often, the aims were not clear enough to serve as a starting point for scientific investigation. And the objectives set were particularly liable to be imprecise. There were a variety of reasons for this. The objectives often represented a compromise of divergent views of individual governments, reached 'at the lowest common denominator of precision', and often stated in the most general terms. The terms used at international meetings were subject to semantic difficulties in that the same terms may mean different things to people speaking different languages, and thinking from a background of different national traditions. The objective of research might be stated in resolutions drawn up in a hurry at the end of exhausting meetings, and were often less important than the more directly operational parts involving measures by governments, or requested because no operational agreement had been reached, and to keep the subject alive.

In preparing period reports, there was always a danger of over-emphasizing the more ephemeral changes since the last report was made. The importance of more long-term factors might be underrated, which did not change spectacularly from one year to the next. A further difficulty in judging problems of economic policy derived from the fact that no measures worked solely in the direction of the single objective it was designed to achieve. Frequently, certain important secondary effects, often of a non-economic nature, were overlooked or regarded as not the concern of economists and left for others to deal with. Forecasting raised special problems. Documents had to be prepared well in advance of meetings and deadlines for preparation were set back further by the need to translate them into several languages. The necessity to use only carefully verified data increased further the time lag between economic research and its consideration for policy application. For these and other reasons, forecasting for an international secretariat was particularly dangerous. The incorrect assumption might, perhaps quite wrongly, cast doubt on its technical analysis. Moreover, assumptions about the future were often emotionally coloured. Perhaps the best course was to be 'short on forecasting, but long on assuming'.

When it came to providing advice on policy, economists working in international organizations were in a different position from their counterparts in national governments. Between them and the governments' decision to take their advice stood the governments' own economic advisers. Hence, less was expected in the way of direct advice on decisions. The strongly federal nature of international organizations in an age of national sovereignty also set close limits to direct action advice and evaluation of analysis. In addition, within the international staffs, there was a division between policy-makers and professional economists working as technicians. For these reasons, the latter rarely carried out their own analysis to a final policy conclusion. Their job was rather to put the alternatives clearly and for the rest to rely on the inherent logic of the argument where they themselves were convinced of the rightness of certain actions. Another critical difference was between advice provided by staff from international organizations which had the financial resources to act as an inducement or condition for sovereign governments to follow, as in the case of the Bretton Woods institutions, and those at the United Nations and other organizations that had little other than technical advice and assistance to offer.

Economists should not limit themselves to working out the answer to the problems of economic policy. They should also be concerned with the problems and difficulties of putting it into effect. In international organizations, where action consisted more of recommendations to sovereign member states, attempts were made to find universally accepted solutions. Hence, economists tended to concentrate research on issues where there was a 'general coincidence and community of interests' between all countries. This 'bias' seemed natural and unobjectionable as long as it did not imperceptibly lead to the underrating of the importance of national resistance, which may exist in spite of an underlying long-run international community of interest.

The many aspects of a problem of economic policy could not be examined by study alone. A large number of factors, not subject to precise definition, had to be brought into relation with each other in such a way that a conclusion emerged. It was of the greatest importance, therefore, to discuss the problems and issues involved with professional colleagues, officials and representatives of interested parties. Similarly, it was helpful to listen to the debates of councils and commissions and to study the records of debates. Conversations with officials of the organizations and groups affected by the measures contemplated, or already in operation, could be particularly revealing. Finally, economists working for international organizations ought to achieve 'some degree of emotional identification' with the purposes of their organizations as set out in its charter. While competent technical services could be given without this emotional commitment, 'in the end a mere technician is all too likely to be deterred by the many hurdles which loom between thought and action'. Singer's experience throughout his work at the United Nations was to prove the wisdom of these views.

What follows is an illustrative, summarized account of some of Singer's main pioneering activities while at the United Nations. It gives an indication of his significant, personal contribution to a number of major initiatives. His efforts led to the establishment of important UN institutions that have endured to this day. They also resulted in the formulation of basic concepts and ideas, which have been of considerable benefit both for a better understanding of the problems of developing countries and for implementing practical steps to assist them in their economic and social development. Many of his ventures required long hours of work, and often team-work, negotiations, persistence and compromise, and a vision on a regional or global scale.

7
Distribution of Gains from Trade and Investment: The Terms of Trade Controversy[1]

Early pioneering

It gives some idea of Singer's immediate and total commitment to his new work that within a short time after his arrival at the United Nations he was to produce a pioneering study for which he became perhaps most well-known as a development economist.

The report of the first session of the UN Sub-Commission on Economic Development, whose members were appointed in June 1947 to consider the problems of economic development in under-developed countries, stated:

> The recent rise in the price of capital goods and transport services has made the task of economic development particularly difficult in the case of the under-developed and least developed countries. The Sub-Commission therefore considers it important that a careful study be made of the prices of capital goods and of the relative trends of such prices and of prices of primary products, so that it may be in a position to make appropriate recommendations concerning the problem. (Cited in UN, 1949b, p. 1)

As a result, the UN secretariat began a study of the terms of trade. The original objective was to address a short-run problem, not to examine the long-term historical trend in the terms of trade. During the Second World War, a number of developing countries had run up export surpluses that could be used to import capital goods for development purposes. Subsequently, the prices of capital goods had risen making export surpluses worth less in terms of imports than they had been when they were earned. This raised the question as to whether developing countries' terms of trade could be expected to continue to deteriorate in this way, and the implications for their economic development.

A strong influence among Singer's early colleagues in the United Nations secretariat was the director of the UN Statistical Office, Folke Hilgerdt, a Swedish economist who had already shaped the League of Nations publication on the *Network of World Trade* (Singer, 1984c, p. 80). Working with him was Carl Major Wright, a Danish economist who was particularly interested in the relationship of primary commodity prices to trade cycles and economic growth in the industrial countries. Two other staff members in the trade section of the UN Economics Department were Walter Chudson from the United States and Percy Judd from Australia, an expert in the details and economics of commodity agreements and for many years the secretary of the UN Interim Co-ordinating Committee on Commodity Problems. Discussions with these four colleagues quickly drew Singer's attention to the problems of the terms of trade between industrialized and developing countries, and to link the new development work in the United Nations with the more advanced work in the field of trade analysis.

Through Hilgerdt's work at the League of Nations in a series of studies on commerce and commercial policy (League of Nations, 1945), and then that of Gunnar Myrdal, Singer became familiar with the possibility of cyclical and structural 'backwash effects' of conditions in industrial countries on the trade of the primary exporting countries, with prices and terms of trade acting as 'mechanisms of transmission'. The statistics of international trade between 1871 and 1938 produced by Hilgerdt during his work at the League of Nations showed that between those dates the price index of manufactured articles had fallen significantly less than that of primary products. Both Singer and Hilgerdt expressed concern over what the data seemed to imply. (Singer had already shown an aptitude for analyzing long-term data series in his PhD work at Bonn and Cambridge, which covered urban land values over the period 1845–1913.)

While mainstream economics concentrated on the problems of allocative efficiency where, as Singer put it, 'comparative advantage ruled supreme', Singer's interest from the beginning of his work on the terms of trade was more in the direction of 'distributive justice or efficiency', following in the footsteps of Alfred Marshall, R. H. Tawney and Beveridge. This reflected his past concern with unemployment and the welfare state, foreshadowed a future interest in basic needs and the problems of children in developing countries, and brought out his natural predisposition as a 'dissenting economist' (Singer, 1984c, pp.280–81; Arestis and Sawyer, 1992, pp. 526–32). To think of the distribution of gains as only the amount of labour saved by specialization was to neglect an essential element. The assumption of equal exchange in impartial 'fair' markets seemed to be in conflict with the facts of unequal markets and technological power. As Singer put it, 'The dice were loaded against one of the trade partners.' As in other such situations, 'acts of positive discrimination were called for, hence the attempt to create an ITO [International Trade Organization]'.

In looking at the data on terms of trade between primary commodities and manufactures (at the time, still a satisfactory proxy for trade between rich and poor countries), Singer quickly dissented from the classical position that the terms of trade would move in favour of primary products as a result of scarcities and increasing marginal costs of production for primary products, and of increasing returns and technical progress in manufacturing goods. This conventional view was related to an optimistic assumption that inequalities in international income would tend to diminish. In Keynesian thinking, there would be diminishing marginal efficiency of capital accumulation in the industrial countries and high rates of return on capital in the developing countries, which, through trade and capital flows, would lead gradually to income equalization. Like others, Singer had initially, and unquestioningly, shared this Keynesian view. The data he now obtained from Hilgerdt seemed to him incompatible with that position.

Singer proclaimed his 'new discovery' in 1949, first in an advance report which was presented to the UN Sub-Commission on Economic Development in February and later in that year in a UN report for general circulation (UN, 1949a). He presented a paper on the subject to the annual meeting of the American Economic Association in December 1949, which was subsequently published in the *American Economic Review* in the following year (Singer, 1950b). He had also sketched out the results of his findings in a paper delivered to the general seminar of the graduate faculty of the New School for Social Research in New York on 23 December 1948 (Singer, 1949b). The pioneering, visionary and provocative nature of this work (and the fact that it was to lay the ground for other major initiatives that Singer was subsequently to pursue) is such that it deserves to be analyzed here in some detail.

Singer began by pointing out how the importance of foreign trade to developing countries had been obscured. He emphasized that 'International trade is of very considerable importance to under-developed countries, and the benefits which they derive from trade and any variations in their trade affect their national incomes very deeply' (Singer, 1950b, p. 473). At the time, economists frequently expressed the opposite view that trade was less important to developing than to industrial countries. He ascribed this view to a 'logical confusion – very easy to slip into' between the absolute amount of foreign trade (which was known to be an increasing function of national income) and the ratio of foreign trade to national income. There were a number reasons for this. Foreign trade tended to be proportionately most important when incomes were lowest. Fluctuations in the volume and value of foreign trade tended to be proportionately 'more violent' in the trade of developing countries and, therefore, *a fortiori* also more important in relation to national income. And *a fortissimo*, fluctuations in foreign trade tended to be 'immensely more important' for developing countries in relation to that small margin of income above subsistence needs which formed the source of capital formation, for which they often depended on export surpluses over and above consumption goods required from abroad.

An additional factor may have been the great discrepancy in the productivity of labour in the developing countries between those working in occupations catering for exports and those involved in domestic production. The former, as carried out in mines and plantations, were often highly capital-intensive and supported by a great deal of imported technology. By contrast, the latter, especially in food and clothing, was often of a very primitive subsistence nature. This gave rise to a dualistic economic structure. Since the proportion of people employed in export-related trade was often lower than in industrial countries, the conclusion was mistakenly drawn that foreign trade was less important to them, since it implicitly assumed rough equivalence of productivity in the export and domestic sectors.

Moreover, there were 'large self-contained groups' in the developing countries outside the monetary economy who were not affected by any changes in foreign trade. By contrast, the repercussions from changes in foreign trade in industrial countries were more widely, and thinly, spread. Another factor was that some developing countries included the transactions of foreign companies in their foreign trade statistics at transfer prices rather than at their market value.

Singer next turned his attention to the drain on the benefits of foreign investment in developing countries. This raised the question of ownership. The facilities for producing export goods in developing countries were often foreign-owned as a result of previous investment in those countries, and did not become part of their internal economic structure. In reality, they were the 'outposts' of the economies of the more developed investing countries. The main secondary multiplier effects of this investment took place where the investment had come from, in the industrial countries themselves, and not in the developing countries. Developing countries had the chance to use the royalties or other income derived from foreign investment to transform their internal economic structure but this was often missed, as demonstrated by the fact that disparities in labour productivity between the export and domestic sectors were not reduced.

Singer went further. He reasoned that if the principle of opportunity costs was applied to the development of nations, the import of capital into developing countries for the purpose of making them into providers of food and raw materials for the industrial countries may have been not only rather ineffective in giving them the normal benefits of investment and trade but could have been 'positively harmful'. Domestic industries might have developed in the developing countries if they had not become specialized in the export of food and raw materials, thus providing the means of producing manufactured goods elsewhere with superior efficiency. While he recognized that it was a matter of speculation that in the absence of highly specialized export-oriented development, any other kind of development would have taken place, the possibility could not be assumed away. Export-oriented development might have absorbed what little entrepreneurial initiative and domestic investment there was, and might even have tempted domestic savings abroad. He argued that the comparison should be not 'what is with what was' but with 'what might otherwise have been', which he described as 'a tantalizingly inconclusive business'. What could be said was that the process of traditional investment taken by itself seemed to have been insufficient to initiate domestic development unless it appeared in the form of the migration of people.

Showing the strong influence of Schumpeter, Singer stated that the principle of specialization along the lines of 'static comparative advantage' had neither been generally accepted in the developing countries, nor generally intellectually accepted in the industrialized countries. In the economic history and life of a country, a most important element was the causal mechanism by which 'one thing leads to another'. The most important contribution of an industry was not its immediate product or its effects on other industries and immediate social benefits (as pointed out by Marshall and Pigou) but perhaps, beyond this, its effects on 'the general level of education, skill, way of life, inventiveness, habits, store of technology, creation of new demand, etc.'. By specializing on exports of food and raw materials, and thus making the developing countries contribute further to the concentration of industry in the already industrialized countries, foreign trade, and the foreign investment that went with it, may have spread static benefits fairly over both. But they may have had very different effects if seen from what Singer called 'the flow of history' rather than static comparative advantage. Of the former school of thought, he considered that the 'protection of infant industries' argument was 'but a sickly and often illegitimate offspring'. Had developing countries developed their own manufacturing industries, this would have provided 'growing points for increased technical knowledge, urban education, and the dynamism and resilience that goes with urban civilization, as well as the direct Marshallian external economies'. Under different circumstances, commerce, farming and plantation agriculture might also have proved capable of being such 'growing points'.

Thus, Singer argued, economic history had been unkind to the developing countries. It removed most of the secondary and cumulative effects of investment from the country in which the investment took place to the investing country. And it diverted developing countries into types of activity offering less scope for technical progress, and internal and external economies taken by themselves, and withheld a central factor of 'dynamic radiation', which had revolutionized society in the industrialized countries.

Singer went on to identify a third factor 'of perhaps even greater importance', which had reduced the benefits to developing countries of foreign trade-cum-investment based on the specialization in food and raw materials. That factor related to the terms of trade. The long-term trend of prices had been heavily against the sellers of food and raw materials and in favour of the sellers of manufactured goods. The capital-exporting countries therefore received repayment on the investment in the developing countries in a number of ways, including: the possibility of building up exports of manufactures, and thus transferring the labour force from low- to high-productivity occupations; enjoyment of the internal economies of expanding manufacturing industries; the 'general dynamic impulse' radiating from industries in a progressive society; the fruits of technical progress in primary production as main consumers of primary commodities; and contributions from foreign consumers of manufactured articles to the rising incomes of producers of manufactured goods. By contrast, the developing countries received no such benefits. The major proportion of their imports was made up of processed food and high-technology luxury consumer goods. The prices of these commodities had risen so much in the immediate post-war period that any advantage developing countries might have had from favourable prices for primary commodities and low prices of capital goods had been 'wiped out'.

Singer drew the following conclusions from his analysis:

- In the interest of the developing countries, world national income, and perhaps ultimately the industrialized countries themselves, the purpose of foreign investment and trade ought to be redefined as producing gradual changes in the structure of comparative advantages and of the comparative endowment of different countries rather than developing a world trading system based on existing comparative advantages and existing distribution of endowments. (He noted that this was perhaps the real significance of the movement toward providing technical assistance to developing countries of the time, and for changing the future international division of labour.)
- The main requirement of developing countries seemed to be to provide for some method of income absorption to ensure that the results of technical progress were retained in those countries, as they had been in the industrial countries. Perhaps the most important measure required in this field was a reinvestment of profits in the developing countries themselves, or the absorption of profits by fiscal measures and their utilization for the financing of economic development. The absorption of rising productivity in primary production in rising real wages and other real incomes could be brought about provided that the increment was utilized for an increase in domestic savings and the growth of markets of a kind suitable for the development of domestic industries. This, in turn, could lead to the introduction of progressive social legislation. But higher standards of wages and social welfare were not a highly commendable cure for bad terms of trade, except where the increment led to domestic savings and investment. Absorption of the fruits of technical progress in primary production was not enough. What was wanted was absorption for reinvestment.
- A flow of international investment into developing countries would contribute to their economic development only if it was absorbed into their own economic system, i.e., if a good deal of complementary domestic investment was generated and the requisite domestic resources found.

- The general policy conclusion was the importance for developing countries of diversification of exports into manufactures as intensively and as rapidly as possible in a process of 'industrialization'. Singer's paper fitted into the mainstream of development thinking of the time, as development and industrialization were treated as virtually synonymous (Singer, 1998f).

Singer was not without his detractors. Bela Balassa, for example, questioned the validity of Singer's findings on the basis of the choice of the time period studied and noted that 'results for a relatively short period are affected to a considerable extent by the choice of the initial and the terminal years'. Replacing the UN price index with that of the World Bank for non-fuel commodities, he found a higher average price increase for primary products than Singer had using UN data. He also questioned Singer's policy prescription for industrialization on the grounds that, apart from petroleum, there were few commodities whose prices developing countries could increase and thereby reduce the volume of their exports (Balassa, in Meier and Seers, 1984, pp. 305–11). Rostow found Balassa's view 'authoritatively refutes Singer's technical argument' (Rostow, 1990, pp. 411–14).

But Singer also found strong and positive allies. Unknown to him, Rául Prebisch (who became executive secretary of the UN Economic Commission for Latin America (ECLA) and later the first secretary-general of the UNCTAD secretariat) had reached similar conclusions (Prebisch, 1950). This he had done after he had read Singer's work for the report that was presented to the UN Sub-Commission on Economic Development, which had been sent to ECLA in Santiago, Chile 'by three different channels between December 1948 and April 1949' (Toye and Toye, forthcoming). Henceforth, their names were to be linked in what became known as the 'Prebisch–Singer thesis', which is generally taken to be the proposition that the net barter terms of trade between primary products and manufactures have been subject to a long-run downward trend. The continuing significance of the Prebisch–Singer thesis is that it implies that without major changes in the structure of the world economy, the gains from trade will continue to be distributed unequally between nations exporting primary products and those exporting mainly manufactures. Inequality of per capita income beween the two types of countries would also be increased, rather than reduced, by the growth of trade. Divergence instead of convergence would therefore occur between them.

Prebisch and Singer probably arrived at their respective explanations of primary commodity terms of trade decline independently, although Singer reached this empirical fact first. Singer presented his explanation, in embryonic form, in a paper presented to the general seminar of the graduate faculty of the New School for Social Research in New York on 23 December 1948, which was published in the New School's journal in the following year (Singer, 1949b). That paper contained the basic idea of a *structural* difference between countries where increased efficiency of production led to higher incomes and those where it led to falling product prices. Prebisch was the first of the two to propose a theoretical mechanism to account for secular decline. Prebisch identified industrial and primary production with groups of countries which he described as 'centre' and 'periphery'. He advanced a cyclical-cum-structural mechanism to explain the decline in terms of trade, which was more complex than the purely structural interpretation of Singer (Prebisch, 1950). In terms of the dissemination of these ideas, both benefited from the other (Toye and Toye, forthcoming). Singer also found a 'sympathetic bond' with Gunnar Myrdal (who at the time was executive secretary of the UN Economic Commission for Europe) as his work fitted well into Myrdal's own thinking.

In defence of his paper, Singer emphasized another point. It was meant to be less of a projection and more a *policy guide*. Developing countries were advised to diversify out of primary exports wherever possible, by developing domestic markets and by industrialization. The latter could be either import- or export-substituting, or a combination of both. In 1949, when Singer presented his paper, the prospects for export-substituting industrialization seemed a long way off and an import-substituting strategy was therefore emphasized more. There was much industrialization in the developing countries after 1949, and especially after 1960 as more countries gained their independence. While we do not know what the data would have been like without such action, Singer claimed that 'the deterioration in terms of trade would presumably have been even sharper than it was' (Singer, 1984c, p. 283).

The UN Sub-Commission on Economic Development discussed Singer's report at its third session in March/April 1949. The report showed that by 1938, the relative prices of primary goods had deteriorated by about 50 points, or one-third, since the 1870s, and by about 40 points, somethat less than 30 per cent, since 1913. While the Sub-Commission accepted, somewhat grudgingly, the statistical evidence produced by Singer, it rejected the conclusions he had drawn. Its report stated:

> The Sub-Commission is constrained to point out that the study under review contains certain conclusions in regard to the price relationship between developed and under-developed countries which, in its opinion, do not represent a correct picture of the actual position. As a result of the discussion, the Sub-Commission agreed that while the document contained an adequate study of relative price trends of primary commodities and manufactured goods, it was necessary to broaden the scope of the study into the terms of trade between under-developed and industrialized countries, including prices and quantities traded, and in extending it, to cover the most recent movements in these fields. (UN, 1949b, p. 12)

This negative reaction was stimulated for two main reasons. First, the statistical evidence presented showed that while the terms of trade of under-developed countries had improved between 1938 and 1946–8, it revealed exactly the reverse when placed in a longer historical perspective. Second, was Singer's finding that under-developed countries were helping to maintaining a rising standard of living in industrial countries without receiving any equivalent compensation. This was potentially politically explosive. The sub-commission used Singer's acknowledgement that the picture presented by the report was 'in some ways incomplete' to disclaim its radical conclusions (Toye and Toye, forthcoming).

Distribution of gains from trade and investment revisited

Singer was to 'revisit' his original distribution of gains from trade and investment thesis on several occasions in later years, when he put more emphasis on relations between types of countries, rather than types of commodities, and on the distribution of 'technological power' in more contemporary terms, in responding to some misunderstandings, and to answer some of the criticisms, of his original paper (Singer, 1958b; 1971m; 1975i; 1984c; 1992k; 1998f; Cairncross and Puri, 1975, pp. 58–66; Sarkar and Singer, 1991k; Sapsford, Sarkar and Singer, 1992k). He recognized the shortcomings in his original work in the search for truth and solutions to the problems of developing countries.

Over three decades after writing his original paper, Singer returned to his original thesis (Singer, 1984c; 1991n). He recalled that he had then discussed the problems of unequal gains from trade and investment largely in terms of different commodities and their attributes. Like other economists of the day, particularly Prebisch and Myrdal, he thought of industrialization as 'the great saviour', the escape from the dependency of the primary producers into 'true development' as producers of manufactured products. He realized that what he did not foresee at the time was the possibility that even national industrialization (including import-substituting industrialization specifically geared to the home market) could become the basis of a continuing and self-reinforcing relationship of dependency. With the benefit of hindsight, he acknowledged that he failed to take account of two critical factors: the characteristics of a dominant technology based upon what he called 'R & D [research and development] monopoly' in the investing (namely, industrial) countries; and the 'structure of centralized decision-making' in multinational corporations.

These factors were first pointed out by Kindleberger in 1956 (Kindleberger, 1956). The investing (industrial) countries were the seats of multinational corporations, the homes of modern technology, with economically integrated societies in which marginal groups were definable minorities (who also participated in the gains from progress, at least through social welfare). These countries would tend to be the chief gainers from any kind of relationship with borrowing (developing) countries, whatever the kinds of commodities would be, primary or manufactured. The borrowing countries would not gain for lack of a modern appropriate technology, except perhaps for groups who were geographically part of the borrowing country but drawn into the 'nexus' of the investing country.

Singer also acknowledged that the possibility that foreign investment might be 'positively harmful' to the borrowing country, which was explicitly visualized in his original paper, was based on not much more than 'wild speculation'. He had assumed that foreign investment and the export sector would be 'enclaves' or 'outposts' of the investing (industrial) country with little interacting multiplier or spread effects to the borrowing (developing) country. On reflection, Singer put this process more strongly and systematically. There would be interaction between enclaves and outposts with the rest of the economy of developing countries but this would be of a kind that would lead to a polarization or 'sharpened dualism' within the economy of the borrowing country. This would clash with objectives of national planning and integration designed to reduce poverty and promote more equal income distribution. The mechanism might produce an effective 'engine of growth' but, as he put it, would 'pull the car in an undesirable direction, perhaps towards a precipice and catastrophe'.

Therefore, Singer saw that the 'salvation' of the developing countries lay not in industrialization based on the technology of the advanced countries but in the Schumpeterian vision of 'technological leadership'. At Bonn, he had been brought up on Schumpeter's theory of economic development and the idea that quasi-monopolistic profits were made by those producing new and sophisticated goods requiring high technological power. It did not seem such a big step to translate this idea from internal to international relations and from simple divergences in GNP growth rates to unequal exchange and changes in the term of trade. He saw the way forward lay in building up indigenous scientific and technological capacities within the developing countries, or in other ways of reforming the system of concentrating R & D on problems and methods irrelevant or harmful to the developing countries. With that objective in mind, he recommended that 'The target must be to bring the objectives of R & D expenditure into line with the distribution of the world's population.' If that was achieved, 'the uneven distribution of gains from trade and investment will begin to look after itself'. Failing that, Singer felt that none of the remedies contemplated in his original paper would really work.

Singer developed this argument further. The traditional view was that the factor endowment of a country determined its production mix and technology. For developing countries, abundant labour and scarce capital would have important consequences. They would lead to a concentration and specialization on labour-intensive products and to the utilization of labour-intensive technology. This, in turn, would lead towards full employment, more equal income distribution, saving of scarce capital, and gradual factor price equalization. (Singer pointed out that trade restrictions concerning labour-intensive manufactured products and heavy tariff barriers against the processing of primary commodities in developing countries prevented this process from operating in so far as it depended on the international division of labour.) Rather than factor endowment, it was technology developed appropriately for the industrial countries (which was capital-intensive, labour-saving, and raw material saving and substituting) which imposed constraints and determined the production mix and use of the factor endowment of developing countries. The foundations of the problem were, therefore, inappropriate technology and factor use rather than factor endowment *per se*. Unemployment and inequalities due to concentration of scarce capital on 'modern' products resulted as the natural outcome of this situation.[2] He therefore proposed that it would be more realistic to replace the chain: factor endowment – product mix – technology – factor use; with the sequence: technology – factor use – unemployment – unequal income distribution.

Singer next underlined the importance of access to information, which 'like technology, feeds upon itself' and was 'self-compounding'. As he put it:

> If you do not have enough information to begin with to know where to look for the information that you need, or to know what new information could be assembled, your initial inferiority is bound to be sharpened and perpetuated. And if innovation becomes increasingly complex and difficult to comprehend, the information gap is bound to increase further. (Reynolds and Singer, 1975, p. 379)

Thus, unequal bargaining situations would affect all relations between the investing and borrowing countries, with the exceptions of aid or technical assistance directed towards equalizing access to information to the developing countries, or strengthening information-gathering capacity (which gave an early indication of Singer's interest in pre-investment theory and technical assistance – see later).

Another factor, which Singer later felt was insufficiently emphasized in his original paper, was the chronic shortage of foreign exchange of developing countries, excepting those with oil. Here, Singer recognized that he failed to follow through on the implications of his original thesis concerning the deteriorating terms of trade, which made the typical developing country highly dependent on foreign investment or aid, even for its import-substituting industrialization programme. This position of dependency would tend to create a situation in which real net export proceeds or real net import savings, even from successful industrialization, would be low and insufficient after allowing for the repatriation of profits, dividends, management fees, and salaries and transfer pricing, which would result in unfavourable terms of trade, and other transactions for developing countries generally.

Regarding income distribution, Singer considered that technical progress more suited to the advanced than the developing countries undermined the classical (Ricardian) theory of income distribution when applied to the international sphere. The concentration of technical progress of a specific kind within richer countries as the basic determinant of the uneven distribution of gains from trade and investment led

Singer to realize that simple manufactured products (of the type capable of import substitution in developing countries) shared many of the characteristics that he originally attributed to primary commodities.

The 'product cycle' school in international trade theory had correctly, and more relevantly, drawn attention to a different principle of distinction. Import substitution shifted the geographical location of manufacturing plants but increasing technological dependence arising from the one-sided distribution of technical progress ensured that the real terms of trade continued to go against the developing countries in favour of the advanced countries from which the intermediate inputs flowed. This was particularly obvious where the relationship was between a multinational corporation and its subsidiary in a developing country. Singer therefore concluded that when all the dynamic effects were taken into account, or counted in appropriate factor and market prices, the net marginal social productivity of import-substituting production might be zero or negative, and that some kinds of export-oriented industrialization might also not provide an escape. He had originally taken it for granted that new manufacturing industries would prove to be the 'growing points' in a developing economy, in line with the prevailing 'infant' industry theory. But the new industries were not the true 'infants' of the developing countries themselves. Moreover, domestic and potential entrepreneurs in the developing countries displaced by the rich country's technology were not as obviously marginal as he was originally inclined to believe. He blamed the process on export specialization in primary products rather than import-substituting industrialization based on rich country technology.

There had been much discussion about 'engines of growth'. The report of the Brandt commission (Brandt, 1980), with its emphasis on mutual interest and interdependence, was based on the view that during the 1950s and 1960s, the industrial countries were the 'engine of growth' for the developing countries but that these roles might be reversed and eventually the latter could serve as an engine of growth for the rest of the world. Singer's original paper had thrown doubt on the first part of this view. It implied that even during those two decades, by providing the industrial countries with steady supplies of primary commodities (and simple manufactures and labour), on terms increasingly favourable to the industrial countries, the developing countries provided an 'engine of growth' for the industrial countries throughout the twenty-five 'golden years' after the end of the Second World War, not least by enabling them to concentrate on high-technology lines of activity and to consolidate their technological leadership.

Singer's original paper was based on a view of commodity markets in which less emphasis was placed on the traditional neoclassical competitive market paradigm and more on bargaining and financial power, and control of processing, marketing and distribution. By the early 1980s, this view was being shared by other economists and the Prebisch–Singer thesis was seen as being a 'rich area for theoretical exploration' (Helleiner, 1981). Singer's original paper also tried to incorporate foreign or 'transnational corporate' investment activity into the model, as indicated in its title – 'The distribution of gains between investing and borrowing countries'. It thus implied a concept of the terms of trade based upon the nationally retained value from exports rather than on conventionally measured prices for export products. It mixed together, without clear distinction, elements in the supply/demand analysis (such as Engel's law and low income elasticity), which pointed to deteriorating terms of trade and elements relating to market structure and technological–financial power. Singer recognized that this may have led to misunderstandings and contributed to criticism. With the benefit of hindsight, he felt that he should have avoided the use of 'terms of trade', with its narrower professional meaning of net barter terms of trade relating to prices only, and used instead 'framework of trade', or some similar concept. That, in fact, was why he had omitted 'terms of trade' from the title of his original paper and referred instead to 'the distribution of gains between investing and borrowing countries'.

Singer appreciated that his thesis of deteriorating terms of trade 'touches raw nerves and rouses strong resistance', and led to diversions to factors that were difficult to measure (which did not go to the heart of the matter, even empirically), such as changing quality of manufactures, new commodities, falling transport costs, factoral terms of trade, and so on. In the last resort, he was quite ready to accept the conclusion that:

> While many of the criticisms of the doctrine that the terms of trade of primary producers steadily deteriorate appear to be damaging, the core of the doctrine may well survive the onslaughts. This core is that in the world economy there are forces at work that make for an uneven distribution of the gains from trade and economic progress generally, so that the lion's share goes to the lions, while the poor lambs are themselves swallowed up in the process. (Streeten, 1981, p. 217)

Singer's original paper did not question the basic doctrine of comparative advantage that trade was a positive-sum game resulting in gains to the trading partners, as indicated in its title 'Distribution of

Gains ...'. But it seemed to him to be legitimate to ask the further question, 'Who gains?' This led him to consider the possibility that in a certain institutional and power set-up, the longer-term and dynamic impact on one of the trading partners could be negative and that at least 'temporary delinking' might be preferable until a better basis for trade, with more evenly distributed gains, could be developed – an extension of the old infant-industry argument into an 'infant-economy' argument.

Analyzing his original paper in terms that he did not use earlier, Singer took a dual position. First, international trade between primary exporting developing countries and industrial countries was as much a question of power relationships as of classical markets and comparative advantages, and domestic power relationships *within* industrial and developing countries were as relevant as power relationships *between* industrial and developing countries. Second, the impact of trade of the type prevalent when he wrote his original paper included not only the 'engines of growth' effects emphasized by the classical economists and the theory of comparative advantage, but also potential 'backwash effects' related to a more dynamic concept of comparative advantage. Such effects on developing countries may, under certain conditions, offset, or more than offset, any engine of growth effects.

These backwash effects would be strengthened by a further factor, which was not discussed in the original paper but to which Singer turned immediately after he had written the paper, namely, the chronic instability of primary commodity prices and export proceeds (Singer, 1952b). If trade, or the foreign investment that went with the development of primary product exports, was not the engine of growth, Singer posed the question 'What was the engine of growth?' As we have already seen, the two answers to which he was pushed were: a shift from primary products to manufactured goods; and the development of a system of international aid. The shift to manufactured products he envisaged was mainly by way of import substitution – export substitution came later in the newly industrializing countries. The chief argument for giving priority to industrialization seemed to be the dynamic advantages. But again with the benefit of hindsight, Singer agreed that the limits of the import-substitution strategy were not fully realized when he wrote his original paper. Yet when developing countries became large net food importers, import substitution in the name of rural development and promotion of food security became very popular and part of the established wisdom, an indication that the objections were perhaps more to 'industrialization' than to 'import substitution'.

Using the index of thirty primary commodities exported by developing countries (excluding gold and petroleum) deflated by the UN index of manufactures exported by developed countries calculated by the IMF research department, Singer traced the empirical trend of terms of trade between 1957 and 1982. These data showed that over that period, the terms of trade of developing country primary exports in relation to developed country manufactured exports had deteriorated by 32 per cent. This deterioration applied to all four major groups of primary commodities: food by 27 per cent; beverages by 28 per cent; agricultural raw materials by 45 per cent; and metals by 28 per cent. Taking the four-year average 1957–60 as the basic figure, the overall deterioration was reduced to 26 per cent and the other sub-indices were reduced accordingly. Comparing 1957–60 with 1978–81, the deterioration was still 14 per cent. Singer therefore concluded that there could be no quibbling over what the tendency of terms of trade had been, provided the exclusion of oil was accepted. The remarkably uniform data for the four groups of primary commodities suggested some common factors at work. This general impression did not exclude the recognition of cyclical factors that complicated the selection of dates for measuring trade. Looking at the full set of 120 annual data for 1957–81, Singer found that 20 showed an improvement over 1957, two showed no change, but 98 showed a deterioration.

Singer concluded that the deterioration of terms of trade of developing countries could be attributed to the combined effects of three factors: the relative deterioration of unit values for primary commodities exported by developing countries in relation to primary export unit values of developed countries; the relative deterioration of manufactured export unit values of developing countries relative to manufactures exported by developed countries; and the lower proportion of manufactures in total exports of developing countries (for which unit values had increased more), and a higher proportion of primary commodities in their exports (for which unit values had increased less). Singer recognized that the terms of trade controversy had arisen because the debate over the course of the terms of trade had been 'shunted onto the wrong track' by disputing the question as to whether they had deteriorated historically. He found support for his original contention that the relevant question was not what the terms of trade are compared with what they were, but what they are compared with what they should and could have been (Streeten, 1982, p. 8).

Recognizing that direct action to improve terms of trade by producers' associations was difficult, Singer suggested other possible policy alternatives, including: changing the underlying bargaining relations; emphasizing collective self-reliance by more intra-developing country trade and investment among developing countries; national delinking (autarky/import substitution); and more export substitution.

In 1991, Prabirjit Sarkar, a visiting fellow at IDS from Calcutta University in India, suggested to Singer that the analysis of the Prebisch–Singer thesis be taken a stage further by examining the manufactured exports of developing countries and their terms of trade (Sakar and Singer, 1991k; 1993i). They noted that since the terms of trade deterioration hypothesis was first proposed in 1949, the commodity composition of exports of developing countries had undergone a major change in the direction of dominance of manufactures in their non-fuel exports, with strong growth in the volume of their manufactured exports. But this did not allow developing countries to escape unequal exchange relations with the industrial countries. Their barter terms of trade in manufactures showed signs of weakness rather than improvement and failed to reflect the respective productivity trends leading to deterioration in factoral terms of trade. Why was this?

Some evidence was found of decline in the unit values of manufactured exports of the developing countries to the industrial countries but this was less than the rate of decline in the unit values of primary products in relation to manufactures. A compensatory factor was the higher rate of growth in the volume of manufactured exports of developing countries. For many developing countries, however, this had served to finance debt payments rather than imports. Their finding suggested that the 'real core' of the Prebisch–Singer thesis was the loss of productivity gains. This applied to both primary products–manufactures and manufactures–manufactures trade. Instead, the debate had focused on the movement of barter terms of trade, which had led to the on-going statistical debate. Their finding fitted in well with that reached by Spraos (Spraos, 1983). The difference in the rate of growth of labour productivity in the total manufacturing sectors of developing countries and industrial countries was indicated in the actual difference between the rate of growth of labour productivity in the export-oriented manufacturing sectors of the two groups of countries.

It was beyond the scope of their analysis to examine whether export orientation improved factor productivity and whether low factor productivity and policy emphasis on 'forced' import-substitution went hand-in-hand. But Singer and Sarkar pointed out that export-orientation was not always a 'natural' phenomenon (governed by 'free' market forces). It was often 'forced' on the developing countries by domestic and/or international policy-makers. Different forms of export subsidy, real devaluation of currencies, and other devices were often used for export promotion. Just as import-substituting output expansion may be limited by the growth of the domestic market, so output expansion in the export-oriented sector of developing countries may also be limited by protectionism, anti-dumping laws and increased regionalism in the markets of industrial countries. Hence, the rate of growth of productivity in the total manufacturing sector of developing countries, and specifically in their import-substituting sector, was less than that in the export-oriented sector. In sum, they maintained that the terms of trade of developing countries deteriorated not only in their exchange of primary products for the manufactures of industrial countries but also in their exchange of manufactures for the manufactures of industrial countries. The Prebisch–Singer thesis therefore also extended to trade in manufactures between developing and industrial countries, as it did in its country and commodity dimensions.

The Prebisch–Singer thesis vindicated

The Prebisch–Singer (P–S) thesis was to create a growth industry in the development economics literature. Being in direct contradiction with the then prevailing orthodoxy, it is not surprising that their hypothesis attracted criticism from a number of quarters. The ensuing criticisms, which initially focused on the adequacy of the particular statistical series analyzed and issues related to the treatment of transport costs and changes in the quality of commodities, left the hypothesis largely undented, in the sense that they failed to destroy its empirical validity. Spraos cut through the then prevailing controversy, both economic and statistical, and showed that on the basis of reasonable and sensible assumptions and interpretations, the P–S thesis remained intact up to the late 1970s, albeit with a rate of decline perhaps rather less than implied by the estimates reported in the original papers (Spraos, 1980). Subsequent work in the 1980s was to further vindicate the thesis (Sapsford, 1985).[3]

Since the mid-1980s, the debate has shifted to the statistical arena. Such was the interest generated by the P–S hypothesis among econometricians and time-series statisticians that 'it has established itself as one of the major test beds on which they routinely evaluate their latest methods of trend estimations!' (Sapsford and Chen, 1998b, p. 27). Subsequent studies have largely upheld their original work leading to the conclusion that 'There can be few hypotheses in economics which have stood the test of time, not to mention the onslaught of increasingly sophisticated statistical techniques, as well as the P–S hypothesis' (Sapsford and Chen, 1998b, p. 29). The studies listed in Table 7.1 are those considered to have been the most influential. The balance of evidence for and against the P–S hypothesis contained in this sample of studies is not appreciably different from that presented in the wider literature as a whole (Sapsford, 1990; Sapsford and Balasubramanyan, 1994). Ten of the studies listed provided support for the P–S hypothesis in that they revealed the presence of a negative and statistically significant trend in the net barter terms of trade between primary products and manufactured goods. This is quite remarkable considering the different time periods analyzed, the different data series studied, and the widely differing array of statistical techniques employed.

Subjecting the P–S hypothesis to a new and novel set of data series, called a 'knowledge-based terms of trade index', it was found that the statistical evidence provided 'strong (and novel) support indeed for the hypothesis advanced almost a half century ago' and that 'There can surely be very few hypotheses in economics that could pass this knowledge-based sort of test with such flying colours!' (Sapsford and Chen, 1998b, pp. 31–2).

Singer last revisited his and Prebisch's thesis 50 years after he had first proclaimed his 'new discovery' (Singer, 1998f). The real objective of his original thesis was to argue for a tendency for international trade and investment to be factors contributing to international *divergence* rather than convergence between industrial and developing countries.

Table 7.1   The Prebisch–Singer hypothesis: statistical evidence

Date	Author	Reference	Trend
1950	Singer	*American Economic Review*	Negative
1950	Prebisch	*United Nations ECLA*	Negative
1980	Spraos	*Economic Journal*	Negative
1985	Sapsford	*Economic Journal*	Negative
1985	Thirlwall and Bergevin	*World Development*	Negative
1988	Gilli and Yang	*World Bank Econ. Review*	Negative
1989	Cuddington and Urzua	*Economic Journal*	None
1991	Powell	*Economic Journal*	None
1992	Ardeni and Wright	*Economic Journal*	Negative
1992	Sapsford, Sarkar and Singer	*J. of International Dev.*	Negative
1993	Bleaney and Greenaway	*Oxford Economic Papers*	Negative
1994	Reinhart and Wicham	*IMF Staff Papers*	Negative

Source: Sapsford and Chen, 1998b, p. 28.

He recognized that this was only one of many factors and that his original thesis left open the possibility that other forces making for convergence might be stronger and would outweigh the tendency towards divergence. However, by pointing in the direction of divergence, his thesis served to modify the prevailing optimistic view of the time that there must eventually be convergence, i.e., that the developing countries would grow faster than the richer industrial countries. He recalled the arguments for the prevailing optimistic assumption of convergence. One was to assume a more favourable capital–output ratio in the poorer countries. Another was that developing countries could use the existing technology produced in the industrial countries without having to go through the cost and pain of Schumpeter's 'creative destruction'. A third argument was the historical evidence that showed clear examples of the catching up process: Germany catching up with England by way of infant industries initially protected; Japan catching up with other members of the OECD club; and, more recently, the example of the East Asian 'tigers'.

The assumption of a tendency towards global convergence, implicit in the neoclassical production function, the theory of comparative advantage, and the Stolper–Samuelson thesis of an equalization of factor prices, was statistically tested by a number of analysts. The general result was that on a global scale, taking all developed and developing countries for which data were available, there was no visible tendency towards convergence. Divergence seemed to rule, in line with Singer's original thesis. There were some notable exceptions to this simple picture of divergence. There had been some conspicuous examples of catch-up by initially very poor countries, such as Korea and Taiwan, supported by massive foreign aid. Conditional convergence has taken place in recent years among countries with similar levels of education and technological capacity. And there was some evidence of convergence if the unit of comparison was persons rather than countries, in which case China and India dominated the picture and both countries had in recent years increased faster than the technological leaders. In that sense, there has been some recent convergence for the typical poor persons in the world, but how widespread and sustainable that was remained controversial.

The divergent elements operating the world economy recognized in Singer's original thesis are no longer such a heretic proposition as they were half a century ago. It is not unusual now to read that divergences and inequalities between and within countries have increased. The question is how much more unequal can world income distribution become before the resulting political instabilities and flows of migrants reach a point of directly harming the well-being of the citizens of the rich world and the stability of their states (Wade, 2001).

The new growth theory emphasizes that investment has increasing rather than decreasing returns, and that knowledge and technology feed upon themselves. It also recognizes that the process of globalization has losers as well as winners, and that the former tend to be the poorer and more vulnerable countries, and groups within countries. And such terms as 'vicious circles of poverty', 'marginalization', 'poverty traps', 'social exclusion' and 'endogenous growth', permeate the development literature. A new element has been added to support Singer's original thesis – the debt pressure under which the poorer countries are compelled to export and earn foreign exchange 'at any price'. The 'fallacy of composition' ensures that the efforts of each country individually to improve its income terms of trade by increasing its own market shares must be at the expense of other countries under similar pressure. The practice of the Bretton Woods institutions to urge countries to be 'outward-oriented' and improve their debt servicing capacity and balance of payments by increased exports, and to do this on a country-by-country basis, without much co-ordination between the different structural adjustment programmes, further strengthens the 'fallacy of composition'. The increased power of multinational corporations to shift production between developing countries, or out of them altogether, has introduced another element of 'racing for the bottom' in production and export costs. In all these respects, Singer saw that his original thesis had now 'joined the mainstream'.

One indication of this is that the Prebisch–Singer thesis is now incorporated into the advice given by the Bretton Woods institutions to developing countries. They are warned to be prudent even when export prices are temporarily favourable, and to guard against currency overvaluation. They are also warned to remember that the outlook for commodity prices is not favourable and that windfalls will tend to be temporary, with subsequent larger relapses. Singer noted that this was exactly the warning that his original thesis gave. The emphasis on 'volatility' was also fully compatible with his thesis. While a long-term declining trend might be of the order of one per cent per annum, year-to-year fluctuation might average something in the nature of 15 per cent a year. In some ways, therefore, volatility was a much greater, and more immediate, problem for macroeconomic policy in developing countries with a long-term declining trend. While diversification into manufactures did not offer a reliable escape from declining long-term terms of trade, it could dampen volatility. The volatility of prices or unit costs of manufactured exports was distinctly lower than for primary commodities, although it was higher than the volatility of the exports of manufactures from the more fully developed countries. The process of divergence, not convergence, continues.

8
Special United Nations Fund for Economic Development (SUNFED)

After 1949, Singer became much involved for almost a decade in a major initiative to increase the flow of resources to developing countries through the United Nations. This was a natural outcome of one of the policy conclusions of his work on the long-term prospects for the terms of trade of developing countries – to compensate for declining terms of trade (and lagging import capacity) by financial transfers (Singer, 1984c, pp. 296–303).

Financial transfers could take many forms, including investment by multinational corporations, bank lending and official development assistance (ODA). Singer pointed out that to rely on multinational corporations ran the risk of introducing cumulative elements into trade imbalances, if transfer pricing, export restrictions, lack of local training and local capacity for research and development (R & D), and repatriation of profits were not controlled by codes of conduct, countervailing power, or enlightened policies (all factors that he had pinpointed in his terms of trade thesis). The cumulative factor arose when trade imbalances made the resources of multinationals attractive. But their activities contributed to new trade imbalances, most clearly seen in the case of transfer pricing that directly affected terms of trade. The alternative of bank lending led to indebtedness, which could reduce significantly the export earnings of developing countries available for imports that were essential for development, and was equivalent to declining terms of trade. Hence, bank lending, like direct foreign investment, as a remedy for poor terms of trade, could be self-defeating. It both postponed the problem and intensified it. That left ODA, which Singer described as 'the natural avenue to which the interest of the United Nations, and my own with it, turned in those years as a result of trade pessimism' (Singer, 1984c, p. 296).

Singer described how the idea was born for a soft financing facility in the United Nations to assist development in the developing countries, as grants or at low rates of interest. It developed at the same time as work on terms of trade progressed 'with a clear intellectual link between the two' (Singer, 1984c, pp. 296–303). As he explained, it is difficult to realize now how revolutionary, even 'subversive', this idea was considered at the time. The limited, near-commercial, lending operations of the International Bank for Reconstruction and Development (IBRD) were the most that was permitted by an institution firmly under western (and especially United States) control. By contrast, the United Nations was at most entrusted with technical assistance work, endorsed as Point Four in President Truman's inaugural speech in January 1949 (see later). The official policy of the industrial countries, particularly the United States and the United Kingdom, was 'trade not aid'. The battle lines were drawn between most, though not all, of the industrial countries and the developing countries, with many of the former against aid and most of the latter for trade liberalization and in favour of aid (Hadwen and Kaufmann, 1960; Kaufmann, 1980).

Singer's personal involvement in SUNFED, along with others in the UN secretariat, took a number of forms. It was not the only assignment he took up during the decade from 1949 during which attempts to establish SUNFED were made. But he was fully committed and involved. He served the UN Sub-Commission for Economic Development as a member of the Development Section of the UN Economic Affairs Department and prepared reports and worked with rapporteurs, committees, groups and bodies concerned with SUNFED. Although the UN secretariat was at pains to point out that the idea for SUNFED originated with, and was pursued by, representatives of member nations, the UN secretariat, including Singer, strongly supported them in their cause. Reports pursuant to UN General Assembly resolutions on SUNFED were prepared by groups and individuals appointed by the General Assembly with the assistance of the small UN secretariat, of which Singer was a constant figure throughout the tortuous trail of hopes and endeavours.

The idea of establishing a special UN development fund took shape during the third session of the UN Sub-Commission on Economic Development in March–April 1949. Its chairman, Dr V. K. R. V. Rao, Singer's friend and former fellow PhD student at Cambridge University, proposed that an international agency should be set up, to be called the 'United Nations Economic Development Administration' (UNEDA), with five fields of activity:

> [1] technical assistance to under-developed countries, [2] co-ordination of technical assistance as extended by the U.N.and the specialized agencies, [3] assistance to under-developed countries in obtaining materials, equipment, personnel, etc. for economic development, [4] financing or helping to finance schemes of economic development which cannot be financed from the country's own resources and for which loans cannot be asked on strictly business principles, and [5] the promotion, and, if necessary, the direction and financing of regional development projects. (UN, 1949b).

The US representative on the subcommission did not concur with Rao's proposal. He said that the US government should look primarily to American private enterprise and should rely fundamentally on the IBRD for financing or collaborating in financing development projects not readily susceptible for implementation by purely private financing. (The IBRD also reacted negatively to Rao's proposal and suggested that the functions proposed for the UNEDA either came within the Bank's terms of reference or did not need to be performed.) Since no immediate unanimous support in the subcommission seemed attainable, Rao submitted this idea as his own personal proposal, which was appended to the report of the subcommission (UN, 1949b). The proposal did not get any further. The UN Economic and Social Council (ECOSOC) and the UN General Assembly concentrated their debates and decisions on the establishment of an Expanded Program of Technical Assistance (EPTA). However, ECOSOC did adopt a resolution (222 (IX) D), which recognized that the economic development of developing countries required not only expanded technical assistance but also assurance of an increased flow of international capital for financing economic development.

Rao would have seen Singer's work on the terms of trade and his proposal for countering developing countries' declining terms of trade with soft financing. He discussed his proposal with Singer, who served the subcommission as a member of the UN Economic Affairs Department. Singer saw to it that Rao's proposal was not forgotten and had it reproduced in a simultaneous UN secretariat report on *Methods of Financing Economic Development in Under-Developed Countries*, which was presented to ECOSOC (UN, 1949d).

A major step forward was taken at the sixth session of the UN General Assembly in 1951–52, which adopted a resolution (520 A (VI)) in which it requested ECOSOC:

> to submit to the General Assembly at its seventh regular session a detailed plan for establishing, as soon as circumstances permit, a special fund for grants-in-aid and for low-interest, long-term loans to under-developed countries for the purpose of helping them, at their request, to accelerate their economic development and to finance non-self-liquidating projects which are basic for their economic development, and to prepare a series of recommendations on the way in which the fund should be set up. (UN, 1952a).

Singer and other members of the UN Department of Economic Affairs prepared a detailed working paper which set out a series of alternative approaches to assist ECOSOC in responding to the UN General Assembly resolution.[4] The paper addressed the question of the composition and size of the fund, its operations, and the manner in which the fund may be controlled and administered, which clearly revealed the thinking and objectives of the UN secretariat. Regarding the composition and character of contributions to the fund, while it was recognized that convertibility would greatly simplify the fund's operation and administration, it appeared unnecessary for the accomplishment of its objectives. Since the principal purpose of the fund would be to assist under-developed countries to procure the goods and services required for their development programmes, and since the contributing countries would be the source of such items, it appeared unnecessary to insist on full convertibility of contributions. That condition would seem to be satisfied by according reasonable freedom to the fund's beneficiaries to buy, within the contributing countries or with their domestic currencies, the kinds of supplies required. In addition, bearing in mind the desirability of universal participation in the fund, insistence on completely convertible contributions would severely limit the number of participating countries participating, and hence its size. A decision would also have to be made as to whether contributions should be assessed or voluntary. If the former, payments would be made an obligation by international agreement, for which a formula for assessment would have to be agreed upon. If voluntary, a special procedure for pledging contributions, such as an international conference, would have to be established.

Pragmatically, the working paper noted that decisions concerning the composition and manner of contributions to the fund would have an important bearing on its size, irrespective of any estimates of the needs of under-developed countries. A number of estimates had already been made, reflecting: different conceptions of the speed at which economic development should or could proceed; and its pattern; geographical coverage; the role of foreign capital in the economic development process; and within the total of foreign capital, the role which grants-in-aid and low-interest loans should play.

A group of experts reporting to the UN secretary-general in 1951 on measures for economic development of under-developed countries had mentioned a figure of $3 billion a year in grants-in-aid 'to be reached eventually' (UN, 1951a).[5] A United States estimate put a ceiling of half a billion dollars annually (US, 1951). Other factors had a bearing on the fund's size. The fund would remain for a period of years, 'perhaps several decades', and would require periodic replenishment as it would provide both grants-in-aid and long-term, low-interest loans, but it was difficult to foresee what the circumstances would be when the need for replenishment arose. The UN General Assembly had suggested that ECOSOC keep in mind 'the utilization of any savings that may accrue from any programme of disarmament, as one of the sources of contributions' to the fund. It was estimated that aggregate world expenditure on armaments was well in excess of $80 billion a year, and still rising. If only 5 per cent of this expenditure was shifted to the resources of the fund, it could be 'greatly increased beyond what would otherwise appear likely'. The UN secretariat suggested that to start the operations of the fund, 'a minimum of $200-300 million from at least 15–20 contributors might appear reasonable' with the proviso that, once established, every effort would be made to obtain additional contributions.

The UN secretariat recalled that, as defined in the General Assembly resolution, the purpose of the fund was 'to help under-developed countries to accelerate their economic development and to finance non-self-liquidating projects which are basic to their economic development'. Within this context, ECOSOC might wish to recall several basic and important features in making its recommendations on the operations of the fund.

- First, both the General Assembly and ECOSOC had repeatedly recommended to under-developed countries that in order to accelerate their economic development they should adopt integrated programmes of development, based on the harmonious development of their natural resources and involving effective mobilization of available domestic capital, and designed to raise the living standards of their population as a whole. It was also recognized that the elaboration of technically sound integrated programmes of economic development was necessarily a protracted undertaking.

- Second, under-developed countries were responsible for their own economic development.
- Third, international grants-in-aid were required if economic development was to proceed at a more satisfactory rate than in the past.
- Fourth, whether or not a development project was revenue producing or non-self-liquidating was rarely a proper test of its importance to a country's development.
- Finally, in accordance with the general principles of the United Nations, assistance from the fund should be made available to all countries irrespective of political structure, race or religion, and provided in ways that conformed to the interests of the people of under-developed countries, with a view to strengthening their economic and political independence, and should not serve as a means of foreign economic and political interference in their internal affairs

Concerning the administration of the fund, it was recalled that in its resolution, the UN General Assembly had requested ECOSOC to keep in mind that the creation of a new international organization should be considered only if a careful examination of existing organizations proved that the functions required of the fund could not be carried out by them. Co-ordination with other existing organizations would also be necessary. Representatives of the IBRD had repeatedly pointed out that properly placed grants, by raising the creditworthiness of under-developed countries, could improve their prospects of qualifying for normal loans from the Bank and other sources. Co-ordination between the fund and the IBRD would therefore be advisable. Similarly, the integration of financial and technical assistance to under-developed countries required close co-operation between the fund, EPTA and the UN specialized agencies.

At its fourteenth session in the summer of 1952, ECOSOC responded to the working paper of the UN secretariat by establishing a committee of nine members to prepare a detailed plan for the operation of an international fund for grants-in-aid and for low-interest, long-term loans.[6] The committee drew closely from the UN secretariat working paper in preparing its report. Among its main recommendations (UN, 1953a),[7] the committee proposed that the fund be designated the 'Special United Nations Fund for Economic Development' (SUNFED), which should start with contributions for an initial two years and be replenished by annual contributions thereafter. Contributions should be voluntary and pledged by governments according to their own assessment of their ability to contribute. Irrespective of the ultimate size of the fund, which the committee was unable to estimate, the fund should not be established until a minimum amount equivalent to $250 million had been pledged for its initial operations by at least 30 contributing governments. Only countries which were members of the fund could qualify for its assistance. Governments assisted by the fund should strive for the effective mobilization and utilization of their internal and external resources to promote their economic development. They should also formulate integrated economic development programmes, and should avail themselves fully of the technical assistance services offered by the UN system and from other sources. Assistance from the fund should only be given to governments at their request. The fund's operation should not serve as a means for foreign economic and political interference and should be directed towards economic development which raised the welfare of the population as a whole. And the fund should have a separate administration and work in close proximity with the United Nations.

Singer worked closely with members of the committee. He recalled that the subject of its report was at first entitled 'United Nations Fund for Economic Development'. It was only shortly before translation and printing that he realized that the initials of the fund would read 'UNFED'. That was too close to the mark, and would no doubt be used by critics (including in the IBRD) to discredit and ridicule the whole idea. At the last minute, it was decided to come back to the use of the term 'special fund' on which the UN General Assembly resolution of 1951 had requested studies. Thus, 'special' was rapidly prefixed, and 'UNFED' became 'SUNFED'. On reflection, Singer felt that perhaps the title UNFED should have been retained, 'thus proclaiming ourselves as realists' (Singer, 1984c, p. 301).

In the high politics of the case, Singer was aware from the outset of the crucial role that the IBRD could play in the acceptance or otherwise of the concept of a UN special development fund. In an attempt to satisfy the concerns of Bank staff, he prepared a comprehensive list of the economic arguments for economic grants-in-aid, limiting his discussion to the measurability of the criteria implied in each case, to the necessary conditions in the under-developed countries corresponding to such criteria, and to the effect of choosing one criterion on the allocation of grants. The response from the IBRD was negative.[8] Its view was that any system of grants to under-developed countries, under which allocations were made more or less automatically, could not be very effective, 'no matter what safeguards were written into the charter of the special fund'. It was also strongly opposed to the provision of long-term, low-interest rate loans since 'they would tend to impair the integrity of other international obligations' and, in any event, 'could be equally well served by a judicious combination of grants and loans of the type made by the Bank'. Already by December 1952, the writing was on the wall. Singer stated that 'it cannot yet be taken for granted that the IBRD would wish to be entrusted with the administration of the IDA (International Development Authority)'.[9]

A new element was introduced into the debate on the establishment of a UN special development fund in 1953, which was to prove to be its undoing. On 16 April, President Eisenhower stated:

> This Government is ready to ask its people to join with all nations in devoting *a substantial percentage of any savings achieved by real disarmament* (emphasis added) to a fund for world aid and reconstruction. The purposes of this great work would be: to help other peoples to develop the undeveloped areas of the world, to stimulate profitable and fair world trade, to assist all peoples to know the blessings of productive freedom. The monuments of this new kind of war would be these: roads and schools, hospitals and homes, food and health. (UN,1953a, p. 14)

At the ECOSOC session following President Eisenhower's statement, the US representative proposed that the following declaration be adopted:

> We, the governments of the States Members of the United Nations, in order to promote higher standards of living and conditions of economic and social progress and development, stand ready to ask our peoples, *when sufficient progress has been made in internationally-supervised world-wide disarmament, to devote a portion of the savings achieved through such disarmament* (emphasis added) to an international fund, within the framework of the United Nations, to assist development and reconstruction in under-developed countries. (UN,1953b)

This proposal was adopted by ECOSOC, submitted to the eighth session of the UN General Assembly, and incorporated into a resolution (724 A (VIII)), which was adopted, with six abstentions, on 7 December 1953. The effect was to link the establishment of the special fund to the problem of universal disarmament, which considerably reduced its prospects, at least in the immediate future. During discussions in the Second Committee which preceded the General Assembly's adoption of the declaration, representatives of the under-developed countries urged the industrialized countries to waive this essential precondition of internationally supervised disarmament and establish the special fund without delay. With this in mind, the General Assembly passed another resolution, 724 B (VIII), on the same day, inviting governments and UN specialized agencies to transmit to the UN secretary-general their detailed comments both on the recommendations of the committee of nine and on the 'degree of moral and material support' which may be expected from them for the special fund. Raymond Scheyven of Belgium, who at the time was president of ECOSOC, was appointed to examine the comments received, with the assistance of the UN secretariat, and present a report on his findings to the UN General Assembly.

Singer was designated by the UN Department of Economic Affairs to work closely with Scheyven in preparing his report. Scheyven asked Singer to prepare for inclusion in his report a full statement of the arguments for establishing a special fund that would make grants-in-aid and low-interest loans, a detailed and fully supported statistical statement on the economic situation of under-developed countries, including the degree of poverty prevailing, the problem of financing economic development in general, and the particular aspects with which SUNFED would deal.[10] In the course of his work, Scheyven visited Washington, DC where the US government repeated its view that the special fund should be financed from the proceeds of disarmament. In a meeting with the IBRD president, Eugene Black expressed the views that: the case existed for grants; the Bank knew of worthwhile projects which could go forward on a grant basis, or with grants plus Bank loans; and the Bank would be able and willing to administer such grants. However, he remained unalterably opposed to low-interest, long-term loans as he felt they would reduce a borrowing country's creditworthiness.

Scheyven duly submitted his report to the UN General Assembly, which contained the information Singer had been asked to prepare (UN, 1954a). Crucially, it also contained an analysis of the replies received from governments concerning the proposed special fund. Under-developed country governments wanted the fund to be set up immediately, without waiting for disarmament, and would be prepared to make contributions to it. Some industrial country governments (Denmark, Italy, Norway and The Netherlands) expressed the view that it would be regrettable to make the creation of the special fund contingent on the general reduction in armament expenditure and were ready to provide contributions. Others (Belgium, France, Japan and Luxembourg), in supporting the establishment of the fund, made their contributions to it dependent on meeting a number of conditions. A third group of countries (Canada, Federal Republic of Germany, New Zealand, Sweden, Switzerland, United Kingdom and the United States of America) either maintained, as an essential condition, that sufficient progress must be achieved in internationally supervised world-wide disarmament before any contributions could be made to the fund, or took the even more reserved position that, at least in present circumstances, the establishment of a new international organization would not be desirable. Accordingly, Scheyven concluded that 'the essential conditions for the establishment of such a fund in the near future do not at present exist'.

The protagonists for the special fund did not give up the fight. After Scheyven's report was discussed at length at the eighteenth session on ECOSOC in 1954, the Council unanimously adopted a resolution, 532 A (XVIII), which recommended that the UN General Assembly should urge governments to review their positions regarding support for the special fund 'in accordance with changes in the international situation and other relevant factors'. The UN General Assembly passed yet another resolution, 822 (IX), in December 1954 requesting Scheyven to prepare a further report:

> giving a full and precise picture of the form or forms, functions and responsibilities which such a special United Nations fund for economic development might have and especially the methods by which its operations might be integrated with the development plans of the countries receiving assistance for it. (UN, 1954b)

The report should also consider the working relationship of such a fund with the UN Technical Assistance Board, the IBRD and other UN specialized agencies concerned, the UN regional commissions and existing programmes in the field of economic development. On this occasion, Scheyven was to be assisted by an '*ad hoc* group of experts', selected by the UN secretary-general in consultation with Scheyven, as well as by the UN secretariat.[11]

A critical stage had been reached in the long-drawn-out saga to establish SUNFED. On 10 December 1954, in an internal memorandum, Singer wrote 'The present stage in the SUNFED work is important.'[12]

A number of governments were rethinking their positions, Scheyven was setting out on a new stage in his mission, a new *ad hoc* group of high-ranking experts would bring their minds to bear on the problem, and the UN secretariat would be called upon to render more assistance. Exchanges of opinions had cleared much of the preliminary ground and had indicated in what direction agreement may, or may not, be possible. He thought that at this stage 'new thoughts and new ideas would be useful, provided they are constructive in the sense of providing areas of agreement rather than disagreement'. He therefore set down 'some thoughts' first to provoke discussion within the UN secretariat and then with Scheyven and his group of experts.

His first suggestion was that in the first place SUNFED might be thought of less as a mechanism of its own but rather as a *'system of international consultation and agreement'* (original emphasis) in the dispensation of soft assistance to under-developed countries. He noted that the precedent of grants-in-aid to under-developed countries was well established, both bilaterally and multilaterally, but not through international organizations. Would it not be possible for donors and recipients of grants-in-aid to be brought together under the auspices of the United Nations to discuss the principles and operational techniques of such assistance? He had two analogies in mind, the Colombo Plan and commodity stabilization, e.g., disposal of surpluses, where the principle of international consultation and co-ordination of policies was generally recognized.[13] An international consultative arrangement embracing all grant assistance would not necessarily increase the sum total of such assistance, although it might ultimately do so if such consultation led to greater confidence in its ultimate value, and its readier acceptance. It might also be a valuable rehearsal for an ultimate SUNFED, if and when it was established. And, he added, it might also lead to further exchanges of opinion among governments 'a little closer to reality' than general discussion in ECOSOC and the UN General Assembly.

Singer's second suggestion related to the absorption and use of grants-in-aid by under-developed countries. He saw the obvious analogy of the Marshall Plan and its successful absorption and utilization by European countries. At the end of the Second World War, the United States came to the assistance of European countries in a massive reconstruction effort that involved the largest aid programme in world history. Under this European Recovery Programme, more popularly known as the 'Marshall Plan' (after its originator, President Truman's secretary of state, George C. Marshall), $13.5 billion of aid was provided between

1948 and 1952 (3 per cent of the US annual GNP for each of the four consecutive years), almost a third of which consisted of food, feed and fertilizers. On that occasion, the technique used was based on the principles of joint organization and constant consultation.

Singer's third thought related to the debate between grants-in-aid and long-term, low-interest loans, which had led to opposition to SUNFED by some key governments and institutions, including the IBRD. Perhaps the committee of nine had been 'psychologically wrong' in starting off with low-interest, long-term loans and then whittling them down by introducing the principles of readjustment, renegotiation and waivers. Singer suggested that perhaps a better approach would be to start with grants-in-aid but then 'whittle them up', e.g., by making provisions for assisted countries in specified conditions or categories to make fairly substantial subsequent contributions to SUNFED, or by having fairly strong provisions for counterpart funds which might be utilized, or even transferred back, under specified conditions and situations. Another way of reconciling the principle of recovery of funds with the removal of the objectionable 'fuzzy loans' would be to utilize the resources of SUNFED as a contribution or subsidy to amortization payments made by under-developed countries in respect of sound projects which only through the SUNFED subsidy were capable of carrying the rate of interest payable to such institutions as the IBRD. In that case, what would be a grant from the SUNFED point of view, was in fact recovered by the IBRD. Not only would this avoid any semblance of competition with other institutions but it would strengthen creditworthiness and be an inducement to under-developed countries to take all the loans they could get on a commercial basis. In fact, it would lower the limits of 'self-liquidation' which projects must display before they could be financed, 'as should be the essence of SUNFED's existence'.

Singer's final thought related to technical assistance. He noted that there was an almost universal desire to strengthen the UN technical assistance programme. Indeed, many governments who were sceptical of SUNFED preferred to build upon the UN technical assistance programme instead. These viewpoints need not be irreconcilable. Perhaps it was possible to think of a separate addition to the UN technical assistance programme which would be specifically designated as a testing-out mechanism for the possibilities and usefulness of a future SUNFED. A moderate addition to the technical assistance funds ('perhaps a further five million dollars or so') would be sufficient to send experts to each applicant to look for, and appraise, projects within the scope of SUNFED.

In a briefing note for the UN secretary-general in March 1955, Singer drew attention to the contrasting views in Scheyven's committee concerning the key issues of loans versus grants and the administrative structure of SUNFED.[14] He noted that the importance of the first of these issues 'should not be under-estimated', since the type of financial operation engaged in would have a considerable bearing on SUNFED's administrative structure. The IBRD would probably not wish to administer SUNFED if it engaged in low-interest or local currency loans. Regarding administrative structure, Singer noted that three different alternatives were emerging: to establish SUNFED as a quasi-autonomous body; to integrate the staff and administration, but not control, of SUNFED into the IBRD; and to establish SUNFED as a governmental control board in New York, with individual projects allocated to the IBRD or other UN specialized agencies as decided by the controlling board.

The divisions in the committee on the affiliation of the fund with the IBRD were 'quite sharp'. It was clear to the committee that the IBRD wished to administer SUNFED but did not want to give the slightest commitment to try to promote SUNFED with the US administration. If SUNFED was entirely integrated with the IBRD, it might lose much of its popular appeal and support it had already gained in some countries. Singer indicated that the 'uncompromisingly negative position' of the US towards making immediate contributions to SUNFED, whatever its administrative structure, had not weakened. Scheyven's alternative approach was to collect promises of say $50 million from West European countries and start SUNFED operations without US participation. The indications were that the best hope of gaining US co-operation lay in starting SUNFED as a largely European initiative by countries that had benefited from the Marshall Plan.

Singer again worked closely with Scheyven, and with the committee of experts, in the preparation of their report to ECOSOC and the UN General Assembly, during the course of which he made an enduring friendship with Jan Tinbergen of The Netherlands. Their report showed unmistakable signs of his hand throughout its recommendations, which were made on behalf of the entire committee and not only of Scheyven (UN, 1955a). It endorsed most of the recommendation of the report of the committee of nine and in some cases took them further. They suggested that the General Assembly should decide to establish the special fund for a five-year period so that countries could take a decision at the end of that period in the light of experience and the results achieved. They recognized that countries might be reluctant to commit themselves for an indefinite period and would thus have an assurance that they would be able to reconsider their commitments within a reasonable time if the operations or organization of the fund were not fully satisfactory to them. The committee left it to the General Assembly to decide the initial sum and minimum membership with which the special fund might start operations, adding that it might not be desirable to wait until a sum of $250 million had been collected before starting the operations of the fund, which had been recommended by the committee of nine.

The special fund would provide under-developed countries with grants or loans repayable in local currency as well as in the currency in which they were given, at low rates of interest, but not on indeterminate and extremely liberal terms. And it advised caution in the use of contributions in kind as 'its task might become so difficult as to hinder effective operation'. As the fields of interest of the fund and the IBRD would be clearly defined, the two agencies would be able to work together in the financing and development of under-developed countries. They would be able jointly to finance a single project or economic development plan in an under-developed country, which would lower the overall interest rate payable by a debtor country, and reduce the drain on the aid resources of both agencies. Repayment in local currency of loans from the fund would also enable it, to some extent at least, to replenish its resources without having to call for the continuous replenishment of the entire fund, and would thus reduce the burden on contributing countries.

In carrying out its functions, the fund would make use of the concerned UN bodies, who would examine all requests for its assistance. The creation of a new international bureaucracy would thus be avoided and its secretariat kept to a strict minimum. Co-ordination would be effected through an executive board and a joint committee in which the fund's director-general, based at UN headquarters in New York, would be required to co-operate closely with the UN secretary-general and the president of the IBRD.

The saga continued. After examining their report, the UN General Assembly passed yet another resolution that kept the quest for SUNFED alive. Expressing 'its great appreciation of the work performed by Mr. Scheyven, assisted by the Secretary-General and the Committee of Experts', the General Assembly requested the Secretary-General to invite countries to transmit to him 'not later than 31 March 1956' (within three months) their views relating to 'the establishment, role, structure and operation' of SUNFED, for which a list of questions was annexed to the resolution (UN, 1955b). The resolution added, for the first time, that such views and replies 'may provide material *for the statutes of the Fund* when it is decided to establish such a Fund' (emphasis added). Clearly, the protagonists for the fund must have felt that they were within sight of the winning post. An *ad hoc* committee composed of representatives of 16 governments was appointed by the president of the General Assembly to analyze the replies received from governments.[15] The establishment of a governmental committee was also considered by the proponents of the fund to be a big step forward in comparison with previous resolutions under which groups of experts had made reports.

But analysis of the 57 replies received showed no substantial change in the positions adopted by countries the last time that they were requested to present their views. Critically, certain key countries, especially the United States, expressed their continued opposition to the establishment of the fund despite strong domestic support, including some from unlikely quarters.[16] Undeterred, another draft resolution (doc. A/C.2/L. 315) presented by 39 countries, which called for the early drafting of statutes for SUNFED, was circulated in the second (economic and financial) committee of the General Assembly on 1 February 1957.[17] Ironically, it fell to Paul Hoffman, the former administrator of the Marshall Plan, the largest aid programme in history, now a US delegate at the UN, to repeat the United States' objection to the drawing up of statutes for the fund 'lest it create false hopes that a decisive step is being taken toward the establishment of a great new program of economic assistance through the United Nations'. He added, 'It seems to me that a decision to draft statutes will prove to be merely a paper plan which cannot be made effective for lack of resources. ... [Therefore], the United States will not be able to participate in drafting of the statutes of the proposed fund.'

The *New York Times* castigated the United States' decision. In an editorial on 1 February 1957, it deplored the renewed United States opposition to SUNFED and suggested that, given his background as a former administrator of the Marshall Plan, Hoffman was possibly unhappy in having to announce that opposition. It stated that with a $40 billion defence budget, it was preposterous that the United States could not afford to contribute $80 million to the proposed level of $250 million for the fund. It noted that Hoffman, in stating United States opposition:

> did not really explain why this was so. It is supposed that Washington is not satisfied with the form SUNFED is taking. If this

is the case why not bring out a better plan? We are not poor in money or in generosity. Why should we be so poor in faith, courage and compassion that we must wait for general disarmament before we join our UN neighbours to do some helpful things that politics and other reasons keep us from doing unilaterally?

The embarrassment of the US position was carried further by the statements of several industrial countries, notably France and The Netherlands, in favour of SUNFED, and the recollection that the US had originally opposed the creation of the International Finance Corporation (IFC), but subsequently reversed its positions. The IFC was established in 1956 as an affiliate of the IBRD to aid private capital investment projects in the less developed countries.

Matters were finally brought to a head when it was decided to proceed with drafting the statutes for SUNFED by a governmental committee under the chairmanship of U Thant, who at the time was the Burmese delegate to the UN but was later to become secretary-general (UN, 1957). Once matters had reached this stage, some kind of action became inevitable and 'the little band of SUNFED activists for the first time felt that all our efforts, and all the abuse, over eight years or so had not been totally in vain' (Singer 1984c, p. 302).

Two somewhat contrasting versions of what then took place have been given as viewed from the UN on the one hand and the US government and IBRD on the other. From the UN perspective, Singer identified V.K.R.V. Rao and Hernan Santa Cruz as the true 'grandfathers of IDA'. The US government and the IBRD were seen to do a U-turn in their opposition to a soft-financing facility for underdeveloped countries. Seeing the relentless pressure to establish SUNFED, the US government agreed to a soft-financing window in IBRD where, owing to its voting structure which was determined by the level of contributions, the US would effectively retain control over its use. This would not have been the case had SUNFED been established under UN auspices, where decisions were made according to a voting structure based on one country, one vote. At the same time, Eugene Black, the president of IBRD, who had been adamantly opposed to the Bank acquiring a soft-lending function, reversed his position. And instead of SUNFED, IDA (the International Development Association) was born as the soft-loan affiliate of the IBRD.

The perspective was different seen through the eyes of US government and IBRD officials. The historians of the World Bank recognized that IDA could be viewed as a significant indirect result of the vigorous campaign to establish SUNFED, and that it stands 'as living proof that the "international power structure" is responsive to persistent peaceful pressure' (Mason and Asher, 1973, p. 380).[18] Black recognized that IDA 'was really an idea to offset the urge for SUNFED' (Weaver, 1965, p. 28). But other pressures were identified by Mason and Asher (1973, pp. 386–9).

In 1954, the US food aid programme was authorized to sell US surplus agricultural commodities, accept inconvertible local currencies in exchange, and make loans and grants for economic development with the funds acquired. As US food aid grew, its local currency holdings increased to a politically embarrassing level. While there was confusion as to the real economic value of these funds, a search began for ways to draw down the holdings, or transfer them to other hands. Senator Monroney of Oklahoma, not known for his international financial experience, announced in February 1958 his intention of introducing in the US senate a resolution calling for the establishment of a soft-lending facility in co-operation with the IBRD. He envisaged the establishment of a competently managed, non-political, agency to which the US could transfer substantial quantities of local currency holdings. With these, and other, resources, the agency could make long-term loans at low rates of interest, repayable in local currencies, to supplement IBRD loans.

Black publicly endorsed the idea, which was supported by the US government and adopted by the US senate. The most compelling argument for a new international facility was the outlook for the developing world if there were no soft loans and/or grant aid. The debt burden of the less developed countries was mounting and the role of the IBRD was limited if it continued to be authorized to make loans only at conventional rates of interest to creditworthy countries unable to borrow in the private market. Once the validity of this line of argument was conceded, the question shifted to the auspices for a soft-loan facility. The rich countries that would have to provide the resources held the decisive vote. As between the UN and the IBRD, the preference of the potential major contributors, particularly the United States, was clear. In a letter dated 31 July 1959, the US secretary of the treasury proposed to the president of the IBRD that draft articles of agreement for an 'International Development Association' be prepared, which were unanimously agreed by the Bank's governors on 1 October 1959. IDA came into force in 1960. A more recent history of the World Bank described IDA as 'one of those phenomena that underscores the role of happenstance in history'. It changed the Bank 'as nothing else had up to that time. It radically increased the Bank's roll of clients and its potential resources' (Kapur *et al.*, 1997, vol. 1, p. 14).

In Singer's view, the UN was to lose potentially significant power and influence in matters of economic development of the developing countries and become something of a 'residual' organization with the loss of SUNFED. But SUNFED protagonists could draw some satisfaction from the fact that their endeavours had played an important, even crucial, role in the creation of IDA as well as the IFC, which increased considerably the level and scope of World Bank assistance.

The United States and the United Kingdom from the beginning of the debate on SUNFED in 1949 'combined hostility to soft financing with hostility to the idea of a rival to the World Bank'. To what extent the Bank's original opposition to the general principle of soft-loan financing was one of conviction or political tactics Singer found difficult to say. He, and some of his colleagues, were under no illusion that if or when it came to a matter of choice, any new soft-financing facility would go to the World Bank, not the United Nations (Singer, 1984c, pp. 298–9). He recognized, with an element of pathos, that 'it fell to us in the UN secretariat to play the role of the "radical", "politically naive", "amateurish", "inexperienced", "utopians" (all adjectives used throughout the SUNFED saga)' but in the event the cause of SUNFED was kept alive 'until it became acceptable, when it was time for the "responsible", "pragmatic", "experienced", "professional", "well-tried" institution [the World Bank] to move in and take over'.

The historians of the World Bank attributed to what Singer called 'the wild men of the United Nations' the function of frightening the conservative donors sufficiently to look to IDA, and earlier to the IFC, 'as a welcome escape from less welcome schemes' (Mason and Asher, 1973). It was even suggested that some of the 'more sophisticated' leaders of developing countries deliberately put on the pressure for SUNFED in order to induce the rich countries 'to counter this pressure by supporting the creation of a soft-loan affiliate of the World Bank and by providing it with ever-increasing financial resources' (Reid, 1973, p. 134). Singer was 'quite satisfied' with this distribution of roles as 'fall guys' for the World Bank and 'happy' with the respectability acquired by the idea of soft multilateral financing, all the more since the UN got the valuable consolation prizes of the UN Special Fund and the UN World Food Programme. As we will see below, Singer was to have a hand in both of them.

But Singer was to suffer personally for his close involvement with attempts to establish SUNFED. At the height of the McCarthy witch hunt for communist sympathizers, the UN came under particular scrutiny. A McCarthy committee room was even opened in the UN building to interrogate UN staff who were suspected of being communists. Singer became the target of sharp attacks by the McCarthyites.[19] SUNFED was characterized as a 'Socialist UN plan to disarm and bankrupt the United States' (Widener, 1956). Singer and others closely associated with attempts to set up SUNFED were subjected to deliberate and orchestrated character-assassination in the McCarthy-controlled press through false and misleading information. SUNFED was said to involve $50 billion over a period of 15 to 20 years, of which the US taxpayer would be called upon to put up about 70 per cent. Singer, who was described as special adviser to the UN Bureau of Economic Affairs and representative of the UN secretary-general, was identified as a key figure on SUNFED at the UN. Details were given of his past work for the Fabian Society on unemployment, his support of the Beveridge plan and the welfare state in Britain, and his work at the Ministry of Town and Country Planning in London for the British Labour government after the war as proof of his left-wing, socialist views, and his association with fellow-travellers in the UN secretariat. Criticism even took on an element of farce when the McCarthyites used as proof the fact that Singer's Fabian pamphlet in support of the Beveridge plan for social welfare in Britain in 1943 was published with a red cover and that it began with the question 'Are pounds, shillings and pence meaningless symbols?' (Singer, 1943b).

Singer's friends and colleagues rallied to his defence. An article on SUNFED was published under the name of Philippe de Seynes, under-secretary of the UN Department of Economic and Social Affairs, in an attempt to set the record straight (de Seynes, 1956). Singer was assured by his superiors and senior colleagues that they had no doubts about the falseness of the accusations made against him. He offered to submit to an inquiry to clear the allegations made against him. As a United Kingdom citizen, he was advised that he should not appear before the McCarthy committee. Singer was shaken by this experience and contemplated leaving the UN. His faith in the integrity of the UN was restored when Dag Hammarskjöld was appointed secretary-general and when he removed the McCarthy committee from the UN building.

Singer's wife provided strong support throughout this troubled period. She was actively involved in protests against the discrimination of women in New York through a branch of the Women's League for Peace and Freedom. She also worked voluntarily for an organization for better housing and for attacking discrimination against black people in the house rental market. But she was careful not to undermine Singer's position at the United Nations.

9
Pre-investment and the UN Special Fund

At its session in the summer of 1957, when ECOSOC had agreed to urge the UN General Assembly to establish SUNFED, the United States fully expected the General Assembly to vote for SUNFED, leaving the US delegation (with Canada and the United Kingdom) isolated in opposition, unless a constructive alternative were found. The alternative proposed by the US, and modified during the debate, was the creation of a UN Special Fund, which the General Assembly decided to establish by its resolution 1291 (XII) on 14 December 1957.

Paul Hoffman was recognized as the 'intellectual father' of the UN Special Fund having spelled out its role in the symbiotic relationship between pre-investment and investment activities, revealed a major gap in the investment process, and pointed to the need for better international arrangements to finance and execute pre-investment studies. In an article published in *The New York Times Magazine*, he suggested that a UN experimental fund of $100 million should be set up to be used for surveys of mineral, water and soil resources and for a limited number of pilot projects (Hoffman, 1957). His views were influential because of the respect he enjoyed as a former administrator of the Marshall Plan, as a member of the US delegation to the United Nations, and as a successful businessman. The Special Fund was set up to finance project studies and analysis, natural resource surveys and pilot projects in the borderland between technical assistance and investment. Singer noted that Hoffman's proposal was readily acceptable to both the proponents and opponents of SUNFED. Both camps hailed it as a victory, but in reality it was more a victory for the opponents, who had out-manoeuvered the proponents (Singer, 1984c, p. 302).

The proponents hoped that the Special Fund would be a stepping stone to the eventual establishment of SUNFED, but this was not to be.

The blowing-up of the pre-investment function was described, with some justification, as 'a mystique well beyond its intrinsic importance in the investment process' (Mason and Asher, 1973, p. 592). Singer argued that from the UN point of view it was a politically necessary and useful 'mystique'.

A close and cordial relationship was established with the IBRD. Discussions had taken place between the UN and the Bank on the latter's role in the proposed Special Fund even before it was established. A consultative board was set up consisting of the UN secretary-general, the president of the Bank, and the executive chairman of the UN Technical assistance Board (David Owen – see later) who met with and advised the managing director of the Special Fund.

Singer was appointed chairman of the preparatory UN secretariat group set up for the establishment of the Special Fund. He helped to develop the concept of 'pre-investment' as an example of what he called the 'new pragmatism' (Singer, 1964b, pp. 18–25). Pre-investment was the term used to denote a host of allied activities essential to laying the base for subsequent economic development. These included: surveys of a country's natural resources; industrial feasibility studies; the inculcation of knowledge and new skills in the working population; the building of national and regional institutions; and improvement of development planning. Such activities could be seen to smooth the way for subsequent economic expansion and maximize the productivity of the capital invested. Because their effects were often not directly visible, but were manifested indirectly through the productivity of the subsequent large-scale investment, they were often neglected by developing countries, whose governments (like those providing bilateral aid) were under pressure to show quick results. The result was seen in dams that leaked; irrigation systems that watered unsuitable soils; and factories without adequate transport facilities, supplies of raw materials, or trained labour. Hoffman recognized that in underlining the importance of pre-investment activities, Singer 'has performed a service for development planners all over the world' (Singer, 1964a, p. x). Singer took charge of the preparatory work for the Fund until the arrival of Paul Hoffman as its managing director. Subsequently, Singer undertook a number of assignments for the Special Fund and for the UNDP (set up in 1965 through the amalgamation of the Special Fund and EPTA), including a mission to Kenya which formulated UNDP's 'country programming' procedure.

Singer and other proponents of SUNFED were, however, to suffer one further disappointment in the long battle for UN control. When it became clear that IDA would be set up as an affiliate of the World Bank, the UN secretary-general, Dag Hammarskjöld, with Singer's encouragement, began urging the Bank's president, Eugene Black, to agree to a special institutional link between IDA and the UN (Mason and Asher, 1973, p. 569). He suggested that the consultative board set up for the UN Special Fund might also be used to co-ordinate IDA and UN activities. Black firmly rejected this suggestion. He recognized, however, that the creation of IDA would intensify the need for close co-operation at the working level. A liaison committee was established in 1961 for an informal exchange of information between the Bank and the UN as a whole. Periodic meetings of not less than four times a year were envisaged but the committee became inactive.

10
Technical Assistance

Another issue to which Singer attached considerable importance, following from his work on the terms of trade, was the provision of technical assistance to under-developed countries in order to build up their national capacities for economic development. When he arrived at the UN, its principal functions were seen to be to convene conferences, collect and analyze data, set standards and undertake studies. The development section of the Department of Economic Affairs, which became Singer's responsibility, was also in charge of a very small technical assistance programme with a total expenditure of about $1 million a year. In January 1949, when working on budget proposals for the next year, Singer recalled debating with colleagues whether they should risk proposing a 10 per cent increase in the technical assistance programme from $1 million to $1.1 million when a major event took place, which caused them to dramatically alter their perspective and resulted in a UN Expanded Programme of Technical Assistance (EPTA).

At his inauguration on 20 January 1949, US President Harry S. Truman caught everyone by surprise when he called for a 'bold new program' for making the benefits of American science and industrial progress available to under-developed countries. It was the first mention of what became known as the 'Point Four Program' (McCullough, 1992, pp. 730–31). President Truman said:

Fourth – we must embark on a bold new program for making the benefits of our scientific advance and industrial progress available for the improvement and growth of underdeveloped areas. More than half the people of the world are living in conditions approaching misery. Their food is inadequate. They are victims of disease. Their economic life is primitive and stagnant. Their poverty is a handicap and a threat both to them and the more prosperous areas. For the first time in history, humanity possesses the knowledge and the skill to relieve the suffering of these people. Much of the aid that is needed can be provided most effectively through the United Nations ... much ... can be provided directly by the United States. (US, 1949)

President Truman followed his inaugural address with a message to the US congress on 24 January 1949 recommending the enactment of legislation to authorize an 'Expanded Program of Technical Assistance for the Underdeveloped Areas of the World'. The aid needed was seen to fall into two related categories: technical, scientific and managerial knowledge necessary for economic development; and production goods, machinery and equipment and financial assistance to create 'productive enterprises'.

The effect was electrifying. David Owen, the UN under-secretary-general for economic and social affairs, Singer's friend who had recruited him to the UN, on hearing about Truman's proposal, rushed to him to order a rewriting of the UN estimates for technical assistance, which emerged as the UN proposal for an Expanded Program of Technical Assistance (EPTA) with an annual expenditure of $150 million. EPTA was launched in 1950. Although the level of expenditure was to fall far short of the original proposal, EPTA was to give the entire UN system an operational role. It enabled the staff of the UN agencies to travel extensively throughout the developing world and put them in touch with the daily lives of large numbers of ordinary people. Singer himself was to benefit in being able to undertake many missions to under-developed countries and take part in training programmes for their national personnel.

At the top of the EPTA pyramid were two pieces of administrative machinery: a Technical Assistance Committee, an intergovernmental body of ECOSOC, responsible for reviewing the annual programme submitted to it by a Technical Assistance Board (TAB), an inter-agency body composed of representatives of the secretariats of the participating UN agencies with an executive chairman appointed by the UN secretary-general. Resident representatives were appointed to reside in under-developed countries by the TAB executive chairman, in consultation with the heads of the participating UN agencies to represent EPTA and provide co-ordination at the country level. David Owen was appointed executive chairman of TAB and Philippe de Seynes, a French national, replaced him as head of the UN Department of Economic and Social Affairs in 1955, with Singer as his special adviser.

Singer identified new directions in the organization of technical assistance activities within the United Nations system in what became known as the 'blue book' of proposals for action in the UN development decade of the 1960s, which mirrored his own experience (UN, 1962, pp. 102–3). Through EPTA, there was a growing participation of the staff of the UN system (in New York, the UN regional commissions, and the UN specialized agencies) in technical assistance activities. The tendency of substantive research and operational services to merge facilitated the application of the results of research to practical problems and, conversely, helped to determine the lines along which research could usefully be developed. Following the recommendations of the UN General Assembly concerning the decentralization of the economic and social activities of the United Nations and the strengthening of the UN regional commissions, their functions in providing substantive support to technical assistance projects and in carrying out administrative tasks were developed. Singer himself was to take part in these functions when he became director of the Policies and Programming Division of the United Nations Economic Commission for Africa (see below). The appointment of regional and interregional advisers whose services could be made available simultaneously to a number of countries also proved to be an effective way of enlarging the range of services to developing countries. Singer was to serve as senior UN interregional adviser of development planning.

A further method for the effective utilization of the technical assistance resources of the UN system was identified by Singer. He proposed the employment of groups of experts to be responsible for a particular project or sector, covering all the relevant fields in which external assistance was requested. This method was especially valuable in the fields of national development planning, the preparation of national statistical or demographic surveys, and the exploration of natural resources and community development. In many of the newly independent countries, the number of public administrators and an institutional basis for national development were inadequate. An important task for the UN development decade was to expand technical assistance through OPEX, the UN programme for the provision of operational and executive personnel. The establishment of training facilities and the training of national personnel for national development planning and the implementation of development projects were seen as priorities in a number of developing countries. Again, Singer was to take part in training programmes as part of his early assignments outside New York (see below).

Singer saw the need to co-ordinate the technical assistance activities of the UN system not only to avoid duplication but to bring to bear on specific problems the combined knowledge and techniques available within the system. He was, therefore, an early advocate of the need for a technical assistance co-ordinating agency as well as the co-ordination of technical assistance with development planning (Singer, 1964g). Although this was resisted by some of the UN specialized agencies, the UN Special Fund and EPTA were amalgamated in 1965 to form a new UN body, the United Nations Development Programme (UNDP), with Paul Hoffman as its administrator, Arthur Lewis (the distinguished development economist and later Nobel Laureate) as his deputy, and David Owen as associate administrator. Singer found this development 'almost too much of a good thing; I felt thoroughly enthusiastic about this addition to the UN family' (Singer, 1984c, p, 299).

11
Multilateral Food Aid

With the failure to establish SUNFED, Singer and others turned their attention not only to the UN Special Fund but to other possible sources of soft financing for developing countries which might be provided through the UN system, including food aid. He was to play an important role both in the creation of the UN World Food Programme (WFP), initially as a three-year experimental programme (1963–65), and in its continuation thereafter.

It was while undertaking his work on SUNFED that Singer's emerging interest in food aid occurred. As he described it:

> it was also in casting around for possible financing for SUNFED that I became very interested in 1954 in the establishment, under Public Law 480, of the U. S. food aid program and the possibility of an international food aid program which had begun to emerge in Rome. (There was also a direct link with the local counterpart funds arising from P.L. 480 and the financing of IDA.) This interest led to my involvement in laying the ground for the U.N./FAO World Food Programme, and it has remained an active interest. (Singer, 1984c, p. 301)

The FAO and UN had been advocating the establishment of a multilateral food aid agency, which, for different reasons, both US presidential candidates in the election campaign of 1960, vice president Richard Nixon and senator John F. Kennedy, also supported (Wallerstein, 1980, pp. 38–42). The chance came when, following a proposal made by President Eisenhower at the United Nations on 22 September 1960 (UN, 1960a), the UN General Assembly passed a resolution on the 'Provision of food surpluses to food-deficit peoples through the United Nations system', and invited the FAO director-general , in consultation with the UN secretary-general, to undertake a study on how this might be done (UN, 1960b). The FAO director-general appointed a group of five 'high-level, independent experts' to assist him in preparing the study, which included Singer. [20] Singer held a special position in the group. He enjoyed the confidence of the executive heads of both the UN and FAO, and was appointed chairperson. He brought to the group the unique and profound experience he had gained in working on the proposals for SUNFED as well as a UN Expanded Program of Technical Assistance (EPTA), and a special interest in a multilateral form of the US food aid programme (PL 480).

Certain basic considerations influenced the group's report and harked back to Singer's early work in the United Kingdom on unemployment and the welfare state and in the United Nations on the terms of trade thesis. Information available at the time indicated that over half of the world's population was either undernourished or malnourished. The world food problem was therefore seen as one of deficiencies, not surpluses. Under-development was recognized as the basic cause. Poverty for many alongside prosperity for a few was previously a general phenomenon, nationally and internationally. While steps were being taken in the industrialized countries to remedy this imbalance, it remained a grim reality in the under-developed world. Equality of opportunity, full employment and a minimum of subsistence were accepted parts of the social philosophy of the welfare state in developed countries. But nothing similar obtained within the international community as a whole. The basic aim should therefore be to apply the principles of social progress within rich countries to the world as a whole.

In a spirit of optimism that matched the time, particularly with the advent of the Kennedy administration in the United States (see below), the group considered that the resources to implement such a far-reaching programme were already available. It estimated that a transfer of two-thirds to three-quarters of one per cent of the Gross National Product (GNP) of the developed countries over a period of five years, and probably less for another decade, would provide sufficient means for helping people in developing countries help themselves. This represented a much smaller international redistribution of income than national income redistribution achieved through progressive taxation in many developed countries, and much less than achieved under the Marshall Plan. The group pointedly added that to think that the developed world could not spare that amount for an international programme of economic aid was to show 'failure of imagination and failure of will'.

A central part of the expert group's case was that surplus food could form an important part of capital in its original sense of a 'subsistence fund'. If sufficient food could not be supplied to meet increased demand from the additionally employed construction workers, either more resources would have to be spent on food imports or the amount of additional investment would have to be reduced. Additionally employed workers would have to be fed during the construction period, before the fruits of the labour could supply their needs, or enable them to buy their subsistence. Without such a fund, additional investment would not be possible, and inflation would become rampant. Food surpluses used for economic development would eventually enable hungry people to produce either their own food or other products to buy food. Freedom from hunger could ultimately be achieved only through freedom from poverty.

The group estimated that about $12,500 million of agricultural commodities would become available as 'surpluses' over a five-year period for use outside normal commercial market channels. It recommended that two-thirds should be used for economic development programmes, including national food reserves and an international emergency food reserve. The aim would be to provide developing countries with a positive incentive for maximum national efforts to increase the rate of growth. The remaining food aid would be used to promote social development including land reform programmes, school feeding, support for poor students in secondary and higher levels of education and in training programmes, and relief and welfare programmes for the old, handicapped and destitute. A country programming, not project, approach was advocated for determining the criteria for the productive use of aid capital, including food aid, which would also take fungibility into account. Singer and others exposed the weakness of project aid whereby aid tied to a particular project in reality releases funds for another project which the donor had not appraised or approved (Singer, 1965c).

While recognizing that the major part of international aid would continue to be provided bilaterally, the group recommended that it should be supplied within a multilateral framework. This would ensure that bilateral and international aid activities would be provided within coherent and consistent country assistance programmes. The chief constraint was the capacity of developing countries to absorb surplus food supplies into their economies at a high level of efficiency. Planning and programming machinery in the developing countries, the international aid organizations and in donor countries needed to be developed to take better, and more immediate, advantage of the availability of food surpluses to further economic and social development.

Given such a like-minded group, the wealth of documentation, the support provided by the FAO secretariat, and the prodigious work output of Singer, it is hardly surprising that the group's report was handed to the FAO director-general in February 1961 only 19 days after the commencement of its work in Rome. When presenting the report to the FAO director-general (B. R. Sen) and to the UN secretary-general (U Thant), Singer was doubtful about the title of the group's report, 'An Expanded Program of Surplus Food Utilization', and raised the question whether it should be something more 'developmental and humanitarian'. The expert group was very much aware of the earlier vision of the first FAO director-general, Sir John (later Lord) Boyd Orr, in proposing the creation of a 'world food board'. Singer recalled that 'Although, like much of Keynes' vision at Bretton Woods, this proved to be Utopian, I can say we felt that in a modest way we were following in the footsteps of both Boyd Orr and Keynes.' He also recognized the debt the expert group had to the earlier work of FAO on the use of food surpluses, particularly the pilot study conducted in India (FAO, 1955).[21]

The views of the expert group were taken fully into account in the report of the FAO director-general (FAO, 1961). Although a number of its recommendations were well in advance of their time, their value was subsequently recognized. Crucially, they were well received by officials in key positions in the United States. For example, in a memorandum to President Kennedy, the US ambassador to the UN at the time, Adlai Stevenson, described it as 'one of the most remarkable documents on the subject'.[22] Willard Cochrane, director of the US Department of Agriculture's Agricultural Economic Service, found it 'an excellent report. The analysis of the role of food aid in economic development is in my opinion, highly competent and informative. I know of no better analysis in the literature on economic development.'[23] The political climate was so opportune that within less than a year after the expert group submitted its report, WFP was established on a three-year experimental, later on a continuing, basis following a proposal made by George McGovern who, at the time, was the first director of the US Food for Peace programme and special assistant to President Kennedy (Shaw, 2001b).[24] Not all of the recommendations of the expert group were adopted. WFP was confined to providing food aid for development projects and emergency operations and was debarred from adopting a country programming approach until much later, thereby restricting the scope of its activities.

Subsequently, Singer was to play a key role as the UN secretary-general's representative in maintaining the interest of the United Nations in WFP as a joint UN/FAO undertaking. As he enjoyed the confidence of both parties, Singer drafted the joint views of the UN secretary-general and the FAO director-general in recommending the continuation of WFP at the end of its three-year experimental period (1963–65).[25]

12
First UN Decade of Development

With the inauguration of President Kennedy in January 1961, a new and positive relationship was established between the UN and the US in what has been described as the 'halcyon days' of the world body. A newly accepted principle of international solidarity and burden-sharing in development co-operation had expressed itself in a greater willingness to give assistance to developing countries. In this favourable political climate, President Kennedy, in his first address to the UN General Assembly on 25 September 1961, proposed that the 1960s be designated the 'United Nations Decade of Development'. He said:

> Political sovereignty is but a mockery without the means of meeting poverty and illiteracy and disease. Self-determination is but a slogan if the future holds no hope. That is why my Nation, which has freely shared its capital and technology to help others help themselves, now proposes officially designating the decade of the 1960s as the United Nations Decade of Development. Under the framework of that Resolution, the United Nations' existing efforts in promoting economic growth can be expanded and coordinated. New research, technical assistance and pilot projects can unlock the wealth of less developed lands and untapped waters. And development can become a cooperative and not a competitive enterprise – to enable all nations, however diverse in their systems and beliefs, to become in fact as well as in law free and equal nations. (US, 1961, p. 623)

The UN General Assembly responded by passing a resolution on the 'United Nations Development Decade' (1710 (XVI)) on 19 December 1961.

Singer drew on consultations with, and on a mass of inputs from, agencies and organizations throughout the UN system, to draft the 'proposals for action' for the report of the UN secretary-general on the UN Development Decade, which also reflected Singer's own views and experience (Singer, 1986h, p. 35; UN, 1962). The main economic objective for the decade was to create conditions in which the national incomes of the developing countries not only would increase by 5 per cent a year by 1970, but would continue to expand at that annual rate thereafter. If this was achieved (and if population growth continued to rise in developing countries at the then current rate of 2 to 2.5 per cent annually), personal living standards could be doubled within 25 to 30 years. This objective was considered to be attainable, given a greater willingness in both developing and developed countries to make the efforts and sacrifices required.

As a result, there had been increasing appreciation of the need for a number of what Singer called 'new approaches' during the UN development decade. Earlier, the emphasis had been on increasing savings and investment in physical capital as key requirements for accelerated economic growth. Now, development was defined as 'growth *plus* change' (original emphasis). Change, in turn, was social and cultural as well as economic, and qualiative as well as quantitative in nature.The concept of national planning for social as well as for economic development was central to all the proposals for intensified action by the UN system during the development decade. It was now generally appreciated that 'the purpose of a development plan is to provide a programme of action for the achievement of targets based on realistic studies of the resources available'. Vigorous efforts were more likely to result if national and sectoral objectives were defined and translated into action programmes.

There was greater insight into the importance of the human factor in development and the urgent need to mobilize human resources. Economic growth in the advanced countries appeared to be attributable in larger part than was previously supposed to human development and skills rather than to capital. Widening people's horizons through education and training, and lifting their vitality through better health, were not only essential preconditions for development, but also among its major objectives.

Another issue, described as one of the most serious problems facing developing countries, was increasing under-employment and unemployment (a subject which Singer first confronted on leaving Cambridge and which remained a principal concern after he left the

United Nations). Increasing unemployment was not confined to countries experiencing population pressures, although it was a major aggravating factor. Far-reaching action was required if the fruits of economic progress were to benefit all world inhabitants.

A further issue arose directly from Singer's work on the terms of trade. The disappointing foreign trade record of developing countries was due in part to obstacles hindering the entry of their products into industrial markets, and in part to the fact that production of many primary commodities had grown more rapidly than demand. 'Disruptive competition' from low-income countries may be felt by established industries in high-income countries. Yet, precisely because they were so advanced, the high-income countries should be able to alleviate any hardship without shifting the burden of adjustment to the developing countries by restricting the latter's export markets. A related problem was that of stabilizing international commodity markets on which developing countries depended so heavily. The report pointedly added that progress could be made if the main industrial countries devoted as much attention to promoting trade as to dispensing aid.

Acceptance of the principle of capital assistance to developing countries was one of the most striking expressions of international solidarity as well as enlightened self-interest. If assistance increased to, and maintained, a level of one per cent of the national incomes of the advanced countries during the development decade, as recommended by the UN General Assembly, this would represent another essential contribution to the success of the decade. At the same time, there was need for pragmatism and flexibility in determining the forms of capital flows and aid in relation to both the needs of developing countries and the shifting balance of payments position of assisting countries.

Reference was made to the concept of pre-investment and the UN Special Fund. Many developing countries lacked detailed knowledge of their natural resources, including water, minerals and power. In the development of water resources, in particular, the United Nations system could have a significant part to play. Nearly all the world's great rivers flowed through several countries, and their development was a problem requiring regional and international co-operation. Even where potential investment opportunities were identified, however, it might be impossible to implement them in the absence of one or more of the factors of production, labour, capital and entrepreneurial and technical skills. The UN Special Fund had concentrated on pre-investment work, paying special attention to surveys and feasibility studies of natural resources, technical and vocational training, and the establishment of institutions for applied research. It was estimated that pre-investment expenditure should rise to about $1 billion by 1970, double the level at the beginning of the 1960s.

It was recognized that the potentialities of modern technology and new methods of research and development for attacking the problems of developing countries were 'as yet dimly perceived'. New techniques permitted the solution of most scientific and technical problems once they were correctly posed. But too little effort had been directed towards posing or solving the problems of developing countries. Research on the social problems of developing countries entering upon a period of rapid social change was also needed. If the skills of the advanced countries were to be successfully adapted to the problems and conditions of developing countries, they should be willing and able to make available the necessary resources of skilled personnel. Shortage of highly skilled personnel, not lack of material resources and finance, would be the greatest obstacle to action in developing count-ries unless steps were taken through technical co-operation both to establish close contact with institutions in the advanced countries and to set up appropriate institutions in developing countries.

The success of the UN development decade depended in large part on the application of these new approaches. Precisely because they were new, their implications could not be fully seen. They were expected to change many existing attitudes and approaches, which did not happen to the extent that Singer had hoped and visualized.

13
UN Research Institute for Social Development

During much of 1964, Singer served as the first associate director of the new UN Research Institute for Social Development (UNRISD), which was established in Geneva in July of that year. One of the effects of the 'proposals for action' for the UN development decade, with its emphasis on the importance of the human factor in development, was to stimulate the Dutch government to donate $1 million to the United Nations to set up the institute. Singer played an active part in setting out the institute's initial philosophy, plans and work programme (Singer, 1965a; 1965d; 1966c).

Singer traced the evolution of thinking among development economists after the Second World War, based on his own personal experience. At the beginning of the post-war period, the attention of most economists had not yet been attracted to the problems of under-developed countries, which they tended to believe were matters of interest to other branches of the social sciences, including sociology and anthropology. Then economic development became the big growth sector in the social sciences. In the first flush of enthusiasm, economists tended to think in terms of economic growth models. Those were the days of the Harrod–Domar formula, of average and incremental capital–output ratios, of rates of saving and investment, and of closing and widening gaps in gross national product (GNP). But then came the days of disillusionment. Doubts began to creep in about whether the matter was as simple as that. The doubts were reinforced when quantitative research arrived at the conclusion that capital investment failed to account for much of economic growth and that there was a large unexplained 'residue'. It was found that when dealing with unhealthy, under-nourished, illiterate people, extra food, the eradication of common diseases, and education and training could be more important in raising productivity than physical capital. Singer questioned, 'What then became of the conventional line dividing consumption and investment'? He added, 'The ICORs [incremental capital/output ratio] of the Harrod–Domar formula turned out to be so unstable as to be useless as an instrument of economic planning, even though it took economists many years to draw this obvious conclusion.'

The rate of investment turned out to be determined by investment opportunities but the perception of such opportunities was a matter of the quality of the people, and involved pre-investment work. Moreover, the utilization of such investment opportunities was found to be a matter of the motivation of people, the right kind of communication with them, and of a social structure which permitted people to utilize such opportunities. Thus, development economists, as they began to turn away from their classical economics textbooks and learned more about under-developed countries, were driven back toward an earlier position, that other branches of the social sciences had a lot to contribute to an understanding of the problems of economic development. But there was an important difference. They perceived that the social aspects of development were too important to be left entirely to other social scientists and, as Singer put it, 'the social aspects of development became for economists a growth sector within the general growth sector of economic development'.

Singer graphically described this evolution of thought by a succession of models characteristic of the different modes of approach (Singer, 1965a). In Model I, which he called 'the classical puritan model of growth', at any given time economic growth required a cut in consumption, although in the end it may result in an increase in consumption. Consumption was reduced and the savings were invested in productive capital, which produced both more productive capital and more consumption goods, so that ultimately the cut in consumption could be restored. The cut in consumption was an instrumental variable, the resulting capital formation was the objective, although a final increase in consumption was 'dimly on the horizon'. However, in this strictly classical model, even this 'dim vision of jam the day after tomorrow' was destroyed by the Malthusian increase in population or by increasing inequality of income distribution owing to the fixed quantity of land and other factors.

Next came the 'distinctly less puritan' Keynesian Model II, where consumption and capital formation grew and declined together, tied together by the multiplier and the accelerator. Provided that there were latent or unemployed resources in the economy, 'the best way of making sure of having jam tomorrow is to have jam today'. This model was of great interest to students of under-developed countries. The analogy was striking. Just as in under-developed countries, under-consumption weakened people and stopped them from being fully productive, and set up vicious circles of low productivity–low output–poverty–no savings–continued poverty–continued under-nourishment, and so on, so in the Keynesian Model II under-employment 'gnaws at the vitals of the economy' and set up vicious circles of depression–unemployment–lack of investment–loss of output–more unemployment–more depression, and so on. Singer felt that Model II could not serve as a model of social development in under-developed countries. It was based on the assumption of latent and unemployed resources, or on 'elastic supply functions', patently not the condition of such countries, which were characterized by inelastic supplies and an all-pervading scarcity of resources, or so it seemed on a first approach.

Model III, or what Singer called the 'human investment model', was based on the basic notion of 'human capital' and its role in the development process. It had some obviously attractive features, combining, as it did, the importance of capital accumulation from Model I with the emphasis on the need to increase consumption in Model II. But it also had its own weaknesses. Above all, it treated human welfare as an instrument and the increase of GNP, or the accumulation of physical capital, as a final value. It therefore inverted, or perverted, the true relationship between human welfare and national income or physical capital. In Singer's opinion, the misleading nature of that approach lay in the fact that any improvement in human welfare which led to an increase in income or capital was called 'productive investment', while any increase in human welfare which did not increase income or capital was called 'consumption'. But the whole purpose of increased production was to lead to increased consumption or welfare. Moreover, by establishing a sharp dichotomy between 'human investment' and 'consumptive welfare', Model III deprived policy-makers of the common standards or measurements by which to allocate total resources among different purposes.

This led on to Model IV, or what Singer called the 'Antonine' model.[26] For this model, he took from the 'proposals for action' for the UN development decade of the 1960s that he had drafted the basic thesis that the problem of under-developed countries was not just growth, but development. Development was 'growth plus change', and change was social and cultural as well as economic, qualitative and quantitative (UN, 1962, pp. 2–3). The key concept should be the improved quality of people's lives, which combined growth and change. Improvements in the quality of life represented at the same time: consumption and investment; objective and instruments; and the demand and supply of resources. The model should include provision for common measurements of improvements in quality of levels of living, economic and social. It should contain 'transformation curves of expenditure' into improved levels of living, whether by the direct or indirect route. It should contain provision for a 'feed back process' in which improved levels of living led to higher productivity, which in turn led to higher levels of living. And it should incorporate four types of relevant movement: the direct improvement of levels of living and its value by itself; improvement leading to growth by the translation of higher levels of living into increased productivity; growth leading to improvement through the use of resources for improvement in levels of living and the income elasticity of various components in levels of living; and growth by itself, the predominant concern of Model I.

Model IV contained the approach which initially provided the framework for UNRISD's research programme. Singer identified five problems around which the work of UNRISD could focus: the interaction of social and economic factors and its relationship to economic development; indicators by which the progress of development could be measured; effective channels of communication with people; the role of children and young people in development; and the techniques of cost/benefit calculations for social projects and programmes. He alluded to some tentative first results of the work of UNRISD. There was 'quite striking' confirmation that a high level of social development tended to be a favourable precondition for more rapid economic growth as measured by *per capita* GNP. Better-off developing countries tended to achieve economic growth faster than the poorer ones. This, Singer called the 'First Law of Development: To him who hath shall be given,' which, in the light of UNRISD's findings, he suggested might be rephrased: 'To him who has assembled the social preconditions and who has reached a certain critical social level shall be given'. This suggested and explained a correlation between higher levels of social development and more rapid economic growth.

Another finding from UNRISD's work was that while favourable social levels tended to produce more rapid economic growth, it was also true that more rapid economic growth tended to result in more rapid subsequent improvement in the levels of social development. However, of the two effects, the latter seemed to be the stronger, when examining the data for a specific group of under-developed countries for the decade of the 1950s.

14
Assignments Outside New York

While engaged in the activities of the UN in New York described above, Singer also carried out a number of assignments in developing countries. These included: training programmes in development planning for government staff in developing countries; working with the UN Economic Commissions for Africa in Addis Ababa, Ethiopia and for Asia in Bangkok, Thailand; participating in UN missions to developing countries, including Brazil, the Philippines, Sudan, Thailand and Turkey; and being associated with the development of several UN institutions and activities. Being a UN official, Singer was not allowed to accept gifts from governments as a token of their appreciation of his work. This proved to be fortuitous on one occasion when he was offered the decoration of the 'Order of the White Elephant, Second Class', which he graciously declined.

What follows is an account of some of the assignments he undertook to illustrate the scope and diversity of the work performed, and their operational significance.

Development planning

One of Singer's first operational assignments outside New York was to take part in a training programme on development problems for economists and planners from Asian countries, mainly Indian and Pakistani officials in connection with the IBRD-financed Indus River scheme, at the Asian Centre on Agricultural and Allied Projects at Lahore, Pakistan from October to December 1950 (UN, 1951b; Singer, 1951; 1964a). The centre was sponsored by the Pakistan government, FAO, IBRD and the UN. Singer's attention had already been directed toward the Indian subcontinent by his earlier friendship with his fellow student at

Cambridge, V. K. R. V. Rao. This involved more pioneering work in providing training to national government officials in the appraisal and implementation of economic development projects as part of national development plans and programmes. These were the days of a strong belief in constructive government intervention and planning, derived from Keynesianism and war-time experience, which had been taken up by several Asian countries, especially India. Singer drew heavily on his Keynesian background and his pioneering work on the terms of trade that he had recently completed. It also anticipated his work on SUNFED, the UN Special Fund, and his concepts of pre-investment and fungibility, and pre-dated the publication of the classical theories and textbooks on economic development that were later to appear. His lectures extended to 110 closely printed pages. Only the main points are summarized here.

Basic principles

In order to understand the relationship of individual projects to the national economy as a whole, Singer identified two basic principles of economic development planning, those of 'cumulation' and 'interrelation'. Regarding the former, he reasoned that in economic life 'there was no cause and effect' but 'a movement of cumulation'. The secret of development planning was, therefore, to set in motion 'forces of cumulation'.

Singer then turned to the 'principle of interrelation' by posing the questions: What should a development programme contain? How can it be drawn up? and What is the place of an individual project within the overall development programme? In answering these questions, it was important to distinguish between 'service' or 'overhead' projects, and what Singer called 'directly productive projects'. In the more highly developed countries, there might be no need for a systematic development programme because development might proceed automatically and the principle of cumulation was already at work. They might decide to have a programme for another reason, such as social justice, efficiency, or the dictates of their political philosophy, but development did not depend on the programme or the plan.

The situation was different in under-developed countries. There the cumulative process had not begun and no automatic mechanism could bring it into play. Deliberate action was required. One of the major problems in beginning to draw up a development plan was to decide on the proportion of overhead facilities that had to be constructed in relation to directly productive projects. In under-developed countries, basic overhead services were generally insufficient for a particular new directly productive project or for a longer-range plan of increasing output. In drawing up a development programme, it was most important always to have in mind not only what was currently being done, but what the next step was in the cumulative process. That decision was often based more on political, than on technical or economic, judgements.

The next stage in the planning process was to determine the relationship between public and private projects in development programmes, which Singer described as 'the most important determinant of the efficiency and quality of a development programme'. Singer pointed to the need for research and the importance of timing. One of the most common mistakes in economic development planning was to wait too long without having a programme and when it was drawn up to rush it through without sufficient research. Great mistakes were made, and large sums of money wasted, by not allowing time for research after the outline of a plan had been prepared. 'The important thing is to be patient at the right time and impatient at the right time.'

Singer also addressed the issue of dispersed versus concentrated development in the knowledge that all parts of under-developed countries were never equally developed. While decisions were based on political considerations, from an economic viewpoint Singer's advice was to push ahead with development in the cheapest possible way by starting where the overhead facilities were already available, in the areas that were relatively more developed, and move out into the hinterland at a later stage when the additional resources that had been created could be used.

Some practical problems

Singer identified some practical problems of development planning during the course of his lectures. First, was the allocation of resources for which there were three key questions: What was the present level of resources? How should they be allocated between consumption and development projects? and How much should be allocated for short-term and longer-run projects? A development plan should be based on the size of present resources, not start from the basis of what was needed. The most common single defect of development programmes was to try to start too much at once and to fail to adjust the programme to available resources. In some countries, this had happened so frequently that the whole idea of planning for economic development had become discredited. Reliable statistics were a vital prerequisite for drawing up a good development programme.

Next was the danger of inflation. It was Singer's conviction that a development programme could not be financed by inflation. The limiting factor was not monetary demand but technical factors, and the absence of capital, skills, raw materials, public services and machinery. No country should try to *execute* a development programme which was in excess of the resources available for it, but each developing country ought to *have* a development programme greater than its available resources (original emphasis). There were four reasons for this. First, to have projects in reserve in case the ones that were being implemented were stopped during execution. Second, resources would increase as development got going, which could bring other projects into operation. Third, it was always possible to underestimate present resources, which could be supplemented by foreign aid or in other ways. Fourth, and most important, was the application of the principle of 'opportunity costs'. As Singer explained, 'You must always have rejected a project or a number of projects to be certain that the project you actually undertake is right', or put in another way, 'the costs of a development project are the sacrificed benefits from another project'.

In selecting projects for implementation, Singer raised the question of how far the priorities within the development programme should be influenced by financial considerations. He argued that priority projects should be selected on technical, not financial, grounds. He recalled that Keynes had observed that it is the proper job of finance to see that nothing is ever done on solely financial grounds. The most important task of a financial expert in an under-developed country was to see that the true technical priorities within a development programme were not upset or made impossible by financial obstacles. The priorities within a development programme ought to reflect the real conditions and needs of the country. There were important exceptions to this general rule, e.g., where a project shifts the financial burden to another place where it is easier to carry, or where projects are revenue-producing rather than revenue-consuming to keep them going.

Singer then turned to a question which anticipated the debate for trying to establish SUNFED. Should projects be self-liquidating, i.e., should the cost of development projects be covered, where possible, from their own proceeds? Singer reasoned that self-liquidation was a form of taxation. It could not be judged whether it was good or bad policy to make projects self-liquidating until it was known what (if any) alternative possibilities there were for taxation. If there were no good ones, it would probably be a sensible policy to make projects self-liquidating. The second argument in favour of self-liquidating projects was one of 'fairness'. People who benefit from a particular project should pay for it. But if it benefits the economy as a whole, there was no reason why it should not be paid for through taxation or other forms of financing. The two decisions – whether to undertake a project and who should pay for it – were unrelated and should be taken separately. It might promote economic development more effectively to cover the cost of a project from general taxation and leave some groups to enjoy its benefits without specifically contributing to the capital cost. The only test of a good project was whether it added more to national income than the total resources put into it, which, following the Keynesian principle, should be appraised in *real* rather than monetary terms.

Resources

Singer distinguished between domestic and foreign financing when considering the resources necessary for development programmes. He listed seven uses of foreign finance:

- for the poorest countries, enabling some of the capital-intensive development projects to be implemented without which continued development might not be possible;
- speeding up capital formation;
- planning capital formation over a longer range, provided there is reason to expect a sustained influx of capital from abroad;
- enabling governments to maintain consumption at a higher level than would otherwise be possible;
- reducing or eliminating inflationary pressures;
- reducing balance-of-payments pressures;
- increasing the international division of labour (shades of Singer's terms of trade thesis) by enabling under-developed countries to import goods from abroad and paying for them through increased exports of goods they were presumably fitter to produce rather than being forced to attempt to produce goods they were ill-suited to produce, and removing the need for inefficient high-cost industries, which might become a permanent drag on the economy .

Common defects in development programmes

Singer concluded his lectures on development planning by summarizing the most common defects in development programmes, drawn up at a UN seminar on the formulation and execution of development

programmes, which he attended in Puerto Rico in 1950 (UN, 1950).
These included:

- lack of consistency of development programmes with the total
  financial resources available;
- too much priority assigned to public works projects relative to such
  needs as improvement of food production and general raising of
  productivity;
- emphasis on the public sector at the expense of the private sector;
- establishing 'paper targets' for the private sector without providing
  for measures required to assure that those targets were attained;
- over-emphasis of investment in spectacular, concentrated, large-
  scale projects rather than basic, scattered, small-scale improvements
  not necessarily requiring big capital investment, which in the aggre-
  gate might be as, or more, important than a few big projects;
- insufficient study prior to the implementation of major schemes;
- concentration on specific expenditure resulting in the creation of
  tangible capital, to the neglect of improvements in institutions, in
  the domestic, economic and social climate, and in the standards of
  the traditional government services;
- multiplicity of government controls and inducements that were
  insufficiently harmonized with each other;
- too much concentration on fixed investment and insufficient
  working capital for productive installations, leading to loss of productivity; and lack of clearly defined priorities.

Singer enjoyed the experience of taking part in the training programme for government officials, (and later for the staff of UN and
bilateral aid agencies and NGOs), which he repeated on a number of
occasions. Not only did he feel that this personnel had a vital role to
play in the development process but he learned from them of the problems they encountered, which contributed to his own learning process.
It also assisted his own emerging theory and concept of development,
which was maturing.

Northeast Brazil: problems and experience

Another early assignment outside New York was a detailed study of the
developmental problems of northeastern Brazil, which Singer visited in
1953. His earlier work in the depressed areas of the United Kingdom
came vividly to his mind. Singer had gone to Brazil in 1950 to visit his

brother and had delivered a series of lectures at the Vargas Foundation in Rio de Janeiro on the economic development of under-developed countries, which were published in Portuguese (Singer, 1950a). During his visits, he established what were to become life-long friendships with leading Brazilian economists, including Roberto Campos, then a young Brazilian delegate in UN economic committees, and later, through him, with a number of other Brazilian economists, including Eugenio Gudin, at that time the minister of finance, Octavia Bulhoes, Celso Furtado and Romulo Almeida, who were destined to play major roles in Brazilian development.

One of the first things to establish was that the problems of northeastern Brazil were development problems and not simply a problem of natural disasters caused by recurring drought, which was the prevailing view. It also provided a practical example of his work on the terms of trade as the region was a major source of Brazilian primary exports, and on development financing and the need for regional development banks (Singer, 1952a; 1953a; 1963a; 1964a, pp. 21–90). The prices obtained by exporters of the primary products from the northeast were depressed by chronic overvaluation of the Brazilian currency, while the prices paid for domestic manufactures from Sao Paulo were inflated by heavy protection and resulting inefficiency and high profit margins. Thus, the work on this case study of a depressed area formed a direct link with his concern regarding the terms of trade. It was also directly connected with the establishment of a regional development bank, Banco do Nordeste. This provided a link with work on development financing, and, more specifically, with later involvement in the establishment of the African Development Bank (see below).

The factors accounting for the lack of development of northeast Brazil and their relative importance were thoroughly covered by Singer. He outlined its investment, trade and fiscal problems, made an estimate of the capital required, and drew up a development outline for its economic development. His observations revealed as much about his own thinking and emerging theory and concept of economic development as about the conditions he saw. To a large extent, he felt that the observed disparity in the towns between economic and social standards 'must be attributed to a noneconomic lag'. Workers and similarly placed groups living in extremely bad health and housing conditions had material possessions which seemed to be out of line with their state of health and housing. He found the standard of productivity and economic levels in the town higher, but the standards in the countryside and the social standards of large groups in the towns rather worse, than he expected.

The high quality and competence of a number of the businessmen and industrialists Singer met, reflected in the efficient organization of a number of the factories he visited, impressed him. But he detected that the businessmen suffered from three main weaknesses: a 'mania' for keeping the business in the family; reluctance to seek outside advice or assistance; and neglect of the human factor in production, resulting in the high cost of ill-health, ignorance and illiteracy on productivity. Power shortage was a universal problem. Water problems dominated the agricultural sector. While the large irrigation systems were an essential part of the economic development of the region, the smaller reservoirs were a matter of social relief for the distress created by droughts, and should be handled separately. Deputies and technicians played a leading role in deciding on the location of the main water systems and the general conduct of irrigation policy.

Singer made a number of suggestions for the economic development of the region based on his observations, which anticipated his later views on pre-investment activities. He suggested that there should be greatly expanded research and study of the economic dimensions of land problems, which were badly neglected in comparison with their engineering and agronomic aspects. Improved technical control of the new larger reservoir projects should be established, irrigation legislation passed and/or irrigation basins transferred into public land, and irrigation extended along the Sao Francisco river and in the dry river valleys. Technical research, subsidies for technical improvements, and market stabilization for export crops should be encouraged. Fertilizer industries and high-grade textiles should be developed as first priorities, insecticides and spraying equipment should be distributed to smaller farmers, and demonstration activities strengthened. Technological institutes should be established. Educational improvements and extended activities of social rural housing should be carried out. And a public works programme should be prepared for the next drought period with emphasis on the improvement of railways. From his studies and observations, Singer formed a definitely favourable impression of the developmental potential of northeastern Brazil, which differed sharply from the conventional views held by government officials. But the subsequent development of the region did not come up to the optimistic view that he projected.

African Development Bank

Singer developed a special interest in the development problems of Africa. He attended a regional conference on economic development in

Sub-Saharan Africa held by the International Economic Association in Addis Ababa in July 1961 at which he presented papers on demographic factors and small-scale industry in African economic development (Singer, 1961e and g). He was appointed director of the Policies and Programming Division of the UN Economic Commission for Africa (ECA) on its creation. He was also made secretary of a group of experts and ministerial committee on African development, which led to the foundation of the African Development Bank (ADB) in Abidjan, Côte d'Ivoire, where he served as its chief economist during the initial stages (Singer, 1963a).

The idea of creating an ADB originated in a resolution that was unanimously passed by all African countries in the ECA in 1961. Subsequently, the idea was explored in several ways typical of UN procedures, ranging back and forth between secretariat studies, panels of private and government experts, consultants, ECA committees, and private as well as official consultations, with Singer playing an active and co-ordinating role.[27]

The idea for an ADB had several roots. The need for additional capital for economic development in Africa was undeniable. So was the need for co-operation among African countries, to overcome national and regional divisions that marked the history of the continent and the emergence of African countries into independence. For established international financing and banking institutions, Africa was a difficult area in which to operate owing to lack of knowledge, data, contacts and tradition. The new African countries were often inexperienced in dealing with the established sources of finance, and the flow of aid was hampered by institutional factors and lack of contact points. The successful establishment of the Inter-American Development Bank (IDB) in Washington, DC, catering for the Latin American continent, also gave impetus to the creation of the ADB.

The need for co-operation among African countries was perhaps the most striking argument for creating a regional instrument in financing, as well as in other fields. Leaving aside Egypt, Nigeria and South Africa, there were some 40 countries or countries-to-be, with an average population of four million people per country, of whom perhaps half were outside the market economy and beyond the scope of any orthodox financial approach to development. The remaining two million people, with varying degrees of contact with the market economy, had an average cash purchasing power corresponding to about one-twentieth of that of a European citizen. They represented a cash market equivalent to a moderate size European town but, by contrast, were dispersed often over a wide area. Therefore, a national approach to planning and financing economic development did not make much sense. Not only were African countries too small in the sense of cash markets to form economic units of development but their borders were determined more by political and diplomatic history rather than by economic sense. Singer reasoned that it was against this background that the idea of creating the ADB should be understood.

From the beginning, attention was focused on seven different types of projects, which a fully developed and mature ADB should specifically undertake. These were described as: regional projects; promotion of inter-African trade; promotion of exchange economies; fulfilling the needs of newly independent countries; education and training; promotion of small-scale African industrial enterprises; and development plans and long-range support. Arrangements for dealing with each of these different types of projects was by no means identical, or even similar. Provisions made for financing, and modes of operation of the ADB, would depend on which of the various purposes or gaps it might fill.

From the outset, the ADB could be justified only if it introduced new elements and tapped new sources of finance rather than replace existing sources or undertake existing functions. The principle of 'additionality' of resources might be satisfied in several ways: from contributions from the African countries themselves; by helping to develop internal capital markets in African countries to promote a more satisfactory flow of potential savings into potentially productive investment; by attracting sources of finance outside Africa by creating a more satisfactory liaison between potential borrowers in Africa and potential lenders or investors outside Africa; through ADB contacts, projects and advice; and by the ADB helping to prepare projects, thereby bringing them to the stage of concrete financing propositions and to the attention of potential investors inside and outside Africa. The ADB could therefore carry out a variety of functions. To the extent that it could improve the terms and conditions by which African countries could obtain capital, and thus reduce their balance-of-payments burden, there would again be additionality. The absorptive capacity of African countries for capital would also be increased by an amelioration of the terms on which they could obtain it.

The question of capitalization was initially based largely on the precedent of the IDB, where the legal capitalization was partly from Latin American beneficiaries and partly from North American and European donors. It soon became clear, however, that such an arrangement would lead to difficulties for the ADB, including: how to ensure that the African capital contributions would not be swamped by larger non-African contributions; how to ensure African control and top management of the ADB; how to parcel out the non-African capital subscriptions among East and West, and among former colonial and non-colonial countries; and whom to admit to capital subscriptions and whom to exclude. The solution was to limit the subscription to the legal capital of the ADB, and hence participation in the top board of governors, entirely to African countries. Consequently, its legal capital had to be kept comparatively small. But other issues surfaced, including: Should contributions from all African countries be the same size regardless of their population, wealth and potential? If not, what should be the criteria for assessing contributions? And should voting in the board of governors be proportionate and weighted according to each country's contribution, if different, or based on other, defined considerations? A special problem was that at the time there were several African countries which were still colonial dependencies. Could they become ADB members? Singer noted that it was a remarkable sign of African willingness to compromise and to achieve the ultimate goal of setting up the ADB that these and other questions relating to capitalization were settled amicably and without rancour.

Similarly, thorny questions relating to the management of ADB were solved at the preliminary stage. It was decided that ADB's senior management would all be Africans. At the same time, African governments were also fully aware that it was essential that a management was required which inspired confidence abroad for attracting non-African capital in order to operate on a significant scale and to satisfy the principle of additionality. On the other hand, there was a strong determination that the ADB should be a thoroughly African institution.

Singer realized that the ADB could play an important part in introducing a new approach to Africa's problems that had been missing in the past. That idea was co-operation on a regional level, cutting across the more artificial groupings based on history and politics. He recalled that it was no accident that the idea of the ADB had its genesis in the United Nations, which embodied this new line of thinking in African affairs. Singer reckoned as a further advantage that the history of the ADB was subject to the cautious checks and counterchecks by all sorts of committees and expert bodies and the numerous consultations that were characteristic of UN procedures. Many of the problems and difficulties involved were repeatedly brought to the attention of governments and others concerned. The adjustments and compromises made were the more solid for having been worked out often by the method of repeated approximations. The draft statutes of the ADB which emerged for consideration by the ECA, and later adopted by the conference of African ministers of finance in Khartoum, was therefore not a rash venture, and ensured that the idea of the ADB did not die. But its role in, and impact on, African economic development was to prove to be much less than Singer had originally envisaged.

15
Academic Activities While at the United Nations

Simultaneously with his work at the United Nations, Singer became a professor at the Graduate Faculty of Political and Social Science of the New School for Social Research in New York (Krohn, 1993; Mongiovi, 1996), and later (1965) visiting professor at Williams College in Williamstown, Massachusetts.

Singer described how he owed his association with the New School to Alvin Johnson, a well-known New Dealer under the Roosevelt administration, who was president of the New School and founder of the 'University in Exile', which became the New School's graduate faculty (Singer, 1992j, pp. 8–9). In 1940, during the dark days of the Second World War when Hitler seemed on the point of invading Britain, Johnson had written to Singer offering him help to obtain a priority visa to go to the United States through the American embassy in Dublin, if needed, and a teaching post at the New School. Johnson's attention to Singer had possibly been drawn by Adolph Lowe who had joined the New School from Manchester where he lived as an independent researcher when Singer was at Manchester University. Both were on the Nazi blacklist, which had been published in *The Manchester Guardian.*

Singer replied to Alvin Johnson that he felt it was his duty to stay in England 'on the chance of being useful in one way or other'.[28] He continued, 'England is carrying the whole burden of the defence of civilization and there can be no more honourable service in the world than to serve England in whatever capacity.' Singer felt that Johnson must have had a shrewd idea of what things were like because in his letter of reply he stated that 'If in the course of the year you should find that your services were no longer wanted, I should no doubt be able to extend the offer.' In frustration, Singer noted that while 'the H.O. [Home Office] growls and the police does worse [referring to his internment as an 'enemy alien'], F.D.R. [President Franklin D. Roosevelt] and Alvin Johnson beckon with an inviting democratic smile. Oh Lord what a mix-up all this is.'

When eventually Singer went to the United States to take up his appointment at the United Nations in 1947, he visited Johnson to thank him for his kind action. Johnson said that there could be no better way of showing his gratitude than by teaching at the New School in the evenings after his work in the UN. This Singer was to do until he left the United Nations in 1969. He never considered this additional responsibility a great hardship despite his arduous work at the UN. He welcomed the chance of maintaining his links with the academic world. Furthermore, it gave him the space and opportunity to think about the theoretical framework of economic development within which his work at the United Nations could be placed. And it gave him an opportunity to publish papers in his own name, a practice which was not followed at the United Nations. Initially, much of the demand for his teaching was created by ex-service men and women returning to civilian life after the war. The underlying theory of development for his course showed the strong influences of Schumpeter and Keynes and was based partly on the importance of infrastructure (which drew on the work on Rosenstein-Rodan and Thomas Balogh), partly on the need for balanced growth (where he was most influenced by Ragnar Nurkse), and partly on the ideas of Gunnar Myrdal (with its emphasis on 'cumulative causation' and 'vicious circles'). But the main component of his lectures was, understandably, on international trade problems (based on his work on the terms of trade).

The mechanics of economic development

This led to his pioneering conceptual work in development economics. Some of his early work was brought together in a book, which appeared in the then prominent series on international development by the publishers McGraw-Hill (Singer, 1964a). The collection included a pathbreaking paper on what Singer called the 'mechanics of economic development: a quantitative-model approach' (Singer, 1952e).[29] Singer's model of the process of industrialization in developing countries was based on Harrod's growth theory modified to fit the characteristics of developing countries. He added the rate of annual population increase to the per capita version of the Keynesian growth model to take account of the problems of over-population and 'unlimited' labour supply. Thus, the process of development – measured by the rate of economic development (D) – was defined as growth of per capita income (assuming that it was proportionate to growth of per capita capital), which equalled the net savings ratio (s) times the productivity of investment per unit of capital (p) minus the rate of the annual increase of population (Gn). With three of the four variables set in advance, the resulting formula ($D = sp - G_n$) helped to generate different scenarios of growth for developing countries. This approach emphasized the strategic roles of savings, capital accumulation, and the capital–output ratio in development planning.

In retrospect, Singer found the model showed a major weakness. The pursuit of GNP growth through savings and investment intensified the dual structure of Third World economies, since the model only applied to a modern, typically urban, sector (Singer, 1981a). Hence, instead of reducing the gap between the traditional agricultural sector and the modern industrial sector, the opposite occurred in most developing countries. Growth in output was disproportionately distributed, and scarce capital was pre-empted for capital-intensive investment in urban areas, which consequently had high rates of productivity growth, whereas the rest of the population was deprived of the capital needed for job creation. Thus, in the agricultural sector, surplus labour was the predominant characteristic. At the same time, higher wages in the manufacturing sector attracted labour away from agricultural occupations. The Harris–Todaro model explained how rural workers could be induced to move to the urban centres by the *possibility* of earning higher income (original emphasis), with the result that migration exceeded urban employment opportunities (Harris and Todaro, 1970). In the model, expected incomes were defined in terms of both wages and employment probabilities. Thus, it was possible to have continued migration despite the existence of high rates of unemployment in the modern sector. Migrants unable to find 'productive' urban jobs constituted an 'informal' sector within the modern centres. Paradoxically, attempts to create additional urban jobs aggravated the problem, since still more migrants were attracted by such measures.

The seven pillars of development

Singer later expanded on what he called 'the seven pillars of development', (after T. E. Lawrence's *Seven Pillars of Wisdom* (London: Jonathan Cape, 1935)), based on his work at the United Nations (Singer, 1964m). These pillars included that of *science and technology*, with higher priority given to the solution of those problems which specifically concerned the poorer countries, which was 'capital-saving rather than capital-using'. A second pillar was *human investment*. The crucial factor in development was not the production of wealth but rather the *capacity* (original emphasis) to produce wealth, which was inherent in people. The third pillar was *planning.* The resources of developing countries were so small that they required carefully laid plans in order to make the best use of their limited resources, and to develop policies and strategies which broke the vicious circles of poverty, ignorance and disease. The real objective of planning was to create a 'plausible picture of an expanding economy', into which the public and private sectors, and individuals, fitted their action. But, Singer emphasized, 'the plan must be realistic, the government must mean what it says, and have the capacity to see that the plan is carried out'.

Next, was the pillar of *trade.* The volume of exports of developing countries had not expanded sufficiently to give them the foreign exchange they needed for their development, and the prices of their exports had continued to fall relative to the prices of their imports. Hence, the importance of the pillar of *aid* to maintain developmental investments in the face of unsatisfactory export earnings. The proportion of aid provided through international channels could, with advantage, be increased, and the idea of the aid consortium represented great progress. It was right that all the different sources of aid should be brought together with the aid-receiving countries to discuss not individual projects but the 'total picture', and the possibilities and requirements of each, especially the recipient countries, within the framework of a country aid programme. And with the tremendous surpluses emerging in the richer countries – in food, fertilizers, machinery, equipment and industrial capacity – such aid in kind was not only sensible but necessary, and 'costless, perhaps even beneficial, to those rendering this aid'.

Another hopeful trend, which Singer considered should become one of the pillars of economic development, was the growth of *technical assistance and pre-investment activities.* There were many *latent* (original emphasis) investment opportunities in developing countries but they had to be created and brought to a stage where productive investment could take place. Hence, the crucial importance of the 'industry' of preparing investment opportunities. Finally, there was the pillar of *regional co-operation.* Developing countries should move away from a purely national and fragmented approach to development. Many were too small to create viable economic entities and their borders had often been determined by political and diplomatic history rather than economic factors. There could be no real worldwide development unless this last pillar was in place and the developing countries tackled the job as a joint task with their neighbours.

Singer emphasized that these 'seven pillars of development' would not be easy to construct. They would require time, international co-operation, and a strengthening of international institutions and approaches, a new spirit of human solidarity, and, above all, a growth in intelligence, 'an understanding that a wider spread and better distribution of well-being throughout the world is in the enlightened self-interest of us all'.

Issues in development theory

Singer was to use his time at the New School profitably to review a number of the emerging issues and theories in development economics based on his practical experience in working at the UN and in his many assignments in the developing countries. He was also to reflect on the teachings of Schumpeter and Keynes and on a theoretical framework for his pathbreaking work on the terms of trade. His papers, some of which were published in the journal of the graduate faculty of the New School, *Social Research*, were widely quoted and commented upon by other early pioneering development economists, and included in their textbooks and publications (e.g., Nurkse, 1953; Agarwala and Singh, 1958; Higgins, 1959; Johnston and Mellor, 1961; Schultz, 1961; Meier, 1964).

Economic progress in under-developed countries

Singer's first paper to be published in the faculty journal was a survey of economic progress achieved in developing countries, based on an address to the general seminar of the New School's graduate faculty in December 1948, less that two years after taking up his appointment at the UN (Singer, 1949b). It gave the first indications of his thinking as he embarked upon his tasks at the United Nations and showed that his work on the terms of trade was already beginning to bear fruit. And it showed his ability to put complex issues in simple, but telling, perspective.

Surveying for the first time what undoubtedly was one of the world's key economic problems, that of under-developed countries, an economist, Singer felt, could not 'fail to be struck by the extraordinary neglect in this field by his own science'. Economic research and literature had been 'deeply conditioned by a purely national approach, generally the approach of a major industrialized country'. This concentration, and particularly the focus on short-term problems of economic stability, was perhaps most clearly epitomized in Keynes' oft-quoted statement, 'In the long run we are all dead.' This had particular poignancy when applied to developing countries and their people. For them, it was 'a physiological fact rather than a logical preference'.

The preoccupation of economists with national problems and data, mainly of industrialized countries, had resulted in a general tendency to assume that there had been a rise in per capita incomes throughout the world and some progress toward a more equal distribution of income. Though incomes had risen in some individual countries, at very uneven rates, average or median world income was smaller in 1948 than it was in 1913. The reason for this was that the developing countries, with their expanding populations, acquired a constantly increasing weight. A shrinking proportion of the world population had been rapidly raising its standard of living while the living standard of an increasing majority of the world population had been rising much more slowly or remained stationary. World income had probably deteriorated during the last three generations in respect of all three 'Pigovian criteria': average size, equality of distribution, and stability over time. If the 'average' world income was defined as that of the 'median world citizen', the spectacular improvement which had occurred at one extreme, and which fascinated economists and other observers, was usefully corrected by this contrary view.

Growing inequality in the distribution of world income was at least partly attributable to a major structural change in international economic relations. That change was caused, Singer believed, by the change in price relations between primary materials and manufactured goods, an early indication of the results of his work on the terms of trade. He noted that from published data, it appeared that over the two generations preceding the Second World War, 'the quantum of manufactured goods obtainable from a given quantum of primary commodities declined by more than 40 per cent'. From the point of view of industrialized countries, the price of manufactured goods had not increased in real terms. Rising wages and money prices of factors of production 'had been amply compensated by increased efficiency of production'.

Increased efficiency in the production of primary goods had not been absorbed by rising standards and rising prices of factors of production but by a larger quantum required in exchange for a given volume of manufactured goods. The argument from the point of view of the under-developed countries, which was 'a difficult one to answer', was that *if* (original emphasis) the labour and other resources employed in the production of manufactured goods had been obtained at a stationary standard of living, these manufactured goods would have been available to the under-developed countries 'at perhaps a third of the price actually paid for them'. In this way, the resources required for economic development, or at least the resources required for the initial stimulus to economic development, could have been supplied by multiplying the imports of capital goods, and no reliance need have been placed on 'the precarious, insufficient, and awkward process of foreign investment'.

Singer continued:

The peoples of the industrialized countries have not supported a higher standard of living in the prices which they pay the under-developed countries for their primary goods. Why should it be taken for granted that the people of the underdeveloped countries should support a higher standard of living in industrialized countries through the prices they pay for manufactured goods?

Seen in these terms, the widening gap between the industrialized and developing countries 'should not be laid entirely at the door of domestic weaknesses or handicaps implicit in the economic structure of the underdeveloped countries'. Hence, the increasing inequality in the distribution of world income need not be accepted as inevitable. Singer estimated that a sufficient stream of additional capital goods flowing into developing countries to maintain 'the 1913 quantum relations' over the last generation could have transformed the economic picture of many of those countries.

Another factor in international relations 'had a clogging effect on economic development'. Singer distinguished between what he called the 'seeds' of development (such as the accumulation of industrial capital, the spread of modern technological methods, and the rise in standards of education), and the 'fruits' of economic development (such as better nutrition, lower death rates, luxury consumption, progress in social security, the development of highly complex administration, multiple state intervention). He found the 'awkward fact' that it was very much easier to transplant the fruits than the seeds. It was 'fatally easy' to transplant the end results of economic development in the industrialized countries (medical improvements, low death rates, advanced social legislation, a complex planning machinery) in underdeveloped countries not as end products but in isolation, divorced from the process which created them. Seen in this way, the fruits of economic development had 'a way of putrefying and even checking development itself'.

Singer raised the rhetorical question, 'Wherein, then, lies the special difficulty of setting in motion, within the frame of existing exchange relations between primary and manufactured goods, the process of economic development itself?' To him, the answer seemed to be a system not only of vicious circles but of 'vicious circles within vicious circles, and of interlocking circles'. He identified the 'dominant vicious circle' of low production – no surpluses for economic investment – no tools and equipment – low standard of production, and concluded that 'An underdeveloped country is poor because it has no industry; and an underdeveloped country has no industry because it is poor.'

Summarizing his position, Singer noted that 'We are faced with an immensely difficult problem.' An important step forward would be taken once the unfavourable shifts in world price relations were reversed or countered. Only then could the harm they had wrought in the under-developed countries be mitigated. Action of this nature might reduce the problem to such proportions that the remedies made in the form of assistance to under-developed countries could exert a real effect. Revolutionary changes in technique might help solve the problem, but such a windfall could not be counted on. We might far better face the fact that the problem is formidable and that no line of attack should be neglected. 'Irresistible forces must be mobilized to meet what may perhaps prove, after all, not to be an immovable object.' Writing 12 years later, he considered that 'we can be moderately optimistic about the economic trends in underdeveloped countries as a whole over the generation or so to come – though on rather different grounds from the romantic or dogmatic or philosophical optimism of the economists before World War II. Ours must be an optimism of gradualism' (Singer, 1961h, p. 414). Although a generation was a short time *sub specie aeternitatis*, it was a long time during the revolution of rising expectations. Given sufficient time, we could help the potentially generative forces to work themselves out. 'There is hope in the picture but no certainty.'

Barriers to economic development

The economic doctrines of peculiar barriers to development were stated in a paper Singer prepared in 1948, even before his work on the terms of trade was published (Singer, 1949a). One doctrine was the theory of the 'vicious circle' of low income and inability to save, impairing capital formation. This theme was later taken up by Ragnar Nurkse.[30] Singer also addressed the obstacles to economic development in a paper published in 1953, which drew heavily from his work on the terms of trade (Singer, 1953b). He found Schumpeter's book on *The Theory of Economic Development* a good basis for a survey of the general obstacles to economic development not because it applied to under-developed countries but because it failed to apply. Singer found the differences between Schumpeter's theory and what could be observed in developing countries 'strikingly summarized' in a paper by Henry Wallich,[31] from which he identified three main differences. First, in Schumpeter's theory, the agents of economic development were the innovating and pioneering private entrepreneurs. In the developing countries, they were much more likely to be the government. Innovating private entrepreneurs were either conspicuously absent or were unable to operate within a framework in which the public prerequisites, ranging from law-and-order to essential public utilities, were lacking.

Secondly, according to Schumpeter, the method by which development was brought about was changes in production functions through the introduction of new pioneering techniques used either for the development of new products or for new ways of producing old-established products. In developing countries, economic development proceeded through the introduction and adaptation of old-established technologies to the production of old-established products familiar in the developed countries.

Thirdly, Schumpeter found the generating force of economic development lay in the sphere of supply of new goods or the increased supply of old-established goods, or in the lowering of supply price in relation to market price, and the consequent opening up of profits for the pioneering private entrepreneurs. In the developing countries, the generating force lay much more in the sphere of demand and the desire for increased consumption. According to Schumpeter, changes on the supply side were the causes and increased consumption the effect. In the developing countries, the desire for increased consumption was the cause, and the changes in supply functions were necessary for the desire for increased consumption to be fulfilled.

Singer therefore concluded that we were faced with a picture not of the private entrepreneur adding to the supply of goods by the application of revolutionary technologies, which was the model of earlier economic development in the developed countries, but with the problems confronted by governments trying to give effect to a desire for higher consumption by introducing and adapting known technologies from developed countries. Many of the handicaps to economic development were implied even in this simple model. Where non-Schumpeterian development started off with higher consumption, 'it put the cart before the horse'. In the Schumpeterian world, 'the horse is before the cart'. It was not surprising that movement there was easier, and taken for granted.

The role of the public sector in economic development

Singer emphasized the crucial importance of the public sector (or government) in economic development (Singer, 1964a).[32] This was a commonly held view at the time and reflected the experience of planning during the Second World War and the influence of Beveridge and his ideas of the welfare state. Singer identified nine tasks (not in order of priority or importance) which governments were called upon to fulfil in an under-developed country during the process of development. These tasks included: (1) responsibility for about half of total investments; (2) engagement in direct commodity production either because of its strategic importance or because of its large capital requirements; (3) determination of the pattern and volume of private investment; (4) making current expenditures, which amounted to a minimum of 10 per cent of the national income, and might amount to 20 per cent or more; (5) establishment of national institutions, or providing the setting in which they could be encouraged and flourished, often neglected in development planning, but essential all the same; (6) adoption and pursuit of policies conducive to economic development; (7) rendering a large number of preliminary services without which productive activities would be greatly handicapped; (8) setting the goals of economic development; and (9) drawing up plans for national development.

All too often it was assumed that public investment projects were the most important contribution of the public sector to economic development. Nothing could be more mistaken, and represented an example of what was referred to as the 'fallacy of misplaced concreteness'. More importance tended to be attributed to the physically tangible than the intangible. For this reason, the importance of 'human capital' (skills, training, scientific knowledge, co-operative habits) tended to be underrated. While it was not really sensible to establish any order of priority among the different tasks of the public sector, Singer argued that 'development policies are fundamentally more important than the public investment programme'. Good development policies could create a setting for 'the unfolding of human activities and resourcefulness which will keep creating a capacity for growth, and this will find its expression in development in due course'. Growth brought about in this way was likely to be more enduring and self-sustaining than that brought about by piecemeal individual investments, which could create a dual economy with isolated enclaves in an otherwise backward economy, and fail to have multiplying effects. For this reason, as he was to emphasize later, development plans were more important than projects, especially for the application of external assistance (Singer, 1965c).

Singer turned to the question of public ownership and the line of demarcation between the public and private sectors in making them work together. Like development planning, he observed that the question of public ownership had often been treated as a question of 'economic dogma', and as such had 'aroused all the proper religious passions'. Treated 'pragmatically', it became more difficult to lay down general rules concerning the proper size of the public and private sectors. However, a few general remarks could be safely made. First, the public sector in under-developed countries normally had its hands so full with the manifold roles listed above that it was well advised to leave alone any tasks which could be done just as well, or even better, by the private sector. An exception was where the private sector was dominated by foreign investment, where national interests had to be secured, and where particular sectors or enterprises were of such strategic or social importance that even national private enterprise should not be given such positions of power and influence. Secondly, the question of public and private ownership should be considered separately from that of public or private finance. And thirdly, under-developed countries were usually short of personnel capable of running and managing enterprises.

The dogmatic approach had tended to obscure the fact that the relationship between the public and private sectors was 'essentially complementary, not competitive'. The real question was therefore not one of demarcation but of 'mutual interaction'. This illustrated further functions of government policy in a developing country, to prevent inflationary pressure, and adjust the economy to balance-of-payments difficulties. Any strong pressure of demand on existing resources tended to create inflationary pressure, which should be counteracted by financing investment from genuine public and private savings. The relationship between inflation and economic development was not entirely clear-cut. Inflation could be the result of strong economic development not properly counteracted and could statistically go together with growth. But growth financed by inflation was likely to be less soundly based, and less enduring, than non-inflationary growth. On the other hand, growth itself was a cure for inflation. It was easier to keep prices stable when the volume of goods and services was constantly increasing, and when wage increases could be granted without raising prices as a result of rising productivity. Singer noted that controversy had arisen between the 'monetarists', who emphasized the need for stability as a platform for sound economic growth, and the 'structuralists', who felt that the danger of inflation was inherent in the structure of under-developed countries, and could only be cured by growth. Both approaches contained an element of truth. Perhaps one of the most difficult jobs for a government was to decide what kind of inflationary pressure signified 'self-terminating growth pains', and what pressures were 'unhealthy and to be eliminated'. The combination of maximum growth and maximum stability called for public statesmanship of a high order.

The really important question was not demarcation of the public and private sectors but whether the essential tasks of the public sector in economic development were effectively carried out. If the public sector extended itself too much beyond its administrative capacity, its tasks would not be well done. On the other hand, if the public sector failed to take the necessary action required, and created a vacuum which the private sector did not, or could not, fill, the public sector's tasks would not be well done, and would be considered to be too small. The key problem was the energetic action that was required, including not only public sector activity but also the development of good policies and proper encouragement and assistance to the private sector. The best line of demarcation had to be determined in each country according to its own objectives and circumstances.

Both the public and private sectors were faced with new and unaccustomed tasks in the process of economic development. Adaptation and adjustment in ingrained habits and operations were required, based on fact, not dogma. Traditional methods in under-developed countries were, almost by definition, not the ones most suited for economic development. This did not mean, however, that a violent break with tradition was necessarily required. Evolution, not revolution, was the best slogan. To the extent that it was possible to build upon existing traditions, and evolve them in the desired directions, this might lead to better results and produce the type of development more in accordance with the wishes of the people.

A balanced view of balanced growth

Singer also took on the concept of balanced growth in economic development, both in theory and in practice, which was in vogue in the 1950s (Singer, 1960).[33] Nurkse, for example, argued for a more or less synchronized application of capital to a wide range of different industries because most industries catering for mass consumption were complementary in the sense that they provided a market, and thus support, for each other. The case for balanced growth rested, in his view, on the need for a 'balanced diet' (Nurkse, 1953, pp. 11–17).

Along with others, Singer criticized this concept and suggested that what was needed was a strategy of 'judiciously unbalanced growth'. He noted that the concept of balanced growth, or the maintenance of some kind of equilibrium during the process of growth, meant different things to different people. He distinguished three classes of usage, which he labelled 'non-technical', 'general technical', and 'specific technical'. In non-technical parlance, the term 'balanced growth' was often used to describe such ideas as growth without too much social disruption, broadly based growth, growth which spread its benefits widely, and sustained growth. In the general technical sense, balanced growth referred to the balance between ambitions and the resources available to satisfy them or, more narrowly, the balance between intended savings and investment. In the specific technical sense, the concept referred to the balance between the size of markets, the volume of supply, and the demand for capital, the problem that Adam Smith had raised of keeping the growth of markets and the growth of supply in balance. It was this specific technical use of the term 'balanced growth' that Singer addressed.

To help in the understanding of the problem, Singer asserted that 'we have to construct some kind of fundamental structural picture – model, if you like – of an underdeveloped country'. An underdeveloped country had a clearly defined employment structure with 70 to 90 per cent of the employed population engaged in agriculture, compared with about 15 per cent in developed countries. He recalled that Arthur Lewis had defined the process of economic growth as the problem of transforming a country from a 5 per cent saver into a 15 per cent saver (Lewis, 1955). Referring to the employment structure, and not to the structure of foreign trade or to the composition of the national income of developing countries, Singer reasoned that 'We can, with equal justice, define the process as one of transforming a country from an 80 per cent farmer to a 15 per cent farmer.'

The high proportion of population engaged in farming was another of the vicious circles of developing countries, which reflected low productivity. 'The low level of productivity in farming decrees that the bulk of the people must be in farming in order to feed and clothe themselves, and that they have little to spare over and above their own needs.' By writ of Engel's law, a high per centage of low incomes was spent on food and essential clothing, and the demand for other things was 'limited to a very small percentage of a very small income'. There was thus only a tiny market for those 'other things' and investment in producing them was not attractive. Under-developed countries were also as a rule net exporters of agricultural goods and net importers of other products.

To make matters worse, Singer observed, productivity in agriculture was significantly lower than productivity in the small industrial sector. In fact, he noted that 'for a surprising number of countries the figures come remarkably close to a constant relation of the form

$$a = 2/3 \, n$$

where a was output per employed person in agriculture and n was output per employed person in the economy as a whole'. From this fact followed an arithmetic law 'of considerable political and emotional significance'. If an 80 per cent farmer economy produced only two-thirds of its national per capita average in the agricultural sector, the differential between the agricultural and non-agricultural sectors would be much larger than in a 15 per cent farmer economy (a typical advanced economy) which also produced two-thirds of its national average in the agricultural sector. In fact, in the under-developed country output per worker outside agriculture compared with agricultural output per worker would be in the ratio of 3.5 :1. Thus, a transformation from a mainly agricultural to a mainly non-agricultural economy was not only an essential part of the development process but this structural change also had an important 'multiplier effect'. As the levels of productivity, and of real demand and markets, rose, the structural change from an 80 per cent farmer economy towards a 15 per cent farmer economy, made possible by that rise, would, in turn, generate forces which would themselves tend to raise productivity and real incomes. The effect might become the cause and 'we are in the midst of a hen-and-egg riddle'. Here, Singer concluded, we have the starting point of the doctrine of balanced growth – 'the self-justifying broadening of real demand and markets, the investment which looks uneconomical *ex ante* but becomes economical *ex post*, the shipwreck which helps to set off the wave which will float it off the rocks'.

In spite of its intellectually satisfying features, Singer observed that the doctrine of balanced economic growth had severe limitations in its applicability to under-developed countries. It failed to come directly to grips with a fundamental problem, that of shortage of resources. It might be true that supply of goods, provided it was properly composed and balanced, would create its own demand. But supply of goods meant demand for factors of production and especially for capital. While supply of goods might create its own demand, demand for factors in under-developed countries would not create its own supply. Demand for factors implied in a broad-based investment programme would be in direct competition with other investment projects and other types of expenditure whose direct objective was to increase available resources. If both types of investment could be undertaken simultaneously, all would be well and the doctrine of balanced growth vindicated. But the resources were not available. Singer agreed with the advice to under-developed countries to 'stop thinking piecemeal and to start thinking big' and that the programming approach was better than the project approach (Singer, 1965c). But this should be done realistically within the resources available. As he put it, 'Perhaps guerrilla tactics are more suitable for the circumstances of underdeveloped countries than a frontal attack.'

Finally, Singer called for 'a balanced view of balanced growth'. He recalled that there were 'several distinct roads to economic growth' other than that of balanced growth. In the first place, and most obviously, there was the increase in productivity in agriculture. Second, was improvement of productivity outside agriculture, and specifically in industry. Third, the low-level-equilibrium deadlock of real incomes and markets existed only in a closed economy. In any individual under-developed country with significant foreign trade, some of the markets were abroad and were not limited by low domestic incomes. Fourth, by the same token, a country engaged in foreign trade had established domestic markets supplied by imports from abroad. Import substitution, like export promotion, thus offered an opportunity of growth 'in happy disregard of the need for an investment package'. The protective tariff had historically been a major alternative to the balanced investment package in the early stages of development. Fifth, and related to the improvement of productivity, there was the approach to economic growth via the building up of the economic infrastructure.

Lastly, we should distinguish between balance as the end result at which to aim and balance as the method of approach. 'Where you start with imbalance, you need *further imbalance* (original emphasis) in order to come closer to balance.' The doctrine of balanced growth seemed to assume that in making decisions on the allocation of resources in an under-developed country, we start from scratch. This was not so. Rather, we start with a situation which incorporates the effects of previous investment and developments. This meant that at any given point of time, there were types of investment which were not in themselves balanced investment packages but which were complementary to existing investments, thus bringing the total stock of capital nearer balance. This might leave the concept of the balanced investment package valid, only stretching it over several investment periods. But, as Singer put it, 'The trouble is that life does not stand still.' While aiming at better balance by unbalanced 'bottleneck' investment, conditions change again and at the end of the investment period we are left with a new imbalance. Thus, while we might aim at balance as an investment criterion, we achieve that objective by unbalanced investment.

Alternative approaches were required other than those singled out in the doctrine of balanced growth. Each of those alternative approaches could conceivably resolve, if successfully pursued, the marketing deadlock, which gave origin to the doctrine of balanced growth. Thus, balanced growth should be judged not as the sole cure for the evil correctly diagnosed but one of several possible cures. The objections to the doctrine of balanced growth would be greatly reduced, and finally vanish, as the available resources increase in the course of economic growth. Thus interpreted, the doctrine should stimulate underdeveloped countries to undertake the necessary sacrifices in the early stages of development. It promised them that one day, when resources had become big enough, balanced investment packages would become possible. As Singer put it, 'When they have labored to the top, the balanced investment package will help them to "coast down the other side of the hill", into the promised land of cumulative growth and compound interest.'

Deficit financing and public capital formation

Singer examined the special factors which determined the effects of deficit-financed public capital formation in under-developed countries (Singer, 1958d).[34] He pointed out that the situation was superficially similar to that of developed countries in a depression in that in many under-developed countries a supply of unutilized labour could be assumed to exist at the going wage rate in the 'modernized' sector of the economy. Unemployment could take many forms but one may assume an oversupply of labour in the sense that a potential working force for expanded production existed and that its marginal productivity was nil, or close to nil. There may also be unutilized reserves of raw materials and even of fixed capital equipment, although not to the extent as in an industrial economy in under-employment equilibrium or in depression. Against this superficial similarity, there was the important difference that the more productive employment of this un- or under-employed labour force was obstructed by something more than a shortage of effective demand.

The difficulties of transforming latent resources into actual output in under-developed countries were more deeply rooted, and differed among them. Analysts had disagreed about what these difficulties were. Singer pointed to those difficulties in his work on the terms of trade. A common factor of all the obstacles was that they related to deficiencies of effective supply rather than of effective demand. Where essential public services and communications were among the obstacles, public capital formation assumed particular importance in creating the preconditions for an expansion of output, which might add to the importance of public investment, financed, if necessary, by deficits.

Public investment 'could be economically justified only for its impact on productivity, for lowering cost curves and increasing the elasticity of supply curves, not for raising demand curves'. Hence, the monetary income effects of deficits incurred to finance public investment were not the main purpose but an 'unintended by-product'. If output could not be expanded under the impact of rising demand, the case for deficit-financed public investment was obviously weakened, and may be reduced to an argument of political or administrative expediency. The expansion of public services was essential, and better ways of doing this might be barred for political and administrative reasons. The income effect of a deficit would normally be at best 'a helpful accessory'. The redistribution of income in favour of profits, as well as the broadening of demand, might possibly serve to assist in the movement toward the main objective, e.g., by adding a further inducement to private investors to take advantage of the opportunities presented by lower cost as a result of the provision of better public services. But 'the lowering of the real cost curve remains the chief objective'.

The marginal rates of savings and taxation in under-developed countries were often, but not necessarily or universally, very low. This could be attributed to a number of factors, but whatever the reasons, the multiplier must often be assumed to be quite high. To this should be added that often there were no surplus foreign exchange reserves, so that the capacity to run an import surplus was small, while the marginal propensity to import may be high. Where foreign exchange, especially accretions of foreign exchange, was largely reserved for producers' goods, and there was little or no home production of those goods, the availability of imports became a determinant of investment.

Thus, an increase in the import surplus may be associated with inflationary pressures. This assumed that the attempt to step up investment would not, and could not, have been made without the availability of more imported capital goods. In this sense, an increased import surplus would *de facto* increase, rather than diminish, inflationary pressures, since the increased investment based on it required also domestic resources and raised domestic incomes.

The marginal rate of savings or taxation may be particularly low where the increase in incomes associated with deficit-financed public investment accrued partly in kind. For example, where previously unemployed or under-employed farmers were drawn from the country-side as a result of deficit-financed public works or construction of urban public utilities, the real per capita income of those remaining on the land was increased. But this increase could take the form not of higher money income through additional sales but of increased consumption in kind. Since those drawn from the countryside would also have a high propensity to consume, and specifically to consume food, the multiplier could become *pro tanto* very high, and the inflationary gap may express itself sharply in terms of food shortages.

Thus, while the multiplier was likely to be high in under-developed countries, the response of supplies to price increases and pressure of demand was likely to be small. The factors reducing productivity or lowering elasticity of supply were simultaneously tackled. There may be an expansion of supplies hand-in-hand with the deficit-financed public investment. Alternatively, the public investment may itself be specifically directed toward removing some of the obstacles. But this possibility was limited by the fact that not all of the obstacles holding back supply could be affected by public investment. Singer therefore concluded that productive public investment directed toward reducing obstacles to increasing supply in the more immediate future, or simultaneously with an attack on those obstacle by other means, 'provided the classical case in defense of deficit financing'.

Added to low productivity and low elasticity of supply when confronted with increased demand was the factor of resource immobility, i.e., a low capacity of shifting resources from one use to another or from one sector to another. Superimposed upon the difficulty of increasing supplies of a given sector from the resources already committed to it, was the further difficulty of augmenting the resources committed by reducing the resources committed to another sector. An under-developed country had neither much capital to depreciate nor a large volume of fresh resources from growth. Resource immobility had an important implication. To set free resources to the extent of, say, 5 per cent of national income in order to augment investment by that amount, it was not sufficient that the same amount of resources should be taken away from consumption or private investment or current public expenditure. If the resources thus set free could not be transferred into the resources required for additional investment, the sacrifice would *pro tanto* have been made in vain. An increase in investment by 5 per cent of national income could involve curtailments in other directions of perhaps 8 or 10 per cent of national income. This situation had some resemblance to the multiplier effect involved in curtailing domestic incomes in order to achieve certain required reductions in total import demand.

The comparative immobility of resources between sectors in under-developed countries, combined with a greater elasticity of supply within each sector, had consequences which could be expressed in various ways. Global pressure of demand on resources was more dangerous and more liable to lead to inflation, and hence, to maintain stability, under-developed countries may have to forgo, at least partially, the use of one of the instruments which might otherwise be conducive to economic growth. Measures to increase the mobility of resources were a precondition for raising the degree of pressure of total demand on resources, since that pressure would inevitably require adjustments in the allocation of resources between sectors. The burden of adjustment which would be thrown on imports would tend to be correspondingly greater, and the difficulties of achieving an expanded balance of supplies from domestic production would lead to an increased need to add to supply through imports.

Singer warned against the use of deficit financing of public invest-ment in under-developed countries faced with a combination of high multipliers, low elasticity of supply and resource immobility 'unless these three characteristics are modified prior to, or simultaneously with, the deficit-financed expenditure'. This warning could be fortified by reference to other characteristics of under-developed countries, which led to the general conclusion that deficit-finance proposals should be regarded with 'acute apprehension … in most, or nearly all, actual combinations of circumstances that are likely to be encountered in underdeveloped countries'.

There remained 'the exceptional combination of circumstances' for employing deficit financing; for example:

- where there was a special opportunity to increase food production and other consumer goods, 'conspicuously and rapidly', with the

aid of public works, and bridge the interval by drawing on a previously accumulated surplus of foreign exchange;
- where there was a very high marginal rate of savings or taxation; where the underlying deflationary tendencies offered scope for public deficits; and
- where better alternatives to deficit financing, such as increased taxation, were politically or administratively impossible, or where their broader economic effects were especially harmful, and yet where some forms of productive public investment were an absolute precondition of economic progress, leading to political and social stability.

But even where deficit financing led to increased capital formation, Singer reasoned that the dangers of deficit financing should be 'weighed against the dangers of economic stagnation or deterioration'. Singer went further. 'Where the need for public investment over and above what present revenues permit is so crucial and imperative, it is difficult to see why the effort to overcome the obstacles obstructing the use of less dangerous methods of financing could not also be made.' A determination to achieve the end would seem to presuppose a determination to make possible the best means. He therefore concluded that 'it would appear that the circumstances justifying deficit financing as a deliberate choice would be rather special and the justified doses [should be]closely circumscribed'.

Human factors in development: the notion of human investment

Singer was an early and strong proponent of the importance of the human factor in development even before his work on the proposals for action for the UN first development decade of the 1960s (UN, 1962). Then (in 1962), he spoke of 'a shift in our whole thinking about … development' from physical to human capital, which T. W. Schultz, among others, energized and broadened into acceptance (Schultz, 1961). This was before he became the first associate director of the UN Research Institute for Social Development in 1964. He was among the first development economists who regarded social development as a key growth sector. Out of this concern arose his 'notion of human investment' (Singer, 1966c).

The concept of 'human capital' in the history of economic thought was by no means a recent discovery (Kiker, 1967). It was grounded in the thinking of several classical economists. Smith, Say, Senior and Mill all saw clearly that the category of 'capital' should include, explicitly or implicitly, the skills and abilities of human beings, and that outlays on the formation of those skills should properly be treated as capital formation expenditures. Singer noted that Friedrich List placed the notion of human capital near the centre of his infant-industry argument on trade protection for development purposes. Later writers also dealt, in various ways, with the problem of defining and estimating the productive value of human skills although, probably as a reaction to the 'dismality of older economic theory', they were reluctant to discuss explicitly the notion of investment in human beings.

Many people shrank from thinking of human beings as 'capital' from which a return was derived. Terms such as 'human capital', 'human investment', and reference to children as 'durable goods', used to describe the formation of human skills and their contribution to production, were regarded as 'not very happy ones'. This reaction Singer attributed to a misunderstanding. He regarded J. S. Mill's 'cogently beautiful definition':

> The human being I do not class as wealth. He is the purpose for which wealth exists. But his acquired capacities, which exist only as a means, and have been called into existence by labour, fall mightily, as it seems to me, within that designation. (*Principles of Political Economy*)

as a basis for reconciling the dignity of human beings with their instrumental function. Singer considered that these words reflected quite accurately the foundation on which a valid approach to human resources could be based. Nobody should suggest that people should be treated only as instruments of production, as 'living machines', or that an improvement in human welfare, which did not lead to increased productivity in the future, should be classed as 'wasteful and unproductive'. He emphasized consistently that an improved life was the entire purpose and point of economic development, a fact worthy of emphasis because it was sometimes lost sight of. However, people were not only the purpose of the entire system, they were also instruments by which the end could be achieved.

To the question whether social or human factors were preconditions for economic growth, or whether economic growth was the precondition for social and human development, Singer replied 'both'. It was another case of 'the chicken or the egg'. In a feed-back process, it all depended where you started from, which was a matter of choice. Experience and research had shown that only a comparatively minor part of economic progress could be attributed to the input of material or physical factors of production. Most was due to the 'intangible', 'residual' or, in other words, the 'human' factor. This realization had opened up new approaches to development by using the vast latent human resources of the developing countries.

The shift in emphasis from the role of physical capital toward that of people had also drawn attention to the problems of children. This was to remain a major concern for Singer from his earliest days at the United Nations and was to lead to his long association with UNICEF. He recalled how this came about.[35] Shortly after he arrived at the UN in 1947, Maurice Pate, the then executive director of UNICEF, approached David Owen, head of the UN Economic Affairs Department, with a request that one of the economists in his department might take an interest in the activities of UNICEF, which was about to be transformed from a UN emergency agency for children to one dealing with their long-term needs. David Owen passed the request to Singer in the development section of his department stating that working with UNICEF might recall their common experience in working on the unemployment problems of the depressed areas of Great Britain , and give what later came to be called a 'human face' approach to his department's development work. Singer was busy at the time, primarily working on his study of the terms of trade. Moreover, he considered that the subject was of little relevance to someone who was supposed to be a development economist, especially one who had had little experience of working among, or on the needs of, children. So he did not respond immediately to Pate's request.

Shortly afterwards, Singer went to Harvard University to visit Schumpeter. While there, and 'almost by accident', he heard a lecture given by Nevin Scrimshaw, a nutritionist at the Massachusetts Institute of Technology, on the effects of malnutrition among pregnant women and young children on their subsequent physical and mental development, leading to a waste of investment on education and training in later life by reducing human capacities. This struck Singer 'like lightning' and caused him to realize the importance of child welfare not only as an 'humanitarian good thing' but as 'a central thing in development economics'. On returning to the United Nations, Singer replied positively to Pate's request. 'Children suddenly seemed more important even than the terms of trade.' So he put aside the work he was doing and produced a study for UNICEF on *The Role of Children in Economic Development* (Singer, 1947a). This was one of the first major tasks that Singer completed at the UN and resulted in a continuing interest in the subject and an association with UNICEF.

Low productivity of human investment in developing countries was due in part to malnutrition during early childhood. As Singer graphically put it, 'An invitation to the "banquet of life" is not very appealing when the menu consists of a forty per cent chance of surviving birth and childhood, followed by forty or forty-five rachitic and mentally retarded years of near starvation' (Schiavo-Campo and Singer, 1970a, p. 92). But although one of the most important factors, malnutrition was not the only social problem of relevance to national development. He noted that other development analysts had referred to other factors, including the value system and motivation instilled in children (Hagen, 1962).

At a conference organized by UNICEF at Bellagio, Lake Como in Italy in 1964 on planning for the needs of children in developing countries, Singer presented a paper on the role of children and youth (Singer, 1964f). Attention was drawn again at the conference to widespread malnutrition among children of one to four years of age in the poorer countries, and the fact that the damage done to physical and mental development was irreversible, no matter how much their situation improved later. They would therefore never be able to take proper advantage of educational facilities, even where these improved, and they would never become fully effective producers. The conference also addressed the problem of employment for young people emerging from the spreading primary school system in developing countries. They were dissatisfied with traditional village life and tended to drift to the towns where there were few employment opportunities. Singer saw at this point how the fields of human resources and technology interconnected. Employment and training was needed for young people as well as appropriate technology. He quoted from the 'proposals for action' for the UN development decade of the 1960s that he had written for the UN secretary-general:

> Emphasis on the mobilization of human resources as a pre-condition for achieving the aims of the development decade, and as a necessary area for intensified international action, does not perhaps need much general argumentation at this time. Educated and trained people are always the chief, and in the longer run the only, agents of development. The unutilized talents of their people constitute the chief present waste, and the chief future hope, of the developing countries. High priority must accordingly be given to establishing educational systems well adapted to the economic and social needs of the developing countries. (UN, 1962, p. 25)

According to Singer's notion of human investment, the fundamental problem was no longer the creation of wealth, but 'the creation of the capacity to create wealth'. This insight had been made possible by 'a shift in our whole thinking about the problems of growth and development'.

Singer also addressed the special concern of planning for the needs of children in a paper prepared for a UNICEF conference on 'Planning for Children and Youth in Asia' in Bangkok, Thailand in 1966 (Singer, 1966b). He argued that children's problems occupied a special position among planners not only because they made up a large segment of the population of developing countries, the cost of the upbringing was high, and they were the 'wave of the future', but also because, as he continued to repeat, 'development is not only growth, but also change'. The children of today were the producers, entrepreneurs, consumers and even the planners of tomorrow. Planning for children was a much wider concept than might be initially conceived. Even basic planning decisions on the rate of physical investment amounted to decisions for or against children. Allocating more resources to investment meant that a higher level of consumption would be enjoyed by the younger generation in later years, and less consumption by today's adults. This assumed that the purpose of present investment was future consumption. But this point should not be taken too far. A cut in consumption required in order to increase investment could fall with particular hardship on children, as the structural adjustment programmes carried out by developing countries in the 1980s, often with the support of the World Bank and the IMF, were to show (Shaw and Singer, 1988g). And much investment, if short-lived, would benefit mainly the adult population. Singer therefore considered that, in practical terms, probably the best approach would be to embody the needs of children in planning processes that linked the concern for children with institutional arrangements made for manpower planning and to include the development of children in a broadening of the term 'manpower'.

The needs of children would be neglected in sectoral planning, where each sector was planned by a different government department because the development of children was typically inter-sectoral. And all sectoral planning tended to exaggerate the importance of tangible and quantifiable things and underestimate the intangible and non-quantifiable, especially human quality. The case for special orientation of development plans toward children could be made on 'very simple social grounds'. Children were members of larger-than-average families where per capita income was less than average. Poor people, on the whole, tended to have more children. And poorer, rural people tended to have more children than richer, urban people. The average child in a given country at any given time tended to be worse off than the average adult. Yet, on economic and planning grounds, it ought to be the other way round. Providing higher standards for children today would benefit the economy more lastingly than the high standards for adults. But providing different standards for adults and children was not easy. It would be possible, however, to slant development planning in the direction of things consumed by large families, where most of the children would be found.

Another important question was whether the needs of children should be dealt with directly or as members of their families and communities. Children formed an important part of the family, in the nucleus or extended sense. It was through the family that the strongest impact was made on the child. Any development plan aimed at children should therefore be carried out with the family's preponderant role in mind. Only when a child was old enough for formal education was a more direct approach possible. It would be impossible in most societies to isolate children and to design a sectoral programme for their development alone.

Finally, Singer emphasized that much of what was required could be done at little or no cost in one of three ways: through better education and advice, for example on feeding and training children; by using resources that were not utilized, such as the spare time of fathers and mothers which could be systematically used for the improvement of conditions of their own children; and through the motivation of direct, tangible benefits for children, which was usually very strong among families and villages in developing countries, to mobilize latent resources.

Education and economic development

Singer observed that it was 'surely one of the most dramatic reversals in the history of human thought that at present (1961) we have thrown overboard the belief in a coming stationary state for the developed countries and replaced it by a picture of the possibility of indefinite progress' (Singer, 1961b).[36] Up to the Second World War, economists from Adam Smith to Keynes were, for different reasons, practically unanimous in forecasting that economic growth in the more developed countries would first slow down and then come to a standstill. Singer found the reason for this transformation in the terms 'technical progress' and 'human capital', and the relationship between education and economic development. This new insight had been made possible by a major shift in thinking about the problems of growth and development. The fundamental problem was 'no longer the creation of wealth but rather the creation of the *capacity* to create wealth' (original emphasis). Once a society had acquired that capacity, the creation of wealth itself became almost incidental and followed 'quasi-automatically'.

The capacity to create wealth resided in the people of a country. It consisted of 'brain power' and was based on the application of research to the problems of production and the best organization of the economic institutions of a country, systematically pursued and applied. The history of the post-war years had shown that given this underlying capacity and systematic application of research, economies could make up for gaps or destruction in their physical capital equipment in a surprisingly short time. It had also shown that systematic application of brain power seemed to transcend in its importance for economic development the distinction between different economic and social system, however important and fundamental those differences may be in other respects.

One factor of the development of research and brain power as a built-in growth element was the systematic expenditure of about 1.5 to 2 per cent of the national income on 'research and development' (R & D), excluding military R & D. The educational level of the population also made that application, with its necessary adjustments, possible, as did the level of expenditure sufficient to create a flow of new investment opportunities that could maintain the productivity of new capital accumulation at a high level.

At the beginning of the 1960s, total new investment in the underdeveloped countries was of the order of about $10 billion a year. In Singer's opinion, it ought to have been double that amount to convert them into progressive economies. The actual figure was only a fraction of that amount, as were the international resources available as aid for that purpose.

Two points were important to note. First, such a systematic expenditure on brain power and the application of its results to production were not subjected to the law of diminishing returns. On the contrary, it was governed by increasing returns. Secondly, as the total body of knowledge extended, the linkage effects of any new additions to the stock of knowledge were multiplied. New knowledge linked up with previous new knowledge to produce quite unexpected new combinations of progress, and new knowledge linked up with previous failures could convert them into success.

Beyond the financing of R & D and related training, there was the much larger cost of general and vocational education and training. Singer argued that much of the cost of educational investment consisted of the loss of time, and hence of earnings, by high-school students,

students in higher education, and full-time trainees. Considered in that way, education was true investment in the 'pure sense', i.e., a sacrifice of production now for the sake of higher production in the future. Calculations of the yield of the investment in education in terms of the additional earnings of individuals as a result of investment in education had shown that it was at least as productive, if not considerably higher, than investment in physical capital. The yield of educational investment was higher in under-developed than in developed countries. In the developing countries, the loss of time of persons going through the process of education was less highly valued than in developed countries. In addition, the yield differential between skilled and trained people and others was much higher than in developed countries. This was based on the assumption that the educational output was adjusted to the needs of the economic system and that graduates and trainees obtained jobs corresponding to their education and training, and could make a proper contribution to national production.

The educational basis was an absolute precondition for the fruitful application of R & D to the process of production. It was only where the working force at all levels was sufficiently literate, educated, trained, and mobile to take advantage of new advances in techniques and organization of production that the creation of a built-in 'industry of progress' became possible. That could not be achieved overnight. It was probably best thought of as a long-term objective to be achieved over three or four generations. This left open many questions of more immediate educational policy. But as in other branches of development planning, the problem was that so many things had to be done at the same time. The productivity of new capital investment had to be raised immediately by providing the complementary inputs of trained workers who were taken for granted in the more developed countries. The more obvious gaps in the ranks of business administrators and technicians, in both the public and private sectors, had to be filled. The educational basis of literacy, and educational institutions, especially in secondary and higher education, had to be created. And the essential first step of teacher training had to be taken.

Where resources were limited, as they were at the beginning of the 1960s in the newly-emerging developing countries, Singer suggested that it made sense to select those projects in educational investment which made the greatest short-term contribution to economic output, provided this did not interfere with the long-term development of the educational system. This did not in any way detract from the long-term importance of educational investment or from the fact that education was of great value in itself. The role of education in a progressive society could not be exhaustively measured by a direct cost/benefit analysis. For example, where the introduction of general elementary education could not be made in the whole country simultaneously, those regions of the country where economic development was expected to be more strongly concentrated could be selected for priority development.

In the short run, the educational deficiencies of under-developed countries could be dealt with by measures other than the development of the educational system. Apart from the stop-gap measure of employing foreign experts and technicians, lacking skills could be substituted for by mechanization. But this was generally shortsighted because it perpetuated the disadvantages of under-developed countries which had low marginal productivity of capital because of the absence of skills. It prevented them from developing a technology of production appropriate to their resource endowment, developing learning processes, and adjusting their resource endowment and techniques of production to each other harmoniously.

Another possible short-cut method was by providing technical assistance through international co-operation. But even this was not the fundamental solution. What the under-developed countries needed was technological progress corresponding to their specific situation, meaning a relative shortage of capital and a population which was not so highly sophisticated and trained to begin with. Only in that way could the situation be created in which by harmonious interaction knowledge of a suitable kind can enable the population to take full advantage of progressively advanced and more complicated degrees of knowledge. There were areas of knowledge in developed countries which were capable of transfer or suitable application to under-developed countries. Moreover, technical assistance could also be used to assist them in making their own type of investment in human capital and in R & D. But while technical assistance might help under-developed countries to achieve built-in progress, it could never substitute for it. True progress, based as it was on human investment, had always to be a domestic product, even though it could be nursed, assisted and stimulated from abroad.

A blueprint for development?

At the end of his period at the United Nations in 1969, Singer reflected on his profound intellectual and practical experience. He gave his 'perspective' on international development, in collaboration with Salvatore Schiavo-Campo, an Italian national who, like him, had had a long association in responsible positions in the United Nations and later went to the University of Massachusetts in the United States (Schiavo-Campo and Singer, 1970a, pp. 3–14). Of all the value judgements which, explicitly or implicitly, underlaid economic policies, they considered that none was more defensible than considering the poverty of two-thirds of the world's population as the priority problem for international economic policy and analysis. A hopeful indication of the economists' sense of relevance was that during the more than two decades that they had been at the United Nations, a considerable amount of scholarly work had been done on questions of economic development. Yet, a theory of economic development had not emerged, at least not in the same sense that could be identified in a price theory, or a pure trade theory, or even a theory of growth. For, they re-emphasized, 'development is not merely economic growth: it is growth accompanied by structural social and economic change'. It was therefore perhaps inevitable that the impossibility of using a *ceteris paribus* approach to problems of development should engender difficulties in constructing a unified theoretical framework. A country in the process of development could best be compared with a giraffe: 'difficult to describe but very easily recognized'.

Many of the valuable textbooks on economic development that had appeared had been characterized by attempts at comparative and thorough examination of all issues and major arguments relating to economic development. But the lack of a general theory impaired their value as a text which a student could follow reasonably well as an integrated whole, and which had a unified, though necessarily partial, view of the development process. A more frankly subjective treatment was therefore needed in a *perspective* (original emphasis) on economic development, with its emphasis on the role of human resources and social factors, technology, trade and aid.

Despite its importance, and almost three decades of work on the subject, the concept of development, and the conditions which defined 'under-developed' areas and their prospects for economic growth, remained 'tantalizingly vague'. The word 'development' could not be applied equally to economic progress in all countries. Economic progress of the poorer countries could not proceed in a continuing and self-sustaining fashion unless it was 'preceded, accompanied and followed by changes in the social and economic structures of these countries'. Hence, economic development was *growth plus change* (original emphasis). But how could that be achieved? A unified, generally applicable 'blueprint for development' was conspicuous by its absence. This was by no means a discredit to economic science, as the ingredients of such a blueprint, as well as their relative ordering, were imperfectly known. But, as in medical science, while the detailed answer was still unavailable, some clues had emerged to provide at least partial solutions, to be interpreted differently in different cases. Economic development problems could be solved. Improving the general framework of analysis would increase chances to find workable solutions applicable to specific countries. But none of these solutions could transform the poorer countries overnight.

Singer's own perspective on development revolved around three main themes: development should be viewed in an international context; social factors should be incorporated into economic development analysis; and economic development should be seen as a dynamic process, which called for structural change and modification of the conditions of production. He noted the circular nature of economic development problems with their 'vicious circles within vicious circles, all interlocking with one another'. This was a restatement of the well-known proposition that in economics everything depended upon everything else, which applied with particular force to developing countries. This, in turn, underlined the need for development planning, which many developing countries had adopted regardless of their political and economic philosophy.

Part III
The Later Years (1969–2001)

'Hans's life has been anything but cloistered. He has made frequent journeys half around the world. There are few of the developing countries that he has not visited and still fewer that he has not advised. He must have addressed a wider variety of academics in a wider variety of places about a wider range of subjects than any other economist, living or dead. He has moved from continent to continent, expounding, advocating, and devising strategies of economic development. His influence has been felt as much by word of mouth in the succession of countries where he has lectured as through the pile of working documents and published reports that survive like a spoor from his travels.'

(Sir Alec Cairncross, in Sapsford and Chen, 1998a, pp. 13–14)

16
Work at IDS

One might have imagined that the drama of Singer's life and work would be over at the end of the second act when Singer retired from the United Nations in 1969. Not a bit of it! The third act has proved to be just as exciting, and productive, as in the previous years, and Singer's output and activities even more prolific, as Sir Alec Cairncross has described. It is little wonder that he regarded Singer as 'better known in the developing countries than any other economist' (Simmons, 1985). The challenge for the biographer is how to do justice to, and convey to the reader in the space available, the extraordinary scale, depth and variety of his writings in the last 30 years as well as in the years before.

When Singer retired from the UN, he had the opportunity to take up a senior appointment in another UN body or a professorship in a university in the United States or elsewhere. Instead, he was attracted to the Institute of Development Studies (IDS) at the University of Sussex in the United Kingdom where he had old friends and where he could help in building up a new development institute. He was appointed fellow at IDS in 1969, and professor later emeritus, at the University of Sussex. There began his third career as researcher, teacher, consultant, conference lecturer, reviewer and correspondent to newspapers, journals and academics around the world, and a colleague who seemed to find time for the most junior of students. In many ways, this was a natural continuation of his work at the United Nations. It was fortuitous for both the Institute and the man. The aims of both of 'combining vision with practicality' matched perfectly (Singer, 1992e, p. iii). IDS was founded in 1966. When Singer arrived, the Institute was still in its formative years. Singer found a similar collegiate spirit to that in which he had flourished at Bonn and

Cambridge. Under the directorship first of Dudley Seers, then Richard Jolly, and later Mike Faber, John Toye and Keith Bezanson, and among the IDS fellowship, he found a congenial environment in which to continue his extraordinary and varied output.[1]

In addition to making a significant contribution to the work and activities of IDS, which quickly became recognized as one of the world's leading institutes of development studies, Singer became in constant demand by governments, multilateral and bilateral aid agencies and non-governmental organizations for his creative intelligence, profound knowledge and wise advice. He is remembered with respect and affection by the cohorts of students who have passed through IDS in the past three decades as a source of almost unlimited help and inspiration through his dedication and generosity of time and attention to their work.

What follows is a summary of some of his main concerns and interests that he has written about since 1969. Singer was able to devote his entire attention to his intellectual and academic interests thanks once

4.   Cutting the cake. Celebration of Sir Hans Singer's 90th birthday, at the Institute of Development Studies, University of Sussex, with his wife Lady Ilse Singer, 7 December 2000 (*The Institute of Development Studies*)

again to the home stability and comfort provided by his wife Ilse. She established a home, which has remained unchanged since it was purchased in 1968, where she and Singer received their many friends and visitors. Ilse also took up her own voluntary work again including organizing the sales of UNICEF cards throughout the area and recording 50 years of fundraising. She also took part in the feminist movement which involved the lobbying ot funds to establish a women's refuge and joining the protest against the use of nuclear weapons. Although she was disinterested in all forms of pompous glory, she welcomed the knighthood bestowed on her husband in recognition of the hard work he had put in over many years for the benefit of the people of developing countries. Singer and his wife became paid-up members of the British Labour Party on their return to Britain after service in the United Nations in 1969.

17
Employment and Redistribution From/With Growth

The ILO World Employment Programme

It was particularly fitting that the first subject that Singer took up again on arriving at IDS was that of unemployment, the subject of his first employment after taking his doctorate at Cambridge (see Chapter 4). He undertook a consultancy with ILO in Geneva between the end of his UN career on 1 January 1969 and his arrival at IDS in April of that year on its newly launched World Employment Programme (WEP) (Morse, 1968; Singer, 1970e).[2] This became an important element in the first years of his affiliation with IDS, starting with participation in a conference in Philadelphia, United States in 1969 on the occasion of the 50th anniversary of the ILO and the 25th anniversary of the Philadelphia Declaration which reconstituted ILO. His personal involvement related mainly to work as a consultant to ILO, with special responsibility for the Asian branch of WEP in Bangkok, Thailand. This involved visits to Bangkok and led to holding a training course (jointly with Ronald Dore who at the time was also a fellow at IDS) on employment problems in Asian countries at the UN Institute for Planning and Development there.

Singer's consultancy with ILO helped to lay the foundation for the World Employment Programme (WEP) (Singer, 1992d). WEP was launched by ILO in 1969 as its major contribution to the UN Second Development Decade of the 1970s. It was launched with a flourish. But there was just one problem. No one at the time of the launch knew quite what the WEP should do. So David Morse, the director-general of ILO at the time who created the WEP, called in Singer and Walter Galenson, a professor in labour relations at Cornell University in the United States, and later Dudley Seers, director of IDS at the time, to

158

help define WEP's objectives. They helped to write the ILO director-general's 1969 ILO conference report, which contained a general description of the WEP, and later were engaged in describing its contents and work programme.

The general objective of WEP was to provide specific guidelines to national decision-makers and planners concerning policies and measures to reduce unemployment and under-employment by accelerating the creation of productive jobs. Singer assisted in the identification of specific policies and measures to improve the employment situation, to examine their relative importance, and to assist countries with their implementation through pilot employment missions, regional employment teams, country employment projects and action-oriented research. Morse received a visit from the Pope, and the Nobel Peace Prize on behalf of ILO, for his initiative.

Changing concepts of unemployment

Singer identified five main factors that accounted for widespread and increasing unemployment in the developing countries at the beginning of the 1970s.[3] These factors were:

- the 'relentless increase in population', which, according to his calculations, would require the developing countries to provide for annual additions to their labour forces of three per cent or so a year, compared with of the order of 1 per cent in the richer countries;
- the 'overwhelming' concentration of science and technology in the richer countries, resulting in rapid increases in the overall capital intensity of 'modern' techniques, and a corresponding absence of any real incentive toward the creation of labour-intensive or small-scale technology, or a technology adapted to tropical conditions or products;
- the resulting 'quantum jump' in labour productivity when 'modern' technologies were imposed upon age-old traditional techniques, resulting in the 'large-scale destruction of traditional employment';
- the preference for urban life, and a wage and income structure, in developing countries which created urban–rural income differentials of a 'considerable magnitude', making unemployment or under-employment in the towns acceptable, or even preferable, to agricultural work; and

- the prevailing social structure in the countryside, which deprived a high proportion of the rural population of access to land and other complementary inputs necessary to utilize their own labour and take advantage of new techniques for raising productivity, resulting in mass migration to urban areas 'so characteristically interwoven with the unemployment process in developing countries'.

In September 1971, Rita Cruise O'Brien and Richard Jolly organized a research conference at IDS on 'Urban Unemployment in Africa'. Singer presented a paper on 'Rural employment as a background to rural–urban migration in Africa' (Singer, 1971k). The conference, at least for the large number of social scientists from rich and poor countries who participated, 'represented a turning point in the intellectual perception of the urban problems of Africa' (Weeks, 1973b, p. 3). Common agreement was reached that analysis of African urban problems could no longer be seen primarily in terms of lack of jobs, 'unemployment', which was recognized as only one manifestation of unbalanced urban growth, rather than the central problem which other phenomena either led to or stemmed from. Two positions emerged from the conference: an 'orthodox' view, which tended to stress the overriding importance of unemployment and the constellation of human problems implied in the western definition of that social and economic state; and an 'unorthodox' view, which was profoundly sceptical as to whether the problems before the conference had anything to do with unemployment, except peripherally, and brought out the importance of the informal sector in urban Africa.

Perhaps the most important reason for turning away from the earlier and more optimistic type of thinking represented by Ragnar Nurkse and Arthur Lewis arose from a stronger realization of the overwhelming impact of population increase combined with the world-wide progress of capital-intensive technology. As a result, the problems facing African countries were specified in quite a different way from earlier analyses. The problem was not so much how to withdraw labour surplus from the countryside for urban employment without reducing agricultural output. That was essentially a static problem appropriate to an economy with stationary population and slowly developing technology. In the dynamic context of the time, the problem was rather how to find increasing employment for a rapidly increasing rural population, and to raise agricultural output more than in proportion to the increase in the rural population, in order to reduce the impact on rural poverty. At the same time, increased employment opportunities were needed for an even more rapidly increasing urban population in the face of an increasing capital-intensive technology, which, among other things, cast the growing informal urban economy in a different light.

Singer's paper, with its almost exclusive emphasis on unemployment, a sharp rural–urban dichotomy, and the shunting aside of definitional, methodological, measurement and ideological issues, was seen as representing a mainly orthodox view. But it already had 'unorthodox' traces. In analyzing rural unemployment in developing countries, Singer noted that the development economists of the late 1940s and 1950s were aware of the interrelationship between the rural unemployment situation and the problems of urbanization, industrialization, modernization and economic development in general. Rural unemployment in that context was visualized as an economic asset rather than an economic evil. Ragnar Nurkse regarded surplus rural labour as representing hidden savings power, which with organization could 'turn labour into capital' (Nurkse, 1953). In Arthur Lewis' classical model (Lewis, 1954), subsequently developed by Fei and Ranis (Fei and Ranis, 1964), rural unemployment existed in the form of a labour surplus which could be removed from the land without reducing agricultural production.

The existence of this labour surplus made it possible to keep urban wages low in some kind of fixed ratio to average rural incomes, with marginal rural incomes in the strict sense being zero, as a corollary of the assumed 'unlimited supplies of labour' in the Lewis model. This, in turn, encouraged the use of labour-intensive technologies and generally encouraged industrialization and development by providing high profit margins, which could be invested in further capital accumulation. Thus, urban employment was maximized both through the encouragement of labour-intensive technologies but also, more importantly, through a high rate of capital accumulation and maximum incentives for the development of an entrepreneurial class. The existence of rural unemployment, therefore, provided favourable conditions for its own elimination through industrialization, urbanization and development. Once this elimination was achieved, a new stage was reached. Both urban and rural average incomes rose together; 'the age of the welfare state had arrived'.

This description of the model, which Singer recognized was 'almost a caricature', brought out some of the essential features in earlier thinking. Clearly, it made a great deal of difference in what form the surplus labour appeared. The method and degree of reorganization of agriculture needed to 'squeeze out' the labour surplus would be quite different, and even the proper type and rate of urban development could be affected.

But these were essentially secondary problems of organization and policy rather than primary problems of analysis. Many critics of this traditional view 'hammered away' at the multiplicity of the different forms in which a labour surplus appeared, and the possibly insurmountable difficulties in the way of 'squeezing it out' without loss of output (see, e.g., Schultz, 1964). Thus, the notion of the existence of a *general* (original emphasis) labour surplus became questionable.

The really crucial attack on these earlier notions came from rather different quarters. It was quite clear that in the case of Africa, the Lewis–Fei–Ranis model did not seem to fit the facts. Urban wages in the modern sector seemed to 'float happily upward' to a high multiple of average rural standards. At the same time, the rural labour surplus did not remain 'bottled up' in the countryside until urban employment opportunities were ready. Instead, a flood of migration to the towns took place. The clear-cut dichotomy of rural labour surplus/urban employment became blurred by the co-existence of a rural labour supply in some form or other with an urban labour surplus. A new model was required, which Singer considered was best provided by Michael Todaro, developed in Kenya, representing an advance in understanding of the interrelationship between rural unemployment and economic development (Todaro, 1969). In essence, the Todaro model represented a different, and rather more pessimistic, picture of the development process. The rural unemployed 'did not stay safely bottled up decently out of sight of urban politicians and where [they] can be somehow looked after by the traditions of sharing, extended family, communalism or tribalism'. Moreover, high wages in modern industry presented an obstacle to labour-intensive technologies, to rapid capital accumulation and high profits so that there was 'no built-in tendency for labour surplus to liquidate itself', even though it might be more evenly distributed between town and country.

Perhaps the most important reason for turning away from the earlier and more optimistic views presented by Nurkse and Lewis came from a stronger realization of the 'overwhelming impact of population increase combined with the overwhelming world-wide progress of a capital-intensive technology'. Analytically, Singer considered that the Nurksian problem remained – 'to convert the waste of manpower into socially useful output'. But much of that output should represent permanent employment on the land and in agricultural production. Apart from the question of 'co-operant factors', specifically land, another key element in rural employment (as in all employment) was the availability and use of an appropriate technology which would utilize the abundance of labour in African countries.

The ILO pilot employment mission to Kenya

Singer was invited in 1971 by Louis Emmerij, who had become director of the WEP, to lead a pilot mission to Kenya where the changing concepts of unemployment were put to the test. This was the first pilot comprehensive employment strategy missions to an African country under the ILO World Employment Programme. Two missions had already been carried out in Colombia and Ceylon (now Sri Lanka) under the leadership of Dudley Seers. These WEP pilot country missions were envisaged to study, with the help of other agencies in the United Nations system, the causes of unemployment and to bring out what

5.   Honorary Degree of Letters, University of Sussex, Hans Singer with Richard Jolly, 24 January 1990 (*University of Sussex*)

needed to be done internationally as well as nationally to overcome them. The reports of these missions had several purposes. They were intended not only to give the government concerned an analysis of its unemployment problem and suggest a programme of action but also to provide guidance for the aid and trade policies of international organizations and donor agencies, and to indicate priorities for research.

The Kenya mission led to another pathbreaking report (ILO, 1972), and to the concept, which Singer inspired, of distribution from, later with, growth (Jolly and Singer, 1973j; Singer and Jolly, 2000a). Singer was well prepared. He had already led a UNDP mission to Kenya, which pioneered UNDP's country programming approach, and had written a paper on technical assistance to Kenya (Singer and Doss, 1969d). The IDS 1971 conference had served to sharpen his views on employment in the African context. And during his ILO consultancy, he had helped to fashion the aims and philosophy of the WEP. Singer visited Nairobi in August and October 1971 to discuss the forthcoming mission with the ministers for finance and planning and government, and with labour and other officials. Further visits were made in December 1971 by Richard (now Sir Richard) Jolly, who had been appointed as a professorial fellow at IDS, and joint chief of mission, and Louis Emmerij, who at the time was designated deputy chief of ILO's Employment Planning and Promotion Department. They were joined by Dudley Seers, director of IDS, who had led the first two WEP pilot employment missions to Colombia (ILO, 1970) and Ceylon (now Sri Lanka) (ILO, 1971). The mission consisted of 26 full-time members and 22 part-time members from UN bodies (including ECA, FAO, ILO, IBRD, UNCTAD, UNDP, UNESCO, UNIDO, UNRISD and WHO) and from African, British, European and United States universities and development institutes. The mission was guided and supported by Kenyan officials, led by Philip Ndegwa, who at the time was permanent secretary in the Ministry of Finance and Planning.[4]

It is not the purpose here to summarize the contents of the mission's report, which in its published form runs to 600 pages and contains 31 technical papers (ILO, 1972), but rather to focus on its pioneering and innovative features. However, some background to the mission's report, as described by its two leaders, is necessary in order fully to understand those features (Singer and Jolly, 1973j). Like the earlier WEP missions to Colombia and Ceylon, the Kenya mission soon discovered that Kenya did not have one employment problem but many, and that the nature and causes of these problems could not be investigated without making a broad analysis of the structure of the economy and the trends in its development. Extreme differences in income, productivity, and access to resources and government services created imbalances between the structure and location of the jobs in demand and the type and location of available work opportunities. The rapid growth of the population, not to mention that of the urban population and of school outputs, far exceeded the growth of wage-earning employment. These internal imbalances were linked to extreme imbalances between the Kenyan economy and the world economy in trade, technology, and the conditions governing private foreign investment. Many of the imbalances were inherited at the time of independence in 1963; others had grown up since that time. All of them underlay Kenya's employment problems.

Just as the causes of the problem were broad and fundamental, so was the strategy needed to deal with them. Thus, of necessity, the report of the Kenya mission took into account a wide range of policy measures with implications for virtually every sector and group in the economy. The underlying theme was a 'coherent strategy' for diminishing the imbalances in the economy through its complete restructuring. The resources for this restructuring would be found from 'a redistribution of the fruits of growth'.

In examining Kenya's employment problems, the mission found that the most striking feature was the overwhelmingly rural character of employment. At the time (1971–2), the rural population accounted for some 90 per cent of the total population. But urbanization was taking place at nearly 8 per cent a year, one of the highest rates in the world. The urban population still maintained strong links with the countryside. (About 20 per cent of all urban wage earnings were remitted to the rural area, the proportion being even higher in the case of the lower wage incomes.) This placed the question of the disparity between urban wages and rural incomes in a somewhat special context, and meant also that rural/urban terms of trade and the nature and sources of rural incomes should be viewed in a different light. In one sense, the preponderance of the rural sector formed the basis for a positive employment policy. Small farms showed both larger labour inputs and higher output per unit of land, in food and cash crops. Thus, there was a 'welcome harmony' between more employment, greater equality and higher output. This provided a powerful reinforcement for the over-all strategy of 'redistribution from growth'.

However, one reason why the employment problem had become much more acute in the years since independence was that the traditionally strong links between the countryside and the urban population had begun to weaken. Historically, the employment system evolved from the tendency towards a high labour turnover in urban employment due to the return to their villages of middle-aged and even younger workers after a period of urban employment, which created numerous vacancies for new entrants to the labour market (Nigam and Singer, 1974j). To counteract this tendency, a tradition of high urban wages, relative to rural incomes, was established in order to induce workers to stay on in regular urban employment. As circumstances changed, this led to the distortion of factor prices, creating dualism and inequalities in the Kenyan economic structure. In the absence of a corresponding rise in rural incomes, jobseekers were attracted to the towns far in excess of the work available. At the same time, high wages were both caused and supported by the prevalence of capital-intensive technologies in the modern urban sector, which created fewer jobs. This, in turn, led to the growth of an 'informal' urban sector in an attempt to reconcile the limited number of jobs in the modern urban sector with the increasing number of jobseekers and the inadequate rural incomes.

As a result, the Kenya mission gave special attention to positive policies based on the existence and potential of this informal sector, which provided income-earning opportunities for a large number of people. Though it was often regarded as unproductive and stagnant, the mission saw it as providing a wide range of low-cost, labour-intensive, competitive goods and services, without government subsidies and support, in fact with restrictions imposed from the outside. The mission broke new ground in that it focused on the 'working poor' rather than on unemployment in the strict sense, or even of 'disguised unemployment'. Its report gave major emphasis to, and original treatment of, the informal sector, and to the removal of inequality.[5] The informal sector was often ignored. In some respects it was helped, and in others harassed, by the authorities. Enterprises and individuals within it operated largely outside the system of government benefits and regulations. Thus, it had no access to the formal credit institutions and the main sources of foreign technology transfer. Many of the economic agents in this sector operated illegally, though often pursuing similar economic activities to those in the formal sector. The consequences were twofold. The risk and uncertainty of earning a livelihood in this low-income sector were magnified, and the regulations ensured a high quality of service and commodities for the wealthy few at the expense of the impoverished many.

Despite the vitality and dynamism that the mission saw in the informal sector, it did not delude itself that it would develop successfully under the conditions of the day. Although it had the potential for dynamic, evolutionary growth, under the existing nexus of restrictions and disincentives, 'the seeds of involuntary growth' had been sown. Unlike the determinants of growth of the formal sector, the determinants of the informal sector were largely external to it. What policies should therefore be followed to cause evolutionary growth? The mission predicted that irrespective of policy change, the informal sector would grow in the next 15 years. If existing policy continued, the growth would be involuntary, the gap between the formal and informal sectors would widen, and the employment problem would then be worse.

A model was developed to identify the major factors determining employment in the informal sector. The model took into account the linkage and product substitution effects, which the mission felt were quite significant in Kenya and should be strengthened in the future. A four-sector model of the economy was used, which distinguished between smallholder agriculture, the informal (non-agricultural) sector, the private formal sector and the government sector. The mission report discussed in detail the ways of increasing the final demand for informal-sector products and strengthening linkages between the informal and other sectors. Data were lacking but a very rough calculation indicated that there was considerable scope for employment in the informal sector in Kenya.

Issues of poverty reduction, income distribution and growth were brought together in a concept that was called 'distribution from growth', which was made the integrating core of the report. The story of how the concept was born, as told by Richard Jolly, is very revealing (Jolly, in Sapsford and Chen,1998a, p. 175). Towards the end of the mission, when the members who were engaged in writing its report gathered after dinner in one of the small lounges of the Fairview hotel in Nairobi, Singer announced that he had an idea, which might serve as an integrating theme for the whole report. He said that the challenge was to achieve a rapid increase in the incomes of the poorest quicker than could be achieved by relying on growth alone. With a population growing at about 3 per cent a year, even with a 6 per cent annual growth rate it would take 25 years to double the incomes of the poorest. If the increments of growth were deliberately channelled into forms of investment directed towards increasing the incomes and production of the poorest, their incomes would rise more rapidly. The process of redistribution from the increments of growth would mean adding to the incomes and assets of the poor without having to take away from others' income, thereby avoiding both economic disruption and political opposition. Singer sketched out his idea with numbers scribbled on the back of an envelope. He assumed a growth rate, estimated the shares of income of the poorest, guessed at a capital–output ratio, and showed that it would be possible for the incomes of the poor to advance very rapidly. Far from being impressed with this approach, the other members of the mission 'rocked and roared with laughter'. 'Such is the recognition accorded to a new idea by fellow professionals at their moment of birth.' But next morning, having slept on it, they were all convinced, and the rest, as they say, is history.

Singer's model of 'redistribution from growth' was designed to redistribute gains in the incomes of the rich to investments which would raise the incomes of the poor until the latter's income per head had doubled.[6] The mission proposed temporarily stabilizing the real incomes of the top 10 per cent of total incomes. The resources gained would be invested in programmes required to attain a minimum income target for the poorest rural and urban households, especially in labour-intensive, employment-oriented projects benefiting the unemployed and the working poor. By this strategy, it was estimated that the incomes of the poorest 40 per cent of the rural population, and the poorest 25 per cent of the urban population, could be increased by 50 per cent within five years and doubled within twelve years at most. In terms of the *realpolitik* of the strategy, it was pointed out that those who benefited would number almost two-fifths of the country's population, all of whom were Kenyans. Those who would pay the price would be the top 1 per cent of income receivers, all the 'power elite', but not all Kenyans, some being expatriates and non-Kenyan citizens. A system of quotas was envisaged to ensure access by the poorest to job opportunities, and to health, education and other government services. This was seen as an investment strategy, channelling redistributed resources into productive investment in permanent opportunities for earning reasonable incomes for the poor, not into income transfers for consumption.

The mission's report was delivered to the Kenyan government and was published for more general consumption. It became the most cited of the WEP country mission reports and one of the most cited publications on development of the 1970s. It was reported that over 20,000 copies were distributed. Unlike many UN documents, more copies were sold than given away. It was distributed widely to civil servants, members of the National Assembly and others concerned. With the help of the Swedish International Development Authority (SIDA), several thousand copies of the report were sold in Kenya at a highly-subsidized price. The Kenyan government prepared a sessional paper on employment policy in which the recommendations of the mission's report were considered in detail and the government's position on them clearly stated. And for two days, the report was at the centre of debate in the Kenyan National Assembly. As part of the follow-up action taken in the wake of the Kenya mission, study and policy seminars were held at Limuru, Kenya organized jointly by the Institute of Development Studies at the University of Nairobi, IDS at the University of Sussex, and the ILO World Employment Programme (Emmerij, 1974).

The report of the Kenya mission was also to have a wider effect. It became a model for subsequent WEP country mission reports and the embryo of the 'basic needs' approach that was later adopted for the ILO world conference in 1976 on 'Employment, Growth and Basic Needs: A One-World Problem'. According to the World Bank's historians, it was to have an influence on Bank policy relating to poverty alleviation. At a meeting with the Bank's president, Robert McNamara, in June 1973, Mahbub ul Haq, who later became the chief architect of the UNDP annual *Human Development Report*, explained the underlying concept as one of 'redistribution of growth', rather than of existing income or wealth, a definition borrowed from Singer's formulation for the Kenya mission report. This became 'the signature concept of the Bank's approach to poverty alleviation' (Kapur *et al.* 1997, vol. 1, p. 263).

It was also to lead to international work on the theme. A joint study was undertaken by the World Bank's Development Research Centre and IDS in 1974 on redistribution with, rather than from, growth, or policies to improve income distribution in developing countries in the context of economic growth (Chenery *et al.*, 1974).The change in the title of the concept (from redistribution *from* to *with* growth) was significant. Singer's original concept had advanced to become an integral part of the growth process. In the original version of the Kenya mission report, growth was put first as essential for providing the resources for distribution. However, the concern for equity is common to both versions. The relation between growth and equity has remained a major feature of development economics ever since, more recently becoming an element in the strategies of 'adjustment with a human face' and 'human development'.

Singer explained that the emphasis in the Kenya mission report on redistribution *from*, rather than *with*, growth was related to the assumption of a high growth rate of 7 per cent a year. Such an assumption seemed justified at the time, when Kenya was considered one of the most successful economies in Africa. In projecting such a high growth rate, it was natural to rely on growth first for providing the resources for equity. The mission was in fact most concerned with the relationship between growth and the wider sharing of benefits, specifically through wider and more productive employment and raising the incomes of the 'working poor'. While recognizing the possibility of trade-offs between growth and greater equality, the report also pointed out areas of complementarity, where greater equity would help to increase output and growth, and foreshadowed some of the later discussion on 'human capital' and 'human development'. An equity-oriented approach was also considered necessary for the national integration of the new state and its political stability.

The strategy of 'redistribution from growth' contrasted sharply with the 'trickledown' strategy which was still part of the development orthodoxy of the time – and, for many of the more orthodox economists, still is. However, it was criticized on two counts. First, that the projected Kenyan growth rate was unrealistic, a kind of *deus ex machina* which made the many suggestions of the mission's report incapable of implementation (Thorbecke, 1973). In defence, Singer pointed out that Kenya had for nearly a decade demonstrated its capacity to grow at 6.5–7 per cent and the mission could not foresee the major changes which soon occurred in the international context to reduce that rate drastically. Secondly, the mission was accused of 'political naivety' when it expected those in power to acquiesce to a strategy which was deliberately fashioned to transfer the benefits of growth to the poorer sections of the population and not to themselves (Leys, 1975). This required 'enlightened political leadership', which Philip Ndegwa had called for throughout his career.

Writing with hindsight almost three decades after the Kenya mission, Singer and Jolly argued that the mission's proposals came at the end of the 'golden age' of the Keynesian consensus (Singer and Jolly, 2000a). Fixed exchange rates had already been abandoned in 1971, and within months of the publication of the mission's report, oil prices had risen more than three times. The possibility of maintaining rapid economic growth in Kenya rapidly faded, the terms of trade sharply declined, and Kenya's debt mounted. These problems continued throughout the 1980s, compounded by growing political difficulties. Notwithstanding these impediments, some elements of progress were maintained in basic health and education, which represented, at least partly, implementation of some of the recommendations of the mission's reports and a modest degree of redistribution of human capital in favour of the poorer sectors of Kenya.

Ironically, Singer and Jolly noted, the informal sector had grown even more that the Kenya mission envisaged, though much less as a positive force for poverty reduction and more as an employment sector of last resort. Internationally, the informal sector was to receive much more attention in analysis, policy and action following the mission's report. With the preoccupation with adjustment, the concept of 'redistribution with growth' was to be relatively neglected in the literature, although with some revival, especially in interpreting the dramatically successful experience of the Asian economies. Frequently, emphasis was to be given to the need for much greater international action to tackle debt, commodity prices, and other severe pressures that have pressed down on the economies of Sub-Saharan African countries. Singer and Jolly projected that when these international pressures are eased, and the prospects for rapid economic growth return, 'redistribution with growth', and the other messages of the Kenya report, may still find their place.

In 1973, Singer joined with Richard Jolly and Dudley Seers to review the work of the three WEP employment missions to Colombia Sri Lanka and Kenya (Jolly, Seers and Singer, 1973e). One important conclusion was that aggregative analyses of employment problems were not very meaningful. Moreover, there should be concern with 'the patterns of all human activities, through different stages in people's lives'. The focus of concern was therefore shifted from economic activities (from 'unemployment' or even 'employment' problems) to concern with all forms of economic and social deprivation, and the role of employment strategy in their cure. Another dimension which was opened up was awareness of the political dimensions of problems, which raised questions such as: what weight a government actually gave to employment objectives; what freedom of manoeuvre it possessed given its relationships to key interest groups, both domestic and foreign; what costs would be involved in adopting an employment-oriented strategy; and how those who would benefit from such a policy could be made more vocal and more powerful. The heart of employment strategy lay not in making economic projections, or finding ways of removing biases toward capital intensity, but in the balance of political forces, and the capacity of political leadership in government and outside to mobilize support in ways which make changes successful. This justified the interdisciplinary approach adopted by the missions to take account of the practical requirements of policy and its social and political, as well as its economic, implications.

International policies and employment

The other main source of the problem was the international context, including the impingement on developing countries of foreign technologies, consumer tastes, attitudes, commercial and directly political influences. This raised questions fundamental to any country's policy: What exactly was its room for manoeuvre? and What international constraints were really preventing the operation of a far-reaching employment policy, including a much more selective approach to foreign capital? This would not be possible unless the political and administrative situation permitted the planning offices and government departments to focus more consistently on the creation of productive employment as a means towards eliminating poverty, with sufficient mobilization of popular support to ensure implementation.

Singer addressed these international policies and their effects on employment under five main headings (Singer, 1973c).[7] It was no accident that *trade* was placed first, which he considered was the main avenue along which to look for a major contribution to the unemployment problems in developing countries. Through trade, developing countries could find an outlet for their abundant labour and enable them to remedy their deficiencies in capital through imports. Unfortunately, trade had not played this major role. The industrial countries had not opened their huge markets to the labour-intensive manufactures on a duty-free or preferential basis. But the developing countries also needed to make painful and difficult adjustments in their present policies and outlook to take better advantage of present, and potentially larger future, export opportunities. This required outward-looking policies and willingness to take risks, and to study foreign markets and tastes.

A second factor was *aid*. Singer distinguished between the general case for additional aid to contribute to fuller employment in the developing countries, and the specific case for adjusting the forms and methods of aid so that a given volume of aid became more 'employment-intensive' in its impact. A third factor was *private foreign investment*. Its impact on employment could be increased in several ways, including: by using labour-intensive rather than capital-intensive technology; being prepared to handle large masses of local labour rather than using capital as the 'line of least resistance'; resisting demands for wages much higher than the prevailing wage rates and the resource endowment of a country would justify; and through the provision of secondary local employment by ordering locally equipment, spare parts, operational raw material, etc., rather than importing them from abroad through local subsidiary or licensing agreements, which was one of the original motives of the foreign investment. This list was by no means complete. There were also countervailing forces at work, including the deliberate policies of foreign firms. But it helped to indicate some of the changes in foreign investment policies which might be needed to increase their impact on local employment.

International liquidity was a fourth factor. A 'great step forward' had been taken by the world community through the creation of special drawing rights (SDRs). A little of that progress had rubbed off on development in that the less developed countries, contrary to the original intentions, at least participated in the SDRs to the extent of their IMF quotas. Singer considered that perhaps more important was the widespread conviction that SDRs had been safely and irrevocably established, and their potential for world development could be safely utilized, without damage to their original and primary purpose. In Singer's view, the balance of payments objection to increased aid to the less developed countries was never too convincing, except possibly as a question of redistributing the overall burden of aid among the richer countries. It could always be pointed out that as long as the less developed countries did not use aid to increase their foreign exchange reserves, there was never a valid balance of payments argument against increases in overall aid. With the creation of SDRs, the richer countries, taken together, would not have a balance of payments deficit, but a positive balance of payments surplus. The case for linking this new progress in international relations with a step forward in development assistance seemed very strong. But what better direction than to link this even more specifically with the objective of providing constructive employment for the young in the less developed countries? (Cairncross and Puri, 1975).

For the fifth factor, Singer returned to another of his prominent interests, the problems of *science and technology* for employment in the developing world. A dominant fact of international life was that the richer countries accounted for practically all the world's scientific and technological innovations, which militated strongly against employment creation in the less developed countries. Surely, Singer argued, the first step in a global partnership should be to use the 'wonderful and dreadful machinery' of science and technology for the economic development of developing countries. It is to that subject that we now turn in describing the next major work that Singer took up on his arrival at IDS.

18
Science and Technology for Developing Countries

Singer stressed the importance of science and technology for development as one of the policy outcomes of his work on the terms of trade (see Chapter 11). He saw this not only as an external factor but also an internal one in the development equation, which has remained a primary concern for him.

Singer identified the growing international inequalities in command over modern science and technology as one of the causes of 'dualism' both within developing countries and between them and industrial countries in a paper prepared for a 'Conference on the Dual Economy' held in Glasgow, Scotland in September 1969 (Singer, 1969e). He argued that tendencies within the field of science and technology, including their increasing capital intensity and their dominance by the needs of the richer countries and lack of direct relevance for the needs of developing countries, were closely associated with growing unemployment and under-employment in various forms within developing countries. Increasingly, the relevant forms of 'dualistic fission' ran along the lines of employment versus unemployment rather than the more traditional distinction between rural and urban, and traditional and modern, sectors.

The tendency for technological developments to produce internal dualism in developing countries was further strengthened by a number of factors, including the association of modern technology with foreign investment that he had recognized earlier in his original work on the terms of trade. Singer reiterated that the forces making for dualism were deeply rooted particularly in science and technology. Much more radical action than a mere redress of discriminatory practices, or correction of prejudices, was needed. He noted that the limited applicability of western concepts was illustrated by the focus on the productive use of scarce capital in developing countries rather than on the mis-utilization of the capital available. The better utilization of existing capital was a problem parallel in importance with a more appropriate technology. Both together held out prospects of approaching development problems along more Keynesian lines than was often realized. Singer therefore concluded that 'the utilization of existing capital together with the development of more relevant technology held the key to solving the most important type of dualism in developing countries'.

Christopher Freeman, head of the Science Policy Research Unit (SPRU) that had been set up at the University of Sussex, shared Singer's views. SPRU and IDS joined forces to form a group of consultants, known as the 'Sussex group', with Singer as chairman, to assist the UN Advisory Committee on Science and Technology in making its proposals for the application of science and technology for development during the second UN development decade of the 1970s.[8] The group produced what was called *The Sussex Manifesto: Science and Technology to Developing Countries during the Second Development Decade* (Singer *et al.*, 1970b), which was incorporated into the report of the UN advisory committee (UN, 1970).

The group described what they called the 'triple schizophrenia' that existed in the world as background to its work. First, was the growing gap between the richer one-third and the rest of humanity, which was by no means the only evidence of divergence in the world. Second, less discussed, but equally important, was the growing divergence *within* the under-developed world between the upper half – the middle third of humanity – and the really poor bottom third. And third, there was also growing divergence within the individual under-developed countries themselves, between the 'haves' and 'have-nots'.

When looking for a common cause for this 'triple divergence', the 'most plausible and the most important' seemed to the group to lie in the field of science and technology. Contrary to what Keynes, and other economists before him, had almost universally accepted and forecast, the accumulation of scientific and technological knowledge, which was continuing at an accelerated pace, had not made the task of development progressively easier for poor countries, or led to greater international equality or convergence. Quite the contrary. The development of science and technology had contributed powerfully to these divergences in several ways. Practically all world expenditure on science and technology took place in the richer countries and was, quite naturally, directed to solving their own problems by methods suited to their own circumstances and resource endowments. The problems of the poorer countries were not the same. The accumulation of knowledge was in directions broadly irrelevant, or sometimes harmful, to the poorer countries, as in the case of the development of synthetic substances for the natural products on which they depended for their export earnings. While more knowledge had accumulated, it had on average become less suitable for the development of poorer countries. For them, it was not only the volume but the composition of knowledge that counted.

The remedy did not lie in increasing scientific and technological expenditures in the under-developed countries themselves. These expenditures were much too small and scattered to be effective and suffered from a critical shortage of trained personnel. To be more effective, they would have to be multiplied to a degree well beyond the resources of most developing countries, placed on a regional rather than national basis, particularly in Africa, and directed towards the development of the necessary trained manpower. The process of transfer of technology also had built-in institutional features, which made the technologies transferred of the capital-intensive type, suitable for the richer countries, rather than the labour-intensive type that the poorer countries needed. The three main institutional instruments for the transfer of technology were trade, private foreign investment, and financial or technical assistance. All three were biased towards capital-intensive technology more suited to the conditions of richer countries.

The introductory statement for the World Plan of Action for the Application of Science and Technology to Development, prepared by the 'Sussex group', began with the premise that the developing countries must have their own scientific and technological capability. This indigenous capability was necessary not only for increasing production but, more importantly, for improving the capacity to produce. There were vast gaps in the developing countries between actual production and the production potentials through the application of science and technology. The underlying problem arose from the international division of labour in science and technology and the orientation of world scientific effort to the problems and objectives of interest principally to the advanced countries. The consequences of the inherent weakness of scientific institutions in the developing countries were exacerbated not only by an 'external brain drain' but also by an 'internal brain drain' of scientific workers in the developing countries who tended to work on problems which were irrelevant to their environment.

To solve these problems, four main and interrelated groups of proposals were made, which constituted the framework for the World Plan of

Action. First, developing countries should build up their indigenous scientific and technical resources. The research and development (R & D) effort of the developing countries should be increased to about 0.5 per cent of GNP. But this would yield economic and social benefits only if various measures of institutional reform were properly executed. In particular, the build-up of science and technology must be planned and oriented to requirements, new policy-making institutions established, universities and other higher educational institutions reformed to increase the supply of highly qualified manpower, and research and other scientific organizations thoroughly reformed so that the manpower could be rationally and usefully employed. Secondly, the advanced countries ought to give direct financial and technical assistance to the build-up of indigenous science in the developing countries. This assistance should reach 0.05 per cent of their GNP during the second UN decade of the 1970s, which implied that about 5 per cent of their total aid would be for science and technology. At the same time, a reorientation of R & D and other activities of the advanced countries was also essential, with about 5 per cent of their total R & D expenditure devoted to the specific problems of the developing countries during the 1970s. A change in the context of the education of scientists in the advanced countries was also required with direct action to build 'science for development' into the professional and reward structure of the scientific community. Thirdly, to overcome problems of communication and access, the scientific and technological efforts of advanced and developing countries should be 'coupled' and an international technology transfer bank established as a valuable, if partial, solution. Finally, it was stressed that the full realization of the economic and social benefits of these policies depended on complementary institutional changes in the developing countries themselves.

The problems of technology transfer were classified under two main headings: the suitability or appropriateness of the technology transferred; and the terms and conditions under which such transfers took place (Singer, 1970c). Concerning the former, Singer saw technology transfer as a one-sided business, 'a one-way street', from advanced to developing countries, hence the inappropriateness of much of the capital-intensive technology that was transferred. He admired the work of E. F. Schumacher, the chairman of the Intermediate Technology Development Group in London, who first introduced the concept of 'intermediate technology' in a report for the Indian Planning Commission in 1963. Schumacher emphasized that 'small is beautiful' and stressed the importance of smaller-scale, labour-intensive, and the more natural or organic, technologies developed for Third World countries. Singer also supported attempts at 'technical co-operation among developing countries' (TCDC), the subject of a UN conference held much later in Buenos Aires, Argentina in September 1987, which developed a TCDC 'world plan of action'.

Singer considered that the terms and conditions of technology transfer were 'very serious' for developing countries. Much of the cost of imported technology was concealed, especially since technology imports often took place as part of a package or in the form of machinery and equipment. Estimates of the annual payments made by developing countries for the transfer of technology were 'very high'. They probably cancelled out a major part of total aid flows, and absorbed a considerable share of the export earnings of developing countries. Such high transfer costs were particularly bitter and controversial since it could be argued that the achievements of science and technology should be 'the common property of mankind' and, subject to proper protection and payment to the inventor, made freely available. But a large part of technology transfer was controlled by multinational corporations, an essential part of whose operations was to obtain the highest returns on the technology they transferred. This formed the basis for the further strengthening of their own R & D capacity and leadership, which in turn resulted in a further increase in their profitability and higher returns.

The terms and conditions of technology transfer were the result of an extremely imperfect market. Countries importing the technology often did not have sufficient knowledge of the alternative technologies available or alternative sources of the same technology, nor the national capacity for debating technological matters on equal terms with the representatives of multinational corporations and salesmen. Any move to make the market more perfect, and the bargaining position of the two sides more equal, was to be greatly welcomed. The tying of aid also played a role in narrowing down the choices of technology. The ultimate solution lay in strengthening the technological capacities of the developing countries themselves.

Singer called for international co-operation in the provision of appropriate technology to Third World countries. He noted that the international debate was mainly concentrated on the transfer of 'modern' or 'advanced' technology, largely at the wish of the developing countries themselves. The basic resolution on the 'New International Economic Order' (NIEO) of the UN special seventh session in 1975 pointedly, and repeatedly, specified 'advanced technology' as the object of its concern.

There had also been an increasing groundswell of opinion that more attention should also be paid to technology suitable for the small-scale or informal sector of developing countries.

In a consultancy for ILO in 1977, Singer focused on technologies related to the basic needs strategy that ILO had developed which encompassed the provision of food, shelter, clothing and other basic necessities of life (Singer, 1977b). He noted that the alternative technologies available from within the Third World countries, or from the earlier economic history of industrial countries, or deliberately created as what was called 'intermediate technology', tended to be inefficient since they were not backed by the full force of modern science. For this reason, developing countries were highly suspicious of, often antagonistic to, attempts to emphasize the question of suitability of transferred technology. They wanted to 'modernize' and share in the benefits of modern science. Attempts to preach alternative technologies to them sounded like 'paternalistic or neo-colonialistic conspiracies', to condemn them to something 'second-best' or 'only good enough for them'. They saw the industrial countries wielding power and enjoying high income levels because they were using 'modern' technology. Hence, in the international debates, which tended to centre around a code of conduct on technology transfer, discussion concentrate on the terms and conditions, rather than the suitability, of technology transferred.

The questions of suitability and terms and conditions of technology transfer were in fact related to each other. Some of the restrictive conditions made the technology less suitable than it would otherwise be. This applied to such restrictions as prohibitions on the adaptation of the imported technology; prevention of the use of imported technology as a basis for local R & D development; and clauses stipulating that the results of local technological research and development based on the imported technology must be transferred to the owner or supplier of the technology. Singer considered that such restrictive clauses were particularly objectionable and their reform or elimination rightly occupied a high place on the agenda of the international discussion around a code of conduct.

19
UNICEF and Children's Well-Being

Singer continued his association with UNICEF, and his strong interest in the well-being of children in developing countries, after he joined IDS. He took part in training programmes for UNICEF staff, and contributed to major UNICEF studies on children's concerns.

UNICEF wanted to portray widely the well-being and development of children not only as a social and human obligation of national governments and the international community, which was generally understood, but as a key factor in economic development, which was less appreciated. At the beginning of the 1970s, and the UN Second Development Decade, it was still not sufficiently realized that children were a country's most precious resource.

Children in the strategy of development

Because of his previous association and interest, Singer was requested by UNICEF to prepare an 'executive briefing paper', for joint distribution by the UN Centre for Economic and Social Information and UNICEF, on *Children in the Strategy of Development* (Singer, 1972d).[9] Singer began by asking, 'What was the real purpose of development'? With variations in precise formulation, he found that it was generally defined as 'a better life in the future for the people of a country'. The people of the future were, of course, the children of today and those still to be born, which put the spotlight on 'children in the strategy of development', the subject of his publication. He considered that perhaps the most powerful and universal motive was the desire by parents to provide a decent life for their children, preferably a better life than they had experienced. This was a source of strength, motivation and participation that had hardly been drawn on in any systematic way.

Looked at from another angle, children were the retainers of the intellectual inheritance of humankind. Given differential birth rates, five out of six of the world's children were born in developing countries. The chances of them realizing their full intellectual and physical potential were severely limited by their compounded, negative, human environment. An unacceptably high number would die prematurely in infancy, or would have their physical and mental development stunted by malnutrition and disease. They would fail to get to school under qualified teachers, and would live in environments in which their gifts were not detected, and so would have no chance of being fully developed. Singer asked, what was the loss to the world at large of giving only a small part of our potential limited stock of talent and genius a chance of making a contribution to the future development of humankind? UNICEF, in partnership with other members of the United Nations system and individual nations, had a role to play in a strategy of world development which was not often fully appreciated in its full significance.

As he had done earlier while in the United Nations, Singer emphasized the importance of planning to meet the needs of children. But a fundamental change was required in the outlook to planning, which, in essence, should focus on the present and future capacity of a society to create wealth directed toward improvement in the quality of life for the maximum number of people. This would lead to an accelerated rate of production growth and result in socio-economic development. To reach these goals, a successful development strategy should place much emphasis on investment in human resources. This brought into focus the vital importance of planning effectively for the provision of adequate resources to be devoted to the upbringing of the children of a country.

Perhaps 'the most crucial decision' that a country had to take was the allocation of resources between its present generation of producers, and the future generation, as represented by its children. The more a country was willing, and able, to spare resources for child development sufficient to give each individual child a better preparation for life, the higher its chances of achieving a decisive break-away from the vicious circle of poverty and economic stagnation. Ultimately, it was improvement in the quality, and productivity, of the next generation of producers which would enable the poor countries to reach a higher level of economic activity. 'The children of today are the producers of tomorrow . ... The possible investment opportunities in the long term plan must be based on the potential that is represented in the children of today' (Schiavo-Campo and Singer, 1970a).

Special concern for the needs and welfare of children might be indicated on grounds of economic equality and social equity. This was primarily because the existence of several young children was likely to move a family into poverty, and secondarily, because on the whole poor people tended to have more children than rich people. Hence, a re-allocation of resources in favour of children would automatically lead to a reduction of inequality in income distribution. Furthermore, if development meant the introduction of social change, children were the prime agents through which important cultural and normative changes could be brought about. Too often, adults resisted new methods and techniques. It was much easier to bring up children so that as young adults they would more readily adopt efficient techniques and new social relationships. Therefore, Singer suggested that planners should aim at bringing about the preconditions for such attitudinal changes through the education of children. But he noted the needs of children were often ignored, or shelved, in the plans and policies of many countries. Children were a weak and vulnerable group with no voting power, influence or direct political say. Mothers, or even both parents, also rarely constituted an organized political pressure group. If tightly pressed for resources, it was always easy to ignore children's requirements. It was therefore important that social and political groups be formed which articulated children's interests and concerns.

The needs of children had been articulated in the *Declaration of the Rights of the Child*, which had been unanimously adopted by the United Nations General Assembly in 1959 (UN, 1959). Since the resources available to meet children's needs were limited, a clear and unambiguous priority list of resources should be established as well as priorities for the different needs within each category by attaching 'orders of importance' to the needs of children. Criteria could be used to evaluate the relative importance of different needs, including the gravity of the problem, the proportion of children affected, effects on other spheres, and so on. The priority list would be different for children living in different environments, and in different age groups. The priority needs of children living in rural areas might be different from those living in towns and cities, while a number of needs would be in common. And those priorities changed constantly. Education and vocational training were important in the higher age-groups, whereas health and nutritional needs were of greatest significance for infants and pre-school children. Different priorities should be charted out for different geographical regions. Singer stressed that varying cultural and environmental requirements should be kept on mind, as well as the different age groups. And looked at in a global perspective, the overall magnitude of providing for the needs of children was immense.

In conclusion, Singer welcomed the growing recognition that development was a social as well as an economic process, and the shift 'from planning for goods to planning for people'. It was appropriate and necessary that top priority be accorded to the formulation of a strategy of investment in human resources. Expenditure on children was 'the most important part of human investment'. Insufficient attention had been given to the problems of children and hence to the development of consistent national policies. A shift from economic to socio-economic planning would serve to increase awareness of the issues involved. Expansion in the efforts of the developing countries themselves, and in the assistance of the developed world, for child development was required. International agencies, specifically UNICEF, had a recognized and important role to play in this field.

The impact of world recession on children

In 1984, Singer was invited by UNICEF to join a team of analysts, led by Richard Jolly, UNICEF's deputy executive director for programmes at the time, who produced what became recognized as a seminal report which showed the full and staggering effects of the recession on children in many parts of the developing world (UNICEF, 1984).[10] Singer played a key role in providing an historical perspective and in analyzing the basic causes that had led to the world recession. A number of its recommendations contained unmistaken imprint of his concerns and perspectives.

Based on country cases studies,[11] the study showed the differential impact of the world recession on children. The situation in Sub-Saharan Africa was found to be particularly serious, which was described as a 'fourth world' region. Its economic and social development had lagged far behind the levels attained by other developing regions. The combination of the world's highest birth rate and rate of population increase, and the inheritance of acute deficiencies in skills and institutions at independence in the 1960s, had made it difficult for the region to close the gap. In addition, the impact of the recession on the region was far sharper than in other regions.

The study constructed an analytical framework to illustrate the effects of the economic recession on child welfare (see Figure 19.1). It was recognized that this framework had its limitations. It was highly

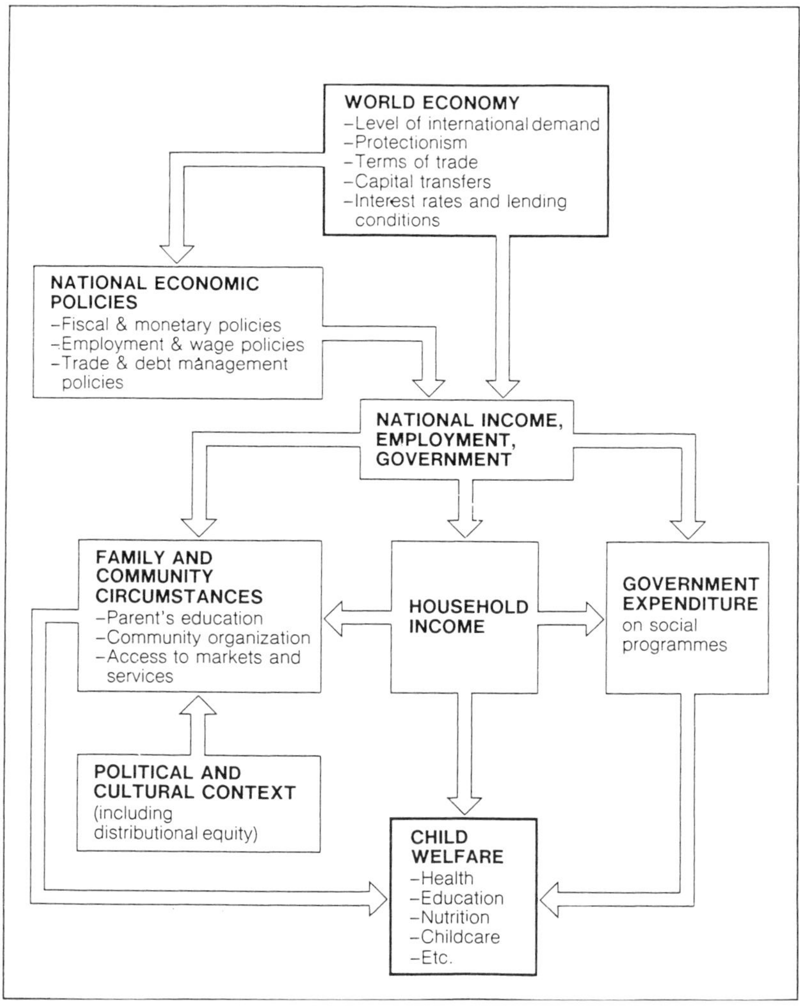

Figure 19.1　How the recession reaches the child (*Source*: UNICEF, 1984)

simplified. It did not differentiate the impact of the recession by countries with different socio-economic characteristics and did not separate
the influence of long-term trends from short-run fluctuations. It
emphasized three dominant types of influences on child welfare:
family and community circumstances; household income; and government expenditure on social services. The study also identified four

ways of measuring children's status, each with different implications for child welfare and with different time lags. First, was the effects on incomes and resources for children. Recession in many countries (rich and poor) had led to an increase in unemployment, particularly in urban-based industry and in the export-dependent sector. Per capita income had fallen in an increasing number of countries. Real household income had been reduced drastically even in countries with some system of unemployment or welfare payments through the combination of rapid inflation and growing unemployment, in come countries by as much as 30–40 per cent. There were indications that the fall in real incomes had been particularly severe for the poorest groups. Cuts in social services were often the first to take place. Cuts in education and food subsidies seemed to precede those in health services. And because of transport and other problems, cuts in services were much sharper in rural than in urban areas. In summary, the deterioration appeared to be 'widespread, unambiguous and, in some cases, extremely severe'.

Second, was the impact on the availability of services. Certain countries were affected by an absolute decline in the amount of services offered, including in the United States. In some countries, fees were introduced for services, reducing their availability to poor people. In others, cuts in social expenditure resulted in a qualitative rather than quantitative decline in the services rendered.

Third, was the impact on child survival and welfare. Children living below the poverty line showed an upward trend. Where the recession had been particularly severe, infant mortality rates had increased. In other cases, the decline in infant mortality apparently had been slower than it would have been in the absence of recession. There was a deterioration in nutrition indicators. And stagnant or deteriorating health conditions were found in a number of countries despite notable declines in mortality. In sum, while a dramatic and general deterioration in child survival was not evident, with the exception of Africa and other poor countries and regions, warning signals concerning various aspects of child welfare were becoming more and more frequent and raised fears about the future for particularly vulnerable groups. Finally, there were other signs of the effects of the recession, including increasing child labour, child abandonment and vagrancy, youth delinquency, and female-headed families.

The study concluded that taking into account the limited data available and the matter of time lags, four findings emerged: first, that some of the worst effects of the crisis were not perceived because they were not measured; second, that the worst consequences of the recession in terms of child welfare might still lie ahead; third, that the initial signs of deterioration should be seen as important warning signals of much more serious problems that could perhaps be avoided only if concerted action was taken immediately; and finally, that a responsible and cost-effective response to these warnings should include in most countries the building up of a better reporting and statistics system for the continuous monitoring of the health, education and general well-being of children, especially those of the poorest, most vulnerable, communities.

Two broad areas of action were required: action to offset the serious consequences for children (and others) of recession; and action to restore momentum in the long-term development effort. Both areas required changes in policy and practice, within countries and internationally. The starting point was a broader approach to adjustment policy at both national and international levels, which would comprise five elements. First and foremost, a clear recognition of the importance of preserving a minimum level of nutrition, household income and basic services as a means towards protecting and maintaining human investment and welfare. Second, the maintenance or creation of a network of basic services and support for young children, the most vulnerable group of the population and also the one most important for the economic, social and political future of a country and, at the same time, and in most respects, the one least costly to protect. Third, a serious restructuring within the health, education and related social services to achieve greater cost-effectiveness and internal efficiency in the provision of those services. Fourth, more and creative use of community action and the informal sector, which tended to use more local and low-cost resources and fewer high-cost and imported supplies. And finally, more concern with income distribution, especially in the sharing of the burden of economic adjustment and cutbacks.

It was at the national level that the first moves should be made. Three broad areas for national action were identified: measures to maintain levels of household income and employment; sustain basic services; and restore or sustain momentum in long-term development, with a focus on the basic needs of poorer families. In addition, the study called for national action towards a 'child health revolution'.

In terms of international action, the study emphasized several major areas. A greater measure of co-ordinated action by the main industrial countries was called for to stimulate a higher level of world economic activity, lower interest rates, and reduce import barriers and import restrictions, especially for the poorer countries. A change in international financial institutional arrangements was suggested to prevent the main burden of adjustment from falling on the poorer countries and to introduce a broader approach to adjustment and conditionality that protected the living standards of the poorer and most vulnerable sections of the population. Measures to reduce the risk of war, and to achieve some shift from military and armaments expenditure to development, in both developed and developing countries, and a higher level of ODA, were called for, as was expanded and more effective co-operation among developing countries.

The study ended with the view that the world needed to be confronted with the consequences of current economic policies and the possibilities of clear alternatives. We were used to describing the flows of money and wealth, with their effects on human life seen as incidental consequences. If we started instead with the focus on people, the same international links could be traced in a wholly new light. The human consequences would be brought to the fore, with the economic numbers becoming background. When this glimpse of another reality became an accepted and legitimate preoccupation of international and national economic policy, more hope could be taken for the welfare and future of the world's children.

In many ways, the study set the scene for another seminal study by UNICEF on *Adjustment with a Human Face*. This was first launched by Richard Jolly in the Barbara Ward Lecture at the 18th Society for International Development world Conference in Rome, Italy in July 1985, with the inspiration and support of the distinguished economist Barbara Ward, and Jim Grant, the executive director of UNICEF at the time. The study was published in 1987 (Cornia *et al.*, 1987).

20
Food Aid and Food Security

Of all the many issues and concerns that Singer has addressed in his long career, one of his greatest contributions has been to the international debate on food aid.[12] There are few aspects of the subject that he has not touched on at one time or another. The epistemic community of food aid specialists has recognized that no other person has had such a dominant impact on the subject (Hopkins, 1992). As we saw earlier, he played a strategic role in the creation of the World Food Programme, the food aid organization of the United Nations system (Shaw, 1998a; Shaw, 2001a). And his consultant services have regularly been sought by bilateral and non-governmental food aid programmes as well as by WFP itself. For his role and services, he was given the WFP *Food for Life Award* in 2001.

Singer's views on food aid as providing an opportunity as well as a challenge to achieving food security for the neediest people in the poorest countries have given a balanced assessment and reasoned account when much of the criticism of food aid has been based on polemical argument and anecdotal evidence. He has played a major role in sorting through the debris of the international debate on food aid that has often generated more heat than light to identify the issues, review the evidence, and suggest areas where new fronts might be established or old ones reopened. Although areas of controversy and disagreement have remained, he has helped to demarcate the boundaries of consensus and uncover the inconsistencies and prejudices.

On his arrival at the IDS after his work at the United Nations, he stimulated the creation of an informal 'food aid cluster' at the Institute. He also initiated a series of food aid seminars for which IDS became famous. And he encouraged and inspired many to work on food aid and related issues. Much of his own work on food aid after 1969 has been conducted with members of the food aid cluster and others at IDS and elsewhere.[13]

Dissenting view

Early interest in food aid could be attributed to what could be called Singer's 'dissenting view', which characterized much of his work in other fields (Arestis and Sawyer, 1992, pp. 526–32). Many economists and development practitioners were contemptuous of food aid, considering it very inferior to financial assistance. Moreover, food aid seemed to be entirely a North American matter and linked to United States interests in getting rid of burdensome surpluses, subsidizing US farmers, and promoting and developing US export markets. In addition, food aid was met with much scepticism and resistance because of its alleged disincentive effects in recipient countries, by lowering domestic food prices, encouraging negative government policies, and thus discouraging local food production.

Singer dissented from these views for a number of reasons. There seemed to be no sound empirical evidence that the enormous volume of food aid that had gone into Western Europe under the Marshall Plan after the Second World War, and into many developing countries, had prevented them from increasing their own domestic food production. As Singer foresaw, the availability of food surpluses would not remain limited to North America but would become widespread among other developed countries, thus making possible a co-ordinated and fully multilateral food aid system. The debate about whether food aid was 'inferior' to financial aid was to him beside the point. Food aid was available whereas financial assistance was limited. The question was therefore whether food aid could achieve positive results in terms of economic growth, employment creation, and relief from hunger and poverty. Even though food aid had 'evil origins' in the agricultural policies of developed countries, which led to the accumulation of surpluses and were harmful to developing countries, Singer felt that this need not prevent 'plucking the flower of development from the nettle of surpluses'. To him, the disincentive effects attributed to food aid were not inherent but were the result of bad planning and administration. Properly designed and managed, food aid could be used to promote local agricultural production.

Multilateral food aid

Singer has remained a strong supporter of food aid supplied through multilateral channels. Despite its difficulties, he considers that the

World Food Programme (WFP) deserves a high place in the list of UN achievements (Singer 2001a; Shaw and Singer, 1998b).[14] He singled out five major achievements of the WFP. First, by giving it a multilateral dimension, WFP has helped to depoliticize food aid and use it as an instrument for achieving universally recognized objectives both as development aid and as relief assistance in conflict and emergency situations.

Secondly, Singer acknowledged that WFP has helped to establish a policy framework for food aid both for development and in times of emergency. Guidelines and criteria were approved by WFP's governing body which, although not always followed by bilateral food aid programmes, still provide the best available policy framework for food aid globally (WFP, 1979). As part of its functions, WFP also administers the International Emergency Food Reserve (IEFR), the only international facility available to respond quickly to emergencies whenever and wherever they occur (WFP, 1978). Although the IEFR has not lived up to its original expectations, it now includes an Immediate Response Account (IRA), a cash reserve to purchase food to respond to emergency food needs quickly. Both the IEFR and the IRA are still too small and unpredictable, and their use not fully multilaterally controlled, to ensure that all emergency needs are satisfied speedily. But the framework for effective action is in place once the political will to expand and use these facilities is fully generated.

Thirdly, Singer observed that WFP successfully pioneered the project approach to food aid through labour-intensive food-for-work programmes and the development of human resources through providing support for nutrition, health, education and training projects for vulnerable groups and abjectly poor people in the most needy countries, even before the mobilization and development of human resources were fully recognized as key factors in development. Fourthly, Singer noted that WFP has emerged as the principal international channel for emergency food aid and a natural co-ordinator in large-scale and complex emergency food relief operations following both natural and man-made disasters.

Finally, with its dual functions of providing both development and relief assistance, Singer sees WFP well placed to play a major role in what has come to be called the 'continuum' between relief and development. Singer considers that there is still much to be done to create a link between relief and development. Food aid could be visualized as a means for preventing conflicts and resolving tensions before they developed into full-scale emergencies. He sees a future task for

WFP to stimulate the international community to remove the artificial dichotomy between emergency and development assistance in the process from crisis to recovery and development, and to broaden the humanitarian consensus from acute, short-run, emergency relief to the full circle of disaster prevention and preparedness linked to rehabilitation, reconstruction after emergencies and development.

Food aid for development

The 'most complete guide and assessment of the literature' on food aid for development is still that carried out by Singer with the co-operation of Simon Maxwell and Edward Clay, which was commissioned by WFP in the 1970s and 1980s (Ruttan, 1996, p. 188, ff. 91; Singer, 1978c; Maxwell and Singer, 1979f; Clay and Singer, 1985c). Singer and his collaborators identified four main potential advantages of food aid. It could lift a constraint on growth and self-reliance by providing the real resources necessary to expand investment or dampen inflationary repercussions of the implementation of development plans. It could particularly benefit disadvantaged groups, notably through nutrition improvement and food-for-work or food subsidy programmes. It could help governments set up food reserve and price stabilization schemes. And it was at least partly additional in the sense that in its absence financial aid and commercial imports would not be forthcoming.[15]

Against these four advantages, there were four potential disadvantages. Food aid could have a disincentive effect on local agricultural production: through the price mechanism; by its adverse effect on government policy; or by attracting agricultural labourers to food-for-work sites. The allocation of food aid among recipient countries reflected the economic, political and military interests of donor countries rather than criteria of need. Food aid could result in greater dependence than self-reliance. And food aid could be second-best, expensive, double-tied, dependent on surpluses, irregular, bureaucratic, and inappropriate.

Singer argued that a closer examination of these eight aspects of the food aid debate showed that these effects could take place, but were not inevitable. An important task was to specify the conditions under which food aid could promote development in the developing countries, for which he established 'guiding principles' that are of continuing validity. Food aid could be useful in those cases where food shortage was a constraint on growth or on the more equal distribution of income, without causing disincentive. It was most useful when it substituted for commercial imports that a country would have made, thereby releasing foreign exchange for other developmental purposes. Food aid was best deployed in general support of a broadly-based, poverty-oriented development plan. It should be planned in advance and its availability should be guaranteed. Food aid should preferably consist of commodities which were indigenous to the recipient country or part of the normal diet. It should be complemented by other forms of aid. And resources generated from the sale of food aid commodities should be used for developmental purposes.

Writing 20 years after the report of the expert group which he chaired (see Chapter II), Singer identified six 'guiding principles for the next 20 years' (Singer with Simon Maxwell, 1983d). These were: more food aid, particularly to remedy malnutrition and to offset the rapid rise in food imports to Sub-Saharan Africa; more food aid in the form of cereals; more programme food aid; more food aid through multilateral channels; greater efficiency in food aid administration and operations; and better international arrangements for food aid.

Programme food aid, pricing, and counterpart funds

Singer and Edward Clay were commissioned by the United States Agency for International Development (USAID) to carry out an assessment of the developmental impact and effectiveness of US PL 480 Title 1 bulk supply food aid in 1982 (Clay and Singer, 1982c). The overall assessment was that recognition of what were called 'donor-end' problems in the programming and operations of food aid played an important part of a balanced perspective on food aid. They also helped explain the considerable diversity of findings and views on the impact and developmental potential of food aid. This diversity could be attributed to two effects of food aid pulling in opposite directions. First, food aid reduced the immediate pressures on the recipient country economy. Secondly, food aid increased the resources of a country for development in general, and increased domestic food production (or improved storage and distribution) in particular, which could lead to reduced dependency and greater self-reliance. Which of the two effects prevailed depended, primarily, on the policies of the recipient government, and secondarily, on the policies of food aid donors, including the extent to which the balance of resources and concessionality moved the overall impact of food aid from a negative to a positive outcome.

Greater obstacles and complexities in the effective use of food aid were also to be expected in the shift of food aid toward poorer countries and communities. Using food aid as an instrument in a basic needs strategy, linked to better income distribution and poverty reduction, also created problems in the targeting of food aid and the use of counterpart funds from the sale of food aid commodities. Targeting on the really poor was notoriously difficult in that they were handicapped in their access to food-aided projects and programmes. And meeting the nutritional needs of the poor was not identical with promoting overall poverty-oriented development. Assessment of the impact of food aid was made difficult by the fact that food aid was only one of many factors in a complex structure that determined rural–urban terms of trade and income distribution. Food aid was difficult to identify as a separate factor and its relationship to other factors was often indirect and disputable. No food aid agreement, however detailed, could cover all these complex factors and interrelationships. At best, it could create a presumption that the direct and indirect impact of food aid was in reducing poverty and strengthening self-reliance and the forces making for sustained development.

Concerning pricing policies for food aid commodities, the best 'general advice' (subject to the overriding importance of specific country objectives and conditions) was that 'where possible food aid should be sold at domestic prices which in turn should not be below international prices' (Singer and Clay, 1983c). Any subsidies connected with food aid should preferably consist of large subsidies or free distribution for specific groups of target recipients rather than a small subsidy spread over a large indiscriminate group. In this way, any spill-over from the subsidized market to commercial channels could be minimized. Food subsidies for consumers should also be matched by incentives to domestic producers. Governments receiving food aid should also have an overall development and food policy that treated domestic food production as a priority throughout. This was ultimately more important than a sophisticated and complex pricing strategy which could not be made effective. Policy aspirations should not outrun managerial capacity and an understanding of the food system.

As early as 1961, Singer exposed the 'multiplier fallacy' of counterpart funds resulting from the sale of food aid commodities and the 'illusion' of the project approach to external aid (Singer, 1961f; 1965c; Schiavo-Campo and Singer, 1970a). He revealed the 'myth' that local currency funds accumulated from food aid sales represented real resources and that their subsequent use, and possibly repeated reuse, could multiply the effects of foreign aid. This had to do with the 'crucial importance' of the nature and effectiveness of the original aid transaction, which was determined by the quality of the planning and use of aid at the time and the surplus food injected into the economy of the receiving country. If the aid was effectively used *at that stage* (original emphasis), it helped to mobilize the domestic resources of the receiving country. The subsequent use of counterpart funds could not add to the effectiveness of the use of the aid or remedy any failures in such use at the time the aid was given.

Similarly, insofar as the counterpart fund were used for specific projects rather than general budgetary support, the 'illusion' of the project approach may be added to illusions about the real nature of counterpart funds. Singer felt that the project approach was itself basically illusionary since, whatever the project label may be, aid really financed the marginal project that would be cut out if the foreign assistance was not provided. The illusion of project aid could, to some extent, be reduced if aided projects were discussed and selected within the framework of a general review of the broad policies of a recipient country and use of the overall resources at its disposal. But Singer also realistically saw that in the 'tangled world of aid policies and economics', the concreteness of aided project was necessary to approve aid, even if it was 'the fallacy of misplaced concreteness'. Perhaps the educational and political value of donors and recipients working together on the formulation, appraisal and execution of specific development projects was sufficient to justify the drawbacks. Abandonment of the project approach to aid giving did not exclude control of the purposes, sectors and uses to which the aid was applied. On the contrary, non-project aid in many ways provided more effective leverage to the aid giver since it was eagerly sought by many countries and the release from project tying would often be accepted as an aspect of 'softness' in aid.

Food aid and the well-being of children

A strong motivation for Singer's interest in food aid was the role it could play in terms of human resource development and particularly the physical and mental development of young children. It also related to his concern with the ethics of aid and his work for UNICEF on children in the strategy for development (see above). Singer considered that the moral case for aid was strengthened by concentration on vulnerable groups, particularly children, but also people living in abject poverty in the poorest countries and refugees and displaced persons, the victims of man-made disasters (Singer, 1983h).

Singer (with Richard Longhurst) set out his views extensively in a major paper on the role of food aid in promoting the welfare of children in developing countries, which he presented to a joint UNICEF/WFP workshop held in New York in November 1985. The workshop's objective was to obtain a clearer and more comprehensive understanding of the various ways by which food aid could help alleviate the problems of children in the developing world, especially in the times of economic recession that were experienced throughout the 1980s (Singer and Longhurst, 1986f). The authors concluded that with effective design and management, food aid could bring real benefits to children. Children in developing countries were, almost by definition, always poorer than the average adult. But mainly because large family size was an important element in poverty, and family size was also a negative function of educational and income levels, there were added social difficulties in realizing the needs of children in intra-household food distribution. The special characteristics of food aid as a form of development assistance were of particular relevance to children. These included: its fungibility as a resource; the speed with which it could be committed; and its political acceptability as aid by both donors and recipients. Food aid had greater flexibility than other forms of aid in circumventing the barriers that might prevent it from reaching children, particularly if provided to women, who had greater control of the use of food than cash in the household, and a high propensity for child welfare. But food aid alone could not be expected to have significant benefits unless combined with other inputs related to health, education and living environments.

A particularly dangerous result of the rapid and radical economic adjustment measures inflicted on developing countries by external and internal pressures in the face of economic recession was that these countries were forced to concentrate on very short-term actions. Provision for children was, in economic terms, a long-run investment to which a country struggling for survival found it difficult to assign proper priority. Keynes' dictum that 'in the long run we are all dead' acquired a pungent meaning for countries in an adjustment crisis. The pressures to sacrifice long-term investment in human capital were strengthened by the fact that the negative effects on child development remained invisible in the absence of appropriate data, monitoring and evaluation, and could only be fully felt at some time in the future. The most vulnerable groups, particularly children, were least able to make their interests and needs felt in domestic and international discussions on adjustment and economic strategies, which focused largely on obtaining 'a financial seal of approval'. But, Singer argued, they should also have a 'human seal of approval' so as to bring about what came to be called 'adjustment with a human face' (Cornia *et al.*, 1987). Within such a macroeconomic framework, it was preferable that additional resources (including food aid) should be provided in conjunction with, and as an integral part of, the adjustment process, rather than as a result of separate and unrelated discussions carried out during or after adjustment negotiations, before the human damage was done.

Structural adjustment and economic reform: the role of food aid

It was a natural progression that took Singer from his concern for children, particularly in the context of economic recession, to a wider interest in the roles of food aid in structural adjustment and economic reform and their effects on poor households and communities, particularly in Sub-Saharan Africa (Shaw and Singer, 1988g; Singer 1990f; 1991e). With passion and outrage, Singer and others were especially critical of the structural adjustment programmes of the IMF and the World Bank and the social costs they brought to poor people in developing countries. In many adjustment programmes, children and vulnerable groups were put under severe pressure. To take an extreme example, Singer argued that if malnutrition among young children increased and led to irreversible loss of physical and mental capacity, this could in no sense be described as 'laying the foundation for viable future economic growth', the purported reason for adjustment programmes.

Mutual benefits could be forthcoming from an association of food aid with adjustment programmes. The adjustment process could be strengthened while food aid provided within the adjustment framework could be more effective. But this did not imply that food aid could be used like some kind of 'magic dust' to work wonders and overcome the mistakes and errors of badly designed adjustment programmes. However, food aid did have special characteristics which were particularly appropriate for addressing the macroeconomic difficulties of developing countries, and the microeconomic concerns of the poor in those countries, by counterbalancing the tendency for adjustment programmes to be unduly austere and contractionist, rather than expansionist. But emphasis on the protection of vulnerable groups against 'austerity' should not be taken as support for a purely 'corrective' function of food aid under which an adjustment agreement is first negotiated and then food aid is rushed in as special hardships became apparent. Rather, food aid should be included as a resource, both generally and with specific functions, in adjustment agreements from the very beginning.

Food aid could make a number of contributions to structural adjustment (Singer, 1991e). These included: contributing to overall available resources, to cushion the austerity of the adjustment process; setting free foreign exchange, thereby helping with the stabilization of balance of payments as a necessary preliminary to resumed economic growth, sustaining incomes and employment of the poor, especially during the difficult transition period from retrenchment to resumed growth; protecting the vulnerable from the harsh short-run impact of stabilization and adjustment policies by maintaining essential economic and social services for them during the transition period; reducing budget deficits and inflation, which were important elements in stabilization and adjustment; helping to provide domestic food stability and food security, an essential political precondition for making adjustment acceptable and viable; supporting essential reform measures and sectoral programmes often related to food production; and helping, through counterpart funds, to provide local finance for projects and programmes within a structural adjustment context. With such a multitude of possible objectives and effects, it was important to be clear about intentions, and to choose the forms of food and financial aid, and other methods and combinations, in the light of the main objectives.

Intellectual investment and the disincentive controversy

Intellectual investment in the subject, in Singer's view, has been less than might be expected given the magnitude of food aid that has been provided. With notable exceptions, development economists have tended to avoid the subject, or have come to it with a preconceived dislike, largely because it is perceived as 'surplus disposal' as opposed to 'development assistance'. The issues have been blurred by participants in the policy debate who produced populist literature on the world food problem that emphasized philosophical and moral arguments and the duty and responsibility of developed countries to 'feed the hungry-poor' (Ruttan, 1996, p. 187).

In the latter part of the 1970s, Singer, with Paul Isenman, clearly revealed the contradictions in the economic literature on food aid (Isenman and Singer, 1975m). They observed that many economists appeared to view food aid and non-food aid from 'remarkably different perspectives'. Most economists seemed to believe that aid recipients should use non-food aid to increase investment, employment and output in accordance with well-thought-out development plans and/or signals provided by market forces. They would be horrified if the aid were used instead for short-term consumption increases or for low-priority development projects with uncertain impact. Yet, paradoxically, because of concern about disincentives and a lack of sufficient emphasis on how food aid could in fact add to employment and investment (and, perhaps, because of the particular association of food with basic human needs), many of these same economists urged that food aid virtually be required to be used for short-term consumption or for *ad hoc* 'additional' projects not included as top priority in development plans. At the same time, food aid was criticized because it benefited consumption instead of investment. While it was inconsistent to insist, implicitly, that food aid not be used for investment and to criticize food aid for not contributing to investment, both these views, each apparently reasonably derived from valid policy concerns, were well established in the 'conventional wisdom' of food aid. Yet increased consumption, when it meant, for example, improving nutritional levels of pre-school children or alleviating near-starvation among adults, could have a bigger impact on future output than a good deal of what was included under the accounting category of 'investment'. But the justification for food aid need not lie solely or primarily in such humanitarian consumption uses. Food aid, balanced with non-food assistance, could also contribute to increases in investment, employment and output.

Isenman and Singer illustrated their arguments by reviewing some of the analytical issues and literature relevant to the concern about the potential disincentive effects and risks of food aid, which they shared, with particular reference to the case of India.[16] That country had been one of the largest recipients of food aid. They examined both the price and policy effects of food aid on Indian agricultural production.[17] They found that the depressing effect on prices was much less than some analysts had expected, partly because food aid was used to increase government food distribution which, being subsidized, added to net food demand. However, they felt that the large-scale food aid supplied by the United States should have been phased in more gradually (by stockpiling more and distributing less). Nevertheless, they found the short-term price effect on food production in India to be 'very limited', the medium-term income and price effect on food production in India (taking account of the effect of food aid on growth) 'probably positive', and the medium-term effect on overall output, employment and nutrition 'strongly positive'.

Regarding the policy effects of food aid, Isenman and Singer distinguished between criticism of the policy effect of aid and criticism of policies supported by aid but caused by political and economic factors far more powerful than aid. In the Indian case, the political and economic factors, which up to the middle of the 1960s led to the preference for heavy industry over agriculture, were far more powerful than food aid which, at most, played a supportive role. When there was a reorientation of Indian priorities toward agriculture after the mid-1960s, food aid was used to help the process not only by saving foreign exchange that would have been spent on commercial imports but by directing a significant part of the funds generated from the sale of food aid commodities in India for investment in the infrastructure needed for the Green Revolution. This resulted in a spectacular growth in Indian food production by raising crop yields through irrigation, technological progress, and the use of high-yielding seed varieties. This, in turn, required a policy commitment on the part of the Indian government and considerable resources, which food aid helped to provide.

The Indian example served to illustrate several general points about food aid. Food aid could be used to support both 'good' and 'bad' agricultural policies. It would be quite unrealistic for either critics or proponents of food aid (or other forms of aid) to take it for granted that it was necessarily a major or determining cause of such policies. If a country had a strong commitment to agriculture, and the political will and sound policies to carry out that commitment, it was likely to use food aid (and other forms of aid) in ways that supported its agricultural development effort. If not, food aid (and other aid) would be used to further whatever alternative economic objectives the government wished to pursue. There had also been a rather paradoxical difference in the conventional views of the disincentive effects in recipient policy of food aid and non-food aid. Non-food aid to India was far larger than food aid and went primarily to support industry and related infrastructure. It would therefore be inconsistent to criticize food aid to India (or any country) on grounds that it led to underemphasis on agriculture in relation to industry unless the same criticism was directed to non-food aid. Isenman and Singer concluded that it would be quite reasonable for donors and recipients to discuss mutual concerns about possible disincentive effects of large food aid programmes and what might be done to prevent them. There might be advantages in carrying out such discussions under the aegis of a multilateral agency, or a multi-donor consultative group, rather than on a bilateral basis.

Redefining food aid in a liberalizing global economy

The conclusion of the GATT Uruguay round of multilateral trade negoti-ations in 1994, the signing and ratification of the Final Act at the end of the negotiations, and the setting up of the World Trade Organization (WTO) provided a major opportunity for establishing a new food aid regime within a liberalizing global economy (Singer, 1996e; Shaw and Singer, 1995e). At the outset, this raised some basic questions, including what should constitute food aid. Should it encompass the large volume of transactions in the 'grey area' between food aid, as defined under the FAO *Principles of Surplus Disposal* (FAO, 1954), and statistically recorded, and outright commercial trade in food commodities?

Singer pointed to what he called the conceptual and statistical 'quag-mire' in food aid. Under present statistical convention, food aid is dis-tinguished from food trade or commercial transactions by an element of concessionality. The Development Assistance Committee (DAC) of the Organisation for Economic Co-operation and Development (OECD), which comprises the major donor countries, agreed on a benchmark of 25 per cent below the commercial price as an arbitrary definition of the grant element in Official Development Assistance (ODA). Some immediate problems have arisen for food aid. As Singer pointed out, the international price for food is not a textbook free-market price with a significant reference function. Subsidizing domes-tic agriculture in the major industrial countries has resulted in surpluses and surplus capacities, which have enabled and induced them to tie their aid to food. They have also depressed the commercial price of food in international trade. Hence, the 25 per cent concession-ality limit that might define food aid is not 25 per cent off a truly free-market price, but 25 per cent off a world price that is itself at a discount to what a commercial process would be in a free, fully liberal-ized market. If it were, many more transactions would come to be defined as 'food aid'.

A large part of so-called food 'trade' does not take place as straight market transactions at international prices but is conducted through a labyrinth of various forms of bilateral agreements that provided dis-counts from the 'commercial' international price (itself reduced by overhanging surpluses and domestic production subsidies) in many direct and indirect ways. This made it difficult to quantify globally such transactions as export credits, guarantee and export enhancement programmes, and linkages with other trade concessions or with financial aid.[18]

Under the Final Act, export subsidies and domestic agricultural support measures are to be partially and gradually reduced. However, it is doubtful whether these reductions will catch all the hidden and indirect subsidies involved. If all the benefits from lowered prices were passed on to food-importing developing countries, Singer estimated that food aid would be approximately doubled compared to the 'statistical' food aid figure. With more radical assumptions, moving from partial to full market liberalization, and defining any discount from the much higher fully liberalized commercial international free-market price for food commodities as 'food aid', the true volume of food aid thus broadly defined would be further increased.[19]

However, the food aid implicit in the artificial lowering of international food prices and trade discounts, which Singer referred to as the food aid that 'dare not speak its name', is not targeted on the food-needy but is 'broadly and blindly' given across the board to all commercial importers, regardless of need, mainly for donor short-run political and commercial, market protection and penetration, purposes. The really needy, almost by definition, are not commercial importers or purchasers.

However, there is a countervailing element where the current definition of food aid could be said to be excessively wide. Part of the programme food aid that replaced commercial imports represented, in effect, financial aid in that it set foreign exchange free. The same could be said to apply to countries receiving emergency food aid for many years continuously, although in their case it was less likely that commercial imports could have been afforded. Another dimension in which food aid statistics may be overstated related to its value. Donors tended to value their food aid contributions at their budget costs, but these costs were inflated by the subsidies and high domestic prices involved in their own agricultural policies. Yet another possible over-valuation of food aid related to triangular transactions and local purchases whereby food commodities were procured in developing countries to be used as food aid. It was by no means clear how there transactions should appear in aid statistics. For example, if a donor country bought maize in a developing country to be used as food aid in another developing country, the receiving country was designated as the food aid recipient country. But the case could alternatively be presented as donor-financed trade between the two developing countries, which could result in double-counting. What should it be? To count it only as food aid might understate the financial aid provided: to count it as financial aid runs the opposite risk.

This last example illustrated that the real 'quagmire' in food aid was conceptual rather than statistical. When dealing with subsidized and financially-promoted trade, what part was 'trade' and what part 'aid'? What is, or should be, the grant element that distinguishes trade from aid? And where is the borderline between financial and food aid? The more the definition of food aid was broadened, the more it became clear that food aid must be understood and handled not in isolation, as in the past, but as an element in world food security and trade, and co-ordinated with financial and technical assistance. A shift towards a broader conception of food aid would be all the more necessary as one of the outcomes of the GATT Uruguay round and the implementation of the Final Act. It would also be necessary as the historical links of food aid with surplus disposal and the resulting popularity of food aid, especially among the farming communities in the major food-exporting developed countries, were weakened as a result of the liberalization of agricultural policy.

Singer considers that cutting the historical links between surpluses and food aid could be a 'blessing in disguise'. This link had always been a flawed motivation for food aid leading to major tensions between donors' domestic agricultural interests and the developmental needs of developing countries, and to the controversy and criticisms surrounding food aid. Much had been made of the possible disincentive effects of food aid on policy-makers and producers in food aid recipient countries. Less had been heard about the disincentives created by policy-makers in the developed countries and the continuation of harmful agricultural policies on the grounds that some of the resulting surpluses could be 'disposed of' as food aid. If as a result of the GATT Uruguay round, the hidden food aid was forced out into the open and placed under the disciplines of food aid established under the Final Act, it could then be purposefully targeted on developmental and humanitarian concerns for needy countries and people, rather than donor short-run political and commercial objectives. This would not only help to clear up the conceptual and statistical quagmire in food aid but, more importantly, would be a major step in dealing with the problem of hunger and, by extension, with the reduction of poverty in the developing world.

Development tool or obstacle?: Responding to the food aid critics

Singer is well aware of the shortcomings and limitations of food aid, which he helped to reveal. Equally, he is concerned with the mistaken and misguided criticisms to which food aid has been subjected, and has played an active role in responding to the critics (Singer, 1987h; 1988n; 1990e; Clay and Singer, 1985c; Raffer and Singer, 1996a, pp. 80–7). Published in 1987, his book on food aid, written with John Wood and Tony Jennings, remains the best balanced account on food aid available (Singer *et al.*, 1987b).

Food aid has been criticized as being 'second class' aid and an inferior substitute for financial assistance. Genuinely untied financial aid is preferable to food aid. But most financial aid is tied, explicitly or implicitly, and when tied to food imports (aid for food) is better than financial aid tied to dubiously required high-priced capital goods or to armaments. Singer questioned whether a distinction could be make between financial and food aid. Financial aid was in fact the first step in the aid process. The next step was to convert the money provided into development goods and services. This raised a host of issues and problems, such as the sources of origin of the aid goods, and their procurement and utilization. In that sense, all aid was commodity aid. Food aid, properly executed, could be commended for simplifying procedures by cutting out the first, or financial, stage of the transaction and coming directly to the substantive second stage of commodity transfer.

There were other reasons for doubting whether there was a real distinction between financial and food aid and to presume that food aid was always inferior. It was best, therefore, to judge food aid on its own merits rather than compare it with the costs and benefits of financial assistance. Where food aid substituted for commercial imports, it saved the recipient government the foreign exchange that would have been spent. Thus, the food aid provided was directly equivalent to financial aid and, moreover, was financial aid unconditionally available to the recipient government. Where food aid was monetized (sold) in the recipient country, this further blurred the borderline between financial and food aid.

Where food aid was additional to financial aid, the comparison was superfluous. There were political and commercial as well as humanitarian and legal reasons (such as international commitments under the Food Aid Convention or the European Union's common food aid programme) which made donors inclined to give food aid where they would not give an equivalent amount of financial aid. Food aid, if properly targeted, had the advantage of directly addressing the needs of poor, food-insecure people, and of being more gender-friendly to women, and thus to their children. A higher proportion of food aid went to the poorer developing countries and benefited poor people than financial aid.

The potential disincentive effects of food aid on agricultural production in developing countries through adverse policy and price effects have been at the 'storm centre' of the food aid debate. Concerning the policy effect, Singer questioned whether developing countries would, in the absence of food aid, have shown less 'urban bias' and done more to increase their own food production. The forces making for 'urban bias' were deeper and went beyond the existence of food aid. It could even be argued that without food aid governments would squeeze their local farmers even harder to extract surpluses for the growing urban population. Conversely, part of the food constraint relaxed by food aid could allow governments to relax the monopoly grip of parastatal marketing organizations and permit farmers to sell their surplus food at free-market prices.

Criticism of developing countries for neglecting their own food production, and for urban bias, did not come well from countries which themselves had shown such distortions and extreme forms of 'rural bias' in their own agricultural policies. Structural adjustment should be a two-way business. In the overall picture, the 'disincentive' due to low international prices (in turn due to overhanging surpluses resulting from the European Union's Common Agricultural Policy (CAP) and similar protectionist policies in other major food-exporting developed countries), which encouraged imports, was more important than any disincentives due to food aid. Nor did such criticism come well from neo-liberal critics who preach the virtue of 'outward orientation' for developing countries. Replacing food imports by domestic production was an act of import substitution. The use of land for export crops rather than food for domestic consumption was the result of 'outward orientation' and the pressure to earn foreign exchange to repay increasing debts.

Food aid provided plenty of opportunity for those governments keen to promote their own food production to do so. Where food aid replaced commercial imports, the foreign exchange released could be used to import the inputs required to increase agricultural production and to produce the consumption goods that farmers need as an inducement to sell surplus food. Governments could also use the revenue derived from food aid sales for the promotion of domestic agriculture. Relaxation of the food constraint provided by food aid also enabled the recipient government to be more expansionist in its general policies. This, depending on the pattern of expansion, would increase the demand for local food and hence raise prices.

Where a government could not be trusted to use the relaxation of the food constraint in a manner favourable to domestic food production, donors could make the provision of food aid conditional upon a shift of policy in that direction. This could be done in a number of ways, for example by providing food aid directly for agricultural purposes; as part of a structural adjustment programme; linked with an agreed food strategy; or through the use of counterpart funds in the agricultural and rural sectors.

Singer found the idea that the governments of developing countries eagerly seize on food aid as an opportunity to neglect domestic agricultural production hardly plausible politically. Developing countries were keen to establish and safeguard their national sovereignty. Dependency on food imports, and especially on food aid, is incompatible with this political priority objective. The critics argued that food aid supplied in bulk for local sale provided governments with 'easy revenue'. This could tempt governments into relaxing their efforts to mobilize domestic savings through taxation. There was an inconsistency in this criticism, if at all well-founded. To the extent that the critics were preaching liberalization, greater reliance on the market, and limitation of the public sector as recipes for development, it could be expected that they would welcome this effect of food aid, namely, that it reduced the burden of taxation and enlarged the resources at the disposal of the private sector. Moreover, insofar as a relaxation of the tax grip reduced the tax burden on farmers and the rural sector, it could only help the objective of promoting local agricultural production.

A fall in domestic food prices as a result of food aid and the resultant disincentive to increased agricultural food production was by no means 'pre-ordained'. A recipient government could distribute the additional food to target groups free or at low or subsidized prices while maintaining or even raising prices for local producers. The idea of an automatic disincentive effect of food aid because it caused low domestic prices was based on the assumption of a single and unified market price applying to consumers and producers. However, as with the EU and the US, food prices in most developing countries were subject to active government intervention. It was quite possible for governments in food aid recipient countries to operate a dual price system with low prices for consumers, or selected groups, and higher prices for producers. The fiscal resources to cover a resulting deficit could be obtained from the revenue derived from food aid sale.

An important qualification was that any reduced demand for locally produced food caused by the arrival of food aid from abroad could and should be offset by additional demand resulting from the additional incomes created by food-aid-induced and accelerated development.

Such additional development would benefit local food producers by creating extra demand for food and maintaining or strengthening food prices. Economic history and cross-country analysis had shown that the major past recipients of food aid managed to use large-scale food aid as a basis for vigorous development of their domestic agriculture and had subsequently graduated out of food aid.

Another qualification to the disincentive effect arose from what Singer called 'the structure of food production' in developing countries. Where food was produced from subsistence farming, it would not be affected by any possible impact of food aid on local prices (except through subsistence transactions). Where food was produced by small-scale producers who supplied a marketable surplus in order to cover production and consumption needs and non-food related expenses, a fall in prices could have the effect of increasing marketable surpluses rather than reducing them. If farmers reduced the production of a given crop affected by lower prices because of food aid, land would be set free to produce other crops. Such crop-diversification could be to the advantage of local farmers and the local economy. To assume that a lower price meant less output and higher prices more production was generally an over-simplified application of neo-classical textbook analysis of a perfect capitalist market and was not applicable to the more complex and segmented food markets of developing countries.

Incentives for farmers were governed by a spectrum of factors going well beyond prices alone. 'Getting prices right' was important but not enough: the more expert advice was 'getting elasticities right'. Other types of neglect or discrimination were often more important than poor domestic terms of trade (prices obtained versus prices paid) of local food producers, as distinct from export crops, in causing a decline in local food production. The response of farmers was determined not by prices as such but by what they could buy with the price obtained. If the additional resources represented by food aid were used for additional imports or domestic production of, say, fertilizer, and its subsidized distribution to farmers, the profit margin for local food producers could be maintained or improved even if local food prices fell. The same applied to the availability of consumption goods and their accessibility in rural areas. If the revenue from food aid was used for that purpose, it could have a more powerful incentive to farmers to increase production and marketed surpluses than a higher price.

Singer responded to other criticisms of food aid, namely, that it distorted consumption patterns, and it fostered urbanization and population growth. It could lead to a taste for expensive foods that cost more per unit of energy and that could not be produced locally. Conversely, it could lead to a more efficient diet. Food habits were not immutable and could be changed by many factors, such as government import and pricing policies, changes in the relative pries of food commodities, increasing incomes, transport and logistical improvements, migration to urban areas, changes in fuel costs, and women's participation in income-earning activities outside the home. To the extent that food aid substituted for imports which would have occurred anyway, the cause of change in consumption habits must lie elsewhere (Cassen, 1986, p. 160). Moreover, the criticism would not apply to food aid provided through triangular transactions, local purchases and exchange arrangements under which the staple foods of the developing countries were supplied as food aid.

Similarly, many factors were at work which led to increasing urbanization and population growth. Family size was affected by a number of socio-cultural factors but was by no means as irrational or biologically determined as many had thought in the past. In very poor countries and communities, children, who became net positive economic assets at a young age, were the best insurance against a disastrous reduction in family earnings through disability or old age. Contrary to the Malthusian view, birth rates among the poor went down, not up, as their standard of living (which in the poorest countries meant initially their standard of eating) rose (Singer, 1976b). While development led to a transitional period of sharply lower death rates before birth rates fell, the sooner and faster the death rate declined so too would the birth rate. Where food aid made a positive contribution to employment, nutrition, and other aspects of the development process, it could be said to be making a positive contribution to reducing population growth irrespective of whether a country had an official and effective family planning programme.

In conclusion, Singer recognized that, as with all forms of aid, the disincentive effects of food aid were possible and should be guarded against, but they were by no means unavoidable, and were certainly not automatic. As with all aid, the policy environment was critical, as well as the precise ways in which food aid was used. Food aid provided an opportunity to promote growth and reduce poverty in developing countries. This opportunity may be taken or it may be wasted. That depended on the way food aid was given and the way in which it was absorbed. It depended on the purposes of the donor countries and the policies and efficiency of the recipients. Only careful analysis of situations in specific countries, at specific periods of time, could tell whether disincentive effects had occurred and whether such effects had been compensated, or over-compensated, for by the developmental benefits of food aid.

Future directions

Singer identified certain lines of possible future development in the field of food aid (Singer *et al.*, 1987b, pp. 193–205; Raffer and Singer, 1996a, pp. 85–7). One possible, and desirable, development was to use food aid to solve some of the intractable problems of the debt burden and balance of payments difficulties of developing countries. The methods of adjustment and conditionality of the IMF and World Bank structural lending programmes had been generally criticized as being too harsh and having undesirable social consequences. They had even been counter-productive in undermining, rather than promoting, future growth, calling for 'adjustment with a human face' (Cornia *et al.*, 1987). It has also been recognized that in return for the painful adjustments expected from developing countries, they should be given a greater *quid pro quo* in terms of additional resources. Food aid in structural adjustment lending had caught the attention of those concerned. It could have the special advantage of representing both additional resources to ease adjustment and also of being capable of providing particular relief for vulnerable groups, such as children, landless rural people, unemployed and other victims of 'tough' adjustment policies.

A second desirable and likely development was the increasing concentration of food aid on Sub-Saharan Africa (Singer, 1990f). The net food import needs of the sub-region have rapidly increased and were projected to increase further. *Per caput* food production had fallen and its revival would be a long-term business, calling for additional aid, including food aid. At the same time, Sub-Saharan Africa carried the heaviest debt burden and was the most affected by the weaknesses in primary commodity prices.

Thirdly, and related to a concentration on Sub-Saharan Africa, there was a developing consensus on a broader definition of emergency aid to include disaster prevention and preparedness at one end and reconstruction and rehabilitation after disasters at the other. As emergency aid represented an uncontroversial aspect of food aid, this could provide a basis for substantial additions to food aid flows, which in turn would assist the development process. The insight that famine was often caused by a breakdown of incomes or other 'entitlements' providing access to food (Sen, 1981), should further support such protective and non-controversial extensions of food aid. For example, rural public works schemes supported by food aid, or by proceeds from food aid sales, could be well designed to maintain rural incomes. They could also be planned so as to cover specifically the 'hungry months' before the harvest and could be stepped up at times of crop failure.

Another line could be the wider use of the potential of monetization or food aid sales. Food aid commodities could be sold in urban areas and the revenue used for rural investment, strengthening the demand for locally produced food. Monetization could also help to finance the non-food costs of food aid supported programmes such as emergency food aid, food-for-work schemes, and nutrition improvement programmes for mothers and children. All these projects require financial as well as food resources but some food agencies, such as the UN World Food Programme, suffered from cash shortages. A related desirable development would be better linkage and combinations of financial and food aid, including better co-operation among the aid agencies concerned.

Greater use should be made of the mechanisms and modalities that resulted in the procurement of food commodities in the developing countries themselves for use as food aid. A number of developing countries had exportable food surpluses. They have been hard hit by the protectionist agricultural policies of the major food exporting developed countries and by the resulting low international food prices. Short of a revision of these protectionist policies, developing country food surpluses should be bought at remunerative prices for use in deficit areas, perhaps in combination with the establishment of regional buffer stocks in which internationally financed regional surpluses could be held under international control. Such an imaginative approach could be supplemented by methods to encourage transfer of surplus food from surplus to deficit regions within developing countries, which would require investment in transport and logistics as well as the encouragement of financing local reserve stocks.

Finally, WFP's governing body should play a more effective role in co-ordinating the policies and programmes and establishing institutional coherence among all those involved in food aid than it has done in the past. By providing a multilateral framework, food aid from all sources could be provided coherently and conflict and duplication could be avoided. Singer concluded that as long as food aid was badly administered by donors and/or recipients, it could have no real benefit. One basic precondition was the creation of a framework on the part of donors, ideally including a revision of their protectionist policies, that enabled 'food aid to be given for the right reason to the right countries in the right way'. Similar improvements were necessary on the recipients' side: food aid should be increasingly devoted to two essential purposes, 'to reduce poverty and to help develop domestic food production'. Such were the challenges – and the opportunities – of food aid.

21
The United Nations and the Bretton Woods Institutions

Singer retained his interest in, and affection for, the United Nations after his retirement from the UN. He has constantly championed its increasing importance as a world body for addressing global issues and problems, securing global development, and attending to the interests of the developing countries. At the same time, he has been a consistent and sharp critic of the Bretton Woods institutions, the IMF and the World Bank, and of their divide from the rest of the UN system (Singer, 1988e; 1989k; 1990h; Jolly and Seniger1995i).

The new international economic order

As he had followed closely the thinking of Keynes and his associates and events that led up to the Bretton Woods International Monetary Conference in the United States in 1944, Singer was repeatedly called upon to provide an historical perspective to the 'new international economic order' that was to emerge after the Second World War. He was also able to give the historical background to the rift between the UN and the Bretton Woods institution, which he had personally witnessed.[20]

The sequence of events that led up to proposals for a new international economic order after the Second World War was particularly important. Much of the foundation of the United Nations was laid during the early phases of the Second World War, some before the United States had even formally entered the war (Emmerij *et al.*, 2001, pp. 19–21). The first of the specific steps that led to the establishment of the United Nations was the Inter-Allied Declaration, signed in London in June 1941 by representatives of 14 governments, nine of which were in exile. With the Atlantic Charter, signed by US President Roosevelt and UK Prime Minister Churchill in August 1941, and the Declaration

6.   Keynes speaking at the International Monetary Conference, Bretton Woods, New Hampshire, United States, July 1944 (*The Institute of Development Studies*)

of the United Nations of January 1942, signed by 26 governments, this provided the vision for the United Nations Organization. The name, 'United Nations', was proposed by Roosevelt and agreed by Churchill. At conferences held in Moscow in October 1943 and Teheran, Iran in December of the same year, world leaders signed declarations proclaiming the necessity of establishing an international organization at the earliest practicable date. At the Dumbarton Oaks conference in Washington, DC in September 1944 and a conference held in Yalta in the former Soviet Union in February 1945, world leaders agreed on proposals relating to the aims, structure and functioning of a world organization. This early vision was reflected in the outcome of the San Francisco conference in 1945. The UN was to operate on the principle of one-country-one-vote. At the time, the present Third World countries, with the exception of those in Latin America, were still largely colonies, hence the voting principle of one-country-one-vote that was agreed upon was acceptable to most of the industrial countries, which at first raised no objections.[21] The UN, in spite of the reference at the beginning of its charter to 'We the people...', was essentially an organization of governments. It was taken for granted that governments were the genuine representatives of all their people. On that basis, the principle of absolute national sovereignty and non-interference in the internal affairs of individual countries was enshrined in the UN Charter.[22]

Originally, the role of the United Nations was seen as twofold (Singer, 1993j). It was to be the focus of global economic management, centred in the General Assembly and the Economic and Social Council (ECOSOC), both charter organs of the UN. And it was to be the focus of a major aid programme for developing countries, a kind of 'Marshall Plan for the Third World'.[23] This was apart from the peace-making and peacekeeping functions centred in the UN Security Council. The UN Charter reflected the concept of the United Nations as 'the authoritative centrepiece of an international system' (Urquhart and Childers, 1994). Under the Charter, the UN specialized agencies were to be 'brought into relationships with the United Nations', with the UN as the senior and active leader of a co-operative system. It also envisaged that the specialized agencies would be concentrated with the UN in one place under the 'principle of centralization' and architectural plans were drawn up in 1947 for that purpose. But this was not realized. The UN specialized agencies were set up in different locations, with their own autonomies, mandates, financial arrangements and governing bodies, making co-ordination of action within the UN system difficult, if not impossible.

Before the UN was set up in 1945, the International Labour Organization (ILO) already existed, being established in 1919 under the Treaty of Versailles as an autonomous institutions associated with the League of Nations, the charter of the Food and Agriculture Organization (FAO) had been drafted, and ministers of education had met in 1942 to establish what was soon to become the United Nations Educational, Scientific and Cultural Organization (UNESCO). In addition, important additional elements of the new international economic order (NIEO) were agreed to at the International Monetary Conference held at Bretton Woods, New Hampshire in the United States in 1944, which usurped further some of the co-ordinating global economic policy and aid functions of the UN, making it in Singer's view a largely 'residual' body. At Bretton Woods, three 'pillars' for a new world economic structure were proposed by Keynes and modified by the United States delegation (Moggridge, 1992; Skidelsky, 2000). The first pillar was an 'International Clearing Union', as Keynes originally called it, which became the International Monetary Fund (IMF), to provide international monetary co-operation and stability. The second pillar was the International Bank for Reconstruction and Development (IBRD), with the initial focus on reconstruction following the devastation caused by the Second World War. The third pillar was to be an 'International Trade Organization' (ITO). As Singer pointed out, Keynes was a strong believer in the stabilization of primary commodity prices, which was to be one of the main functions of the ITO. He recalled that at one point Keynes combined his proposals for a world central bank and world currency with his proposals for commodity price stabilization by suggesting a world currency based on 30 primary commodities, rather than gold, dollars or special drawing rights (SRDs). This would have stabilized the average price of the 30 commodities included.

As things turned out, little was to remain of the structure of a new international economic order originally visualized at Bretton Woods and San Francisco. And, as Singer explained, 'yawning gaps' have remained: no co-ordination of global economic policies by the UN; no world currency or world central bank, or other source of co-ordinated world liquidity, and no pressure on surplus countries; no commodity price stabilization; and no integrated UN system but rather two separate systems. Even what remained of the proposed NIEO was distorting, serving purposes of debt collection, control of inflation, stabilization and neo-liberal reforms rather than full employment, poverty reduction, resource development and growth.

The IMF developed in directly the opposite way to its originally conceived function. Now it is the deficit countries which are forced to make their own adjustments, focusing all the deflationary pressures on the poorest countries and people. By comparison, pressure on surplus countries is virtually non-existent and largely rhetorical. Keynes' international tax proposal was opposed. Ironically, the United States, the country with the largest deficits, escapes deflationary pressures by serving as a depository for reserves from the poorest countries, thereby extracting even more resources from those countries already squeezed to the margin by limited foreign exchange reserves. Singer observed that, more recently, the IMF has developed into an instrument for using the powerful leverage of the debt crisis to impose policies running directly counter to the Keynesian vision of full employment, adding 'One shudders to think of how Keynes would feel if he knew what has happened to his cherished brain-child of an International Clearing Union.'

Similarly, the IBRD departed from its original role as foreseen by Keynes. As Singer observed, in its original version, the IMF was supposed to be a bank, i.e., a world central bank. By contrast, the IBRD was supposed to be a fund, largely because originally the temporary needs of reconstruction from war devastation were predominant and 'development' was added to its title almost as an afterthought. Singer recalled that Keynes never had any real interest in what are now called the 'developing countries'. 'Development' was added to the Bank's function of 'reconstruction' largely on the insistence of the Latin American countries at the Bretton Woods conference. Reconstruction needs were largely taken care of by the Marshall Plan and other forms of US aid, outside the UN system. Furthermore, reconstruction turned out to be a quicker and less strenuous task than originally assumed. On the other hand, development needs were clearly underestimated in IBRD's original blueprint. Many of the developing countries were still colonies and responsibility for their development rested with the colonial powers. Their voice was not heard at Bretton Woods. In addition, commodity prices were high during and immediately after the Second World War, and were further driven up by the Korean War.

Another major reason for the IBRD's development along quite different and unexpected lines occurred after 1959. In its development work, the Bank was supposed to be limited to project lending. Singer recalled that this was not assumed to be a serious limitation since it was optimistically considered that there was no shortage of high-yielding projects in the developing countries in view of their capital scarcity and abundance of labour and natural resources. It was therefore assumed that it was only a question of identifying, formulating, financing, and monitoring these projects. This was supposed to be the comparative advantage and specific function of the Bank. Programme aid was supposed to be a function of the UN itself.

As explained in Chapter 8, when the attempt to establish a soft financing facility in the UN in the form of SUNFED failed, and instead was transferred to the IBRD in the form of the International Development Association (IDA), this had two major repercussions. First, it enabled the Bank to move strongly into policy-making based on conditional programme lending through structural adjustment and sectoral programmes. Second, it widened the rift in the UN system between the Bretton Woods institution and the other UN bodies.

A point now frequently and conveniently forgotten is that the Bretton Woods institutions were originally set up as specialized agencies of the United Nations, fully within the UN system and subject to co-ordination by the UN. This is still reflected in their Terms of Agreement, which require them to be guided by decisions of the UN General Assembly and ECOSOC. The only relic of this legal position is that the heads of the IMF and World Bank are required to 'report' in speeches to ECOSOC, although, as Singer observed, their reports are more *de haut en bas* than the other way round. Moreover, the secretary-general of the United Nations was for a long time not allowed to address the annual meetings of the Fund and Bank. Singer considers that the divide in the UN system into two components (which in large part was responsible for the Bank receiving the soft-financing facility of IDA, instead of the UN in the form of SUNFED) is due to the different voting systems of the two components. Whereas the principle of one-country-one-vote was adopted throughout the rest of the UN system, in the Fund and the Bank a voting system reflecting the contributions of the donor countries was established, which gave them the ascendancy. A tradition has also been established whereby a US citizen has been appointed head of the Bank, and essentially chosen by the US administration, and a citizen of Western Europe head of the Fund.

At the same time, the shift to policy-making and programme-lending signified another important move, i.e., the shift away from unlimited sovereignty and control by recipient governments to a controlling position by the donor community, exercised through the international financial institutions. This represented their combined power under the 'good housekeeping seal of approval' procedure, by which bilateral aid is conditional upon acceptance of IMF and World Bank policy prescriptions. The original paradigm was that UN bodies, including the Bretton Woods institutions, should be the servants of member governments; nothing was permitted except at the specific request, and with the specific approval, of the recipient government. Singer considers that the main reason why this controlling position of the recipient governments has been undermined is the weakening of their situation as a result of the debt trap and the 'lost decade' of the 1980s. To that extent, economic sovereignty became an empty legal principle, 'comparable to the "freedom" of the penniless to "choose" between starving or doing as he is told'. At the same time, Singer pointedly asserted that the self-confidence of the Bretton Woods institutions sharply increased as a result of their 'whole-hearted embrace of neo-liberal fundamentalism', referred to as the 'Washington consensus' (see later), which gave them 'the zeal and confidence characteristic of religious or ideological conviction that they know the secrets of successful developments and that their knowledge is universally relevant for all developing countries'.

Although successfully negotiated at the UN conference in Havana in 1948, the International Trade Organization (ITO) was never ratified and became a victim of hostility in the US Congress during the

McCarthy era. Singer recalls that four years earlier, when he left the Bretton Woods conference to the cheers of the participants,[24] Keynes was under the firm impression that the ITO would be created, adding:

> It is quite possible, as a matter of counterfactual speculation, that he [Keynes] would not have recommended the agreements reached at Bretton Woods without the ITO, although in the nature of counterfactual speculation this can be neither proved nor disproved. In place of the ITO we have the General Agreement on Tariffs and Trade (GATT) [replaced by the World Trade Organization (WTO) in 1994] but this was Hamlet without the prince: the key function of commodity price stabilization was not included among the functions of the GATT [or of the WTO]. (Singer, 1993j, p. 30)

In the absence of the ITO, primary commodity prices tended to deteriorate to the disadvantage of developing countries. A violent reaction against this trend by oil producers organized in the OPEC cartel played a major causative role in the collapse of the Bretton Woods system and was directly and indirectly responsible for much of the subsequent troubles. In Singer's opinion, 'In this and other matters we would have been well served in following the advice and wisdom of Keynes' (Singer, 1993j, p. 30). He noted that subsequent attempts to fill this gap at least partially (as in UNCTAD's Integrated Programme for Commodities and the IMF's Compensatory Financing Facility) have 'remained more or less stillborn'. The latter became part of the 'neo-liberal tide' and GATT (and its successor, the WTO) became part of the Bretton Woods system in the sense that they were distinguished from the UN system, without a link to any global co-ordination or international governance in the UN.

Critic of the Bretton Woods institutions

Singer has remained highly critical of the work of the Bretton Woods institutions, including: the World Bank's focus on 'outward orientation' as the factor accounting for why certain developing countries have progressed while 'inward oriented' countries have not; the Bank's structural adjustment lending; and the thinking of the IMF and Bank on the behaviour of primary commodity prices (Singer, 1988e; 1989k; Sapsford and Singer, 1998g). Singer's research, and that of others, has shown that the link between outward or export orientation (as opposed to inward orientation or import substitution) and economic performance, which seemed to exist in the more prosperous and expansionist international environment up to 1973, has since been much weakened in the more unfavourable international environment after that date, and particularly after 1981.

According to the Bank's methodology and findings, the economic performance (including GNP growth) of developing countries tended to decline as they moved along the scale from those 'strongly outward-oriented' towards those described as 'strongly inward-oriented'. South Korea, Hong Kong and Singapore were placed in the strongly outward-oriented group. Singer and others questioned the World Bank's findings on grounds that there were many reasons for the success of South Korea, other than outward-orientation. He even questioned whether that country should be placed in the 'strongly outward-oriented' category. But the main point, overlooked by Bank analysts, was that the inward-oriented group of developing countries, and especially those that were classified by the Bank as 'strongly inward-oriented', consisted of countries which were poorer than those in the outward-oriented category. Outward orientation did not work as well for the low-income developing countries, particularly in Sub-Saharan Africa, as it did for the middle-income countries. Singer considered it surprising that the Bank did not think it necessary to introduce income levels as a separate factor in its analysis, nor to consider the risk of export and import instability to which outward-oriented countries with lower income levels were exposed. He also found it 'dangerous', and an over-simplification, to argue the case for outward-orientation and give policy advice on the basis of one country and two city states.

Singer's criticism of the Bank's structural adjustment lending was even more scathing. He questioned whether the Bank was seeking to put a 'human face' or merely a 'facelift' on its structural adjustment programmes. This was in response to the widespread criticism of the Bank's adjustment lending of the 1980s, and the work of the United Nations Children's Fund (UNICEF) and other protagonists of what came to be called 'adjustment with a human face' (Cornia *et al.*, 1987). Singer showed that the Bank's intentions in this regard were at best dubious (Singer, 1989k). In professing to put into practice the lessons of the past, greater weight was to be put on prices and markets. But, as Singer pointed out, this by itself was 'notoriously not welfare-oriented'. It tended to rely on effective buying power, which, in turn, reflected the existing income distribution and worked against the poor, unless there was an equal distribution of assets or other corrective measures, which would reduce the reliance on markets.

The Bank defined its approach as 'to integrate the core of poverty concerns of the 1970s into the growth and market-oriented concerns that marked the first half of the 1980s'. Singer questioned this approach. It indicated that in the Bank's view, its growth and market-oriented concerns had been proved right, and were to be maintained by being 'integrated' (whatever that meant) with the poverty concerns of the 1970s. It was not clear what would constitute the 'core', and what was to be discarded. The sceptic might suspect that the core might be little more than the language of redistribution and basic needs, while the market-oriented concerns would provide the substance. Singer welcomed the Bank's intentions to give a greater poverty focus in its operations, more direct attention to addressing the social costs of adjustment, and particularly the promise of strengthened support for the humanitarian aid programmes of non-governmental organizations. This represented a move away from complete reliance on trickle-down and recognition that more positive poverty action was needed. But there was no recognition of the possibility that the neo-liberal pattern of growth advocated might itself preclude or negate such positive action.

There was an indication of the Bank's intention to provide assistance to governments in designing structural and sectoral adjustment lending programmes that 'to the extent possible' would protect the poor, notably through improvements in the efficiency and targeting of social expenditures. While welcoming this intention, Singer wished that reference had also been made to the maintenance of, and where desperately needed, even increases in, social expenditures. Moreover, the qualification that the poor were to be protected 'to the extent possible' was ominous, and did not sound like any kind of moral imperative, or even high priority, for the protection of the poor.

The Bank's intention to increase collaboration with other agencies, both official and non-governmental, in addressing poverty concerns in the context of adjustment by supporting compensatory nutrition and employment programmes for the poor was welcomed by Singer. But he questioned on whose terms this collaboration was to take place, and whether these programmes were to be a central part of the Bank's lending policy, or merely an add-on for political convenience and acceptance.

The thinking of both the Fund and the Bank regarding the behaviour of primary commodity prices was criticized by Singer and others (Sapsford and Singer, 1998g). It appeared to them that prior to the 1980s both institutions were aware of the statistical evidence relating to the downward trend in the net barter terms of trade in what became known as the Prebisch–Singer thesis but chose largely to disregard it in the light of the reservations that were put forward regarding the apparent adequacy of the statistical series analyzed. Subsequently, work carried out in both the IMF and the World Bank produced strong statistical evidence which supported the Prebisch–Singer thesis of a long-run trend deterioration in the price of primary commodities in relation to the price of manufactured goods.[25]

The acceptance by both institutions of the validity of the declining long-run trend hypothesis and their recognition of the need to properly distinguish in both analytical and policy formulation terms between secular and cyclical movements was welcomed by Singer. He argued, however, that both institutions had paid insufficient attention to potentially important issues concerned with the *interaction* (original emphasis) between trend and volatility. In addition, he saw it as significant that the Bank at least had accepted the existence of what he called an 'adding-up problem', and the need to give proper consideration to what he described as a 'fallacy of composition' problem. If all developing countries followed Bank advice to expand primary product exports, prices would fall even further. This acceptance was especially welcome if it turned out to constitute a first step on the road to a proper analysis of the adequacy of previous policy prescriptions and thereby fed through into improved policies.

Singer called for recognition in both institutions that because the net barter terms of trade between primaries and manufactures were a ratio, algebraic symmetry indicated that policies designed to influence its behaviour, both cyclical and secular, could equally be addressed to its denominator (the price of manufactured goods) as opposed to its numerator (the price of primaries). He reasoned that if the developed countries were serious about overcoming the problems raised in the developing world by both trend and volatility in the real prices of primary commodities, this would suggest that policies might (at least in part) be directed at influencing the prices at which developing countries purchased their imports of manufactured goods. He noted that this issue might be particularly acute for the usually very poor exporters of primary commodities, especially in Africa, since some evidence existed to suggest that such countries paid more for their imports of manufactured goods as a combined result of the lack of competence in procurement, small market size, high transport costs, lack of market knowledge, and corruption. As he put it, 'the ball lay at least partly in the backyard of the developed countries'. But there was no indication that this view had percolated in any real way into the thinking of either the Fund or the Bank.

In both the Fund and the Bank, 'the sands were shifting' but only *partially* (original emphasis) (Singer and Sapsford, 1998g). In the final analysis, movements in the terms of trade forced upon the primary commodity dependent countries of the developing world had effects not only on their economic growth and macroeconomic performance but also on employment, poverty and opportunity in those countries, plus feedback effects on industrial countries. These were therefore important concerns of all countries. The recent work in both institutions was welcome not only because it went a long way toward resolving some long-disputed issues but also because it suggested a rich and promising agenda for further research.

UN reform and revitalization

Singer regretted the fact that, for historical reasons, the UN became largely a 'residual' body in the economic and developmental fields, carrying out functions which were not specifically allocated to other UN bodies (Singer, 1985g). As we saw earlier, the Bretton Woods institutions were created before the UN, thereby pre-empting their important, wide and expanding functions from the UN. Similarly, some of the UN specialized agencies were established before the UN. The tasks of the UN therefore largely developed as a result of filling recognized gaps left in the multilateral system.

As the fiftieth anniversary of the founding of the United Nations approached, Singer welcomed discussion on proposals to reform and revitalize the UN system, including the Bretton Woods institutions. Among other things, he took part in a meeting of the North–South Roundtable of the Society for International Development, which was held symbolically at the site of the original Bretton Woods conference in September 1993.[26] He prepared a paper for the meeting which provided an historical perspective on the Bretton Woods system (Singer, 1993j). An overall policy framework emerged from the meeting to guide human action in the coming decades, to which Singer subscribed (ul Haq *et al.*, 1993). A new concept of human security had emerged, which focused on security for people through development, not security of countries and geographical territory through arms. It was envisaged, correctly, that future conflicts would be more between people than nations, and required socio-economic reforms, not soldiers in uniform. There was both the need and possibility, and the time was

7.   North–South Roundtable of the Society for International Development held at the original site of the 1944 Bretton Woods conference in September 1993 (*Society for International Development*)

ripe, for reform in the international system. In the areas of human development, the beginnings of new approaches could be traced. To achieve greater coherence and support, all four pillars of the international economic and social system needed to be reconstructed and strengthened. And public opinion, including the continuing strong support for humanitarian action, needed to be built upon and extended to focus on eradicating the worst aspects of poverty and moving on to acceptable patterns and lifestyles of sustainable human development.

An agenda for action was drawn up, with five proposals. A 'world social charter' should be produced to give shape to the emerging concept of global human security. In order to provide a decision-making forum at the highest level to ensure global human security, a 'development security council' should be set up within the United Nations to review critical social and economic threats to people all over the globe and to reach political agreement on specific policy responses.

To meet the emerging requirements of global human security, there should be a fundamental change in the framework of development co-operation based on: mutual interests, not charity; greater co-operation, not confrontation, among nations; more equitable sharing, not protection, of global market opportunities; and growing internationalism, not national isolation. Existing institutions needed to be restructured and strengthened. And a UN agency for the advancement of women should be established to protect the vital interests of the world's 'neglected majority'. The ultimate aim should be to build a new global civil society where people matter. Reform of global institutions were a means to achieving that end.

On the occasion of the fiftieth anniversary of the United Nations in 1995, Singer made five specific proposals for its revitalization (Singer, 1995i). First, in order to improve relations between the Bretton Woods institutions and the rest of the UN system, he suggested that thought be given to ways of moving the voting systems of the two parts closer together. He recognized that this would not be an easy matter but pointed out that as long as the differences in voting systems persisted, an unequal distribution of support and resources between the two systems, and erosion of support for the non-Bretton Woods component of the UN system, would continue. Second, the dichotomy between emergencies and development should be ended. The roots of emergencies were not only military and political but also economic and social. This raised questions of preventive action and led to the proposal to create a ' UN economic security council' or possible alternatives. As creating a new principal organ of the United Nations would raise difficult questions, including a change in the UN Charter, Singer considered that priority might be given to considering alternatives, such as extending the mandate of the existing UN Security Council to cover economic and social emergencies as well as military conflict. A separate committee of the Security Council might be established, a parallel to the present Military Committee, but without veto provision. A special concern would be the question of world food security following the gap created by the abolition of the UN World Food Council, the Final Act of the GATT Uruguay Round, and the creation of the World Trade Organization. Among the actions required would be the activation and enlargement of the WFP-administered International Emergency Food Reserve, including the pre-positioning of food stocks in danger spots in advance of actual conflict.

Third, Singer observed that whatever macroeconomic global economic management existed had been moved out of the multilateral system into the hands of the G7 (the group of seven leading industrial countries)[27] Singer did not find this an acceptable solution. The G7 represented little more than 10 per cent of the world's population, and even with the possible future addition of Russia, it would still only represent a small minority. He acknowledged the spreading acceptance that global economic management should in some way, and to some extent, move back to the multilateral framework visualized at Bretton Woods in 1944 and San Francisco in 1945. The creation of a 'UN economic security council' (or the alternatives suggested above) would serve, to some extent, to bring global co-ordination back to the multilateral forum where it was originally intended to be.

Fourth, Singer addressed the need to strengthen the resources of the United Nations. This might be done by reviving political support from powerful countries, perhaps at the price of a change in the UN voting system. Another way might be by giving the UN independent resources which would enable it to tackle the problems for which it has responsibility more effectively and promptly, and perhaps, in doing so, elicit further support. This would serve to break the vicious circle whereby lack of resources resulted in less effective operations, leading to increasing disenchantment with the organization as a force in world affairs, and to the provision of less resources. He noted that the possibility of providing resources for the UN from some form of international taxation was increasingly being raised.[28] But he also noted that UN resources could be increased if member countries paid their contributions promptly, and if they met the targets that were set for aid in resolutions that they had passed both in the UN General Assembly and at international conferences. He called for concerted action by the contributors since otherwise a 'prisoner's dilemma' would be created with each country waiting for the others to contribute.

Singer observed that there were also other latent international resources which could be activated and used for the benefit of international action by the UN. These included: the power, unused since 1981, to issue special drawing rights (SDRs) through the IMF or, alternatively, richer IMF member countries forgoing their quota of SDRs for the benefit of agreed international action through the UN; and the sale of some of the IMF's gold reserves. He acknowledged that ultimately this came back to the question of political will. Once the principle of international taxation or tapping latent resources was accepted, the details would be amenable to international agreement.

Finally, Singer lamented the emerging division of labour in the UN system whereby the so-called 'hard' parts of development (such as money, finance and macroeconomic policy) became the responsibility of the Bretton Woods institutions, and the so-called 'soft' parts of development (such as social factors, poverty reduction, employment and human resource development) were assigned to the rest of the UN system. This, in turn, had resulted in increasing resources being made available to the IMF and the Bank, while resources to the other UN bodies had not grown commensurately. This division of labour was based on the fallacy that the 'hard' parts were more important for development. There has subsequently been increasing realization on the part of the Bretton Woods institutions as well as others that human capital and human resources (presumably the 'soft' areas) are equally, if not more, important, and should be taken equally seriously and equally supported with resources.

22
International Aid to Developing Countries

Singer sought to increase the size of international aid transfers to developing countries, and to improve their efficiency and effectiveness, after he left the UN. In fact, his contribution at the IDS founding conference in September 1966 was on that subject (Singer, 1966a). He addressed a wide range of issues and problems relating to aid and responded to the critics of aid both on the right and the left (Raffer and Singer, 1996a).

Aid targets and definitions

In the 1960s, the best-known volume target for transfering international financial resources to developing countries was the 1 per cent of national income of advanced countries adopted by the United Nations and accepted, at least in principle, by all the aid-giving countries. (Subsequently, a target of 0.7 per cent of GNP was adopted for Official Development Assistance (ODA).) In Singer's view, this was obviously a minimum target. It was equally obvious that some definition of 'aid' was required for the target to be of any meaning. This raised a host of questions concerning both the definition of aid and how it should be measured. For example, should private investment and short-term and suppliers' credits be included? Should grants and loans be equally counted? Should any distinction be made between the flow of aid and financial resources and, if so, where would the line be drawn? Should aid be counted as gross, or net of repayments, and if the latter, what repayments should be taken into account? Should trade concessions be counted as aid? Should aid be measured as the cost to the donor, or the value to the recipient – by no means identical concepts?

An aid target raised other questions. It was obviously crude in that it made no allowance for the differences in per capita incomes, balance of payments, and internal needs and employment situation among the aid-giving countries. Was the target considered to apply to donor countries individually or collectively? Singer suggested that the contradictions could be removed or mitigated in several ways. For example, the aid target could be treated as the actual target for lower-income countries with balance of payments and economic growth difficulties, while those in a better position could be expected to exceed the target, or give their aid in softer forms. Aid recipients could justly claim that balance of payments difficulties and surpluses almost by definition cancelled themselves out for the aid-giving community as a whole since they (the recipients) did not build up surpluses. Which brought back the need to define 'aid', and the question of setting collective or national targets.

On the other hand, an international aid target had obvious virtues. It embodied a number of basic principles, including: international recognition of global responsibility and interest in the advancement of the poorer countries, a reflection, however faint, of the unity of humankind; burden sharing; comparing and measuring the performance of individual countries; and relating aid to aid-giving capacity. The target also showed up the relatively modest burden of the kind and volume of development aid which the richer countries were expected to provide (only a fraction of the quasi-automatic increase in annual income accruing to the aid-giving world), and which the poorer countries were assumed to be in a position to use effectively. The target had the further advantage of protecting the volume of aid against erosions caused by falls in the value of money, and of creating a built-in growth factor within the aid total.

A further merit in setting an aid target was that it forced the international community to face up to the problems and difficulties of interpretation raised above. An alternative to an aid target would be either, at one extreme, calculation of aid requirements through some macroeconomic calculations of 'gaps', or, at the other extreme, some standard of what constituted 'effective use' of aid. Singer saw the difficulties involved in either extreme. While the former 'opened the floodgates', and was also subject to great uncertainty depending upon the projection model and data used, the latter placed the aid recipients at the mercy of more or less arbitrary standards established by aid donors.

Aid and trade

While Singer was a strong proponent of increased aid, he emphasized that it was only one possible method of acquiring the resources and foreign exchange which developing countries needed to finance their economic development. He recognized that even on the most generous definition of 'aid' (equating it with financial resources), it was still 'the junior partner', providing about a quarter of total exports in the 1960s. In this sense, developing countries were more interested in expanding trade than aid but this depended on the kind of trade and the kind of aid that were compared. It might also be argued that the question of more aid or more trade was a 'non-question', in the sense that aid was not intended to divert resources from export use.[29] There was no simple answer to whether aid or trade was better for development. Trade concessions could have as many strings attached (politically or in the form of reciprocal concessions) as aid could (in the form of tying to specific projects and to purchases in a particular country).

Extra trade had the advantage that it could give additional foreign exchange without repayment obligation and thus not add to indebtedness. But so did aid in the form of grants and really soft loans, and some trade set up its own kind of 'indebtedness' in the form of import obligations. And extra trade, in the form of additional volume rather than a higher price for exports, tied down the resources of developing countries, while with corresponding aid, these resources would be available for alternative developmental domestic uses. Against this, the resources absorbed in the production of exports might be specific, and have no alternative home use. Moreover, aid was normally not supplied to enable a country to direct resources away from export use. But aid might also tie down a country's own resources, particularly if it was supplied in the form of project aid, and if a developing country had to divert its own resources to an aided project which would not have been otherwise undertaken.

Trade was considered by liberal economists as the 'time-tested engine of growth with a built-in compulsion to efficiency'. Aid enthusiasts had corresponding faith in the possibilities for using aid as a leverage for more effective and forceful development policies. The arguments for trade or aid could therefore go round and round. So, Singer concluded, the only reasonable conclusion to the question 'more trade or more aid?', *in a general sense* (original emphasis), 'was more or less unanswerable', although he recognized that it still had to be decided in innumerable concrete cases and circumstance.

For a developing country, trade had the presumption of being a more lasting relationship than aid. Combined with the 'skeleton of truth' in the free trade doctrine – that trade forces countries to be efficient and to specialize on lines of comparative advantage and appropriate factor proportions – Singer regarded that it was 'probably sufficient' to make us look at trade as the normal and primary matter under review in the dialogue with developing countries, with aid as the 'supplementary'. But he pointed out that even this general liberal presumption became doubtful if the trade matters under review referred to *prices* rather than *volumes*, and to *preferences* rather than *access* (original emphases). Moreover, the governments of aid-giving countries might be able to do more about aid than about trade, which was a matter of private enterprise and multinational corporations, except where governmental interference, such as tariffs, quotas and preferences, could be brought into the debate.

The relationship between trade and aid suggested to Singer the possibility of a more realistic combined target, with the aid givers being given the option to count agreed additional imports from developing countries resulting from agreed new trade concessions as part of their aid target. He felt that combined targets of this kind might perhaps be worth discussing. The most dramatic link between trade and aid would be for the aid to be given in the form of a subsidy on imports from developing countries. The subsidy would give preference over the local producer as well as over the rival exporter from richer countries, but he recognized that this would be 'politically more explosive'. Looked at from another angle, such a subsidy across the board would be considered as a generalized series of commodity arrangements for the exports of developing countries, but resulting in a fixed addition to the market price obtained by the exporter rather than a fixed price itself. Yet another angle would be to think of such subsidies as an agreed partial devaluation of the currencies of the aid recipient, without the devaluers having to pay the penalty on import prices. But it was not clear whether these different angles helped to make such an approach of direct 'aid to trade' debatable in terms of practical possibilities, or whether it was an economically sound approach.

Aid conditionality

Singer took on the vexed and controversial subject of aid conditionality (Singer1994e; 1995b; Raffer and Singer, 1996a, pp. 153–80). He explained the reasons behind the increasing trend for donors to put conditions on the assistance they provided through programme as well as project aid. First, was the concept of fungibility. Singer (1965c) and others had pointed out that if assistance was provided for a high-priority project, this set free a recipient government's own resources, which would otherwise have gone into that project. The resources thus freed would then finance some other project. Thus, in effect, the aid provided would finance projects which had not be examined or approved, and of which the aid donor was not even aware. This could include such items as military expenditure, additional salaries for high-ranking civil servants, and so on. In addition, project aid was seen to have little effect on the policies of developing countries. For these reasons, the World Bank and others eagerly embraced the concept as an excuse for moving to programme lending with built-in conditionality.

Secondly, experience showed that the success or failure of projects depended not only, or even mainly, on the virtues of the project itself but rather on the general efficiency of the recipient government and its policies. As Singer put it:

> As the rising tide lifts all boats, so a dynamic and growing economy can absorb and turn to advantage even a doubtful project and *vice versa*: where the economy is stagnant and macroeconomic policies counter-productive, even the best designed project will fail to yield its expected benefits and will be engulfed in the general failure. (Raffer and Singer, 1996a, p. 154)

Projects were not carried out in a policy vacuum, hence project lending became more policy conditional and this shifted over into programme lending.

Thirdly, as noted above, there was a general undermining of the national sovereignty of developing countries on which the United Nations Charter was based. The dependence and weak international position of developing countries, and their deteriorating terms of trade, were combined with increasing scepticism about the nature and role of governments in the developing world. This was part of the neoclassical paradigm that came to be known as the 'Washington consensus', which became dominant in the 1980s. Previously, governments were supposed to be the Platonic guardians and best judges of national interest, and aid was supposed to help them in their tasks. Later, in what Singer saw as a 'remarkable reversal', governments were depicted as centres of corruption, policy failures, and rent seekers, while donors and aid agencies acquired a self-confidence of being in possession of the secrets of 'good governance', and the ability to sort out the 'good boys' from the bad.

Conditionality became the instrument to discipline 'bad boys' and convert them into good, based on the firm (and often misplaced) conviction that donors and aid organizations knew what was best for recipient countries and that they had got hold of the 'sacred truth', that is the market-rules principles ('basics') of neoclassical economics.

Singer became a constant and vociferous critic of the 'Washington Consensus', which, to him, revolved around the question of 'ownership' and the assumption of donors and aid organizations that they 'knew the right answers' to developing countries' problems. He argued that if conditionality was imposed on countries against their wishes and their own judgement of what was best for them, they were unlikely to persevere with the aid programmes and fulfil all the conditions. Criticism also stemmed from what became known as the 'fallacy of composition'. Conditionality was based on a common ideology or theory that 'what was good for one country was good for others'. It failed to understand and appreciate that the efforts of each country individually to improve its income terms of trade by increasing its own market share must be at the expense of other countries under similar pressure. And it did not make sufficient allowance for different circumstances, political systems, objectives and cultures.

There were signs in the 1990s that the pendulum was swinging back from the 'Washington consensus' to something like a compromise with the earlier 'Keynesian consensus' but also embodying new concerns, including good governance, democracy, accountability, the environment, human development, human rights and poverty reduction. But the 'rhetoric was running far ahead of reality, as a comparison of the per capita ODA received by democratic and authoritarian regimes shows' (UNDP, 1994, p. 76). Singer observed that applying these aid conditions has proved to be difficult and often contradictory as double standards have been applied. Cutting off aid because people lived in a country whose government violated the principles of conditionality amounted to punishing the population for the actions of their government, and would affect those groups already suffering repression, further deteriorating their lot. Briefly put, as Singer suggested, 'it may matter less to which country aid was given than to whom within that country'.

Aid criteria for allocation and effective use

Other aspects of aid had an influence on criteria for its allocation and effective use. These included: the terms (hard or soft) on which it was provided; its role in removing the debt burden of developing countries (see below); the forms of aid, either through development projects, which raised the problem of fungibility (already discussed), or through development programmes (Singer, 1965c); tied or untied aid; balance of payments obstacles; and multilateral v. bilateral aid (Prendergast and Singer, 1991g).

While the principle that aid should go where it was effectively used was widely acclaimed, in practice this was modified by the multipurposes of aid and by politics. Another modification with important implications was that where conditions were such that aid was not effectively used, aid itself could be used to improve the situation and lay the foundation for more effective use in the future. This could be brought about through technical assistance and training, improved project design and implementation, and changes in policies and administration. Even so, another host of questions was raised. What was 'effective use' of aid, and how should it be measured? Should aid be limited to the 'good performers' (whatever that might mean), or extended to 'improving performers', or further bring in 'bad performers', who might be reformed and improved by aid? Should aid be given on an assessment of past performance or on the prospects for the future, if the two could be separated? Should 'good performance' be assessed in terms of a country's use of its total resources or of the additional resources provided by aid? Should the same performance test by applied to all recipient countries? Should aid be concentrated on the upper range of developing countries where it could be self-terminating with effective use, or on the poorer countries where its effective use would have the greatest impact in terms of welfare? And should the same test of effectiveness be applied irrespective of the source, channel or type of aid provided? What were the best techniques for measuring and improving effective use? Or, as Singer pointedly questioned, was the whole business of devising tests of 'effective use' merely a device to rationalize decisions reached on other grounds, or to sell aid to taxpayers and parliaments, or to maximize returns to the aid-giver?

All these questions had to be answered within the framework of specific constraints. For example, operating on the principle of 'universality', multilateral aid had to be spread fairly widely and thinly so that all member countries benefited in some reasonable and fair degree, which probably operated in favour of the smaller, and against the large, developing countries. Bilateral aid, however, was concentrated on friends and associates, with some thought also given to potential enemies who might be prevented by aid from becoming actual ones.

Within this framework of real constraints, Singer asked how much real scope was left for the exercise of objective criteria of the effective use of aid?

Responding to the aid critics

Singer responded to the 'unholy alliance' of the critics of aid from the left and the right. He accepted that a number of their criticisms had valid elements, and should be taken seriously, but asserted that they should be taken as challenges to improve the quality of aid, rather than as final condemnation of aid, or as proof that aid was doomed to be harmful and counter-productive. But uncritical support and uncritical use of aid could be as harmful as root-and-branch opposition (Singer, 1982e).

The critics of aid were sometimes selective in their examples when they said that certain countries owed little or nothing to foreign aid for their economic success. Many developing countries had owed much of their economic success to foreign aid during crucial periods in their history. Critics objected to aid because many governments admittedly had poor policies and made bad use of the aid received, However, logically, that criticism should not be limited to aid. On the same grounds, criticism could be made of trade. Governments could make bad use of foreign exchange earnings from exports, which were unconditionally at the disposal of receiving countries, whereas in the case of aid donors could exercise some control over the aid provided.

A recurring criticism was that if aided projects were profitable and productive, governments would have no difficulty in raising the necessary funds in financial markets. However, there was a difference between an investment being profitable and productive and an investment yielding the foreign exchange sufficient to repay at commercial rates. Moreover, much of the necessary investment in poorer countries was often in infrastructure, which yielded returns only indirectly and with considerable time lags. A perennial criticism was that aid often went to inefficient or weak governments which patently impoverished their people or retarded economic development. This raised the eternal question of whether or not the people living in countries with bad governments should be penalized by withholding aid. In principle at least, aid could help in making an effort to improve the position of people in spite of their governments, and make an attempt to influence bad governments, assuming agreement could be reached on which governments were good or bad.

Criticism had also been made that the restraint which commercial lenders might exercise on borrowing governments might be undermined by expectations of official aid available for bailing out improvident governments. This could be put in reverse. The restraint which expectations of official aid imposed could clear the way for commercial lending. Loans from the Bretton Woods institutions had played precisely that role in relation to commercial lenders. And an IMF agreement clearly served as a 'signal' of this kind to commercial banks. Singer agreed with the critics that the volume of investible funds was not the most important engine of economic progress. The human capital of a country was probably more important. But external aid, in principle, could just as well be used to build up the human capital of a country, even though he considered that it had not been sufficiently directed towards that purpose in the past.

Ethics of aid

Singer welcomed reviews of aid experience, which forced the advocates and practitioners of aid to rethink and restate their position (Singer, 1988h). He positioned himself in the 'middle ground' of the aid debate; perhaps a little less worried about the critics from the right than those from the left. He felt that the earlier advocates took the arguments for aid, both moral and economic, too much for granted. Singer recognized that it took him over twenty years of participation in the aid debate before he felt compelled to look at the ethics of aid (Singer, 1983h). Here, he identified two separate problems. The first concerned the 'motives' or 'reasons' for which aid was given. Was aid given for humanitarian or charitable reasons or because of a sense of global responsibility, all of which were presumably in the field of morals or ethics, or for reasons of self-interest or politics? The second problem related more to the 'effects' of aid. If aid helped to reduce the poverty of poor people, feeding hungry children, coping with emergencies, or helped a struggling poor country to make better provision for its citizens, then presumably there was a strong moral basis and justification for that aid. On the other hand, if aid was clearly given for reasons of politics or self-interest, and if it helped an oppressive government to maintain control over its citizens, with widespread violation of human rights, then such aid would clearly be 'immoral', or at least 'non-moral'.

However, there could be mixed cases. Aid given for good reasons might be leaked away from the intended purpose and instead benefit a bad government or an opulent elite in the recipient country. Aid might also be given for a variety of motives (as was usually the case) which might be mixed up together and impossible to disentangle. The effects of aid could equally be mixed, some of which helped poor people but another part might be leaked away to the rich, powerful, or oppressive. There were no statistics to decide how much aid was moral and how much was not. Singer's own guess (made In 1984) was that perhaps 20 per cent of all aid was morally supportable, about 20 per cent was clearly not moral, and about 60 per cent belonged to mixed cases. Whether or not such a record justified aid was a matter of judgement, according to what weight was attached to the moral case for aid as against other justifications. What was clear to him was that those making a moral case for aid should be concerned to change the mixture so that more aid was clearly morally justifiable both as a motive and for greater effect, and perhaps more important, that in the 'big bag of mixed cases', the morally desirable element became stronger (Riddell, 1987, p. 4). He supported the call for more and better evaluation of aid but noted that this raised questions concerning both methodology and who should conduct the evaluations. He concluded that the moral case for aid was strengthened by concentration on vulnerable groups and that improved targeting of aid on poverty groups was 'the most important item on the aid agenda for those advocating aid on moral grounds'.

New priorities for aid

In a book written with Kunibert Raffer, associate professor of economics at the University of Vienna, on *The Foreign Aid Business*, Singer identified what he regarded as new priorities for aid (Raffer and Singer, 1996a, pp. 195–212). He lamented the fact that there was no clarity about the purposes of aid. Donors had their own priorities and multipurposes for the aid they provided. The call that he had made many years ago for a 'multilateral framework' for aid from all sources so that it could achieve maximum impact and avoid duplication and conflict has still not been agreed upon. Moreover, he argued that it was not plausible that a single instrument, usually fed from the same single aid budget, and often promoted by the same donor agencies, could fulfil all the diverse, and often contradictory, objectives for which aid was provided. One of the main new priorities for aid should therefore be to distinguish the diverse purposes which aid was assumed to achieve, and to devise instruments properly adjusted for each of those manifold objectives.

Perhaps the most immediate need was for a new look at the 'so fashionable' method of structural adjustment lending. As Singer put it, 'What we need is structural adjustment of structural adjustment!' Project lending had its proper place in the aid picture but its success depended on the domestic as well as the external economic framework which was set by economic policies. If overall policies were sound and the economy grew, most projects were likely to be profitable and effective if properly designed at the beginning. The reverse was also true. The best conceived projects were likely to fail to make their expected contribution in an inefficient and stagnating economic framework. Again, as he put it, 'It is not easy to maintain islands of efficiency in a sea of inefficiency.'

It seemed now accepted that the IMF/World Bank type of adjustment lending and imposed conditionality did not work, especially in Africa, and the poorer countries generally, where it was most needed. 'What was wrong?' In reply, Singer put high priority on copying the success of the Marshall Plan by which massive aid was provided by the United States for the reconstruction of Europe after the second World War. He identified two characteristics of the Marshall Plan which distinguished it from structural adjustment conditionality. First, the programmes and projects submitted for financing under the Marshall Plan were freely developed by the recipients governments of Western Europe and not imposed by the donor, the United States. Hence, there was no question of the 'ownership' of the programmes financed by that aid. The programmes were approved and thus use of the aid money for the approved programmes had to be checked by the donor, but that was all. This was in sharp contrast to structural adjustment lending in which the donor impressed its views on the policies, programmes and projects of the recipients.

Secondly, the proposals for the Marshall Plan were collective in the sense that they had to be agreed by all the aid recipients. Singer contended that by being on a regional basis, the Marshall Plan attained that formidable volume and momentum which gave the recipients the confidence to move into regional co-operation and reform their policies. This laid the foundation for regional co-operation, which resulted in the European Community (later Union). By contrast, adjustment lending was on a country-by-country basis, with practically no allowance being made for what happened in other countries in the same region. Singer felt that it was not inconceivable that the pooling of all aid given to Africa into a single regional programme could achieve a similar momentum in that region. Failing such a major change, Singer suggested that representatives of regional organizations should be present when structural adjustment programmes were negotiated for individual countries in that region, thereby setting them in a regional perspective and fostering regional co-operation. In addition, broader regional agreements would give the recipient side better negotiating power and hence lead to better ownership of the agreed aided programmes in contrast to the striking disparity in negotiating skill and power that characterized structural adjustment lending.

Under the Marshall Plan, the aid relationship was one of partnership and mutual contractual obligations of recipient and donor, whereas under structural adjustment programmes the relationship was clearly one of dependency. Singer called for the regional multilateral banks to play a greater role in future aid. He reasoned that these banks had a closer relationship and more detailed knowledge of local problems and political situations in recipient member countries. They also had a special mandate to promote regional co-operation. A complementary suggestion was for the Bretton Woods institutions to be less centralized in Washington and to have a greater country presence and better links with local institutions in developing countries. This would reduce over-reliance on short-term missions, increase continuing long-term involvement, and make their aided programmes and projects more participatory, and in touch with local institutions and people. (The IMF and World Bank now seem to be moving in this direction.)

The orthodox position was that aid, by increasing investment, would stimulate growth, which would be fairly widespread and 'trickle-down' to the poor. It was admitted that the trickle-down process might be delayed, and that its intensity depended to some extent on the pattern of growth – labour-intensive growth would be more effective in the 'trickle down' process than capital-intensive growth. But essentially the emphasis in the 'aid business' was on growth as a chief objective. Experience, however, had not been encouraging as far as 'trickle down' was concerned. Income distribution in many aid recipient countries had become more unequal. It was not clear whether aid had been a contributory factor but it had clearly not been sufficient to counteract the process of simultaneous growth and increasing poverty. Hence the tendency to seek ways for aid to have a direct impact on poverty alleviation.

One way of doing this was embodied in the notion of 'human development', as expressed in the UNDP *Human Development Reports*, published annually since 1990.[30] These reports have shown that growth of GNP is a poor measure of progress in human development.

Some countries are what may be called 'efficient converters' in converting economic resources as expressed by GNP into human development as expressed by a range of human indicators. They rank higher on the human development index rankings than on the GNP rankings. The opposite is the case with the 'inefficient converters'. This did not mean that growth was irrelevant. Economic growth could be good for human development but that depended on how resources were actually used. Growth was desirable but only as a means, not an end, of development, and hence was not the ultimate aid objective. But the implications for aid were not entirely clear. Should aid donors give priority to the 'efficient converters' on grounds that the aid was more likely to lead to human development? Or should aid be given to the 'inefficient converters', with conditionality to change their policies and give higher priority to future human development? And should aid be more directly related to projects which affected human development, care being taken that in the process of fungibility the aid so provided did not displace national expenditures in desirable priority areas?

Targeting aid on the poor was notoriously difficult. One possibility was to concentrate more aid on the poorest countries but there was no guarantee that those countries would be efficient converters so that the aid would not reach the really poor. Another possibility was to give greater emphasis to social sectors (such as health, education and clean water supplies) that would directly benefit human development but there was no guarantee that within these sectors the resources would be used for the benefit of the poor. Perhaps one of the best ways of giving expression to the attempts to focus aid more on poverty reduction was to make it more participatory by involving local institutions, and the poor themselves. Another way was in the 20:20 proposal under which aid donors committed at least 20 per cent of their aid to selected social sectors, to be matched by recipient governments' commitment that at least 20 per cent of their budgets would go to the same social objectives.[31] This would represent a more 'contractual' approach to aid in which donors and recipients would undertake mutual obligations rather than imposing unilateral conditionality on the aid recipient.

The relationship of aid to the heavy debt burden of developing countries was another area of priority (see below), as was the increasing proportion of total aid budgets that were swallowed up by emergency assistance of all kinds. There was strong humanitarian pressure to use aid money for immediately obvious and pressing purposes and in response to disasters and emergencies given widespread prominence in newspapers and on television screens. But with stagnant or declining aid in real terms, and increasing amounts allocated for emergency relief, aid for developmental purposes was increasingly squeezed (Singer, 1996f). A new aid objective was, therefore, the need to retain the developmental purposes of aid and yet respond to the humanitarian appeal of emergencies. This new objective could best be defined as development of a kind which prevented future emergencies and removed their causes, and which concentrated on the reconstruction and rehabilitation of countries or regions emerging from conflict or natural disasters, in a 'continuum' of aid between development and emergencies.

Both these situations seemed particularly fruitful areas for the application of aid. Reconstruction and rehabilitation provided opportunities for investment at high rates of return and prevention of emergencies turned out to be much less costly than aid required after emergencies had occurred. Singer therefore considered that the situation in which aid for emergencies and aid for development were in direct conflict was 'not a happy one'. A new development paradigm was needed which covered the 'continuum' from prevention to relief to reconstruction and rehabilitation to new development. He felt that we should have learned enough about situations leading to conflicts, civil wars or famine, as well as environmental disasters such as desertification, to be able to devise aid priorities oriented towards preventing such disasters in the future. It would be a matter of education both of governments and the general public, including NGOs, in developed countries to realize that such aid for prevention and reconstruction and rehabilitation was just as worthy of support, and just as urgent and pressing, as emergency aid.

The best reform of the international aid system would be for the developed countries to increase their own growth rates, return to full employment policies, and open their markets to the products of developing countries. In other words, what was needed was for the developed countries to become again the 'engines of economic growth', which they were in the 'Golden Age' of the 1950s and 1960s. This would mean a return to the original proposals of Keynes in preparation for the Bretton Woods conference. In particular, Singer singled out the need for the IMF to become a world central bank which provided the liquidity needed to enable countries to pursue expansionary full employment policies and to restore the symmetrical treatment of surplus and deficit countries originally visualized by Keynes.

23
Debt and Debt Servicing

Singer was an early advocate for addressing the debt problem of the developing countries and the high level of debt servicing that they accumulated in the 1980s. He recalled the history of the debt crisis, which was often forgotten (Singer, 1989m). The immediate cause was the large financial surpluses of the oil producing countries following the two increases in oil prices of the OPEC countries in 1973 and 1979. These financial surpluses flowed into the commercial banks of the US, UK, Switzerland and other industrial countries. Since the industrial countries, taken as a whole, did not have balance of payments deficits, the money was available to be 'recycled' into developing countries. The commercial banks pressured the developing countries to take their newly-found resources at low interest rates, with few questions asked. This helped to maintain their growth rates, in spite of deteriorating terms of trade, as a result both of the higher oil prices and of the concomitant reduced growth rates of industrial countries. At the time, this seemed a viable system and everyone (the World Bank, IMF, OPEC and OECD governments and commercial banks)'were patting themselves on the back and congratulating themselves on how well the world financial system was coping'.

But there was a far deeper reason for the debt crisis. One essential factor was the reaction of the industrial countries to the rising oil prices. They adopted restrictive domestic policies, which reduced demand and slowed down their growth rate (and with it the growth of world trade) from 5-6 per cent in the 1960s to some 2.5 per cent in the 15 years after the first oil price hike in 1973. But Singer traced the origin of the debt crisis even further back to the weakness of the new international economic order established at the Bretton Woods conference in 1944. Keynes' original plans included an International Trade

Organization (ITO) with the dual purpose of stabilizing primary commodity prices and promoting world trade. The ITO, if it had been established, would have stabilized the price of oil. (Keynes' vision had included the creation of a world currency based on primary commodities, including gold and oil, rather than gold, dollars or sterling.) Singer reasoned that if this had been implemented, there would not have been the high volatility in the price of oil and other primary commodities that occurred. Nor would there have been the collapse of primary commodity prices in the 1980s, which made the debt burden impossible for the developing countries to carry. The debt issue was therefore part and parcel of the total picture of post-war development experience (Singer, 1989m).

Three factors ('three cumulative taxes') came together to make the debt situation untenable. First, was the slowdown in the growth rates of industrial countries and their restrictive and protectionist policies, which significantly reduced the exports of developing countries. Second, was the deterioration in the terms of trade of the developing countries, affecting mainly, but not only, their primary exports, and reducing their capacity to import goods to support their development.[32] Thirdly, the rising interest rates from a negative real figure (i.e., relative to inflation) in the 1970s to about 15–20 per cent magnified the debt burden to a degree unforeseen when the debt was first incurred. Singer saw this process as that of a successive tax on the export earnings of developing countries of some 55 per cent or so – first, a 25 per cent tax on account of reduced growth in the world economy, then a 25 per cent tax on the remainder as a result of deteriorating terms of trade, and then another 25 per cent tax on the remainder on account of high interest rates. It was little wonder to him that this triple blow on export earnings made it difficult to overcome the debt crisis through the 'fashionable recipe' of more 'outward orientation' that the Bretton Woods institutions and others prescribed.

By the late 1990s, the market had expressed scepticism about the full debt repayment in the 'secondary market', where debt certificates of developing countries were traded with heavy discounts. The commercial banks made provision against losses due to non–payment of their claims. And the governments of creditor countries took measures to reduce or cancel their claims, particularly those of the 'heavily indebted poor countries' (HIPC). Singer saw that debt reduction or forgiveness was inevitable but that this should be part of a world plan to promote growth and prosperity and not prolong the miseries of the 'lost decade' of the 1980s.

Singer welcomed the Heavily Indebted Poor Countries (HIPC) Initiative launched by the Bretton Woods institutions and other multilateral creditors in 1996, as far as it went (Singer, 1989m). He distinguished between the debt problem of the developing countries, which had been long recognized, and the debt crisis into which it had developed, particularly in the HIPCs, mainly in Sub-Saharan Africa. The HIPC Initiative was recognition of the fact that the debts of those countries were now unsustainable in the sense that they were unable to keep up the necessary flow of repayments on their debts.

This unsustainability had three aspects. First, was a downward-spiralling chain reaction. As a country's backlog of unpaid debt mounted up, so did the debt overhang, which deterred investment and impeded growth, and any chance of poverty reduction. It also reduced financial credibility, which, in turn, meant that no foreign direct investment flowed and higher interest became due on any loans received. Domestic investors also lost confidence and there was a constant threat of the flight of capital. Any new money received was used to roll over existing debts, adding further to the debt overhang and increasing risk for potential investors, hence reducing investment further. Ultimately, the HIPCs became locked into a vicious cycle of increasing isolation from the global market and increasing poverty.

Secondly, debt servicing absorbed a high and increasing percentage of export earnings. If the HIPCs had made all their scheduled debt payments during the decade 1985–94, no less than two-thirds of their total export earnings would have been used up. Even the actually paid debt, which was only 38 per cent of the scheduled payments, absorbed 22 per cent of the export earnings. According to UNCTAD data, while in the developing countries as a whole the ratio of debt stock to exports declined to a perhaps sustainable level of 151 per cent, in the HIPCs it stood at a level of 447 per cent, a clearly unsustainable level (UNCTAD, 1997, pp. 45–6). In addition, the deteriorating terms of trade of the HIPCs had benefited importers in the industrial countries and had been one element in helping to reduce and contain inflation. That factor alone justified special reciprocal action of the part of the creditors. Yet aid to those countries had been stagnant or had declined. Between 1992 and 1996, official aid to developing countries from the industrial countries and multilateral institutions fell by 16 per cent in real terms. Furthermore, there was high instability of primary commodity prices of the order of 15 per cent from one year to another. Because most HIPCs depended on a single or a few primary commodities for their export earnings, this made it hard to achieve macro-economic stability, let alone sustainable development.[33] Therefore, Singer saw one of the ways of making debt service sustainable lay through better and more stable terms of trade.

Thirdly, debt servicing absorbed much of the scarce revenue which ought to have been devoted to health, education, social infrastructure and other 'foundation stones for human and economic development'. The high proportion of government revenue devoted to debt servicing did not sit well with the 20/20 compact agreed at the World Social Summit in Copenhagen in 1995 under which developing country governments should devote 20 per cent of their budgets to poverty-reducing measures in health, education, clean water, sanitation and the like.

All these factors came together to make the debt crisis in the HIPCs an insurmountable obstacle to their development and a major factor in their increasing marginalization and exclusion from the global economy. For Singer, it meant that debt relief for those countries should play a key role in any international agenda for a genuine fight against poverty and for making reality of an all-inclusive global market with opportunities and potential benefits for all.

In spite of its limitations, the 1996 HIPC Initiative was a new approach to debt relief. It represented an important breakthrough in securing the participation of the multilateral financial institutions alongside bilateral creditors in debt relief action. This participation was an indirect recognition of the shared responsibility for the previous failure to create sustainable development and enable countries to service their debts fully. It also marked a more flexible attitude towards the 'absolute preferred creditor' status of the Bretton Woods institutions. This had been jealously guarded in order to maintain the best possible access to capital markets for raising their finances, and had ruled out overt debt relief on any of the loans made by the IMF or the World Bank. The HIPC Initiative also recognized that there was a creditor problem as well as a debt problem and that for every unsustainable debt there must have been an unsustainable credit in the past.

The HIPC Initiative was designed to remove rather than merely reschedule the debts that had accumulated in the HIPCs. It was also a recognition of the need for greater transparency in giving aid and in the lending practices of the multilateral institutions. Singer hoped that this might pave the way for more independent evaluations, with a possible role for NGOs, and for bringing about procedures that were more genuinely based on negotiation and agreement rather than imposition.

Finally, the HIPC Initiative was the first time that debt sustainability, and the debt relief required to achieve it, was calculated according to a debt service/export ratio. The link between the debt problem and the trade problems of poorer countries had often been ignored but Singer questioned whether the initiative went far enough in this regard. He argued that the ratio between debt servicing and exports should leave room for essential developmental needs to be met and for poverty-reducing measures to be put in place, enabling the HIPCs to escape their marginalization from the global community.

Other weaknesses and gaps in the HIPC, Initiative were identified by Singer. Its details were highly complicated and while there were some signs of flexibility regarding certain HIPCs he felt that the initiative should be 'more ambitious'. There was also a clear need for more certainty about the exact criteria applied in judging a country's eligibility for HIPC assistance. There was also a 'startling absence' in the initiative of any explicit targets for the reduction of poverty and malnutrition. Finally, even with the removal of the debt burden, many other obstacles to development remained for the HIPCs. The HIPC Initiative was therefore a necessary but not sufficient condition for real development. It should therefore not be considered as an alternative to continued aid and investment. The myriad of problems that poor countries faced would not be solved until their social investment requirements were covered. If private investors would not, and domestic governments could not, meet the requirement, there was little alternative to foreign assistance. International development co-operation was therefore not only desirable for moral reasons, but also made economic sense.

Singer looked in detail at the pressures of debt, adjustment policies and deterioration of terms of trade for developing countries, with special reference to Latin American countries (Singer, 1989f). He recalled that the Prebisch–Singer hypothesis on the long-term deterioration of the terms of trade for primary product exporting countries had two elements, which related to the characteristics of both primary *commodities* and primary producing *countries* (original emphasis). He showed that debt pressures related to both elements. Both barter terms of trade and factoral terms of trade were closely interwoven with pressures arising from debt payments. In particular, he maintained that in addition to the resources burden there was an additional transfer burden of debt payment in the form of deteriorating terms of trade. He recalled that this was also the position which was maintained in the debate over German post-First World War reparations by Keynes (based on John Stuart Mill) but contested by Ohlin (based on Ricardo).

Singer argued that not only was there a transfer burden but that in fact it formed an important dimension of the debt problem. In relation to the second element of the Prebisch–Singer thesis, the charateristics of primary producing countries, he argued that diversification or shifts into manufactured exports under debt pressure did not provide a satisfactory escape from the transfer burden but in fact formed a part of it. This emerged particularly in relation to factural terms of trade. Thus, as he put it, 'the debt situation unleashes forces which tend to make for immiserizing growth in the Periphery and for widening income gaps between the Centre and the Periphery' [in Prebisch's language].

The debt situation and the terms of trade problem were 'deeply entangled' with each other in a process of 'mutual causation', which was 'much more so than is usually realized'. Singer attributed the rise in indebtedness to changes in terms of trade in various ways. First, the debt burden was a legacy of the incompleteness and perversion of the Bretton Woods system in the area of commodities and commodity prices. Second, the rapid increase in oil prices in 1973 and 1979, which resulted in enormous OPEC surpluses recycled through the commercial banks in the United States, Europe and Japan, led to debt accumulation in the oil-importing developing countries, especially after 1975/76 when the temporary boom in primary commodities other than oil collapsed. Even in oil-exporting countries, such as Mexico and Venezuela, debt accumulation occurred as their favourable terms of trade and financial surpluses engendered a growth and investment optimism for the future. Third, the debt burden was predictably added to by an additional 'transfer burden' in the form of pressure on terms of trade. And fourth, the worsening terms of trade for primary products after 1975 was a major factor, which contributed to the dimensions of the debt problem. What was less realized was that the deterioration in terms of trade also applied to trade in manufactures. Therefore, the shift from primary to manufactured exports mitigated but did not eliminate the role of deteriorating terms of trade in debt accumulation.

Deteriorating terms of trade and the associated fall in export earnings therefore had a direct role in the accumulation and escalation of debts. Perhaps less well known was the opposite connection, that is the way in which debt pressures were a causative factor in the decline in commodity prices and deterioration of terms of trade. Under the pressure of debt payment obligations, developing countries tried to achieve export surpluses. Such surpluses could be achieved by way of import reduction combined with effective and efficient import substitution but could result in import 'strangulation' and not constructive import substitution. This left export expansion as an alternative route. Debt pressures created a need for earning foreign exchange 'at any price', even at heavy cost, resulting in what were termed 'desperation exports'. This pressure was further added to by the neoclassical (anti-Keynesian and anti-Prebischian) ideology of 'outward orientation' as representing the only recipe for healthy, 'sustainable' growth and development, governing the stabilization and adjustment procedures of the IMF and the World Bank.

Under the double pressure of the need to make debt payments in a hostile international environment, and of the neoclassical adjustment ideology, developing countries were pressed to undergo stabilization and structural adjustment measures, prominently including exchange depreciation and other incentives for intensified exports. The currency depreciations increased export supplies but also made exports cheaper to the customer countries, thus increasing export volumes at the expense of deteriorating terms of trade. This amounted to a 'reverse' transfer of capital, similar and additional to the better-known reverse transfer of capital represented by the debt payments themselves. To the extent that the growth in export volume was bought at the expense of deteriorating terms of trade, it represented a case of 'immiserizing growth'. The real beneficiaries were the importing countries although, on a broader view, they might be ultimate losers in such a no-win, anti-development approach.

Getting the worst of both possible worlds was 'no rational way of running international affairs'. Singer found the IMF and World Bank approach too country-specific in the sense that their country missions were not given any mandate to study the impact on other developing countries. Yet, at the same time, the approach was not country-specific enough in the sense that the recommendations addressed to various countries showed a surprising similarity to each other. This 'fallacy of composition', of expecting that what may be good for individual debtor countries must be good for them all, was particularly serious in the case of competing exporters of primary commodities, facing inelastic demand, so that large price cuts were necessary to achieve given increases in export volumes; and where there was often an oligopolistic supply situation (where a small number of producing countries had a significant market share) this could have marked influence on other countries.

Writing at the beginning of the 1990s, Singer endeavoured to 'glimpse what lay beyond the debt crisis' (Singer, 1991). He considered that the effects of the 'lost decade' of the 1980s on the Third

World had been devastating and would result in 'an almost imposs-ible task for Third World countries to make up for the losses in the coming decades'. He speculated about the long-term trends, favourable and unfavourable, for these countries and expressed doubts whether the predominantly neo-liberal counter-revolution would really serve to lay the foundation of future solid and sustain-able growth. He advocated a more 'eclectic and country-specific approach', in keeping with the perspective on economic development that he had formulated by the end of his time at the United Nations (Schiavo-Campo and Singer, 1970a).

Singer posed the question: What difference would it make to the world in general, and to the developing countries in particular, if by general agreement all debts were wiped out? The chief beneficiaries of the debt crisis seemed to have been the commercial banks and what he called 'that mysterious entity', the world financial system, which had been protected and safeguarded, rather than the developing countries. The first thing to realize was the tremendous devastation which the debt crisis had wrought upon the developing countries. Compared with the GDP growth rate of 1965–80, the developing countries lost heavily during the decade of the 1980s. In manufactur-ing, which Singer still considered 'the flagship of economic develop-ment', the cumulative setbacks in developing countries were even more severe. Not all this economic devastation was due to the debt crisis. The industrialized OECD countries had also suffered their set-backs but these were minimal compared with those of Third World countries, and could easily be made up in the next decade through better economic management on behalf of the G7 countries and by restoring the growth objective to a more equal place relative to control of inflation.

By contrast, to make up for the cumulative losses of Third World countries during the 1980s would require 'nothing less than a miracle'. Singer considered it might have to be spread out over 30–40 years at least. 'So we will be walking in the shadow of the debt crisis for a generation or more.' In spite of the much-vaunted 'outward orienta-tion' achieved during the 1980s, even in the case of trade lost ground had to be made up. Investment in the indebted countries and Third World countries generally had declined heavily. This applied to invest-ment in both physical and human capital. Rather than 'dreaming of a return to paradise lost', Singer felt it more constructive to accept the setbacks of the lost decade of the 1980s and ask: 'Where do we go from here?' and 'How can we do better in the future?' He recognized that economic projections were notoriously tricky and that the record of forecasters was very patchy, to say the least. There was practically no area where plausible optimistic assumptions about the impact on developing countries or equally plausible pessimistic assumptions could be made. Taking courage in both hands, he made the following propositions in 1991:

- The international context for the growth of developing countries would continue to be unfavourable and it would be rash to expect the 'locomotive of growth' which the industrial countries are expected to provide for the rest of the world to move very fast in the decade of the 1990s.

- Domestic development policies could become more pragmatic with mixtures of planning, free markets and experiments with 'social market' systems. This may make development policies much more diverse and trendless, certainly more so than the broadly uniform and identical policies imposed under debt pressures by the Bretton Woods institutions on developing countries. The prospect for developing countries may be much less determined by the international context than by their domestic policies. But developing countries differ sharply in the quality of the domestic policies, hence their future growth rates will differ sharply. This depends on the assumption that the international context will be less important than domestic policies – a proposition on which one could differ and which would be difficult to quantify.

- On financial flows, it would be difficult to be optimistic. If there was full debt relief, it was hard to see private investment and commercial bank lending resuming with any vigour. Official development assistance (ODA) would have to provide the bulk of resources yet this assistance had stubbornly refused to rise above even half the theoretically accepted level of 0.7 per cent of GNP. Furthermore, if the above assumption about sluggish growth in industrial countries for the sake of inflation control was correct, this could mean rising unemployment, and financial resources would be absorbed domestically to cope with social problems since 'charity begins at home'.

- Technology may work as much against developing countries as in their favour. Biotechnology, improved health technology, globalization of production due to improved communications technology, and so forth, may work in their favour. But increased replacement of natural raw material, increased importance of high skills rather than cheap labour, closer integration of R & D with production , would operate against them. Nobody could be sure where the balance would lie. But it may be true to say that countries with good technology policies could gain by maximizing the advantages and minimizing the disadvantages, and vice versa.

The experience of the 1990s was largely to support his propositions.

24
Relevance of Schumpeter and Keynes for Developing Countries

It is perhaps fitting that this review of Singer's work over the past 30 years since he first arrived at the Institute of Development Studies in 1969 should end with his views on the relevance of the works of his two mentors, Schumpeter and Keynes, for developing countries, based on his profound experience during the years he spent at the United Nations (see Part II), just as he recognized their legacies following his days at Bonn and Cambridge universities (see Part I).

In Singer's opinion, while Keynes was clearly the leading economist of his time in terms of impact, both on thinking and shaping the world, Schumpeter was arguably the leading economist of his time in terms of contributions to economic theory and analysis of the capitalist system. Singer regarded it as 'something of a tragedy' that, given their very different personalities and cultural backgrounds, these two great economists 'did not click together' (Singer, 1992j). He wondered what would have emerged if the two had worked together and pooled their ideas. But that was not to be. Singer had no doubt that 'Keynes was the more successful and happier both in his public life and as a private man'. As for who was the greater economist, Singer quotes Stolper who in turn refers to Goethe who, when asked whether he or Schiller was the greater poet, replied 'be glad that there are two of us'.

Schumpeter is most directly identified with his analysis of the vital role of the creative entrepreneur 'who injects into the circular economic flow the dynamic elements of "new combinations"' (Singer, 1992j, p. 63). These new combinations could be the production of new goods or an improved or higher-quality product, use of a new raw material, or a new technology, opening new markets, new methods of business and labour management, etc. In emphasizing this as the key element of economic progress, Schumpeter became the pioneer of what has now become the conventional wisdom of the 'residual factor'. This is the insight that progress is not just a matter of more capital and more labour, but also, and mainly, of a question of 'new combinations'. Although today the 'residual factor' is often associated with innovations and technical progress through R & D (research and development), Schumpeter was emphatic in distinguishing between the innovation and invention on the one hand and the use of new ideas by the entrepreneur on the other. He regarded the latter rather than the former as the source of economic progress. It was no wonder that Schumpeter was so popular in Japan, which initially was weak on innovation but very ready for 'new combinations'.

In this way, Singer considers that Schumpeter occupies an intermediate position in the controversy around whether technical progress is endogenous or exogenous to the economic system. Schumpeter did not believe, like Adam Smith or Kaldor, that the widening of the economic system itself creates conditions of increasing returns and economic progress. He also believed that the source of progress was not the laboratory or the genius of the scientist, but rather the pioneering entrepreneur and his 'swarm of followers' who were themselves part of the economic system. He took this position in his early writing although later he came to attribute more importance to the role of research and development in the laboratories of the big multinational corporations. This was not so much a change of view but an 'adjustment of view' to the increasing 'trustification' and monopolization of production in later capitalism.

Singer identified three areas in which Schumpeter seems most directly relevant to current economic debates and problems. First, Schumpeter's concept of 'creative destruction'. This comes from his analysis of business cycles when the recession following upon the preceding 'swarm of entrepreneurs' introducing new combinations creates a 'leaner and fitter' economy, thereby laying the groundwork for the renewed recovery. Singer observed that all this would sound very familiar in the offices of the IMF and the World Bank. In his view, the idea of structural adjustment is the same as that of 'creative destruction', i.e., *reculer pour mieux sauter*, to cut down today, thus allegedly creating the basis for subsequent sustainable economic growth. Schumpeter's 'creative destruction' is, therefore, in Singer's view, the 'intellectual father of the IMF and World Bank approaches to economic stabilization and structural adjustment'.

Second, Schumpeter provided some support for the 'fashionable view' that 'the market knows better than the state' and that the economy in general, and the innovating entrepreneur in particular, had best be left alone without government interference, which was likely to do more harm than good. Third, Schumpeter proclaimed that it was the producer, not the consumer, who ruled the market. It is not that the consumer wants new things but that he is 'taught to want new things'. The person who is teaching him is the producer in the form of the 'innovating entrepreneur and his swarm of followers'. The medium of teaching is advertising. Schumpeter wanted the free market, not because of consumer sovereignty and choice but because it gave free rein to the dynamic forces of the innovating entrepreneur.

Singer is at pains to point out that both Schumpeter and Keynes were not particularly interested in the application of their ideas to developing countries, about which they were not greatly concerned, and which they never visited. Yet, he believes that, like Schumpeter, some aspects of Keynes' teaching are highly relevant to developing countries, that they are related to his overall philosophy and methodology rather than to the details of his prescriptions, and that they were particularly strong in the international, as opposed to the national or domestic, context (Singer, 1984j; 1985b; 1987a; 1998c). On the relevance of Keynes' overall philosophy and methodology, Singer considered that the best starting point is Albert Hirschman's essay on 'The Rise and Decline of Development Economics' (Hirschman, 1982), which credits Keynes with two major methodological breakthroughs, making Keynes, in his view, 'the founder of mainstream development economics'.

In the first, on the domestic side, Keynes moved away from the classical (and neoclassical) vision of mono-economics (the view that the laws of economics and precepts of economic policy were universal and applied everywhere, and in all circumstances) to a picture of 'duo-economics' (where there was one set of economic relations and policies applicable to conditions of unemployment of resources and another to conditions of full employment). This could be extended to distinguishing the economics applying to developed countries from those in a state of under-development. In the second, on the international side, through his vision of a new order of post-war international economic relations expounded at the Bretton Woods conference in 1944, Keynes developed a framework and a perception of policies by which developing countries could be brought into a network of international relations to the mutual benefit of themselves and the industrial countries.

The shift to duo-economics was important to development thinking in three different ways. First, most generally, Keynes' idea that it was possible, indeed necessary, by macroeconomic policies, and where necessary intervention, to stimulate economic potential which the market mechanism allowed to go waste, was crucial as a basis for development economics of many schools and opinions. Second, and directly, this put the emphasis on the utilization of unemployed (and, by extension, under-employed) resources, and specifically human resources, as a source of economic growth and welfare. And third, and indirectly, the maintenance of full employment by the major industrial countries would sustain commodity prices, and sustained demand from them would make it possible, and safe, for developing countries to expand by Keynesian policies without coming up too soon against a foreign exchange constraint and domestic inflationary pressures.

Another direction in which Keynes' overall philosophy and methodology was directly applicable to developing countries lay in his belief and vision that the limits to economic growth and welfare need not be set by financial resources but only by the availability of real resources. Where these existed, the job of finance was simply to mobilize and employ the available and potential real resources most effectively. In this way, as Keynes put it, proper economic management and proper use of finance can perform the miracle of 'turning stone into bread'. As Singer explained, there were plenty of stones around in the form of unutilized and under-utilized actual and potential resources and the job is 'to turn the useless stones of unused potential into the bread of development'. Singer recalled that Keynes' broad philosophy had been described as 'combining macro management, which is the responsibility of governments, with microeconomic liberalism'. In Keynes' system, once macro management was on the right lines, there was no further need for much micro management. The job was not to abolish markets but to manipulate them so that they yielded the right results in terms of full employment.

The international relevance of Keynes' thinking 'lay ironically and fatally often in those parts of his recommendations which were not implemented rather than those which were'. The foreign exchange gap prevented the application of Keynesian expansionist policies in developing countries. Singer observed that if Keynes' proposals for a new financial and monetary world system expounded at Bretton Woods had prevailed, the foreign exchange constraint for implementing a Keynesian global economy would not have been so fatal. The reference here is to Keynes' proposals made at various times, and under different names, for a world central bank, a world currency, for automatic liquidity, for stable commodity prices, and generally for a world system in which the pressure for adjustment, at times of global unemployment, would be on the balance-of-payments surplus, rather than deficit, countries. This would have been perhaps the greatest Keynesian legacy for developing countries. But, as Singer put it, 'What a contrast to what we actually got!' Initially at Bretton Woods, Keynes had proposed an International Development Board and Inter-Allied Bank. Both were designed for the development of the world economy as a whole. The World Bank and IMF which eventually emerged were but 'barely a pale shadow' of the original plans. Keynes also proposed an International Trade Organization, which, had it been established, would have provided global stabilization measures for primary commodity producers.

Keynes' relevance for developing countries can only be judged by taking into account both the domestic and international relevance of his thinking and proposals. He considered that there is a 'clear logical relationship in this extension'. On the domestic front, Keynes pointed out that the micro decisions made by individual firms and individual workers and consumers, based on their own micro profit/loss calculations, did not usually result in a macro optimum for the whole economy. Keynes described the corrective action that would be needed to reconcile the two. In the same way, Keynes based his approach to the management of the whole economy on the view that action taken by individual countries at what was from a global point of view a micro level in their own national interests, and according to their own lights and conditions, may not lead to a global optimum. He then described the corrective action needed, and the framework and policy instruments for this corrective action. According to Singer, 'Unfortunately, his (Keynes') view did not prevail and even the application of a truncated Bretton Woods system has sadly deteriorated in the recent past' (Singer, 1987a, p. 86).

When Keynes' *General Theory* was published in 1936, the great problems of the day were unemployment, deflation, collapse of commodity prices, international beggar-my-neighbour policies, and so on, but 'of all the problems, unemployment was identified as the basic cause of all the other troubles' (Singer, 1998a, p. 104). So Keynes and Keynesianism were governed by the intention 'never again' to permit a recurrence of mass unemployment. For 25 years after the Second World War, what became known as the 'Keynesian Consensus' enjoyed its 'golden age', under which the world enjoyed full employment, rapid growth, greater welfare and equality and, for a long time, low inflation. The developing countries did well, partly as a result of full employment in the industrial countries, partly as a result of high commodity prices, and partly as a result of applying Keynesian doctrines of high effective demand and promotion of public investment in their own domestic macroeconomic policies. As Singer put it, 'It looked as if the Keynesian Consensus had fully established itself as a permanent solution.'

But this was not to be. The 'golden era' ended in the early 1970s. Rising inflationary pressures undermined its sustainability even before the 'death blow' of the collapse of the Bretton Woods exchange rate system in 1971, and the quadrupling of oil prices in 1973. The objective shifted from the fight against unemployment to that against inflation. And the era of the Keynesian Consensus was superseded by what was called the 'Washington Consensus', a conglomerate of trade liberalization, privatization, deregulation, and observance of fiscal and monetary 'fundamentals'.[34] This also claimed to be a lasting and permanent solution to the problems of the day but after another 25-year cycle it too was shaken to its foundations by the re-emergence of the spectre of unemployment, the evident dangers of social exclusion and rising inequalities, and the doubtful effects of structural and stabilization programmes. As a result, the 'pendulum is swinging back' in the direction of the Keynesian Consensus. Singer recognized that of the two objectives, full employment and control of inflation, the former had the advantage. It dealt with the real economy and real people rather than the financial phenomena of prices. It is inherently egalitarian insofar as moving unemployed people to work is one of the major ways of dealing with poverty. And it can claim to have a 'human face' at least more plausibly than observance of the Washington Consensus fundamentals.

Singer saw the relevance of the international dimensions of Keynesianism for developing countries in 'a single dominant fact'. At the time of writing in 1998, he noted something like a US$500 billion a year resource outflow from developing countries, offsetting many times over the reverse flow of aid. This massive outflow was made up of four major items: terms of trade losses; debt servicing; repatriation of profits and transfer pricing; and capital flight from developing countries. Singer emphasized that under the arrangements which Keynes proposed in his preparatory memoranda for the Bretton Woods conference, and which were partially implemented during the 'golden age' of the 1950s and 1960s, ' these catastrophic drains would not have occurred'.

Regarding the national dimensions of Keynesianism for an understanding of development policy, Singer quoted two examples, that of the concept of disguised unemployment and the Harrod–Domar model of sustained growth. Both were associated not so much with Keynes himself but more directly with two of his closest 'disciples', Joan

Robinson and Roy Harrod. While the concept of disguised unemployment was initially applied to the United Kingdom and industrial countries in general, it soon became apparent that the most important application of the concept was in developing countries. The simultaneous existence of open unemployment, disguised unemployment, and under-employment in various forms was a recognition that unemployment is not a homogeneous phenomenon. Keynes dealt with open unemployment, which was the most pressing problem of the time, as a homogeneous case and suggested a single remedy, that of an increase in effective demand. Yet even within this category of open unemployment there was no homogeneity, as work on the Pilgrim Trust unemployment enquiry (1936–38) and Singer's later publication (Singer, 1940a). were to show. With surplus labour, capital becomes the scarce factor. This led directly to the emphasis on capital accumulation (investment) as the source of economic growth in the Harrod–Domar growth model. As Singer pointed out, 'these two avenues of influence of Keynesianism on development thinking are thus clearly and directly connected'.

Singer found the basis of the Harrod–Domar model 'so simple as to amount almost to tautology'. The rate of growth was determined by the share of investment in output (in equilibrium equal to the share of saving) divided by the capital-output ratio. If, for example, the rate of investment is 12 per cent and the capital output ratio is 3 (that is three units of capital needed to produce one unit of output in all subsequent years), the rate of growth will be 4 per cent. If the rate of population increase is 1 per cent a year, then the rate of per capita income growth will be 3 per cent. As Singer described it, 'Simple, but all the same illuminating and also controversial.' The formula was illuminating because capital accumulation or physical investment was clearly seen as an important element in economic growth, just as disguised unemployment identified industrialization and structural transformation from agriculture as important elements in development. More questionable was the restriction of the concept of investment to physical capital. Development economists, including Singer, later placed more emphasis on the importance of human capital, with better health and education and higher skills, for example, improving the capital–output ratio and increasing the rate of sustainable growth.

By expressing everything in relation to physical capital accumulation, Singer and others felt that the formula could lead to a neglect of other factors important for growth. The role of technical innovation, for instance, as emphasized by Schumpeter, was not easily accommodated in the Harrord–Domar model, which also presented the rate of invest-

ment and the capital–output ratio as two separate, and presumably independent, factors. Subsequent development economists, like Kaldor, have
presented models where growth feeds upon itself with constant or
increasing returns. Myrdal's 'cumulative causation' may also lead to
similar results but in a downward as well as upward direction. Singer
observed that with these new insights, the Harrod–Domar model may be
seen as a 'razor's edge' where a steady rate of growth is achieved almost
by rare accident and the normal case would be either inflation or stagnation, or a combination of both in the form of 'stagflation'.

The model does not show to what extent the crucial rate of investment, and the crucial increase in the rate of investment, needed for full
employment growth are to be achieved by public or private investment. Keynesians, while advocating a mixed economy, tended to stress
the catalytic role of public investment and the complementary relation
between the two. The emphasis on physical capital accumulation also
provided an intellectual basis for aid to developing countries. Aid was
supposed to go into capital formation rather than consumption.
Moreover, aid was supposed to be a transfer from capital-abundant
donor countries with low marginal returns to capital to poorer countries with little capital and hence a favourable capital-output ratio.
Singer noted that political stability, human resources solid financial
institutions, social harmony, the rule of law, and so on, clearly factors
in economic growth, do not explicitly figure in the Harrod–Domar
formula but he felt that both would readily accept them as important
determinants of both the rate of investment and the incremental
capital/output ratio (ICOR).

These two examples of Keynesianism, the concept of disguised
unemployment and the Harrod–Domar formula, have had a deep and
lasting effect on development thinking and policy. Neglect of employment effects, the maintenance of effective demand, a full employment
sustainable growth path, and the promotion of capital accumulation
(physical and human) have had harmful effects in the stabilization and
structural adjustment programmes imposed on developing countries.
Singer saw signs that this is being increasingly recognized and that the
pendulum is swinging back from the 'excesses of the neo-liberal
counter-revolution and towards an updated Keynesian Consensus' –
toward 'more of Keynes and less of Milton Friedman'.

Part IV

An Appreciation

'Lieber Hans, you are an extraordinarily intelligent person. But there are many just as intelligent. You are also an extraordinarily compassionate person,and I must confess that I for one do not have your capacity for compassion. But you are something much rarer still: you are one of the very few people I could call truly good, *ein wahrer Mensch*.'

(Wolfgang Stolper, in Sapsford and Chen,1998a, p. 523)

25
Recognition

By general opinion, Hans Singer is Britain's most highly-respected and most-loved development economist. He is better known in the developing countries than any other economist, and is held in enormous regard. Economists there have put his name forward on several occasions to receive the Nobel prize for economics in recognition of his work for the benefit of developing countries.

Singer is one of that small band of pioneers who have stimulated so many of the ideas that engaged the attention of the world community for much of the last century. He has had one of the most varied and influential careers of any leading British academic. His seminal contributions have helped in the understanding of the problems of developing countries and also of what might be done to solve them. These contributions have been recognized in: six honorary doctorates;[1] an honorary fellowship of the Institute of Social Studies in The Netherlands (1975); the Francis Wood Memorial Prize of the Royal Statistical Society (1939); the Alan Shawn Feinstein World Hunger Award for Research and Education (1994/95); the WFP Food for Life Award (2001); presidency of the New York and London chapters of the Society for International Development; presidency of the United Kingdom Development Studies Association; and a knighthood 'for services to economic issues' in 1994. He was included as one of the ten 'pioneers in development' in a book published in 1984 for the World Bank.[2]

There can be few who have had five *Festschrifts* published in their honour in their lifetimes (Cairncross and Puri, 1975; Clay and Shaw, 1987; Chen and Sapsford, 1997; Sapsford and Chen, 1998a; Sapsford and Chen, 1999). The list of contributors to, and the papers contained in, these volumes give an indication of the breadth and depth of

8.	Degree Congregations of The University of Kent at Canterbury Cathedral on 20 July 1999, with (left to right) Sir Crispin Tickell, Lady Ilse Singer, Sir Hans Singer, Frank Fox (Kent County Council Chairman) and Professor Robin Sibson (*University of Kent at Canterbury*)

Singer's influence in development economics, and the respect, esteem and sheer affection in which he his held by so many friends and colleagues, in diverse professional fields, and in different parts of the world. A book on *Food Security in Sub-Saharan Africa* (Devereux and Maxwell, 2001) was dedicated to him on his 90th birthday on 29 November 2000.

To many who have worked and studied in the field of development economics, Singer may seem more of an institution than a man. But as was recognized many years ago, and has emerged from his many publications, his work shows his driving concern with justice, solidarity with the poor and oppressed, and the optimism of the will that has been the motive force behind his mind. Despite being in close range of much injustice and misery, he has retained his faith in humankind and its ability to create justice and humane societies. He is 'more than an institution or an intellect or a disembodied force for good – he is a committed man with a brilliant mind and a great energy harnessed to his will to serve his fellows' (*The Economist*, 1976).

9. Investiture of Knighthood by the Queen at Buckingham Palace, 22 November 1994 (*BCA and Buckingham Palace*)

This is not to say that Hans Singer has not had his critics and detractors. Even his life-long friend and admirer, the late Sir Alec Cairncross, warned of his powers of persuasion:

> There is a deceptive meekness about Hans, an even-tempered mildness of manner and modesty in debate, that tends to conceal the force of his intelligence and still more his convictions. He gives the impression of a troubled, uncertain and reasonable man who is used to being contradicted and what he says very often implies a contradiction of somebody else even if he thinks it kinder not to say so. The voice is the voice of sweet reason and the words flow on imperturbably. Just because he expresses himself with such apparent moderation, one has to be on one's guard against an uncritical acceptance of his argument. (Cairncross, in Cairncross and Puri, 1975, p. xi)

But Cairncross also recognized that Singer is essentially an economic activist – perhaps one should say 'visionary' – full of what he thinks

10.   Seminar in honour of Hans Singer on his 75th birthday at the Old Ship Hotel, Brighton, United Kingdom, 13 December 1985 (*The Institute of Development Studies*)

should and ought to be done, however improbable it may seem that sufficient support will ever be mobilized. 'After all, he did contribute powerfully to get the IMF and the World Bank to take a more elastic and imaginative view of the contributions they could make to helping the developing countries.'

26
Twists of Fate

It is worth recalling the 'twists of fate' that guided Hans Singer's development as a development economist. He characterized these events as two scenarios, one logical and gradually unfolding, the other fortuitous and accidental, that led him to leave the mainstream and join the then tiny band of 'development economists'. The former scenario could be seen as representing continuity, a life intertwined with that of friends and colleagues. The latter was made up of accidents and coincidences.

It started with his fateful decision in 1929 to switch from medicine to economics at Bonn University in Germany at the decisive moment when he first came under the spell of Joseph Schumpeter and his economics masterpiece, *The Theory of Economic Development: An Inquiry into Profits, Capital, Credit, Interest and the Business Cycle*, and later under the discipline of Arthur Spiethoff. It continued with the award of a two-year postgraduate scholarship to Cambridge University in England in 1934, where he came under another spell, that of John Maynard Keynes, precisely at the time when Keynes was producing his economic masterpiece, *The General Theory of Employment, Interest and Money*, and the supervision of his PhD work by Colin Clark, which maintained his interest, and sharpened his ability, in statistics and econometric techniques.

The 'accidents' 'continued with his first, fortuitous employment on *The Pilgrim Trust Unemployment Enquiry* in the depressed areas of the United Kingdom (1936–38). This made a strong impression on a young economist starting out on his professional career, with its particular characteristics of interdisciplinary study, field work during which he immersed himself in the lives of the unemployed by living with them, team work with a young economist who became a senior colleague in the United Nations, and the formulation of policy that was to lead to practical results. During this time, he came under the influence of two other important figures, Dr William Temple, then Archbishop of York and later of Canterbury, who had inspired the enquiry and from whom he gained the moral and ethical imperatives of development, and Sir William Beveridge, who instilled in Singer the role of the social welfare state in combating the 'five evils' of want, disease, ignorance, squalor and idleness.

The twists of fate continued when David Owen, who had worked with Singer on the Pilgrim Trust unemployment enquiry, was appointed as the first head of the Department of Economic and Social Affairs at the newly created United Nations at Lake Success in the United States, and sought the services of either Alec Cairncross or Hans Singer to help him establish the new department. Cairncross was not available and so Singer was released from his post at Glasgow University, provisionally on a two-year assignment – which was to last for 22 years. The final twist came when on arriving at the United Nations in 1947, in the absence of David Owen who was away on duty travel, he was assigned to work in a small development section which dealt with the problems of developing countries due to a 'linguistic difference' between the American and English usage of the term 'country planning'. Singer had had a brief spell at the Ministry of Town and Country Planning in London in 1946–47. In American parlance, 'country planning' meant national planning, hence his work assignment in the UN department. As the department was not rigidly structured in those early formative days of the United Nations, and given his close friendship with its head, Singer was allowed to roam far and wide in a dazzling array of assignments across the spectrum of issues in development economics and to travel to many developing countries. In addition, simultaneously with his work at the United Nations, he became a professor at the New School for Social Research in New York, and later visiting professor at Williams College in Williamstown, Massachusetts. This maintained his links with the academic world and gave him the space and opportunity to think about the conceptual and theoretical framework of economic development within which his work at the United Nations could be placed.

Whatever interpretation is given to these twists of fate, Singer took full advantage of the opportunities they provided to make a unique and outstanding contribution to the field of development economics. The account below attempts to summarize the various dimensions of that contribution.

27
Body of Work

Singer has produced 450 publications over the 66 years since his first article appeared in 1935 (see Appendix). Their scale, dimension and diversity have been truly remarkable. They have included more than 100 books and pamphlets that he has authored, co-authored or edited, or to which he has contributed. He has produced over 80 reports for 13 organizations in the United Nations system, bilateral and non-governmental organizations, governments and other bodies. And he has published 260 articles. In addition, he has produced well over 100 book reviews and comments and rejoinders on articles in academic journals, and written many letters to the editors that have appeared in national newspapers.

The astonishing dimensions of his work go well beyond their number, and continue to be quoted worldwide. Table 27.1 attempts to give some idea of the themes and diversity of his work.

Inevitably, there is some degree of arbitrariness in listing Hans Singer's publications by subject as many of his works cover more than one topic or issue. Several collections of his papers have been published (including Singer, 1964a; Schiavo-Campo and Singer, 1970a; Cairncross and Puri, 1975; Singer and Ansari, 1977a; Singer, 1998a; Shaw, 2001b).

Singer has produced reports for a number of United Nations organizations (including FAO, ILO, the United Nations, UNCTAD, UNDP, the UN Economic Commission for Latin America, UNEP, UNESCO, UNICEF, UNIDO, UNITAR, WFP and WHO), and for other international bodies and research and development institutes (including the Commonwealth Secretariat, the Inter-American Development Bank, OECD, USAID, the Korean Development Institute, the Bank of Korea, the Indonesian Development Institute, the Pakistan Society of Development Economists, and the Japanese FAO Association).

Table 27.1   Sir Hans Singer: publications 1935–2001

Subject	Number of publications			
	Total	*Books*[1]	*Reports*[2]	*Articles*
Terms of trade and investment	57	10	11	36
Food aid and food security	34	4	11	19
UN (including the Bretton Woods institutions)	34	6	4	24
Employment and unemployment	32	11	6	15
Aid issues	29	8	6	15
Science and technology	23	3	9	11
Industrialization	18	2	6	10
North–South issues	18	3	1	14
Keynes and Schumpeter	12	3	–	9
Debt and debt servicing	11	4	–	7
Perspectives on development[3]	89	33	3	53
Miscellaneous[4]	93	20	26	47
Total publications[5]	450	107	83	260

[1] Includes contributions to books edited by him or written or edited by others.
[2] Includes reports for United Nations and other international bodies, NGOs and governments.
[3] Includes broad and historical views on development, including development planning.
[4] Includes a wide variety of subjects: accountancy; autobiographical material; education; environment; human capital, including children; income distribution; location theory; population; regional perspectives on Africa, Asia and Latin America; social welfare; structural adjustment and stabilization; and urban ground rent and house prices.
[5] In addition, there have been over 100 book reviews and countless letters to the editors of newspapers and comments and rejoinders on articles in academic journals.
Source: See Appendix listing the publications of Sir Hans Singer.

His work has appeared in journals in developing as well as developed countries, and in several languages. He has teamed up with friends and colleagues from developing as well as developed countries in producing a number of the publications. Collaboration with others has arisen from a mixture of motives. On some occasions, it grew out of a common interest, which he enjoyed discussing with those concerned in shaping his and their views. On other occasions, it was to give support to young economists at the start of the careers. There was always the ulterior motive of avoiding the nitty-gritty of publication, like correcting proofs, preparing an index, and discussing details with publishers, which he disliked and left to his co-authors in order to allow him to proceed to the next subject of interest and expand his output. Writing with others increased the range and subtlety of Singer's contribution but it could have been at the cost of losing sharp analytical clarity and blurring the line of argument. Those who have worked with him have experienced the inspiration and reward that this brought.

He writes with fluency and lucidity, with a gift of making even difficult matters seem comprehensible. He cultivated this style so that what he had to say could be clearly understood by decision-makers and politicians as well as by the academic fraternity. As Alec Cairncross recognized many years ago, his is a lively and often witty style that only occasionally lapses into facetiousness. He manages with remarkably few technical terms, and when he does use them, he explains them clearly (Cairncross and Puri, 1975). The profusion of papers is balanced by an equal fertility of ideas. He is never content to take a negative approach and underline what should not be attempted. He is essentially an economic activist, always on the look-out for what might be done and concerned to mobilize support for whatever seems most helpful. His intellectual energy and versatility are remarkable indeed. What he has written is easy to read not because it is over-simplified but because Singer has such a complete command of his subject and the power to communicate his ideas simply and vividly. He has deliberately endeavoured to spread the message of his concerns far and wide, and especially to make them accessible to students, academicians and practitioners throughout the developing world. His moral support and papers led to the *New World Order Series*, which he has co-edited with Neelamber Hatti and Rameshwar Tandon since 1987. The series is planned to reach 25 volumes and contains compendiums of leading works in their field.[3]

In producing his enormous output, Singer has addressed more issues and concerns than any other development economist. This has arisen because he saw the whole canvas, especially after his work on the terms of trade between developed and developing countries and his policy conclusions derived from it, and was drawn to address the panoply of big issues that relate to economic development. At the same time, his natural disposition has always been to respond positively to the many requests that have been made to him. The downside of this is that he has dispersed his efforts widely and has not produced the one definitive work which he carries in him.

28
Special Attributes

What are some of the special attributes that set Singer apart from most of his contemporary pioneering development economists? Perhaps four features are particularly relevant.

The combined influence of Schumpeter and Keynes

Singer is unique in that he came under the direct influence of *both* Schumpeter and Keynes, the two great beacons in his academic progress as a development economist. This high-octane mixture has been a potent driving force throughout his long career. Of the two, Keynes has had the stronger influence. But it is the *combination* of the two forces that has given a unique and decisive form to his views and ideas. Schumpeter's views on the importance of technology and innovation and the role of the entrepreneur, and Keynes' thesis that economics is not a universal truth applicable to all countries and conditions but a framework of thinking to mould to different circumstances, have provided Singer with an enabling framework for much of his thinking. Thus, he considers that there can be no 'blueprint' for development which is applicable to all countries (Schiavo-Campo and Singer, 1970a, pp. 3–14). He also distinguishes between 'economic growth', which applies to income increases within the existing social and economic framework, and 'economic development', which includes the notion of structural change at the economic or social level or both, and was the *leitmotiv* of his book on *International Development, Growth and Change* (Singer, 1964a).

Singer has remained a strong and persistent advocate of Keynesianism and its relevance for understanding the problems of developing countries. He points to disguised unemployment and the Harrod–Domar formula as two examples of Keynesianism which have had a deep and lasting effect in development thinking and policy (Singer, 1998d). He considers that neglect of employment effects (including disguised unemployment), of maintenance of effective demand, of a full-employment sustainable growth path, and of the promotion of capital accumulation (both physical and human), have had harmful effects in the stabilization and structural adjustment programmes imposed on developing countries. He welcomes the signs that this is being increasingly recognized and that the pendulum is swinging back from the excesses of the neo-liberal counter-revolution and toward an updated Keynesian Consensus, and has called for 'more of Keynes and less of Milton Friedman!' (Singer, 1992j; 1997c).

Terms of trade: the fulcrum

Perhaps Singer's best-known contribution to development economics is his analysis of the terms of trade for developing countries incorporated in two works in 1949 and 1950 (UN, 1949a, Singer, 1950b). It contradicted the belief among economists at the time of that the long-run terms of trade was in favour of the primary products and against manufactures, and courageously carried a message of historical injustice: that underdeveloped countries had helped to maintain a rising standard of living in the industralized countries, without receiving a corresponding equivalent contribution towards their own standard of living. He later showed that this deterioration in the terms of trade also extended to the exchange of manufactures of the developing countries for those of the industrial countries (Sarkar and Singer 1991k; 1993i).

Recent work has shown conclusively that Singer was the first to produce the statistical evidence for these conclusions, which was subsequently used by Rául Prebisch in what became known as the Prebisch–Singer thesis (Toye and Toye, forthcoming). This has led to a call to at least rename the concept as the 'Singer–Prebisch thesis'. Singer, himself, has never raised the issue of who first did the original work. Instead, true to character, he has praised Prebisch for his 'unfailing originality', his courage to go against the current mainstream of thought, his combination of thought and action, his ability to go to the heart of things, and the way in which he combined his Latin American background and experience with global insights, features which are reminiscent of Singer's own work (Singer, 1986d).

It is a source of considerable satisfaction to Singer that increasingly sophisticated statistical and econometric analyses continue to vindicate the work that he produced in 1949, making it one of the very few hypotheses in economics that have stood the test of time. But for him, his work on the terms of trade was always more than an exercise in long-run statistical analysis. It was a policy guide in distributive justice which revealed the in-built, long-term inequalities between industrial countries exporting manufactures and developing countries exporting primary commodities, and the need to establish some form of 'positive discrimination', or at least, in today's parlance, 'level playing field', if convergence rather than divergence between them is to be promoted.

His work on the terms of trade was also to be the fulcrum for many other concerns he took up in order to achieve 'distributive justice' for the developing countries, not as separate issues but as interrelated subjects with compounding effect, and fructified in a number of important studies and papers. Hence his concern and interest in:

- *industrialization*, initially import-substituting but also export-promoting, as a means of breaking out of the trap that primary production created for long-term development;
- *science and technology*, from capital-intensive to labour-intensive, to take account of the structural differences between developed and developing countries;
- *investment in human capital*, with the realization that the capacity to create wealth lay inherently in people;
- *planning*, in order to utilize the scarce resources of developing countries by governments with the capacity to carry out realistic programmes with achievable targets;
- *aid*, including technical assistance and pre-investment, to maintain investment in development in the face of unsatisfactory export earnings and to release the many latent investment opportunities in developing countries;
- *regional co-operation*, as many developing countries were too small to create viable economic entities and their borders were determined by political and diplomatic history rather than economic factors;
- *an international economic order* with multilateral global governance, which could ensure a fair distribution of the fruits of progress in the realization that the elimination of poverty and a better distribution of well-being is in the enlightened self-interest of all.

Long service in the United Nations

Singer's long service during the formative years of the United Nations system was also to benefit his progress as a development economist in a number of ways. He carried out a wide range of assignments both at the United Nations in New York and in UN regional institutions and developing countries in Africa, Asia and Latin America. This enabled him to see at first hand the realities of the developing countries, and to discuss with their leaders and planners their developmental problems and aspirations. This practical experience allowed him to set his own conceptual and theoretical intellectual framework against the background of concrete reality. He was also able to see the national and international political dimensions and environment within which developmental issues were discussed and resolved.

Theorist and pragmatist

Out of this milieu, and from his natural inclination to be a 'dissenting' economist, emerged certain perspectives on development that have stood the test of time. These include: the mechanics of economic development; the role of the public sector in economic growth; a balanced view of balanced growth; the concept of pre-investment financing; a programme not project approach to development, which avoids the problems of fungibility; the 'myth' of counterpart funds; the notion of human investment; the interaction of education with economic growth; and, above all, the realization that development is 'growth *plus* change', culturally and socially as well as economically. Even his concept of 'redistribution from growth', which was formulated during the ILO employment mission to Kenya in 1972, was firmly grounded in his UN experiences. Singer is also one of the founding fathers of the structural analysis of development. This explains disequilibrium in the balance of trade and payments, unemployment and worsening income distribution by particular properties of demand and supply functions and the role of institutions. In particular, he analyzed the failure of the price mechanism to produce a satisfactory distribution of income.

A number of common themes have permeated throughout this biography that add up to Singer's vision of development. For him, development is not merely about economic growth: it is growth accompanied by structural social and economic change. The starting point should be people, not money and wealth, which gives a whole new perspective on development. Sustained and equitable development depended not on the creation of wealth but on the capacity of people to create wealth. Hence, his insistence on the importance of the human factor in economic development, and, following from that, on education and training, on science and appropriate technology, on employment and income distribution and the conquest of poverty, on the well-being of children, and on planning and sound institutions, all viewed in an international context in which trade and aid were conducted with distributive justice and efficiency so that all countries, developing and developed, might flourish, and converge instead of diverge.

Singer was one of the earliest development economists to recognize the importance of the human factor in development. This recognition evolved gradually over time. It began with his personal experience in working on the Pilgrim Trust unemployment enquiry, his conversations with Archbishop Temple who constantly stressed the importance of people in the development of their communities and nations, and with the influence of Beveridge and the value of social welfare and full employment in a free society. And it was constantly brought home in his work at the United Nations, and in his discussions with colleagues, including Julia Henderson, head of the social affairs section of the UN Department of Economic Affairs, through his realization of the importance of children in development and his work for UNICEF, and during his visits to developing countries and discussions with national personnel there.

But Singer has never been content just to formulate and understand the theoretical underpinnings of the problems of developing countries. He has actively sought solutions to those problems. He has not been afraid to leave the high ground of development economic theory and (to mix the metaphors) get his hands dirty and his feet wet in the arena of public action. On the contrary, his whole bent has been to see good theory put into sound and effective policies and instruments. He has been very much driven by engagement with policies and institutions. It is notable that a number of his publications have been commissioned by a wide variety of organizations. As a result, this biography is as much about practical applications as it is about the theory of development. Like his mentor, Keynes, before him, it is as an advocate that Singer has been supreme. And, like Keynes, he owes his achievements above all to his ability to think 'orthogonally', at right angles to existing ideas, as a dissenting economist, and his ability to carry discussion on to a new plane and break out into a new dimension, as many of his theoretical concepts have done. In recalling how he developed his analytical abilities, Singer stated 'One tries to look at the world from the viewpoint of the underdog – of the recipient, the victim. You may get insights into the world that are not open to people who look at the world from the top down' (Emmerij *et al.*,

2001, p. 51). During his time at the United Nations, and later, he saw it as a duty to challenge untested assumptions and orthodox conventional wisdom, and has probably done as much as anyone to help in discarding them. He has a vision of the international community, properly disciplined, providing proper care for the neediest in society.

Singer became involved in a large number of pioneering ventures. The list is nothing short of breathtaking and makes impressive reading. Many of the organizations that he helped to set up to tackle Third World problems are still operating today. These have included:

- the terms of trade controversy and the formulation of the Singer–Prebisch thesis, which helped to create the IMF Compensatory Financing Facility, EEC's STABEX, UNCTAD's Special Fund, and a series of international commodity agreements of varying coverage and effectiveness, and led to a growth industry in academic work that has continued to this day;
- the Special United Nations Fund for Economic Development (SUNFED) and the quest for a multilateral source of soft financing, which, although not achieved directly by the United Nations itself, led to the creation of the International Development Association (IDA), the soft-lending window of the World Bank;
- the UN Special Fund and the concept of pre-investment financing, which, with technical assistance and the UN Expanded Program of Technical Assistance (EPTA), led to the foundation of the United Nations Development Programme (UNDP);
- changing the focus of UNICEF from an emergency fund to an organization concerned with the long-term interests and well-being of children through helping in providing a better perspective of children in the strategy of development;
- creation of a multilateral food aid facility and the establishment of the UN World Food Programme;
- appropriate technology and the setting up of the United Nations Industrial Development Organization (UNIDO);
- the importance of the social factor in development and the creation of the United Nations Research Institute for Social Development (UNRISD);
- the foundation of the African Development Bank;
- the early work of the UN Economic Commission for Africa (ECA);
- the proposals for action and the identification of new approaches to international development co-operation for the first UN Decade for Development of the 1960s;

- the concept and content of development planning and the training of national personnel in developing countries.

A number of these organizations now vie with each other to claim him for their own in recognition of the pioneering work he did on their behalf.

Not all that he set out to accomplish was achieved, and there were disappointments along the way. Perhaps the greatest were: the failure to launch SUNFED; the subsequent rejection by the World Bank of the UN proposal for close collaboration and co-operation; the departure of the Bretton Woods institutions from their original roles as foreseen by Keynes; the failure to establish the International Trade Organization; and the development of the UN as a 'residual' rather than a defining force in world economic and social affairs. His personal experience during the McCarthy period was also sobering and caused him briefly to lose faith in the UN as a world organization, but this was restored under the dynamic leadership of Dag Hammarskjöld. Like other pioneers in their different fields, Singer had often simply arrived in the future ahead of everyone else, and it could be frustrating to wait until they caught up.

Some of the UN bodies that he had helped to establish have not performed as well as he had originally envisaged. The targets set for aid to developing countries have still not been met. Governments in developing countries have not filfilled the roles that he had foreseen for them in planning, building up appropriate institutions, and tackling poverty. With hindsight, he realized that he overrated their capacity to do so. He also came to appreciate the recurrent problem of the gap between thought and action. Many of the resolutions passed by the UN General Assembly and other UN bodies, and many of the reports he helped to produce, did not automatically result in tangible programmes of work and positive action.

Singer's contributions toward the evolution of key ideas and concepts about international economic and social development born or nutured under United Nations auspices have been recognized in the first volume to appear of the United Nations Intellectual History Project (Emmerij *et al.*, 2001).[4]

29
Forebears and Roots

In his presidential address to the United Kingdom Development Studies Association in 1990, Singer identified Adam Smith as the 'forebear of Development Studies' (Carty and Singer,1993a, pp. 26–34). He regards him as a development economist in that Adam Smith believed in the 'possibility of progress', however pessimistic we may be about the actual progress achieved. He thought of the progressive state of society as a likely or, indeed, natural outcome, speaking of 'the natural progress of opulence' and being enthusiastically in favour of it. Adam Smith stated, 'The progressive state is in reality the cheerful and the hearty state to all the different orders of the society. The stationary is dull: the declining, melancholy.' Singer regarded this paradigm of a dynamic state of society, with built-in growth, or in Adam Smith's words 'accumulation', as what established development studies as a separate sub-discipline of economics.

Singer traced his own intellectual roots to Schumpeter, Keynes and Beveridge, who were what might be called the first modern generation of development economists (all born in the early 1880s), and to Colin Clark, Rosenstein-Rodan, Myrdal and Tinbergen of the second generation (born about the turn of the century). Singer, born in 1910, belongs, with Bauer, Hirschman and Arthur Lewis (all born in 1915), to what might be regarded as part of the third generation in terms of age, although he owes perhaps more to the first two generations than to his contemporaries (Rostow, 1990). He particularly admires the econometric and planning work of Jan Tinbergen, and has kept a photograph of him in his office at IDS (Singer 1993d; 1994n), and found a natural affinity with Gunnar Myrdal's thesis of 'cumulative causation' with its 'vicious circles' and 'backwash effects'.

Singer 'revisited' the work of his contemporary pioneering development economists at a seminar organized by the University of Zagreb
and the World Bank on 'The Future of Development Economics' at
Dubrovnik, Croatia in May 1999 (Meier and Stiglitz, 2000, pp. 517–19).
The Bank had previously organized a series of retrospective autobiographical accounts of what were called the 'first generation of
development economists (approximately 1970–75)', which included
Singer (Meier and Seers, 1984; Meier, 1987).

Singer quoted Rosenstein-Rodan, who concluded his contribution to
the World Bank's volume on pioneering development economists in
1984 by stating 'We know what has to be done – we have to mobilize
the will to do it' (Meier and Seers, 1984, p. 221). Singer added, 'Since
then, we have become even clearer about "what has to be done" as far
as the ultimate objective is concerned – the reduction and ultimate
abolition of poverty and the reduction of inequality.' But, he continued, this clarity is deceptive in two ways. First, we have come to
realize that 'poverty' is multifaceted and requires action in many
different fields, and by many different actors. Secondly, echoing the
Keynesian vision, Singer noted that we do not 'know' any general rule
of how, and in what sequence, these different facets of poverty should
be tackled in the many different countries, with their different histories, cultures, institutions, resources, climates, ethnic uniformity or
diversity, and so on. Growth expressed as the single indicator of GNP
per capita tempted many development analysts to look for such
general rules, 'but poverty reduction is too complicated and too
country specific'. This reality forced development analysts more and
more 'into the hard slog of detailed analysis of different situations'.
Greater availability of data, and greatly increased powers of modelling
and examining the data, may help but it would be 'preposterous to
claim that "we know what has to be done"' from the myriad of situations that confront us and for every poor person or household in the
world.

Concerning 'mobilizing the will', Singer considered that development analysts had not done the job of providing the knowledge that
would allow politicians to act. More and more attention was being
given to include in the field of development economics the problems
of 'architecture' at many different levels – global, regional, national,
household and personal. The problems of 'governance', including that
of transnational corporations, were increasingly important in development studies. Subjects such as financial regulations, corruption, participation, democracy, gender relations, human rights, prevention of

ethnic conflicts, and credit institutions were all designed to 'mobilize the will'. So were discussions of global governance and the re-examination of the United Nations system and the Bretton Woods institutions and the World Trade Organization. 'How to mobilize the will to do it' had become an integral part of development studies and, Singer prophesized, was likely to become even more important in the new millennium. In the process, development studies was becoming more and more interdisciplinary. And reflecting on his own experience, Singer added that development economists must increasingly help to mobilize the political will to act.

Within this general framework of a shift from paradigm to implementation and governance, from growth to poverty reduction (or rather from growth *per se* to pro-poor growth), with its associated emphasis on distribution and the reduction of inequalities, and from general rules to 'situation specificity', Singer identified a number of areas that he considered would receive increased attention in the field of development studies. These included:

- *Globalization*: to create a genuine, all-inclusive, movement that would convert the global economy from a 'winners and losers' to a 'win-win' force, and, among other things, avoid the marginalization of much of Africa, and provide access to the new sources of information.
- *Urbanization*: which soon will result in the majority of the world's population, including the poor, living in towns, often in megacities, giving an added urgency to the problems of local government, civic participation, the urban informal sector, and urban infrastructure and environment.
- *Environmental degradation*: which Singer recognized as a matter of 'intergenerational equity', leaving to the next generation the same quality of resources as now exists, or even better. This issue added yet another dimension to the need for increased 'multidisciplinarity', for studies of urban environments, and the development of new measures of sustainable development.
- *Footloose and volatile financial flows*: which Singer considers deserves special priority at the global and national levels in view of the magnitude of financial flows and the new techniques that favour volatility, 'unforeseeable' by the pioneering development economists. Singer included under this heading the different problems of providing microcredit in urban and rural areas as a means for creating new opportunities for poverty reduction.

- *Trade in services, technology and brainpower*: a difficult challenge, which 'will have to be met' in view of the new measures of trade volumes, terms of trade, openness, balance of trade, and so on.
- *Child poverty*: and how to target action to eradicate it, which Singer regards 'should be perhaps the most important task for development studies'.

Singer realized that others may want to add to this list of priorities but that even this selective list 'will call for new Pioneers to take up the extended tasks for development studies in the new century'.

30
Continuing Relevance of Development Studies

Singer reacted positively to the question 'Is development economics still relevant?' (Singer, 1997a). In one sense, the question answered itself. Development problems have certainly not disappeared. But those who spoke about the 'demise' of development economics meant something different. They contended that development economics, at least in the old style, is neither a necessary nor a suitable tool for solving today's problems. The contention holds that traditional development economics was misguided, and misled developing countries into adopting harmful policies.

What were the specific accusations against old-style development economics? In the first place, the old approach supposedly assigned an excessive role to government, and placed excessive faith in government planning and in the wisdom of government intervention. Singer recognized that there is much truth in this connection insofar as it refers to the early development economists. But he stressed the historical context in which development economics emerged as a lively, separate, sub-discipline of economics at the end of the Second World War in 1945. Pioneers like Rosenstein-Rodan, Arthur Lewis, Gunnar Myrdal, Ragnar Nurkse and Raul Prebisch, as well as Singer himself, were strongly influenced by economic planning experience in the United Kingdom during the war and the creation of a social-welfare state along the lines of the Beveridge report, central planning in the Soviet Union, the Keynesian demonstration of the possibility of active interventionist macroeconomic full-employment policy, and the experience in the United States of Roosevelt's New Deal. It was assumed that these precedents could be readily replicated throughout the world. As for market forces, it was assumed that they did not exist in developing countries, and had first to be created by government action.

Singer reasoned that few today would deny that there was an important role for the state in economic development, even among the most ardent advocates of market forces. The criticism revolved more around the ability of governments to carry out their assigned functions. According to Singer, the position of the early development economists on the question of state action versus market forces was closely related to their belief in the importance of what Myrdal called 'cumulative causation', that development is largely a matter of the interaction of beneficial circles whereby improvements in one sector led to improvements in other sectors, with a positive 'backwash effect' on the original sector. This concept lay behind such ideas as the search for 'forward and backward linkages', emphasized by Albert Hirschman, input–output studies, and the theories of 'balanced growth' associated with Ragnar Nurkse.

The belief in 'cumulative causation' also implied the possibility of its opposite, the existence of 'vicious circles' in which nothing moves because everything has to wait for action somewhere else. In assuming the existence of vicious circles or 'poverty traps' in developing countries, development economists, including Singer, were clearly influenced by the Keynesian demonstration of the possibility of 'under-employment equilibrium' and his view that some external force, such as government intervention, would be needed to break the vicious circle and create a beneficial circle of expansion. Schumpeter, too, looked for an external force to be provided through the innovator and the enterprising entrepreneur, while others looked to technology and research and development (R & D), or to foreign aid or other external-capital inflows, as Singer had done. But, in Singer's view, governmental intervention, even if limited to fiscal and monetary policy, remained the prime method of breaking the vicious circle and escaping the poverty trap.

Other accusations levelled against the early development economists were that they concentrated too much on savings and physical-investment rates as the determinants of growth rather than on investment in people, and too much on economic growth, ignoring key elements such as income distribution, poverty reduction, environmental protection, access to education, and so forth. Singer, himself, did much to recognize these deficiencies and over time to define the final objective of development as much more than growth in per capita GNP. His thinking evolved to include reduction of poverty, satisfaction of basic needs, creation of greater opportunities for human fulfilment through access to work opportunities and social services, and ultimately an increase in human opportunities or a wider range of choice. He recognized that the first approach of the early development economists was clearly 'too economic', as indeed indicated by the term 'development economics' itself. The backlash against this approach was not long in coming. It resulted in a shift from development economics to 'development studies', and a recognition of ethical, social, and political elements in judging how to approach or measure the true objective of increasing the range of human opportunities.

Rather ironically in Singer's view, the more extreme backlash against the early development economists in the form of the 'neoclassical monoeconomic counterrevolution' is in a way a throwback to the early economistic stages of development economics. The IMF and World Bank stabilization and structural adjustment programmes have been criticized for putting too much emphasis on reducing economic imbalances and for lacking a 'human face'. The neoclassical defence is that economic growth is essential for poverty reduction and other social improvements. While this is understood, there is considerable doubt in current development economics about the implied ease with which economic resources created by growth are converted into human development. The *pattern* of growth is now considered as, or more, important than the *rate* of growth (original emphasis), and certain patterns of growth are viewed as hostile, rather than contributory, to human development. In this way, Singer considers that the history of development economics can be treated as comprising two cycles. First, emphasis on GNP growth in the 1940s and 1950s, followed by emphasis on distribution in the 1960s and 1970s. And second, renewed emphasis on GNP growth in the 1980s followed by renewed emphasis on human development and poverty eradiction in the 1990s.

So ends this account of the long and extraordinary career of a leading elder statesman of development economics who has dedicated his life and work to the service of developing countries. His commitment to the cause of a more equitable international order remains unquenched, and his willingness to nurture this ideal, by force of argument and by personal example, continues to inspire our profoundest respect, admiration and gratitude. I hope that readers will find this biography as stimulating and inspiring as I have in writing it, and that the next generation of development economists will seek to emulate Singer's example. He has provided more than enough 'stepping stones' to help them in their tasks, and has fully warranted recognition as *ein wahrer Mensch*.

Notes

Part I: The Early Years (1910–47)

1. When searching for clues in Hans Singer's formative years for early influences that were to fashion his outlook on life and determine his future work, we are fortunate to have a number of autobiographical accounts, which leaves little to surmise or conjecture (Singer, 1976a; 1984c; 1986g; 1992d; Arestis and Sawyer, 1992; Esslinger, 1997).
2. Original version published in 1912; revised edition in1926. Shortened and revised edition translated into English by Redvers Opie in 1934. For an appreciation of the life and work of Schumpeter, see Marz, 1991; Swedberg, 1991; and Stolper, 1994;
3. Wolfgang Stolper, Schumpeter's biographer, described perhaps the most important messages of Schumpeter's *Theory of Economic Development* as 'History matters. Theory matters. Evolution, not equilibrium, is the central phenomenon. The future is in principle not foreseeable. Theoretical explanations are rational but not deterministic. Extrapolation of the past to the future may work for a time but may then suddenly become misleading' (Stolper, in Sapsford and Chen, 1998a, p. 521).
4. It has also helped many friends and colleagues who have sent their drafts to Singer for comment and found that nothing escaped his attention, including omitted punctuation marks and spelling mistakes.
5. Singer acknowledged that Loesch's work provided the main inspiration for one of his earliest papers, which he wrote with Abba Lerner in 1937 (Lerner and Singer, 1937a). A year earlier, he had also written a paper on the possibility of a mathematical generalization of the relative numbers of towns and villages of different size first discovered by Auerbach in 1913, which he 'rediscovered' using more extensive data (Singer, 1936a). Colin Clark was struck by the predominance of German names in the study of the economics of location. He commented that 'The intellectual challenge of attempting to systematize such intractable material must have a particular appeal to the German mind' (Clark, 1937, p. 279). Clark recognized that the graphical exploration and analysis of town size was very difficult unless the technique of cumulating data and plotting them on double logarithmic diagrams was used. This technique was analogous to the Pareto diagram for analyzing the distribution of income which, like the distribution of towns, was also very highly skewed. He noted that Singer first discovered this in 1936 (Clark, *ibid*, p. 317).
6. Wolfgang Stolper came across Singer's letters to Schumpeter when doing his research on Schumpeter's biography and sent copies to Singer. The first letter sent from Wuppertal-Elberfeld requesting Schumpeter's help was dated 24 October 1933. The second letter, acknowledging Schumpeter's help with 'immense gratitude', was sent from Istanbul and was dated 2 January 1934 (Singer papers, Institute of Development Studies, University of Sussex, Brighton, United Kingdom).

7. Her obituary by Margaretta Jolly appeared in *The Guardian* on 13 March 2001.
8. Singer graphically described his impressions of Cambridge in Singer (1997e). A vivid description of Cambridge and Keynes during the time that Alec Cairncross and Singer were postgraduate students is also given in Cairncross' autobiography (Cairncross, 1998, pp. 41–52).
9. I am grateful to Dr Mark Nicholls, Department of Manuscripts and University Archives, Cambridge University Library for this information. Copies of Rao's and Singer's dissertations (Nos PhD 796 and PhD 803) are deposited in the Cambridge University Library and brief summaries of their contents are included in *Cambridge Dissertations, 1936–37,* pp. 68–70. Rao's thesis was published by Macmillan in 1940 under the same title as his PhD dissertation (Personal communication, 18 June 1996).
10. The study by Paul Lazarsfeld and Marie Jahoda on *Die Arbeitslosen von Marienthal* ('The Unemployed of Marienthal'), published in 1933, argued that people have a fundamental need to work for economic, social and personal reasons. It showed the damaging psychological consequences of unemployment and was taken into account in the work that Singer and his colleagues were to undertake in the Pilgrim Trust enquiry.
11. Singer further elaborated on these issues in two articles in the *Review of Economic Studies* (Singer, 1938j; 1938k).
12. Letter to Alec Cairncross from Hans Singer dated 18 June 1940.
13. Letter to Alec Cairncross from Hans Singer dated 3 June 1940.
14. Reference to the 'University of Madagascar' alluded to one of Hitler's 'solutions to the Jewish problem', which was to resettle Jews on the island of Madagascar. Letter to Alec Cairncross from Hans Singer dated 1 June 1942.
15. David Owen was to play an important role in Singer's career at the United Nations. Apart from being the first assistant secretary-general and head of the UN Department of Economic Affairs, he was the first and only chairman of the UN Technical Assistance Board until it was merged with the UN Special Fund to form the UNDP in 1965, of which he was co-administrator with Paul Hoffman until his retirement in 1969. A pioneer of the United Nations from its very beginning, he never lost his sense of 'practical idealism' during his 24 years at the UN.

Part II: Service in the United Nations (1947–69)

1. I am particularly indebted to John and Richard Toye for their work on the origins of the Prebisch–Singer thesis (Toye and Toye, forthcoming) and to David Sapsford and John-ren Chen for their work in reviewing the considerable number of studies concerning the Prebisch–Singer thesis (Sapsford and Chen, 1998b).
2. Singer saw an analogy here with the Todaro model in which unemployment brings into equilibrium the urban wage rate and the rural living standard (Todaro, 1969). In Singer's model, unemployment brought into equilibrium the available technology and factor endowment of developing countries.
3. David Sapsford worked in the IMF's Research Department in 1984 on an assignment to investigate the likely movements in the barter terms of trade

with a view to making an input into the debate of the time as to whether the Fund might devote increased resources to its Compensatory Financing Fund Facility. His 1985 paper in *The Economic Journal* was a shortened version of the internal document he produced, which showed that 'once the then proper statistical procedures were applied to the data, the evidence in support of the P-S thesis shined through loud and clear. The avalanche of statistical/econometric studies ... thus began' (Personal communication, 19 September 2000).

4. *Methods of Financing of Economic Development in Under-Developed Countries* (1952) (Series RAG-2/170, box 6, UN Archives and Records Centre, New York).
5. The members of the expert group were: Alberto Baltra Cortez, D. G. Cadgil, George Hakim, W. Arthur Lewis and Theodore W. Schultz.
6. The nine members were: S. Amjad Ali (Pakistan), Ambassador and President of ECOSOC during 1952; Fernand Baudhuin (Belgium), Professor of Economics, Catholic University, Louvain; C. V. Bramsnaes (Denmark), member of the Board of Directors and former Governor of the National Bank; Miguel Cuaderno (Philippines), Governor, Central Bank; Sir Cyril Jones (United Kingdom), Director, Mercantile Bank of India, Ltd., London and former Finance Secretary of the Government of India; Leo Mates (Yugoslavia), Ambassador Extraordinary and Plenipotentiary, Permanent representative of the Federal People's Republic of Yugoslavia to the United Nations; Hernan Santa Cruz (Chile), President of ECOSOC during 1950 and 1951 and former Permanent representative of Chile to the United Nations; Eduardo Suarez (Mexico), member of the Board of Directors of the Nacional Financiera S. A. and the Bank of Mexico and former Secretary of Finance; and Wayne C. Taylor (United States), former President of the Export-Import Bank and former Under-Secretary of Commerce. Eduardo Suarez acted as chairman of the group.
7. A copy of the report of the committee of nine is available in the UN Archives and Records Centre in New York, series RAG-/170, box 7.
8. Letter to H. W. Singer from Richard H. Demuth, Director, Technical Assistance and Liaison, IBRD, 9 June 1952 (Series RAG-2/170, box 7, UN Archives and Records Centre, New York).
9. Letter from H. W. Singer to H. J. Dernburg, Balance of Payments Division, Federal Reserve Bank of New York, 2 December 1952 (Series RAG-2/170, box 7, UN Archives and Records Centre, New York).
10. Memorandum from H. E. Caustin, Acting Director, Division of Economic Stability and Development to Roy Blough, Principal Director, Department of Economic Affairs, 14 December 1953 (Series RAG-2/170, box 16, UN Archives and Records centre, New York).
11. The members of the group were: John Abbink (United States), foreign trade consultant; A. Nazmy Abdel Hamid (Egypt), sub-governor of the National Bank; B. K. Madan (India), economic adviser to the Reserve Bank, former executive director of the IMF, and Alternate executive director of the IBRD; Sir Francis Mudie (United Kingdom), former head of the British Economic mission to Yugoslavia; Jacques Oudiette (France), director of the Banque Nationale pour le Commerce et l'Industrie, Paris; Nenad Popovic (Yugoslavia), vice-governor of the National Bank, former executive director

of the IMF, and former alternate executive director of the IBRD; Jorge Schneider (Chile), director of the New York office of the Corporacion de Fomento de la Produccion de Chile, and former executive director of the IBRD; and Jan Tinbergen (the Netherlands), professor of economics, Netherlands School of Economics and director of the Central Planning Bureau, The Hague.

12. SUNFED – A Policy Memorandum by H. W. Singer, 10 December 1954 (Series RAG-2/170, box 7, UN Archives and Records Centre, New York).

13. Singer had in mind the principles for the disposal of agricultural surpluses which FAO had recently recommended in Rome and the establishment of a permanent Consultative Subcommittee on Surplus Disposal (CSD) in Washington, DC to monitor their application (FAO, 1954).

14. Memorandum to Sune Carlson, Director, Bureau of Economic Affairs, 21 March 1955 (Series RAG-2/170, box 17, UN Archives and Records Centre, New York).

15. The *ad hoc* committee was composed of representatives of Canada, Chile, Colombia, Cuba, Egypt, France, India, Indonesia, Netherlands, Norway, Pakistan, Poland, Union of Soviet Socialist republics, United Kingdom, United States and Yugoslavia.

16. For example, Walter P. Reuther, President of the United Automobile Workers of America, gave strong support to SUNFED in his 64 page testimony before the United States Senate Committee on Foreign Affairs on 18 May 1956 (Hubert H. Humphrey papers, Senatorial Files 1914–64, Manuscripts Collection 150.D.12.1. (B), box 637, Minnesota Historical Society, St. Paul, Minnesota).

17. This draft resolution superseded an earlier text sponsored by 18 Latin American countries (doc. A/C.2/L.296) and another sponsored by 20 Asian and African countries plus Greece , the Netherlands and Yugoslavia (doc. A/C.2/L. 300). (UN Press Release GA/EF/371, 1 February 1957).

18. The 1956 decision of the IBRD's board of governors to establish the International Finance Corporation (IFC) can also in part be attributed to a desire of the Bank's principal stockholders to respond in concrete fashion to the mounting pressure in the UN for SUNFED (Mason and Asher, 1973, p. 386).

19. I have used information obtained through personal interviews with Hans Singer and from the UN Archives and Records Centre (Series RAG-2/170, box 16) to reconstruct the personal attacks on Singer and what transpired during the McCarthy period.

20. The other members of the expert group were: Dr M. R. Benedict, Professor of Agricultural Economics, University of California at Berkeley, United States; Dr J. Figueres, ex-president of the Republic of Costa Rica; Dr V. K. R. V. Rao, ex-vice-chancellor, University of Delhi, India, director of the New Delhi Institute of Economic Growth; and Dr P. N. Rosenstein-Rodan, Professor of Economics, Massachusetts Institute of Technology, United States. Singer was designated Principal Officer, Office of the Under-Secretary for Economic and Social Affairs, United Nations, New York.

21. Singer, 'Multilateral Food Aid in Context', personal note, Institute of Development Studies, 30 August 1991.

22. *The Papers of Adlai E. Stevenson: Vol. VIII. Ambassador to the United Nations 1961–1965* (Boston: Little, Brown and Co., 1979, p. 149).

23. Memorandum to the United States Secretary for Agriculture, Orville Freeman, 21 June 1961 (Secretary's Records Section, Food for Peace Program, File IX, US Department of Agriculture, National Agricultural Library, Beltsville, Maryland, United States).

24. George McGovern's proposal, made at the FAO in Rome on 10 April 1961, is reproduced in FAO (1961), pp. 121–2 and in FAO (1985), pp. 315–16.

25. World Food Programme, series RAG-3/2, box 468, UN Archives and Record Centre, New York.

26. Singer used that name in recollection of the 'golden age' in the life of Imperial Rome when, for the first time, the welfare of the whole population became the primary objective of government.

27. Singer prepared a paper, originally for publication in *Revue de Science Financiere*, which was used as information material circulated by the United Nations in connection with the establishment of the ADB. The bank was established at a conference of African finance ministers held in Khartoum, Sudan in the summer of 1963 (Singer, 1963a).

28. Letter to Alec Cairncross from Hans Singer dated 7 November 1940.

29. The pathbreaking character of the paper was illustrated by its inclusion in a volume of contributions of 'basic significance' for the economics of under-development (Agarwala and Singh, 1958).

30. Nurkse said 'On the supply side there is the small capacity to save, resulting from the low level of real income. The low real income is a reflection of low productivity, which in its turn is due largely to the lack of capital. The lack of capital is a result of the small capacity to save, and so the circle is complete' (Nurkse, 1953, p. 5).

31. Henry C. Wallich, 'Some Notes Towards a Theory of Derived Development', paper presented at the third meeting of central bank technicians of the American continent in Havana in 1952. Reprinted in Agarwala and Singh (1958), pp. 189–204.

32. This paper was prepared for a volume on *Public Finance and Policy in Under-developed Countries*, published by the Instituto de Estudios Fiscales (Institute of Fiscal Studies) in Madrid, Spain, in 1964.

33. This paper was originally delivered at the Conference on Economic Development organized by the Department of Economics of the University of Texas at Austin, Texas, in 1959 on the occasion of the seventy-fifth anniversary of the foundation of the university.

34. This paper, in which specific reference is made to the inflationary process in under-developed countries, formed a contribution to a Study Conference on Economic Development in Underdeveloped Countries held at the Institute of Social and Economic Research at the University College of the West Indies in Jamaica in 1958.

35. Interview by Richard Jolly at the Institute of Development Studies, University of Sussex, England, on 13 October 1995.

36. This paper was prepared for a conference of African states on the development of education in Africa, jointly organized and convened by UNESCO and ECA and held in Addis Ababa, Ethiopia, in May 1961.

Part III: The Later Years (1969–2000)

1. Paul Streeten recalls that when Singer was considered for appointment at IDS in 1969, there were voices that said he might be too old. 'As we all know, in the three decades that have passed since, he produced more original ideas, books, articles, speeches than many others in two lifetimes' (Personal communication, 23 August 1996).
2. Note on 'Activities since leaving the UN in 1969' by H. W. Singer dated 1975 (Singer papers, IDS, University of Sussex, England).
3. Note on 'Unemployment in LDCs – The Five Main Factors' by H. W. Singer dated April 1970 (Singer papers, IDS, University of Sussex, England). These views were later reiterated in Singer,1971l.
4. The two leaders of the Kenya mission, Singer and Richard Jolly, paid special tribute to Philip Ndegwa for his contribution to the work of the mission in a *Festschrift* to his memory almost three decades later (Singer and Jolly, 2000a).
5. Singer and Jolly recognized the role played by John Weeks (Weeks, 1973a) for the positive and pioneering view the Kenya mission took of the informal sector, and the earlier work of Keith Hart on the informal sector in Ghana (Hart, 1973). See Technical Paper No. 22 on 'The Relation between the Formal and Informal Sectors' of the Kenya mission report (ILO, 1972, pp. 503–8).
6. Singer's model is described in Technical Paper No. 6 of the Kenya mission report (ILO, 1972, pp. 365–70)
7. This paper was included as Singer's contribution to the *Festschrift* in honour of his friend Jan Tinbergen, director of the Central Planning Bureau, The Hague (1945–55), professor of development planning, University of Rotterdam (1933–73) and Leiden (1973–5)
8. The members of what became known as the 'Sussex group' under Singer's chairmanship were: Charles Cooper (secretary), Christopher Freeman, Oscar Gish, Stephen Hill and Geoffrey Oldham of the University of Sussex, and R. C. Desai, who was designated by the Office for Science and Technology of the UN secretariat.
9. Other publications in the 'Executive Briefing Papers' series included: *A Strategy of Development* by Max Millikan; *The Development Process* by W. Arthur Lewis; *Social Dimensions of Development* by Josef Pajestka; *Our Moral Involvement in Development* by Jean-Marie Domenach; *The Economic Interest of the Industrial Countries in the Development of the Third World* by David Wightman; and *The Future Imperative for the Human Environment* by Hans Palmistierna.
10. Other members of the team were Eduardo Bustelo, Giovanni Andrea Cornia, James Himes, K. N. Raj and Giorgio Solimano.
11. The countries selected for the study included: one least-developed country (Tanzania); two highly contrasting low-income countries (Sri Lanka, small and trade dependent and India, very large and insulated with an important industrial sector); a middle-income, mineral exporting country (Zambia); an oil exporter (Nigeria); two better-off, newly industrial countries (Brazil and the Republic of Korea); three middle-income Latin American countries with

sharply contrasting economic strategies (Chile, Costa Rica and Cuba); and two developed countries (Italy and the United States).

12. Other versions of Singer's contribution to the international debate on food aid appeared in Shaw, 2001a and Shaw, 2001c.

13. Colleagues in the 'food aid cluster' and others at IDS and elsewhere who have collaborated with Singer on food aid and related issues have included: Edward Clay, Reginald Green, Paul Isenman, the late Tony Jennings, Richard Jolly, Richard Longhurst, Simon Maxwell, Kunibert Raffer, Sumit Roy, Bernard Schaffer, John Shaw, Chris Stevens and the late John Wood. Several have became authorities in the subject in their own right.

14. Singer has been joined in this assessment by the former US ambassador to the United Nations, Richard C. Holbrooke, who stated 'the United Nations include "fabulous organizations" like ... the World Food Program' (*The New York Times*, 14 January 2001).

15. Additionality in food aid has been increasingly called into question with the decrease of ODA in real terms and the effect of the GATT Uruguay round and the beginnings of agricultural trade liberalization. However, the uncertain effects of the United States 1996 'freedom to farm' legislation on US agriculture, the postponement of reform of the Common Agricultural Policy of the European Union (EU), which has been largely responsible for the generation of structural food surpluses in EU countries, the enlargement of the EU, and the as yet unfulfilled food aid provisions of the Final Act of the GATT Uruguay round raise doubts as to whether the rapid fall in statistically recorded food aid in the latter part of the 1990s is a structural or short-run phenomenon. Recorded global food aid deliveries fell from 17.3 million tons in 1993 to 7.3 million tons in 1996 but rose again to 14.5 million tons in 1999 (WFP, 2000, p.9).

16. Isenman and Singer suggested that a useful way to visualize the importance of the food constraint to economic development in the developing countries was 'to imagine that the developed-country worker spent two-thirds of his wages on oil products and then consider what a limit this would put on growth in employment' (Isenman and Singer, 1975m, p. 207).

17. At is height, United States bulk food aid supplies to India under Title 1 of the PL 480 food aid programme reached over five million tons of cereals a year between 1964 and 1967. At its zenith in 1966, it was over eight million tons, 16 per cent of net Indian foodgrain production, 80 per cent of net food imports, 58 per cent of the total Indian public food distribution programme, and more than total global cereal food aid in 1997 (Isenman and Singer, 1975m, p. 231, table A1; Shaw and Clay, 1993, p. 59; WFP, 2000, p. 9).

18. In 1993, for example, the value of United States agricultural commodities under credit, guarantee and export enhancement programmes was $7.5 billion, almost three times the value of agricultural exports designated as 'food aid', and accounted for 18 per cent of the total value of US agricultural exports (USDA, 1995).

19. The IMF's Compensatory Financing Facility (CFF), established in 1963, was widened to include coverage for balance of payments difficulties caused by excesses in cereal import costs. In 1988, the IMF's Compensatory and Contingency Financing Facility (CCFF) was established to provide timely financial assistance to member countries particularly primary commodity pro-

ducing countries, that experienced balance of payments difficulties resulting from shortfalls in export earnings or sharp increases in cereal import costs.

20. A detailed description of Keynes' thinking and events leading up to, and at, the Bretton Woods conference is given in the third volume of Skidelsky's biography of Keynes (Skidelsky, 2000, pp. 337–74).

21. The United Nations had 51 members at its foundation in 1945. By the year 2000, the number of members had increased to 189.

22. While the principle of state sovereignty was enshrined in Article 2.7,Chapter 1 of the UN Charter, this same article also states that 'this principle shall not prejudice the application of enforcement measures under Chapter VII of the UN Charter on "Action with respect to threats to the peace, breaches of the peace, and acts of aggression"'. This provision has assumed particular significance as man-made emergencies have increased in incidence, scale and duration, especially within, rather than between, developing countries, leading to an escalation in the peace-making and peacekeeping functions of the UN.

23. Chapter IX of the UN Charter states: 'With a view to the creation of conditions of stability and well-being which are necessary for peaceful and friendly relations among nations … all members pledge themselves to take joint and separate action in cooperation with the organization for promoting higher standards of living, full employment and conditions of economic and social progress and development.' The US Secretary of State, in his report to President Roosevelt of 6 June 1945 on the results of the San Francisco Conference, which established the United Nations, said: 'The battle for peace has to be fought on two fronts. The first is the security front where victory spells freedom from fear. The second is the economic and social front where victory means freedom from want. Only victory on both fronts can assure the world of an enduring peace.'

24. Skidelsky records that as Keynes left the dinner at the end of the Bretton Woods conference, some delegates – 'presumably those from the Anglo-Saxon world' – started singing 'For He's a Jolly Good Fellow', and adds 'The Soviet reaction to these strange rites is not recorded' (Skidelsky, 2000, p. 356). Keynes' contribution to the Bretton Woods conference was intellectually and diplomatically enormous, but in the final result, American power was decisive for the outcome. As Roy Harrod puts it, 'The combination of the purely scientific aptitude for intellectual construction with a keen sense of realities and power of adapting theory to practice, and the combination of these again with persuasive and diplomatic faculties, were surely unique' (Harrod, 1951, p. 585). Skidelsky's assessment, fifty years later, is that the agreement reached at Bretton Woods 'reflected the views of the Americans, not the British Treasury, of White [Harry Dexter White, director of monetary research at the US Treasury, and US chief negotiator at the Bretton Woods conference] not Keynes' (Skidelsky,2000, p. 357). Keynes did not have a free hand at Bretton Woods. His main brief at the time was to obtain a desperately needed loan for Britain from the United States to continue the war effort, in which he succeeded. He saw his original proposals watered down by the United States delegation but did not object in order not to jeopardize the loan.

25. References to the work carried out in the Fund and the Bank on commodity prices are given in Sapsford and Singer (1998g).

26. The meeting was held in the hotel where Keynes had stayed in 1944. Singer saw the plaque on the door of the room noting that Keynes had occupied it during the Bretton Woods conference. It was a sign of the changing times that he also observed a larger plaque had also been placed on the door, which indicated that the head of the New Hampshire branch of the Coca-Cola company had subsequently occupied the room.

27. The G7 leading industrial countries are Canada, France, Germany, Italy, Japan, United Kingdom and United States. Recently G7 meeting have been attended by the Russian Federation. The president of the Commission of the European Union also takes part in discussions.

28. Various forms of international taxation have been mooted. In his original memoranda in preparation for the Bretton Woods conference, Keynes proposed a tax on balance of trade or balance of payments surpluses of 1 per cent a month. Perhaps a leading candidate for consideration is the proposal by Nobel Laureate James Tobin for a tax on international currency transactions. Given the huge volume involved, a very small tax would yield a large revenue; for example, a tax of 0.05 per cent would yield $150 billion a year and would be too small to deter genuine trade or capital movements. Other international taxes have been proposed including on air travel, and exploitation of common resources such as the Artic seas. A system of tradable permits for pollution would also lend itself to finance international purposes, including the UN.

29. Singer recalled that when Senator Taft was asked 'Trade not aid?', he replied that he agreed with the second part.

30. Singer has been a regular consultant for the *Human Development Report* and has contributed background papers and comments.

31. This proposal was unanimously accepted as a target by all countries at the UN World Social Summit in Copenhagen in 1995 but has so far not been implemented.

32. Singer conducted a detailed study into the relationships between debt pressures, adjustment policies and deteriorating terms of trade for developing countries with special reference to Latin America (Singer, 1989f).

33. A study of 79 non-oil-producing developing countries for the period 1970–88 showed that the 20 countries with the best terms of trade record had significantly faster GNP growth than the 20 with the worst record (Thirwall, 1995).

34. The term 'Washington Consensus' is usually attributed to John Williamson, then senior fellow at the Institute for International Economics in Washington, DC, but Singer could also claim a modest part in its genesis.

Part IV: An Appreciation

1. Singer's honorary degrees have included: hon. doctorate, Universidad Nacional del Litoral, Santa Fe, Argentina (1989); hon. DLitt , University of Sussex, United Kingdom (1990); hon. DLitt, Glasgow University, Scotland (1994); hon. doctorate, Universidade Tecnica de Lisboa, Portugal (1994); hon. doctorate, University of Innsbruck, Austria (1998); hon. doctorate, University of Kent, United Kingdom (1999).

2. The other 'pioneers' included in the volume are: P. T. Bauer, Colin Clark, Albert Hirschman, Arthur Lewis, Gunnar Myrdal, Rául Prebisch, Paul Rosenstein-Rodan, Walt Rostow, and Jan Tinbergen.
3. Personal correspondence from Professor Rameshwar Tandon, 8 November 2000.
4. The United Nations Intellectual History Project, under the direction of Louis Emmerij, Richard Jolly and Thomas Weiss and the guidance of an international advisory council composed of 11 distiguished individuals, has two components. The first is a series of commissioned studies and three overarching books about the major economic and social ideas or concepts central to UN activities. The second consists of in-depth oral history interviews with leading contributors to crucial ideas and concepts within the UN system.

Bibliography*

Agarwala, A. N. and S. P. Singh (eds) (1958) *The Economics of Under-Development* (Delhi: Oxford University Press).

Ardeni, P. G. and B. Wright (1992) 'The Prebisch–Singer Hypothesis: A ReappraisalIndependent of Stationarity Hypotheses', *The Economic Journal*, vol. 102, no. 413, pp. 803–12.

Arestis, P. and M. Sawyer (eds) (1992) 'Hans Wolfgang Singer', in *A Biographical Dictionary of Dissenting Economists* (Aldershot, UK: Edward Elgar).

Athukorala, P. (1993) 'Manufactured Exports from Developing Countries and their Terms of Trade. A Re-examination of the Sakar–Singer Results', *World Development*, vol. 21, pp. 1607–13.

Balassa, B. (1984) 'Comments' (on Singer's terms of trade thesis), in G. M. Meier and D. Seers (1984), pp. 304–11.

Beveridge, W. W. (1942) *Social Insurance and Allied Services* (New York: Macmillan).

—— (1944) *Full Employment in a Free Society* (London: Macmillan).

Blaug, M. (1986) *Great Economists Before Keynes* (London: Wheatsheaf).

Bleaney, M. and D. Greenaway (1993) 'Long-Run Trends in the Relative Price of Primary Commodities and in the Terms of Trade of Developing Countries', *Oxford Economic Papers*, vol. 45, no. 3, October, pp. 349–63.

Booth, A. (1985) 'Economists and Points Rationing in the Second World War', *Journal of European Economic History*, vol. 14, pp. 297–316.

Brandt, W. (1980) *North–South: A Programme for Survival*. The Report of the Independent Commission on International Development Issues under the Chairmanship of Willy Brandt (Cambridge, Mass.: The MIT Press).

—— (1983) *Common Crisis. North–South Co-operation for World Recovery. The Brandt Commission 1983* (London: Pan Books).

Cairncross, A. (1993) *Austin Robinson. The Life of an Economic Adviser* (Basingstoke, London and New York: Macmillan and St Martin's Press).

—— (1998) *Living with the Century* (London: Lynx Publishers).

Cairncross, A. and M. Puri (eds) (1975) *The Strategy of International Development. Essays in the Economics of Backwardness by H. W. Singer* (Basingstoke and London: Macmillan).

—— (eds)(1976) *Employment, Income Distribution and Development Strategy. Problems of the Developing Countries. Essays in Honour of H. W. Singer* (Basingstoke and London: Macmillan).

Cambridge University (1937) *Cambridge Dissertations (1936–37), Faculty of Economics and Politics* (Cambridge: Cambridge University Library).

Carlsson, B. and N. Hatti (1999) 'Ekonomportrattet: Hans W. Singer (1910–)' (Portrait of an Economist: Hans W. Singer (1910–)' in Swedish), *Ekonomisk Debatt*, vol. 27, no. 5, pp. 281–9.

---

* Publications by Hans Singer and in association with others are listed separately in the Appendix.

Cassen, R. H. and Associates (1986) *Does Aid Work?* (Oxford: Oxford University Press).

Chen, J. and D. Sapsford (eds) (1997) 'Economic Development and Policy. Professor Sir Hans Singer's Contribution to Development Economics', *World Development*, vol. 25, no. 11, Special Section, pp. 1853–956.

Chenery, H., M. S. Ahluswalia, C. Bell, J. Duloy and R. Jolly (eds) (1974) *Redistribution with Growth. Policies to Improve Income Distribution in Developing Countries in the Context of Economic Growth* (London: Published for the World Bank and the Institute for Development Studies by Oxford University Press).

Clark, C. (1937) *National Income and Outlay* (London: Macmillan).

—— (1940) *Conditions of Economic Progress* (London: Macmillan).

Clay, E. and D. J. Shaw (eds) (1987) *Poverty, Development and Food. Essays in Honour of H. W. Singer on his 75th Birthday* (Basingstoke and London: Macmillan).

Cornia, G. A., R. Jolly and F. Stewart (eds) (1987) *Adjustment with a Human Face. Protecting the Vulnerable and Promoting Growth. A Study by UNICEF.* 2 vols (Oxford: Clarendon Press).

Cuddington, J. and C. Urzua (1989) 'Trends and Cycles in the Net Barter Terms of Trade: A New Approach', *The Economic Journal*, vol. 99, no. 396, pp. 426–42.

de Seynes, P. (1956) 'Economic Development Fund. U.N. Official Explains Origins and Aims of the Proposal', *Herald Tribune*, 1 August.

Devereux, S. and S. Maxwell (eds) (2001) *Food Security in Sub-Saharan Africa* (London: ITDG Publishing).

Emmerij, L. (1974) 'A New Look at Some Strategies for Increasing Employment in Africa', *International Labour Review*, vol. 110, no.3, pp. 199–218.

Emmerij, L., R. Jolly and T. Weiss (2001) *Ahead of the Curve? UN Ideas and Global Challenges* (Bloomington, IN: Indiana University Press).

Esslinger, H. U. (1997) '"… More of Keynes and Less of Milton Friedman". Sir Hans Singer's Contribution to Economics', *Review of Political Economy*, vol. 8, no. 4, pp. 367–78. Reproduced in Singer, 1998a.

FAO (1954) *Disposal of Agricultural Surpluses. Principles Recommended by FAO* (Rome: Food and Agriculture Organization of the United Nations).Revised with latest edition FAO (1992) *Principles of Surplus Disposal and Consultative Obligations of Member States* (Rome: Food and Agriculture Organization of the United Nations).

—— (1955) *Uses of Agricultural Surpluses to Finance Economic Development in Under-Developed Countries: A Pilot Study in India.* Commodity Policy Studies No. 6 (Rome: Food and Agricutural Organization of the United Nations)

—— (1956) *Functions of a World Food Reserve. Scope and Limitations.* Commodity Policy Studies No. 10 (Rome: Food and Agriculture Organization of the United Nations).

—— (1961) 'Report on an Expanded Program of Surplus Food Utilization', in *Development Through Food. A Strategy for Surplus Utilization.* FFHC Study No. 2 (Rome: Food and Agriculture Organization of the United Nations, pp. 69–117). Republished in FAO (1985), pp. 223–343.

—— (1983) *Approaches to Food Security.* Economic and Social Development Paper No. 32 (Rome: Food and Agriculture Organization of the United Nations).

—— (1985) *Food for Development.* Economic and Social Development Paper No. 34 (Rome: Food and Agriculture Organization of the United Nations).

Fei, J. and G. Ranis (1964) *Development of the Labor Surplus Economy: Theory and Policy* (Homewood, IL: Irwin).

Financial Times (1999) 'Reflections of a Knowledge Worker', 27 April, p. 12.

Grilli, E. and M. C. Yang (1988) 'Primary Commodity Prices, Manufactured Goods Prices and the Terms of Trade of Developing Countries: What the Long-Run Shows', *World Bank Economic Review*, vol. 2, no. 1, January, pp. 1–47.

Hadwen, J. G. and J. Kaufmann (1960) *How United Nations Decisions are Made* (Leyden: A. W. Sythoff).

Hagen, E. (1962) *On the Theory of Social Change. How Economic Growth Begins* (Homewood, IL: The Dorsey Press).

Hall, P. (ed.) (1989) *The Political Power of Economic Ideas: Keynesianism across Nations* (Princeton: Princeton University Press).

Harris, J. R. and M. P. Todaro (1970) 'Migration, Unemployment and Development: A Two-Sector Analysis', *American Economic Review*, vol. 60, pp. 126–40.

Harrod, R. F. (1951) *The Life of John Maynard Keynes* (New York: Harcourt, Brace).

Hart, K. (1973) 'Informal Income Opportunities and Urban Employment in Ghana', *Journal of Modern African Studies*, vol. 11, no. 1, March.

Helleiner, G. (1981) 'The Refsnes Seminar: Economic Theory and the North–South Negotiations', *World Development*, vol. 9, no. 6, p. 545.

Higgins, B. (1959) *Economic Development. Principles, Problems and Policies* (London: Constable).

Hirschman, A. O. (1981) 'The Rise and Decline of Development Economics', in *Essays in Trespassing* (New York: Cambridge University Press).

—— (1982) 'The Rise and Decline of Development Economics', in M. Gersovitz (ed.) *The Theory and Experience of Economic Development : Essays in Honour of Sir W. Arthur Lewis* (London: Allen & Unwin).

Hoffman, P. (1957) 'Blueprint for Foreign Aid', *New York Times Magazine*, 17 February.

—— (1964) 'Introduction', in Singer (1964).

Hopkins, R. F. (1992) 'Reform in the International Food Aid Regime: The Role of Consensual Knowledge', *International Organization*, vol. 46, no. 1, Winter, pp. 225–64.

ILO (1970) *Towards Full Employment. A Program for Colombia, prepared by an Inter-Agency Team Organized by ILO* (Geneva: International Labour Office).

—— (1971) *Matching Employment Opportunities and Expectations. A Program of Action for Ceylon* (Geneva: International Labour Office).

—— (1972) *Employment, Incomes and Equality. A Strategy for Increasing Productive Employment in Kenya* (Geneva: International Labour Office).

Johnston, B. and J. Mellor (1961) 'The Role of Agriculture in Economic Development', *American Economic Review*, vol. 51, no. 4, September, pp. 566–93.

Jolly, M. (2001) 'Obituary of Ilse Singer', *The Guardian*, 13 March.

Jolly, R. (1985) 'Adjustment with a Human Face'. The Barbara Ward Memorial Lecture at the 18th World Conference of the Society for International Development, Rome, July (New York: UNICEF).

—— (1998) 'Redistribution without Growth', in D. Sapsford and J. Chen (1998a), pp. 172–82.

Kapur, D., J. P. Lewis and R. Webb (1997) *The World Bank. Its First Half Century. Vol. 1, History* (Washington, DC: The Brookings Institution).

Kaufmann, J. (1980) 'Chapter 10. Turning Failure into Success: The Story of SUNFED, the U.N. Special Fund and the U.N. Capital Development Fund', in

United Nations Decision Making (Alphen aan den Rijn, The Netherlands and Rockville, MA: Sijthoff and Noordhoff).

Keynes, J. M. (1919) *The Economic Consequences of the Peace* (London: Macmillan).

—— (1936) *The General Theory of Employment, Interest and Money* (London: Macmillan).

Kiker, B. F. (1967) 'The Concept of Human Capital in the History of Economic Thought', *Indian Economic Journal*, January–March.

Kindleberger, C. P. (1956) *The Terms of Trade: A European Case Study* (New York and London: Technical Press of MIT, John Wiley and Chapman Hall).

Krohn, C.-D. (1993) *Intellectuals in Exile. Refugee Scholars at the New School for Social Research* (Amherst: University of Massachusetts Press).

Labouisse, H. (1972) 'Foreword', in Singer (1972d).

League of Nations (1945) *Industrialization and Foreign Trade*. League of Nations Series II. Economic and Financial 1945.II.A.10 (Geneva: League of Nations).

Lewis, W. A. (1954) 'Economic Development with Unlimited Supplies of Labour', *Manchester School of Economics and Social Studies*, vol. xxii, no. 2, pp. 139–91.

—— (1955) *The Theory of Economic Growth* (London: Allen & Unwin).

Leys, C. (1975) *Underdevelopment in Kenya* (Los Angeles: University of California Press).

Marz, E. (1991) *Joseph Schumpeter, Scholar, Teacher and Politician* (New Haven, CN and London: Yale University Press).

Mason, E. S. and R. E. Asher (1973) *The World Bank Since Bretton Woods* (Washington, DC: The Brookings Institution).

McCullough, D. (1992) *Truman* (New York: Simon & Schuster).

Meier, G. M. (1964) *Leading Issues in Development Economics* (New York: Oxford University Press).

—— (1987) *Pioneers in Development, Second Series* (New York: Published by Oxford University Press for the World Bank).

Meier, G. M. and D. Seers (eds) (1984) *Pioneers in Development* (New York: Published for the World Bank by Oxford University Press).

Meier, G. M. and J. E. Stiglitz (eds) (2000) *Frontiers of Development. The Future in Perspective* (Oxford and New York: A Co-publication of the World Bank and Oxford University Press).

Moggridge, D. E. (1992) *Maynard Keynes. An Economist's Biography* (London and New York: Routledge).

Mongiovi, G. (1996) 'Emigre Economists at the New School, 1933–1945', in H. Hagemann (ed.), *Die deutschsprachige wirtschaftswissenschaftliche Emigration nach 1933* (Marburg: Metropolis Verlag).

Morse, D. (1968) 'The World Employment Programme', *International Labour Review*, June, pp. 517–40.

Ndegwa, P. and J. P. Powelson (eds) (1973) *Employment in Africa: Some Critical Issues* (Geneva: International Labour Office).

Nurkse, R. (1953) *Problems of Capital Formation in Underdeveloped Countries* (Oxford: Basil Blackwell).

Powell, A. (1991) 'Commodity and Developing Country Terms of Trade: What Does the Long Run Show?', *The Economic Journal*, vol. 101, no. 409, pp. 1485–96.

Prebisch, R. (1950) *The Economic Development of Latin America and its Principal Problems* (Santiago, Chile: United Nations Economic Commission for Latin

America). (Also published in *Economic Bulletin for Latin America*, vol. 7, no. 1, 1962, pp. 1–22).

Reid, E. (1973) *Strengthening the World Bank* (Chicago: Adlai Stevenson Institute).

Reinhart, C. and P. Wickham (1994) 'Commodity Prices: Cyclical Weakness or Secular Decline?', *IMF Staff Papers*, vol. 41, no. 2, pp. 175–213.

Republic of Kenya (1965) *African Socialism and its Application to Planning in Kenya*. Sessional Paper No. 10 (Nairobi: National Assembly, Government of Kenya).

Riddell, R. (1987) *Foreign Aid Reconsidered* (London and Baltimore, MA: Overseas Development Institute, James Currey and The Johns Hopkins University Press).

Robinson, A. (1976) 'The Economic Development of Malthusia', in Sir A. Cairncross and M. Puri (1976), pp. 181–92.

Robinson, J. (1936) 'Disguised Unemployment', *The Economic Journal*, vol. 46, June.

Rostow, W. W. (1990) *Theorists of Economic Growth from David Hume to the Present with a Perspective on the Next Century* (New York: Oxford University Press).

Ruttan, V. W. (1996) *United States Development Assistance Policy. The Domestic Politics of Foreign Economic Aid* (Baltimore, MA: The Johns Hopkins University Press).

Sapsford, D. (1985) 'The Statistical Debate on the Net Barter Terms of Trade between Primary Commodities and Manufactures: A Comment and Some Additional Evidence', *The Economic Journal*, vol. 95, no. 379, September, pp. 781–8.

—— (1990) 'Primary Commodity Prices and the Terms of Trade'. *Economic Journal*, vol. 66, no. 195, pp. 34–56.

—— and V. N. Balasubramanyan (1994) 'The Long-Run Behaviour of the Relative Price of Primary Commodities: Statistical Evidence and Policy Implications', *World Development*, vol. 2, no. 11, pp. 1737–45.

—— and J. Chen (eds) (1998a) *Development Economics and Policy. The Conference Volume to Celebrate the 85th Birthday of Professor Sir Hans Singer* (Basingstoke and London: Macmillan).

—— and J. Chen (1998b)'The Prebisch–Singer Terms of Trade Hypothesis: Some (Very) New Evidence', in D. Sapsford and J. Chen (1998a), pp. 27–38.

—— and J. Chen (eds) (1999) 'The Prebisch–Singer Thesis: A Thesis for the New Millennium', *Journal of International Development*, vol. 11, no. 6, *Policy Arena*, pp. 863–916.

Schultz, T. W. (1961) 'Investment in Human Capital', *American Economic Review*, vol. 51, March.

—— (1964) *Transforming Traditional Agriculture* (New Haven, CT: Yale University Press).

Schumpeter, J. A. (translated by Redvers Opie) (1934) *The Theory of Economic Development: An Inquiry into Profits, Capital, Credit, Interest and the Business Cycle* (Cambridge, Mass.: Harvard University Press). (1st edn *Theorie der wirtschaftlichen Entwicklung* (Leipzig: Duncker & Humbolt, 1912); 2nd edn *Theorie der wirtschaftlichen Entwicklung. Eine Untersuchung uber Unternehmergewin, Kapital, Kredit, Zins und den Konjunkturzyklus* (Munchen und Leipzig: Duncker & Humblot, 1926).

Sen, A. (1981) *Poverty and Famines. An Essay on Entitlement and Deprivation* (Oxford: Clarendon Press).

Shaw, D. J. (1998a) 'The World Food Programme: Linking Relief and Development', in D. Sapsford and J. Chen (1998a), pp. 437–84.

—— (1998b) 'The World Bank's Hidden History. A Review Article', *Canadian Journal of Development Studies*, vol. xix, no. 1, pp. 175–86.

—— (2001a) 'The Opportunity and the Challenge: H. W. Singer's Contribution to the International Debate on Food Aid', *Canadian Journal of Development Studies*, vol. xxii, no. 1, March, pp. 7–31. Also published in Shaw, 2001c.

—— (2001b) *The UN World Food Programme and the Development of Food Aid* (Basingstoke and London: Macmillan/Palgrave).

—— (ed.) (2001c) *International Development Co-operation. Selected Essays by H. W. Singer on Aid and the United Nations System* (Basingstoke and London: Macmillan/Palgrave).

Shaw, D. J. and E. Clay (1993) *World Food Aid. Experiences of Recipients and Donors* (Rome, London and Portsmouth NH: World Food Programme in association with James Currey and Heinemann).

Simmons, M. (1985) 'Creative Force at the UN. An Appreciation of the Work of Hans Singer', *The Guardian*, 29 November.

Skidelsky, R. (1992) *John Maynard Keynes. Volume Two. The Economist as Saviour 1920–1937* (London: Penguin Books).

—— (1996) *Keynes* (Oxford: Oxford University Press).

—— (2000) *John Maynard Keynes. Volume Three. Fighting for Britain 1937–1946* (Basingstoke and London: Macmillan).

Spraos, J. (1980) 'The Statistical Debate on the Net Barter Terms of Trade between Primary Products and Manufactures', *The Economic Journal*, vol. 90, no. 357, January, pp. 107–28.

—— (1983) *Inequalizing Trade* (Oxford: Clarendon Press).

Stolper, W. (1994) *Joseph Alois Schumpeter – The Public Life of a Private Man* (Princeton, NJ: Princeton University Press).

—— (1998) 'Joseph A. Schumpeter: The Man and the Economist', in D. Sapsford and J. Chen (1998), pp. 513–33.

Streeten, P. (1981) *Development Perspectives* (Basingstoke and London: Macmillan).

—— (1982) 'Approaches to a New International Economic Order', *World Development*, vol. 10, no. 1, January.

Swedberg, R. (1991) *Joseph A. Schumpeter. His Life and Work* (Cambridge: Polity Press)

The Economist (1976) 'Tribute to H. W. Singer', 26 June, p. 56.

Thirlwall, A. P. (1995) 'The Terms of Trade, Debt and Development with particular reference to Africa', *African Development Review*, June (Abidjan: African Development Bank).

Thirlwall, A. and J. Bergevin (1985) 'Trends, Cycles and Assymmetries in the Terms of Trade of Primary Commodities from Developed and Less Developed Countries', *World Development*, vol. 13, no. 7, July, pp. 805–17.

Thorbecke, E. (1973) 'The Employment Problem. A Critical Evaluation of the Four ILO Comprehensive Country Reports', in ILO, *Strategies for Employment Promotion* (Geneva: International Labour Organization).

Timmins, N. (1996) *The Five Giants: A Biography of the Welfare State* (London: Fontana).

Todaro, M. P. (1969) 'A Model of Labour Migration and Urban Unemployment in Less Developed Countries', *American Economic Review*, vol. LIX, March, pp. 138–48.

Toye, J. and R. Toye (forthcoming) 'The Origin of the Prebisch–Singer Thesis', in J. Toye, and R. Toye *Trade, Finance and Development*. The United Nations Intellectual History Project (Bloomington, IN: Indiana University Press); also in *History of Political Economy* (forthcoming).

ul Haq, M., R. Jolly, P. Streeten and K. Haq (eds) (1993) *The United Nations and the Bretton Woods Institutions: New Challenges for the 21st Century*. Report of the North South Roundtable Session, Bretton Woods, New Hampshire, United States, September 1993 (New York: North South Roundtable, Society for International Development).

UN (1949a) *Relative Prices of Exports and Imports of Underdeveloped Countries: A Study of Post-War Terms of Trade between Under-Developed and Industrialized Countries*. No. 1949, II, B.3. (Lake Success: United Nations Department of Economic and Social Affairs).(Original title of draft document, *Post-War Price Relations between Underdeveloped and Industrial Countries*).

—— (1949b) *Report of the Economic and Employment Commission on the Third Session of the Sub-Commission held from 21 March to 11 April 1949*. Document No. E/CN.1/65 (Lake Success, NY: United Nations Sub-Commission on Economic Development).

—— (1949c) *Official Records of the Economic and Social Council: Ninth Session*. Supplement No. 11B, pp. 22–24.

—— (1949d) *Methods of Financing Economic Development in Under- Developed Countries*. Document E/1333/Rev/ 1, No. 1949.11 (New York: United Nations).

—— (1950) *Formulation and Execution of Development Programs* (New York: United Nations).

—— (1951a) *Measures for the Economic Development of Under-Developed Countries*. Report by a Group of Experts appointed by the Secretary-General of the United Nations. UN publication sales no. 1951. II. B.2. Recommendation 14, p. 95 (New York: United Nations).

—— (1951b) *Formulation and Economic Appraisal of Development Projects*. Book 1 (New York: United Nations).

—— (1952) *Methods of Financing Economic Development*. UN General Assembly Resolution 529A (VI) (New York: United Nations).

—— (1953a) *Report on a Special United Nations Fund for Economic Development*. UN publication sales no. 1953, II, B.1 (New York: United Nations).

—— (1953b) *Official Records of the Economic and Social Council, Sixteenth Session, 725th Meeting* (New York: United Nations).

—— (1954a) *Special United Nations Fund for Economic Development*. Final Report by Mr Raymond Scheyven prepared in pursuance of General Assembly resolution 724B (VIII). General Assembly Official Records: Ninth Session. Supplement No. 19 (A/2728) (New York: United Nations).

—— (1954b) *Official Records of the General Assembly, Ninth Session, Supplement No. 21* (New York: United Nations, p. 11).

—— (1955a) *Special United Nations Fund for Economic Development. Report prepared in pursuance of General Assembly Resolution 822 (IX)*. General Assembly Official Records: Tenth Session. Supplement No. 17 (A/2906) (New York: United Nations).

—— (1955b) *Question of the Establishment of a Special United Nations Fund for Economic Development*. Resolution adopted by the General Assembly at its 553rd plenary meeting on 9 December 1955 (New York: United Nations).

—— (1957) *Final Report of the Ad Hoc Committee on the Question of the Establishment of a Special Fund for Economic Development*. General Assembly document A/3579 and Add. 1 (New York: United Nations).

—— (1959) *Declaration of the Rights of the Child*. UN General Assembly resolution no. 1386 (xiv) (New York: United Nations).

—— (1960a) *868th Plenary Meeting. UN General Assembly, Fifteenth Session, Official Records, Part I. Plenary Meetings Vol. 1*. Verbatim Records of Meetings of 20 September – 17 October 1960 (New York: United Nations).

—— (1960b) *UN General Assembly resolution 1494 (XV) adopted at the 908th plenary meeting, 27 October 1960* (New York: United Nations).

—— (1962) *The United Nations Development Decade. Proposals for Action*. Report of the Secretary-General (New York: Department of Economic and Social Affairs, United Nations).

—— (1970) *Science and Technology for Development. Proposals for the Second Development Decade*. Document ST/ECA/133 (New York: United Nations).

UNCTAD (1997) *Trade and Development Report 1997* (Geneva: United Nations Conference on Trade and Development).

UNDP (1994) *Human Development Report 1994* (New York: Oxford University Press for the United Nations Development Programme).

UNICEF (1984) 'The Impact of Recession on Children. A UNICEF Special Study' in, UNICEF, *The State of the World's Children 1984* (New York: Published by Oxford University Press for the United Nations Children's Fund, pp. 137–72).

Urquhart, B. and E. Childers (1994) *Renewing the United Nations System* (New York: The Ford Foundation).

US (1949) *Congressional Records. Proceedings and Debates of the 81st Congress. First Session*, 20 and 24 January, 1949, vol. 95, parts 1 and 6, pp. 447–77 and pp. 8397–99 (Washington, DC: United States Government Printing Office).

US (1951) *Partners in Progress: Report to President Truman*. United States International Development Advisory Board (New York: Simon and Schuster).

US (1961) *Public Papers of the Presidents of the United States. John F. Kennedy, 20 January to 31 December 1961* (Washington, DC: United States Government Printing Office).

USDA (1995) 'Agricultural Export Programs: Background for 1995 Farm Legislation'. *Agricultural Economic Report No. 716* (Washington, DC: United States Department of Agriculture).

Wade, R. (2001) 'Global Inequality: Winners and Losers', *The Economist*, 28 April, pp. 93–97.

Wallerstein, M. (1980) *Food For War – Food For Peace. US Food Aid in a Global Context* (Cambridge, Mass.: The MIT Press).

Wallich, H. C. (1958) 'Some Notes Towards a Theory of Development', in A. N. Agarwala and S. P. Singh (1958).

Weaver, J. H. (1965) *The International Development Association: A New Approach to Foreign Aid* (New York: Praeger).

Weeks, J. (1973a) 'An Exploration into the Nature of the Problem of Urban Imbalance in Africa', in *Urban Employment in Africa*, IDS Research Conference, September 1971 (Brighton: Institute of Development Studies, University of Sussex).

—— (1973b) 'Introduction', in *Manpower and Unemployment Research in Africa* (Montreal: Centre for Developing-Area States, McGill University).

WFP (1978) 'Modalities of Operation of the International Emergency Food Reserve'. *Report of the Sixth Session of the Committee on Food Aid Policies and Programmes* (Rome: World Food Programme, Annex IV).

—— (1979) 'Guidelines and Criteria for Food Aid', *Report of the Seventh Session of the Committee on Food Aid Policies and Programmes* (Rome: World Food Programme, Annex IV).

—— (2000) *The Food Aid Monitor*. Special Issue. May (Rome: International Food Aid Information System, World Food Programme).

Widener, A. (1956) 'U.N. Economics', *USA: An American Bulletin of Fact and Opinion*, vol. III, no. 2, 27 July.

Ziesemer, T. (1953) 'Economic Development and Endogenous Terms of Trade Determination: Review and Reinterpretation of the Prebisch–Singer Thesis', *UNCTAD Review*, vol. 6, pp. 17–34.

Appendix
Publications of Sir Hans Singer

Section A: Books and pamphlets

Includes contributions by Hans Singer to books edited by him or written or edited by others. Reports for United Nations, other international bodies and governments are listed separately in Section B. Journal articles are listed in section C.

1936
(a) *Materials for the Study of Urban Ground Rent*, Cambridge University PhD dissertation approved in 1936. Short abstract available in *Cambridge Dissertations (1936–37), Faculty of Economics and Politics* (Cambridge: Cambridge University Library). Results summarized by Colin Clark in his *National Income and Outlay* (London: Macmillan, 1937) and in his *Conditions of Economic Progress* (London: Macmillan, 1940), and in Singer, 1942a.

1938
(a) *Men Without Work: A Report made to the Pilgrim Trust* (with W. F. Oakeshott and A. D. K. Owen) (Cambridge: Cambridge University Press). Reprinted by Greenwood Press, New York, 1968.
(b) 'Local Differences in the Incidence of Unemployment', in *Pilgrim Trust Unemployment Enquiry Interim Report* (with Preface by Dr William Temple, then Archbishop of York).
(c) 'The Regional Distribution of Unemployment', in *Pilgrim Trust Unemployment Enquiry Interim Report* (with Preface by Dr William Temple, then Archbishop of York).
(d) 'Changes in the Distribution of the Industrial Population', in *Pilgrim Trust Unemployment Enquiry Interim Report* (with Preface by Dr William Temple, then Archbishop of York).
(e) 'Transference and the Age Structure of the Depressed Areas', in *Pilgrim Trust Unemployment Enquiry Interim Report* (with Preface by Dr William Temple, then Archbishop of York).
(f) 'Unemployment and Health', in *Pilgrim Trust Unemployment Enquiry Interim Report* (with Preface by Dr William Temple, then Archbishop of York).

1940
(a) *Unemployment and the Unemployed* (London: King and Son).

1943
(a) *Standardised Accountancy* (Cambridge: Cambridge University Press for the National Institute for Economic and Social Research).
(b) *Can We Afford 'Beveridge'?* (London: Fabian Society Research Pamphlet).

1946

How Widespread are National Savings? (London: Circulated as a pamphlet by the National Savings Committee).

1948

(a)   'Some Accounting and Economic Aspects', in *The Working Party Reports* (London: Association of Certified and Corporate Accountants).

1950

(a)   *Economic Development of Under-Developed Countries* (Rio de Janeiro: Vargas Foundation). (Based on a series of lectures delivered in Rio de Janeiro, Brazil (in Portuguese).)

1952

(a)   *O Nord-Este: Estudo Sôbre O Desenvolvimento Economico Do Nordeste* (A Study of the Economic Development of the Brazilian North-East) (Recife: Comissao de Desenvolvimento Economico de Pernambuco). Also published in English as a UN *Technical Assistance Report*, 1953 and in Singer, 1964a.

1954

(a)   'The Economics of Technical Development', *Yearbook of Education*, London.

1955

(a)   *The Role of the Economist as Official Adviser* (with W. A. Jöhr) (London: Allen & Unwin).

1958

(a)   *Economics of Under-Development* (contributor) (Oxford: Oxford University Press).

1959

(a)   'Development Plans in Asia', in R. J. Barr (ed.), *American Trade with Asia and the Far East* (Milwaukee, WI: Marquette University Press).

1960

'The Concept of Balanced Growth in Economic Development: Theory and Practice', in E. Nelson (ed.), *Economic Growth – Rationale, Problems, Cases* (Austin, TX: University of Texas Press). Paper originally delivered at the conference on economic development organized by the department of economics of the University of Texas on the occasion of the 75th anniversary of the founding of the university. Also published in the *Texas Quarterly*, August 1958; in *The Malayan Economic Review*, vol. 3, no. 2, October 1958; and in Singer, 1964a. A Spanish translation appeared in *Revista de economia politica*, September-December, 1962.

1961

(a)   'The Dilemmas of Under-Developed Countries', in W. D. Grampp and E. T. Weiler (eds), *Economic Policy Readings in Political Economy* (Homewood IL: The Irwin Series in Economics, Irwin Inc.).

1964

(a) *International Development, Growth and Change* (New York: McGraw-Hill Series in International Development, McGraw-Hill).

(b) 'An Example of the New Pragmatism: Toward a Theory of Preinvestment', in Singer, 1964a.

(c) 'Reassessment of the Capital Requirements of Under-Developed Countries', in Singer, 1964a.

(d) 'Public Aid: A New Factor', in Singer, 1964a.

(e) 'The Role of the Public Sector in Economic Development', in Singer, 1964a.

1966

(a) 'Some Practical Issues in International Economics', in IDS, *Papers and Proceedings of the Founding Conference* (Brighton: Institute of Development Studies, September). Also in *IDS Communications* No. 6, March 1968 and reproduced as 'Some Problems of International Aid', *Journal of World Trade Law*, vol. 4, no. 2, March/April 1970.

1967

(a) *International Development, 1966*, (co-editor with Nicolas de Kun and Abbas Ordoobadi) (New York: Oceania Publications).

(b) *Disarmament, International Development Economics* (contributor) (Stanford, CA: Stanford Law Society).

(c) 'The Concept and the Role of Capital. Social Development: Key Growth Sector' (Chapter 1), and 'Strategies of Capital Accumulation. A Balanced View of Balanced Growth' (Chapter 3), in S. Tangi and H. P. Gray (eds), *Capital Accumulation and Economic Development* (London: D.C. Heath and Co.).

1970

(a) *Perspectives in Economic Development* (with Salvatore Schiavo-Campo) (Boston: Houghton Mifflin Co.).

1971

(a) *Britain's Role in the Second Development Decade*. Pamphlet prepared for the UK Standing Conference on the Second UN Development Decade, London. (Member of the committee which prepared this report.)

(b) 'International Policy and its Effect on Employment', in R. Robinson and P. Johnson (eds), *Prospects for Employment Opportunities in the Nineteen Seventies* (London: Her Majesty's Stationery Office). Reproduced in Cairncross and Puri, 1975.

1972

(a) 'Overseas Trade and Investment Patterns can Reinforce Exploitation', in M. Wolfe (ed.), *The Economic Causes of Imperialism* (London: Major Issues in History Series, John Wiley & Sons, Inc.).

1973

(a) *New Forms of International Co-operation for Technical Assistance* (with Javed Ansari) (London: Allen & Unwin).

(b) 'La Empresa Internacional Como Exportadora de Tecnología, (Spanish translation of 'The Foreign Company as an Exporter of Technology'), in M. S. Wionczek (ed.), *Comercio de Tecnología y Sub-Desarrollo Económico* (Mexico: Coordinación de Ciencias).

(c) 'International Policies and their Effect on Employment', in K. Wohlmuth (ed.), *Employment Creation in Developing Societies. The Situation of Labor in Dependent Economies* (New York: Praeger). Also in W. Sellekaerts (ed.), *Economic Development and Planning. Essays in Honour of Jan Tinbergen* (London: Macmillan, 1974).

1974

(a) 'Why Do We Need New Approaches?', in D. Wirmark (ed.), *The Rich and the Poor – New Approaches Towards a Global Development Strategy.* International Colloquium organized by the Friedrich Naumann Stiftung and the Swedish Liberal Party, 24–29 November 1974.

1975

(a) *The Strategy of International Development. Essays in the Economics of Backwardness by H. W. Singer,* Sir Alec Cairncross and Mohinder Puri (eds) (London: Macmillan).

1976

(a) 'Early Years (1910–1938)', in Sir A. Cairncross and M. Puri, 1976.

(b) 'Income Distribution and Population Growth', in H. Richards (ed.), *Population, Factor Movements and Economic Development. Studies presented to Brinley Thomas* (Cardiff: University of Wales Press).

1977

(a) *Rich and Poor Countries. Consequences of International Economic Disorder* (with Javed A. Ansari) (London, and Baltimore MA: Allen Hyman Ltd.). Second edition, 1978; Third edition, 1982; Fourth edition, 1988. Also published in Spanish as *Paises Ricos y Pobres* (Madrid: Edicones Piramides, S. A., 1982) and in Portuguese as *Paises Ricos – Paises Pobres* (trans. J. R. B. Azevedo), Rio de Janeiro, Sao Paulo: Livros Tecnicos e Cientificos Editora, 1979).

1978

(a) 'Wirtschaftswachstum oder Bekämpfung der Armut? Dreissig Jahre Wandel im Entwicklungsdenken der Vereinten Nationen' (Economic Growth or Fighting Poverty? Thirty Years of Change in the Development Thinking of the United Nations), in J. Naumann (ed.), *Auf dem Weg zu sozialen Weltwirtschaft* (Berlin: R. Sperber).

1979

(a) 'Environmental Factors in Project Analysis: A Conceptual Note', in H. I. Greenfield *et al.* (eds), *Theory for Economic Efficiency: Essays in Honor of Abba P. Lerner* (Cambridge, Mass.: The MIT Press).

(b) 'Poverty, Income Distribution and Levels of Living: Thirty Years of Changing Thought on Development Problems', in *Reflections on Economic Development and Social Change. Essays in Honour of Professor V. K. R. V. Rao*

(Delhi: Allied Publishers Private Ltd. for the Institute of Economic Growth). Also published, in R. P. Misra and M. Honjo (eds), *Changing Perceptions of Development Problems* (Nogoya: Maurzen Asia, 1981) and in Spanish by Fondo de Cultura Economics, Mexico, 1981.

1981

(a)   'The Role of Human Capital in Development' (lecture delivered at Bristol University, UK, January 1981), in R. M. Garrett (ed.), *North–South Debate–Educational Implications of the Brandt Report* (NFER Nelson). Also published in *Pakistan Journal of Applied Economics,* vol. 2, no. 1, 1983.

1982

(a)   *The International Economy and Industrial Development: Trade and Investment in the Third World* (with Javed A Ansari and Robert H. Ballance) (Brighton: Harvester Press). Translated into Turkish as *Uluslararasi Ekonomi ve Sinai Kalkinma: Ucuncu Dunyara Dis Ticaret ve Yatirim* (Istanbul: Caglayan Kitabevi, 1985).

1983

(a)   'North–South and South–South: The North and ECDC (Economic Co-operation Among Developing Countries)', in B. Pavlic, R. Uranga, B. Cizelj and M. Svatlicic (eds), *The Challenges of South–South Cooperation* (Colorado: Westview Press).

1984

(a)   'Reflections on Our Response to the Poorest of the Third World', in A. Jennings (ed.), *Our Response to the Poorest of the Third World* (Oxford: Pergamon Press).

(b)   'Appropriate Technology for a Basic Human Needs Strategy', in P. K. Ghosh (ed.), *Third World Development: A Basic Needs Approach* (London: International Development Resource Books, No. 13, Greenwood Press).

(c)   'The Terms of Trade Controversy and the Evolution of Soft Financing: Early Years in the UN', in G. M. Meier and D. Seers, 1984. Also *IDS Discussion Paper,* No. 181, November 1982. Published in Spanish as 'La controversia de la relación de intercambio y la evolucion del financiamiento en condiciones concesionarias: los primeros anos en la ONU', in G. M. Meier and D. Seers (eds), *Pioneros del Desarrollo* (Madrid: Published for the World Bank by Editorial Tecnos, 1986).

(d)   'Further Thoughts on North–South Negotiations: A Review of Bhagwati and Ruggie', in J. N. Bhagwati and J. R. Ruggie (eds), *Power, Passions and Purpose. Prospects for North–South Negotiations* (Cambridge, Mass.: The MIT Press). Also in *World Development,* vol. 13, no. 2, 1985.

1985

(a)   'Aid', 'Dual Economy', 'Underdevelopment'. Contributions to A. Kuper and J. Kuper (eds), *The Social Science Encyclopedia* (London: Routledge & Kegan Paul).

(b)   'Relevance of Keynes for Developing Countries', in H. L. Wattel (ed.), *The Policy Consequences of John Maynard Keynes* (New York: M E Sharpe Inc.), and in S. Sharma (ed.), *John Maynard Keynes: Keynesianism into the Twenty-First Century* (Cheltenham, UK: Edward Elgar, 1988).

1986

(a)   'The Ethics of Aid', in M. Wright (ed.), *Rights and Obligations in North–South Relations: Ethical Dimensions of Global Problems* (London: Macmillan). Also in *IDS Discussion Paper* No. 195, 1984.

(b)   'Import Substitution Revisited in a Darkening External Environment' (with Parvin Alizadeh), in *Im Spannungsfeld von Wirtschaft, Technik und Politik, Festschrift für Bruno Fritsch* (Munich: Gunter Olzog Verlag). Reproduced in *RAZVOJ/Development-International*, vol. 1, no. 2, July–December 1986, with amended reprints later. Also in S. Dell (ed.), *Policies for Development. Essays in Honour of Gamani Corea* (London: Macmillan, 1988).

(c)   'Collective Self-Reliance in the Service of Africa's Employment and Basic Needs', in *The Challenge of Employment and Basic Needs in Africa. Essays in honour of Shyam B. L. Nigam and to mark the tenth anniversary of JASPA (Jobs and Skills Programme for Africa)* (Nairobi: Oxford University Press).

(d)   'Raul Prebisch and His Advocacy of Import Substitution', in Homage to Raul Prebisch, special issue of *Development & South-South Cooperation*, vol. I, no. 3, December.

(e)   'Foreword', in T. G. Weiss, *Multilateral Development Diplomacy in UNCTAD* (London: Macmillan, 1986).

1987

(a)   'What Keynes and Keynesianism Can Teach Us About Less Developed Countries' in, A. P. Thirwell (ed.), *Keynes and Economic Development. The Seventh Keynes Seminar* held at the University of Kent, Canterbury, UK, 1985 (London: Macmillan). Also in A. M. El-Agraa (ed.), *Protection, Cooperation, Integration and Development: Essays in Honour of Professor Hiroshi Kitamura* (London: Macmillan).

(b)   *Food Aid. The Challenge and the Opportunity* (with John Wood and Tony Jennings) (Oxford: Clarendon Press).

(c)   'The New International Economic Order: An Overview' and ' The Second Brandt Report: A Common Crisis', in *Economic Theory and New World Order* (with Neelamber Hatti and Rameshwar Tandon (eds)), New World Order Series: Volume One (New Delhi: Ashish Publishing House).

(d)   *International Commodity Policy* (with Neelamber Hatti and Rameshwar Tandon (eds)), New World Order Series: Volume Two (New Delhi: Ashish Publishing House).

(e)   'Terms of Trade and Economic Development', in J. Eatwell, M. Milgate and P. Newman (eds), *The New Palgrave: A Dictionary of Economics*, Vol. IV (London: Macmillan).

1988

(a)   *Technology Transfer by Multinationals* (with Neelamber Hatti and Rameshwar Tandon (eds)), New World Order Series: Volume Three (New Delhi: Ashish Publishing House).

(b)   *New Protectionism and Restructuring*, 2 vols (with Neelambar Hatti and Rameshwar Tandon (eds)), New World Order Series: Volume Four (New Delhi: Ashish Publishing House).

(c) *Resource Transfer and Debt Trap*, 2 vols (with Neelamber Hatti and Rameshwar Tandon (eds)), New World Order Series: Volume Five (New Delhi: Ashish Publishing House).

(d) *Challenges of South–South Co-operation*, 2 vols, (with Neelambar Hatti and Rameshwar Tandon (eds)), New World Order Series: Volume Six (New Delhi: Ashish Publishing House).

1989

(a) *Economic Development and World Debt* (with Soumitra Sharma (eds)), Vol. I (London: Macmillan).

(b) *Growth and External Debt Management* (with Soumitra Sharma (eds)), Vol. II (London: Macmillan).

(c) 'Aid Not Trade? The Evolution of Soft Financing in the Early Years in the United Nations', in J. Kaufmann (ed.), *Effective Negotiation: Case Studies in Conference Diplomacy* (The Netherlands: Martinus Nijhoff Publishers).

(d) 'Lessons of Post-War Development Experience, 1945–1988', *IDS Discussion Paper* No. 260, November. (Originally written for the South Commission.) Also published in W. L. M. Adriaansen and J. G. Waardenburg (eds), *A Dual World Economy* (The Netherlands: Wolters-Noordhoff). Printed in *African Development Review*, African Development Bank, 1989 and in Spanish in *Comercio Exterior* (Banco Nacional de Comercio Exterior, SNC), Mexico, July 1989. Also in, S. Sharma (ed.), *Development Policy* (London: Macmillan, 1992). Included in Singer and Roy, 1993. Reprinted in *Economia do Desenvolvimento Bulletin* No. 1, Instituto Superior de Economia e Gestao/"Economicicas", September 1999.

1990

(a) 'The Vision of Keynes: The Bretton Woods Institutions', in E. Jensen and T. Fisher (eds), *The United Kingdom – The United Nations* (London: Macmillan).

(b) *Towards Economic Recovery in Sub-Saharan Africa* (with James Pickett (eds)) (London: Routledge).

(c) *North–South Trade in Manufactures* (with Neelambar Hatti and Rameshwar Tandon (eds)), New World Order Series: Volume Seven (New Delhi: Indus Publishing Company).

(d) *Trade Liberalization in the 1990s* (with Neelambar Hatti and Rameshwar Tandon (eds)), New World Order Series: Volume Eight (New Delhi: Indus Publishing Company).

(e) 'Food Aid', in C. K. Eicher and J. M. Staatz (eds), *Agricultural Development in the Third World*, second edition. Johns Hopkins Studies in Development (Baltimore: Johns Hopkins University Press).

(f) 'The Role of Food Aid', in J. Pickett and H. W. Singer (eds), *Towards Economic Recovery in Sub-Saharan Africa. Essays in Honour of Robert Gardiner* (London: Routledge).

1991

(a) *Aid and External Financing in the 1990s* (with Neelambar Hatti and Rameshwar Tandon (eds)), New World Order Series: Volume Nine (New Delhi: Indus Publishing Company).

(b) *Joint Ventures and Collaborations* (with Neelambar Hatti and Rameshwar Tandon (eds)), New World Order Series: Volume Ten (New Delhi: Indus Publishing Company).

(c) *Foreign Direct Investments* (with Neelambar Hatti and Rameshwar Tandon (eds)), New World Order Series: Volume Eleven (New Delhi: Indus Publishing Company).

(d) *Adjustment and Liberalization in the Third World* (with Neelambar Hatti and Rameshwar Tandon (eds)), New World Order Series: Volume Twelve (New Delhi: Indus Publishing Company).

(e) 'Food Aid and Structural Adjustment Lending in Sub-Saharan Africa', in E. Clay and O. Stokke (eds), *Food Aid Reconsidered – Assessing the Impact on Third World Countries*. EADI Book Series 11(London: Frank Cass).

(f) 'Foreword', in P. Wignaraja, A. Hussain, H. Sethi and G. Wignaraja, *Participatory Development – Learning from South Asia* (Karachi and Tokyo: United Nations University Press and Oxford University Press).

(g) *Development Perspectives for the 1990s* (with R. Prendergast (eds)) (London: Macmillan for the Development Studies Association).

1992

(a) 'Agriculture-Based Industrialization in Sub-Saharan Africa', in *African Development Perspectives Yearbook 1990/91: Industrialization based on Agricultural Development* (Hamburg: Lit).

(b) 'Impact of Trade Policy Reform in the Shadow of the Debt Crisis', in R. Adhikari, C. Kirkpatrick and J. Weiss (eds), *Industrial and Trade Policy Reform in Developing Countries* (Manchester: Manchester University Press).

(c) *Los Problemas del Desarrollo en Améric Latina – Homenaje a Raúl Prebisch* (with Luisa Montuschi (eds)), (The Development Problems of Latin America – a Homage to Raúl Prebisch) (Argentina: Fondo de Cultura Económica/Serie de Economia).

(d) 'Autobiographical article', in P. Arestis and M. Sawyer (eds), *A Biographical Dictionary of Dissenting Economists* (Aldershot, UK: Edward Elgar), 2nd edn 2000.

(e) 'Introduction', in IDS (1992) *International Governance*. Silver Jubilee Papers. (Brighton: Institute of Development Studies).

1993

(a) 'Adam Smith: Forebear of Development Studies' (Presidential address to the UK Development Studies Association), in A. Carty and H. W. Singer (eds), *Conflict and Change in the 1990s, Ethics, Laws and Institutions* (London: Macmillan for the Development Studies Association).

(b) 'Overall Postwar Development Experience, 1945–89' and 'The 1990s: On to Fortune or Bound in Miseries?', in H. W. Singer and Sumit Roy, *Economic Progress and Prospects in the Third World: Lessons of Development Experience Since 1945* (Aldershot, UK, and Brookfield, VT: Edward Elgar). Also published in Shaw, 2001c.

(c) 'The Impact of Trends in Terms of Trade on GNP Growth' (with J. Edström), in, M. Nissanke and A. Hewitt (eds), *Economic Crisis in Developing Countries: New Perspectives on Commodities, Trade and Finance. A Collection of Essays in Honour of Alfred Maizels* (London: Pinter Publication Ltd).

(d) 'Jan Tinbergen – Champion of World Security and Equity', in A. Jolink and E. Barendrecht-Tinbergen (eds), *Gedeelde Herinneringen (Shared Memories). Essays in honour of Jan Tinbergen for his 90th birthday* (Rotterdam: Published by A. Jolink, University of Rotterdam).

(e) 'Debt Relief for the Highly Indebted Poor Countries', in Christian Aid, *Proclaim Liberty. Reflections on Theology and Debt* (London: Christian Aid).

1994

(a) 'The Bretton Woods Institutions and the UN', in *Briefing Notes in Economics*, Issue No. 8 (London: The American International University in London).

(b) 'Structural Adjustment Programmes: Evaluating Success', in J. W. Gunning, H. Kox, W. Tims and Y. de Wit (eds), *Trade, Aid and Development. Essays in Honour of Hans Linnemenn* (London: Macmillan).

(c) 'Two Views of Food Aid', in R. Prendergast and F. Stewart (eds), *Market Forces and World Development* (London: Macmillan for the Development Studies Association).

(d) 'Prospects for Development', in A. M. Murshed and K. Raffer (eds), *Trade, Transfers and Development: Problems and Prospects for the Twenty First Century* (Cheltenham, UK: Edward Elgar).

(e) 'From Project Lending to Programme Lending: Shifting World Bank Priorities', in J. D. MacArthur and J. Weiss (eds), *Agriculture, Projects and Development: Papers in Honour of David Edwards* (Aldershot, UK: Avebury).

(f) 'Trend and Volatility in the Terms of Trade: Consequences for Growth' (with Matthias Lutz), in D. Sapsford and W. Morgan (eds), *The Economics of Primary Commodities – Models, Analysis and Policy* (Cheltenham, UK: Edward Elgar).

(g) 'An Assessment of the World Bank', in *50 Years of Bretton Woods System: The Role of the IMF, World Bank and GATT in the World Economy* (Friedrich-Ebert Foundation and Richmond College, October).

1995

(a) 'An Historical Perspective', in M. ul-Haq, R. Jolly, P. Streeten and K. Haq (eds), *The UN and the Bretton Woods Institutions – New Challenges for the Twenty-First Century* (Basingstoke and London: Macmillan).

(b) 'Rethinking Bretton Woods from an Historical Perspective', in *Promoting Development: Effective Global Institutions for the Twenty-First Century* (Washington, DC: Pluto Press and Center of Concern).

(c) 'Historical Background to the Bretton Woods System and its Relation to the United Nations System', in B. Etemad, J. Batou and T. David (eds), *Towards an International Economic and Social History – Essays in Honour of Paul Bairoch* (Geneva: Editions Passé Présent).

(d) 'The Future of Food Trade and Food Aid in a Liberalizing Global Economy', in E. Messer and P. Uvin (eds), *The Hunger Report 1995* (Providence, RI: Alan Shawn Feinstein World Hunger Program, Brown University).

1996

(a) *The Foreign Aid Business. Economic Assistance and Development Co-operation* (with Kunibert Raffer) (Cheltenham, UK: Edward Elgar).

(b)   *The World Economy: Challenges of Globalization and Regionalization* (with Marjan Svetlicic (eds))(Basingstoke, London and New York: Macmillan and St Martin's Press).

(c)   'Effectiveness and Problems of Food Aid', in IFIC Seminar Series (95-5) *Food Aid* (Tokyo: Institute for International Cooperation, Japan International Cooperation Agency (JICA).

(d)   'Alternative Approaches to Adjustment and Stabilisation', in S. Sen (ed.), *Financial Fragility, Debt and Economic Reforms* (Basingstoke, London and New York: Macmillan and St Martin's Press).

1997

(a)   'Is Development Economics Still Relevant?', in L. Emmerij (ed.), *Economic and Social Development in the 21st Century* (Washington, DC: Inter-American Development Bank and The Johns Hopkins University Press).

1998

(a)   *Growth, Development and Trade. Selected Essays of Hans Singer. Economists of the Twentieth Century* (Cheltenham, UK: Edward Elgar).

(b)   'A Note on Some UN Achievements with Special Reference to the World Food Programme' (with John Shaw), in M. I. Glassner (ed.), *The United Nations at Work* (Westport, CN, and London: Praeger).

(c)   'Modern Relevance of Keynesianism in the Study of Development', in D. Sapsford and J. Chen, 1998a.

(d)   'How Relevant is Keynesianism Today for Understanding Problems of Development?', in S. Sharma (ed.), *John Maynard Keynes. Keynesianism into the Twenty-First Century* (Cheltenham, UK: Edward Elgar). Also in E. Petitat-Cote, *The EDAI Story: Networking Over the Years 1975–2000* (Geneva: European Association of Development Institutes, 1999).

(e)   *Export-Led Versus Balanced Growth in the 1990s* (with Neelambar Hatti and Rameshwar Tandon (eds)), New World Order Series: Volume Thirteen (Delhi: B. R. Publishing Corporation).

1999

(a)   *Trade in Services* (with Neelambar Hatti and Rameshwar Tandon (eds)), New World Order Series: Volume Fourteen (Delhi: B. R. Publishing Corporation).

(b)   *T.R.I.Ps, The Uruguay Round and Third World Interests* (with Neelambar Hatti and Rameshwar Tandon (eds)), New World Order Series: Volume 15 (Part1) (Delhi: B. R. Publishing Corporation).

(c)   *T.R.I.Ps, The Uruguay Round and Third World Interests* (with Neelambar Hatti and Rameshwar Tandon (eds)), New World Order Series: Volume 15 (Part 2) (Delhi: B. R. Publishing Corporation). (TRIPs = Trade-Related Aspects of Intellectual Propery Rights)

(d)   *Technological Diffusion in the Third World* (with Neelambar Hatti and Ramesgwar Tandon (eds)), New World Order Series: Volume 16 (Part 1) (Delhi: B. R. Publishing Corporation).

(e)   *Technological Diffusion in the Thirld World* (with Neelabar Hatti and Rameshward Tandon (eds)), New World Order Series:' Volume 16 (Part 2) (Delhi: B. R. Publishing Corportation).

(f)   'Preface' to S. Browne, *Beyond Aid: From Patronage to Partnership* (Aldershot, UK: Ashgate).

2000

(a)   'Poverty, Employment and the Informal Sector: Some Reflections on the ILO Mission to Kenya' (with Richard Jolly), in D. Ghai (ed.), *Renewing Social and Economic Progress in Africa* (Basingstoke and London: Macmillan in association with the United Nations Research Institute for Social Development).

(b)   Comment' on Irma Adelman's 'Fallacies in Development Theory and their Implications for Policy' and 'Pioneers Revisited', in G. M Meier and J. E. Stiglitz, 2000.

2001

(a)   'Foreword', in D. J. Shaw, 2001b.

(b)   *International Development Co-operation. Selected Essays by H. W. Singer on Aid and the United Nations System.* Edited by D. J. Shaw. (Basingstoke and London: Macmillan now Palgrave).

(c)   *The Economic North–South Divide. Six Decades of Unequal Development* (with Kunibert Raffer) (Cheltenham, UK, and Northampton, Mass., USA: Edward Elgar).

Section B: Reports for United Nations, other international bodies and governments

Does not include the many internal reports that Hans Singer produced when a member of the secretariats of UN bodies.

1947

(a)   *The Role of Children in Economic Development.* Report at the invitation of the Executive Director, UNICEF.

1949

(a)   *Relative Prices of Exports and Imports of Under-Developed Countries* (Lake Success, NY: United Nations Department of Economic Affairs, December). The advance version, which was made available to the UN Sub-Commission on Economic Development, was entitled *Post War Price Relations in Trade between Under-Developed and Industrialized Countries.* Document E/CN.1/Sub.3/W.5. (Lake Success, NY: United Nations Department of Economic and Social Affairs, 23 February 1949).

1951

   'Economic Development Projects as Part of National Development Programs', in UN, *Formulation and Economic Appraisal of Development Projects.* Book 1 (New York: United Nations). Also reprinted as part of the official proceedings of the Development Institute, Lahore, Pakistan, 1951 and included in Singer, 1964a.

1952

(b)   *Instability of Export Proceeds of Underdeveloped Countries* (New York: United Nations).

1954

(b) 'Population and Economic Development'. Paper presented to the World Population Conference, Rome, Italy. Published in *United Nations World Population Conference*. Vol. V. UN publication sales no. 1955 XIII.8 (New York: United Nations, 1955). Also published in Singer, 1964a.

1961

(b) 'Education and Economic Development', in UNESCO and ECA, *Development of Education in Africa*. Proceedings of a joint UNESCO/ECA conference, Addis Ababa, Ethiopia, May 1961 (Paris: United Nations Educational, Scientific and Cultural Organization and Economic Commission for Africa). Also published in Singer, 1964a.

(c) 'Some Significant Trends in Economic Work of the United Nations'. (Paper presented at New York University). *Annual Review of the United Nations Affairs, 1961* (New York: United Nations).

(d) 'Report on an Expanded Program of Surplus Food Utilization'. (Chairman of expert group which produced this report). Reproduced in FAO, *Development Through Food: A Strategy of Surplus Utilization*. Freedom from Hunger Campaign Basic Study, No. 2 (Rome: Food and Agriculture Organization of the United Nations). Republished in, FAO 1985.

1962

The United Nations Development Decade – Proposals for Action. Report of the Secretary-General, (New York: United Nations).

1963

(a) 'The Project of an African Development Bank'. Paper submitted to a Conference of African Heads of States, Addis Ababa, Ethiopia, 1963 and published in *Revue de Science Financière*, Paris, 1963. Also published in Singer, 1964a.

(b) 'Problems of Industrialization of Under-Developed Countries', in J. Meynaud (ed.), *Social Change and Economic Development* (Paris: United Nations Educational, Scientific and Cultural Organization).

1964

(f) 'Some Neglected Aspects of the Role of Children and Youth in Developing Countries'. Statement and working paper presented at a UNICEF Round Table Conference, Bellagio, Lake Como, Italy, 1964, and reprinted in H. D. Stein (ed.), *Planning for the Needs of Children in Developing Countries: Report of a Round Table Conference* (New York: United Nations Children's Fund).

(g) 'Co-ordination of Technical Assistance and Development Planning: Determination of Priorities'. Paper presented at a UN Technical Assistance Board Seminar on *National Co-ordination of Technical Assistance*, Addis Ababa, Ethiopia, January.

(h) 'Effects of Patents on the Economy of Under-Developed Countries'. Contribution to a UN study on *The Role of Patents in the Transfer of Technology to Developing Countries*. Document UN E/3861/Rev.1. (New York: United Nations).

(i)   'Development Decade – A General Review'. Statement to the Annual Conference of Non-Governmental Organizations, 26–27 May.
(j)   'The Potential Importance of Industrial Estates for African Countries'. Paper prepared for a UN Economic Commission for Africa seminar on *Industrial Estates*, Addis Ababa, June.

1966
(b)   'Methods of Planning for the Needs of Children'. Prepared for a UNICEF Conference on *Planning for Children and Youth in Asia*, Bangkok, Thailand.

1969
(a)   *Social Policy and Planning in the National Development: Report of the Meeting of Experts on Social Policy and Planning* (Rapporteur of Committee). Report for the UN Social Commission and Economic and Social Council, Stockholm, Sweden, September.
(b)   *A Regional Development Plan for the Northern Region of Thailand.* A report prepared for the United Nations and the Government of Thailand.
(c)   *Social Defence Policies in Relation to Development Planning.* (Chairman of the Committee). Report of Meeting of Experts for UN Social and Economic Council, Rome, Italy.

1970
(b)   *The Sussex Manifesto: Science and Technology to Developing Countries during the Second Development Decade* (Chairman of the 'Sussex Group' and co-author of report). Reproduced in UN, *Science and Technology for Development: Proposals for the Second Development Decade.* Document ST/ECA/133 . (New York: United Nations). Also published in *IDS Reprints* 101, 1970 and in Cairncross and Puri, 1975.

1971
(c)   *World Plan of Action for the Application of Science and Technology to Development,* (UN Sales No. E.71.II.A.18) (New York: United Nations).
(d)   'International Aid to Development', in UNICEF, *Les Carnets de l'Enfance/Assignment Children,* No. 14 (New York: United Nations Children's Fund, April-June).
(e)   *Science and Technology to Developing Countries during the Second Development Decade* (New York: United Nations).
(f)   'Forms and Causes of Extreme Underdevelopment' for expert group meeting on *Industrialization in Countries at Early Stages of Development with Special Reference to Small-Scale Industry,* Vienna, 6–10 December. Document ID/WG. 109/2 (Vienna: United Nations Industrial Development Organization).
(g)   *The Great Experiment: Science and Technology in the Second UN Development Decade.* Popular version of the *World Plan of Action for the Application of Science and Technology to Development* (UN Sales No. 71.I.19) (New York: UN Centre for Economic and Social Information).

1972
(b)   *Environment and Development (Founex Report).* UN Preparatory Committee for the Stockholm Conference on the Environment (Member of Committee) (Mouton, Paris and The Hague).

(c)   *Employment, Incomes and Equality: A Strategy for Increasing Productive Employment in Kenya* (with Richard Jolly). Report of UNDP/ILO Employment Mission to Kenya (Geneva: International Labour Office, November).

(d)   *Children in the Strategy of Development.* Executive Briefing Paper, No. 6. Prepared for the UN Centre for Economic and Social Information and UNICEF(New York: United Nations). Also in French, *La Place de 'L'Enfance dans la Stratégie due Développement*, (Document d'Information, No. 6, établi pour l'information économique et sociale de Nations Unies et pour le Fonds des Nations Unies pour l'enfance) (New York: United Nations, 1973). Also published in Spanish as *Los Niños en la Estrategía para el Desarrollo'*, (Documento Informativo para Ejecutivos, No. 6, preparado para el Centro de Información Económica y Social de las Naciones Unidas y el Fondo de las Naciones Unidas para la Infancia) (New York: United Nations, 1973).

(e)   *The Quest for an Employment Strategy in Developing Counties and its Relationship to the Work on Human Resources Indicators.* Paper for UNESCO Committee on Social Planning (Paris: United Nations Educational, Scientific and Cultural Organization, November/December).

(f)   *Distribution of Costs and Benefits of Regional Groupings among Developing Countries* (Geneva: United Nations Conference for Trade and Development).

(g)   'New Forms of International Co-operation for Technical Innovation' (with Brian Johnson and Bruce Mackay). A paper presented at the United Nations Institute for Training and Research (UNITAR) weekend seminar held at the Institute for Development Studies, 30 June–2 July. Published in H. Caustin (ed.), *The Search for New Methods of Technical Co-operation.* UNITAR Conference Report No. 4 (New York: United Nations Institute for Training and Research, 1974).

1973

(d)   *Effect of Taxation on Income Distribution in Developing Countries: Addendum – Studies in Tax Reform Planning.* Document UN ESA/ECOSOC/L1/Misc.2/Add.3. (New York: United Nations).

(e)   'The Pilot Missions under the World Employment Programme' (with Richard Jolly and Dudley Seers). Prepared for the ILO World Employment Programme meeting on *Evaluation of Comprehensive Employment Missions.* Document ILO E.0078.1:11(Geneva: International Labour Office, March). Also published in *IDS Communications* No. 111, June 1974.

(f)   'Population Growth and Income Distribution'. UN document prepared for the *International Symposium on Population and Development*, Cairo, Egypt, June 1973, preparatory to the *World Population Conference*, 1974. Published in *The Population Debate: Dimensions and Perspectives.* Vol. 1. Papers of the World Population Conference, Bucharest, 1974 (New York: United Nations, 1975).

(g)   *Science and Technology in the Second UN Development Decade: International Development Strategy* (Consultant). Document UN E/CA/10. (New York: United Nations, 31 July).

(h)   'Introduction' and 'The European Economic Community and Developing Countries', in *Report of the International Symposium on Growth and World Equilibrium*, Elsinore, Denmark, 6–8 August).

(i)   'Aspects of the Distribution of Income and Wealth in Kenya' (with Stuart D. Reynolds). Prepared for UNESCO Conference on *Human Resources Indicators* and issued as UNESCO Document SHC/WS/3-4, Paris, 1 November 1973. Revised version subsequently issued as *IDS Discussion Paper*, No. 41, February 1974 and published in UNESCO, *The Use of Socio-Economic Indicators in Development Planning* (Paris: United Nations Educational, Scientific and Cultural Organization).

1975

(b)   *Employment and Youth. Commonwealth Youth Programme* Occasional Papers (London: Commonwealth Secretariat).

(c)   'Use of Locally Available Resources in Health and Socio-Economic Developments', in *Paediatric Education in Rural Health*. Paper presented at Reunion Meeting of Past Fellows of the UNICEF/World Health Organization Course for Senior Teachers of Child Health, New Delhi, October 1975.

1976

(c)   'Policies for Urban Informal Sector in Brazil' (joint Consultant and Contributor). Memorandum prepared for *Mesa Redonda sobre Politicas de Emprego paro o Sector Informal Urbano*, Brasilia, 2–6 February 1976 (Geneva: International Labour Office).

1977

(b)   *Technologies for Basic Needs* (Geneva: International Labour Office).

1978

(b)   *Environment and Development: A Conceptual Overview* (with Biplab Dasgupta and Brian Johnson). Report submitted to the United Nations Environment Programme, Nairobi, Kenya, January.

(c)   *A Survey of Studies of Food Aid*. Document WFP/CFA: 5/5-C. Prepared for the World Food Programme (Rome: World Food Programme, March). Also published as 'A Summary Survey of Studies of Food Aid', in H. Schneider, *Food Aid for Development* (Paris: Organisation for Economic Co-operation and Development). Report on the Organisation for Economic Co-operation and Development Centre expert meeting on 'Scope and Conditions for Improved Use of Food Aid for Development', held in Paris, 30–31 March.

(d)   *The Expansion of Processing in Developing Countries and International Policy Requirements* (with Juliette Stephenson). Commonwealth Economic Paper No. 10. (London: Commonwealth Secretariat, October).

(e)   'The Basic Needs Approach to Development Planning; 'New Trends in Development Strategies'; 'The New International Economic Order: An Overview'; 'Poverty, Income Distribution and Levels of Living: Twenty-Five Years of Changes in Thinking about Development'; and 'The Common Fund Debate', in *Seanza Lectures 1978* (Seoul: The Bank of Korea, September 1979).

1979

(c)   *International Cooperation for the Generation and Diffusion of Appropriate Technology and Appropriate Products for Industrialization.* (Consultant). Paper prepared for United Nations Conference for Trade and Development, Geneva, February.

(d)   'Introduction' and 'Policy Implications of the Lima Target', in *Industry and Development*, Special Issue No. 3, Document ID/SER.M/3, for the Third General Conference of United Nations Industrial Development Organization (New York: United Nations).

1980

(a)   'A Note on Brandt: Points of Broader Significance for the UNDP'. A report prepared for, and circulated by, United Nations Development Programme, New York, March.

(b)   *Young Human Resources in Korea's Social Development: Issues and Strategies* (with Nancy O. Baster) (Seoul: Korean Development Institute, March).

(c)   *Commodity Development Activities: Potential for DC/LDC Negotiations* (with P. Mishalani). Report submitted to the United Nations Conference on Trade and Development (UNCTAD), Geneva, April.

(d)   *Research Suggestions for the Proposed UNCTAD Research and Training Centre.* (Consultant). Document prepared for United Nations Conference on Trade and Development (UNCTAD), Geneva, June.

(e)   *International Agricultural Adjustment: Revised Guidelines.* Report submitted to Food and Agriculture Organization of the United Nations (FAO), Rome, July.

(f)   *Beyond the Brandt Report: Some Problems of Trade and Trade Promotion.* Extracts from lecture at United Nations Conference on Trade and Development/General Agreement on Tariffs and Trade, Geneva, 13 August.

(g)   *Basic Needs in an Economy under Pressure: Findings and Recommendations of the ILO/JASPA Basic Needs Mission to Zambia.* (Contributor and Member of Mission)(Geneva: International Labour Office, 1 September). (JASPA = Jobs and Skills Programme for Africa)

1981

(b)   *Poverty, Malnutrition and Food in Zambia.* Country case study for World Employment Programme, Report IV (Geneva: International Labour Office).

(c)   *Innovatory Uses of Food Aid: A Task for the Eighties?* Paper to the World Food Programme, Rome, March.

(d)   *The Brandt Report – A Basis for a Second Korean Miracle?* (Seoul: Korean International Economic Institute, April).

(e)   'The Basic Needs Approach to Development Planning' (in Indonesian: 'Pendekatan Kebutuhan Dasar dalam Perencanaan'), in T. K. Wie (ed.), *Pembangunan Ekonomi dan Pemerataan: Berberapa Pendekatan Alternatif* (Djakarta, Indonesia).

1982

(b)   *Report on the First Policy Seminar on Children* (with others). (Manila, Philippines: United Nations Children's Fund).

(c)   *Food Aid and Development: The Impact and Effectiveness of Bilateral PL 480. Title I – Type Assistance* (with E. J. Clay). A.I.D. Program Evaluation Discussion Paper, No. 15 (Washington, DC: US Agency for International Development, December).

1983

(b) 'Multilateral Aid to Developing Countries' (with Stephany Griffith-Jones), in *Study on the International Financial and Trading System*. Background Papers No. 9. (London: Commonwealth Secretariat, April). Also in *Towards a New Bretton Woods. Challenges for the World Financial and Trading System*. Selected background papers prepared for a Commonwealth Study Group, Vol. 1. (London: Commonwealth Secretariat, November).

(c) *Pricing Policies for Food Aid* (with E. J. Clay). Technical Paper No. 8 for Commonwealth Consultative Meeting on *Food Pricing and Marketing Policy*, London, 3–6 May 1983, Food Production and Rural Development Division, Commonwealth Secretariat in collaboration with Guelph University, Ontario, Canada.

(d) 'Development Through Food: Twenty Years' Experience' (with Simon Maxwell), in *Report of the World Food Programme/Government of the Netherlands Seminar on Food Aid*. Contribution to the 20th Anniversary of World Food Programme seminar held in The Hague, The Netherlands, 3–5 October.

1984

(e) 'The Impact of World Recession on Children' (with others), in UNICEF, *The State of the World's Children, 1984*. Chapter IV. (New York: Published for the United Nations Children's Fund by Oxford University Press).

(f) 'Sub-Saharan Africa in Depression: The Impact on the Welfare of Children' (with R. H. Green), in R. Jolly and G. A. Cornia (eds), *The Impact of World Recession on Children. A Study prepared for UNICEF* (Oxford and New York: Pergamon Press). Published in French as 'L'Afrique Subsaharienne en crise: l'impact de la récession sur le bien être des enfants', in *L'Impact de la Récession Mondiale sue les Enfants, Etude réalisée pour l'UNICEF, Travaux dirigés par R. Jolly et G. A. Cornia)* (New York: United Nations Children's Fund. 1984). And in Spanish as 'Effectos de la recesion en el Africa subsahariana sobre el bienestar de la infancia', in *Effectos de la Recesion Mundial Sobre la Infancia, Estudio especial del UNICEF*, R. Jolly y G. A. Cornia (compiladores) (Siglo XXI de Espana Editores for UNICEF, 1984).

(g) 'Industrialization: Where Do We Stand? Where Are We Going?', in *Industry and Development*, no. 12 (New York: United Nations Industrial Development Organization). Published in French as 'L'Industrialisation: où en sommes-nous, où allons-nous?', in *Industrie et développement*, no. 12 (New York: United Nations Industrial Development Organization). Also published in *Korean Development Policy Studies*, 1984; in *METU Studies in Development*, Vol. 11, Nos. 1–2, METU – Middle East Technical University, Ankara, Turkey, 1984; and in *Industry and Development*, no. 12, 1985. Also in Spanish in *Industria y Desarrollo*, no. 12, 1985.

(h) 'Economists Comment on UNCTAD's Role' (with others).Contribution to a *Symposium on the Future Role of UNCTAD*, in *UNCTAD Bulletin*, no. 205, September.

1985

(c) 'Food Aid and Development: Issues and Evidence. A Survey of the Literature since 1977 on the Role and Impact of Food Aid in Developing Countries' (with E. J. Clay), *World Food Programme Occasional Papers* No. 3 (Rome: World Food Programme, September).

1986

(e) 'The Role of Food Aid in Promoting the Welfare of Children in Developing Countries' (with Richard Longhurst), in J. P. Greaves and D. J. Shaw (eds), *Food Aid and the Well-Being of Children in the Developing World*. UNICEF/WFP Workshop held at UNICEF Headquarters, New York, 25–26 November 1985. (New York: United Nations Children's Fund and World Food Programme).

1987

(f) *The African Food Crisis and the Role of Food Aid in Coping with It*. Address to the World Food Day Symposium, Tokyo, 16 October 1987. Published by the Japan FAO Association, Tokyo (in Japanese and English).

(g) 'A Development Economist's View'. Contribution to the World Health Organization Round Table on *How Should Information on Health Care be Generated and Used?*, in WHO journal *World Health Forum*, vol. 8.

1990

(g) 'How to Foster Diversification, Not Dependence' (with Adrian Hewitt), in *Africa Recovery*, vol. 4, nos 3–4, October–December. Published by the Communications and Project Management Division, United Nations Department of Public Information, New York.

1991

(h) 'Foreword' to G. Standing and V. Tokman (eds), *Towards Social Adjustment: Labour Market Issues in Structural Adjustment* (Geneva: International Labour Office).

(i) *Structural Adjustment and Agriculture: Report of an In-Service Training Seminar for FAO Staff*. Training Materials for Agricultural Planning No. 25 (Rome: Food and Agriculture Organization of the United Nations).

(j) 'UNCTAD in a Changing World', in *UNCTAD Bulletin* No. 12, November/December.

1992

(f) *Research of the World Employment Programme: Future Priorities and Selective Assessment* (Geneva: International Labour Office).

1993

(f) 'Commentarios sobre "Raúl Prebisch, 1901–1971: La Búsqueda Constante"'. (Commentary on 'Raúl Prebisch 1901–1971: the Constant Quest'), in E. V. Iglesias (ed.) *El legado de Raúl Prebisch* (Washington, DC: Banco Interamericano de Desarrollo).

1994

(h) 'New Patterns of Macro-Economic Governance' (with Stephany Griffith-Jones), in UNDP Human Development Report, *Office Occasional Paper* No. 10, New York.

(i) 'Assessment of the IDB Lending Programme, 1979–92' (with Stephany Griffith-Jones, Alicia Puyana and Christopher Stevens). A study commissioned by the Inter-American Development Bank, *IDS Research Report* No. 25.

1995

(e) 'Is a Genuine Partnership Possible in a Western Hemisphere Free Trade Area?', in IDB and ECLA, *Trade Liberalization in the Western Hemisphere* (Washington, DC: Inter-American Development Bank and UN Economic Commission for Latin America and the Caribbean).

Section C: Articles

A number of articles have been published in more than one journal, and in languages other than English. Articles have also been reprinted in various books. Book reviews and letters to newspaper editors are not included. Those articles that appear in books edited by Hans Singer or written or edited by others are included in Section A.

1935

'Can Overcrowding Automatically Disappear?', *Review of Economic Studies.*

1936

(b) 'The "Courbe des Populations" – A Parallel to Pareto's Law', *The Economic Journal*, 1936.
(c) 'Income and Rent', *Review of Economic Studies.*

1937

(a) 'Some Notes on Duopoly and Spatial Competition' (with A. P. Lerner), *The Journal of Political Economy*, vol. 45, no. 2, April. Reprinted in M. L. Greenhut and G. Norman (eds), *The International Library of Critical Writings in Economics, The Economics of Location*, Vol. I (Cheltenham, UK: Edward Elgar, 1995), and in J-F. Thisse, K. J. Button and P. Nijkam (eds), *Location Theory. Volume 1* (Cheltenham, UK: Edward Elgar, in the series Modern Classics in Regional Science).
(b) 'Notes on Spatial Discrimination', *Review of Economic Studies.*

1938

(g) 'The Law of Diminishing Elasticity of Demand', *The Economic Journal.*
(h) 'Prices and the Trade Cycle', *The Manchester School.*
(i) 'Price Dispersion in Periods of Change', *The Economic Journal.*
(j) 'The Process of Unemployment in the Depressed Areas, 1935–38', *Review of Economic Studies*, vol. 6.
(k) 'The Process of Unemployment and Regional Labour Markets', *Review of Economic Studies.*

1939

'The Inflexibility of the Price System', *Manchester Statistical Society.*

1940

(b) 'The German War Economy, I–XII'. A series of 12 articles in consecutive issues of *The Economic Journal*, vols 50–54, December 1940 to June–September 1944.

1941

(a) 'The Coal Question Reconsidered', *Review of Economic Studies*.

(b) 'Some Disguised Blessings of the War', *The Manchester School*, vol. XII, no. 2.

1942

(a) 'Urban Land Values in England and Wales, 1845–1913', *Econometrica*.

(b) 'German War Finance', *The Banker*.

(c) 'The Sources of War Finance for the German War Economy', *Review of Economic Studies*, vol. 10.

1943

(c) 'Beveridge Plan Economics', *Westminster Newsletter* (special issue).

(d) 'The German War Economy', *Manchester Statistical Society*, 1943. (Also in *Review of Economic Studies*.)

1944

(a) 'The National Income', *Discovery*.

(b) 'An Economist's View of Accountants', *Accountancy*, August.

1947

(b) 'Wage Policy in Full Employment', *The Economic Journal*, December. (See also 'Wage Policy in Full Employment – A Rejoinder', *The Economic Journal*, September 1948.)

1948

(b) 'Industrial Productivity in England and Scotland' (with C.E.V. Leser), *Journal of the Royal Statistical Society*, vol. CXI, part IV. Also reprint IV, Department of Social and Economic Research, University of Glasgow, 1950.

1949

(b) 'Economic Progress in Under-Developed Countries', *Social Research*, vol. 16, no. 1.

1950

(b) 'The Distribution of Gains between Investing and Borrowing Countries', *American Economic Review*, vol. XL, no. 2, May. Paper delivered to the American Economic Association meeting in December 1949. Also published in Spanish as 'Comercio poco Desarrollados', *El Trimestre Económico*, Mexico, April–June 1950. Reprinted in *Growth Theory: Articles and Papers*, *Vol. II* (Washington: Economic Development Institute, International Bank for Reconstruction and Development, 1960) and in Singer, 1964a.

(c) 'International Approaches to Modernization Programmes'. Paper presented at the Round Table of 1949 Annual Conference of the Milbank Memorial Fund, 1949, published in the *Milbank Memorial Fund Quarterly*, vol. XXVII, no. 2, April 1950.

1952

(c) 'Capital Requirements for the Economic Development of the Middle East', *Middle Eastern Affairs*, February.

(d) 'India's Five-Year Plan – A Modest Proposal', *Far Eastern Survey*, June.
(e) 'The Mechanics of Economic Development: A Quantitative Model Approach', *Indian Economic Review*, vol. 1, no. 2, August and February 1952/1953. Also published in Agarwala and Singh, 1958, and in Singer, 1964a.

1953

(a) 'The Brazilian "Salte" Plan – A Historical Case Study of Government Borrowing for Economic Development', *Economic Development and Cultural Change*, February. (Reprinted in Spanish in *El Trimestre Económico*, Mexico, April–June 1953.)
(b) 'Obstacles to Economic Development', *Social Research*, vol. 20, no. 1, Spring. Also published in Singer, 1964a.
(c) 'The Theory of Federal Finance – A Comment', *The Economic Journal*, September.
(d) 'Problems of Industrialization of Under-Developed Countries'. Paper presented at the *Conference on Economic Progress of the International Economic Association*, Sta. Margherita Ligure, Italy, September.

1954

(c) 'Working Models of Economic Development, Economic and Financial', *Ekonomi Dan Keuangan Indonesia*, no. 4, April.
(d) 'Problems of Industrialization of Underdeveloped Countries', UNESCO *International Social Science Bulletin*, vol. VI, no. 2.

1957

'Terms of Trade – Barter vs. Factoral – and Gains from Trade', *Contribuicoes a Analise do Desenvolvimento Economico*, Rio de Janeiro.

1958

(b) 'Comment' on C. P. Kindleberger's 'The Terms of Trade and Economic Development', *Review of Economics and Statistics*, vol. XL, no. 1, part 2, Supplement, February.
(c) 'Distributed Dividends, Earnings Cover and the Price of Shares', *The Bankers Magazine*, no. 1370, May.
(d) 'Deficit Financing of Public Capital Formation with Special Reference to the Inflationary Process in Under-Developed Countries'. Paper presented to the study conference on economic development at the Institute of Social and Economic Research, University College of the West Indies, Jamaica, June 1957. Published in *Social and Economic Studies*, vol. 7, no. 3, September. Also published in Singer, 1964a.
(e) 'A Footnote to Professor Kuznets' Quantitative Aspects of the Economic Growth of Nations', *Economic Development and Cultural Change*, vol. VII, no. 1, October.
(f) 'Stabilization and Development of Primary Producing Countries', in *The Quest for a Stabilization Policy in Primary Countries, Kyklos*, vol. II, fasc. 2, and 'Introductory Statement' and 'Epilogue' to Symposium II, *Kyklos*, vol. XII, fasc. 3, 1959. Also published in Singer, 1964a.

1959

(b)   'Differential Population Growth as a Factor in International Economic Development', *The Economic Journal*, vol. LXIX, December.

(c)   'Stability and Progress in the World Economy', *Kyklos*, vol. XII, fasc. 2.

1961

(e)   'Problems of Small-Scale Industry'. Paper presented to the International Economic Association Regional Conference on *Economic Development in Africa South of the Sahara*, Addis Ababa, Ethiopia, July. Published in Singer, 1964a.

(f)   'Use and Abuse of Local Counterpart Funds', *International Development Review*, vol. 3, no. 3, October. Also published in Singer, 1964a.

(g)   'Demographic Factors in African Economic Development'. Paper presented at the conference on *Indigenous and Induced Elements in the Economics of Sub-Saharan Africa* held at Northwestern University, USA, November 1961. Published in Singer, 1964a.

(h)   'Trends in Economic Thought on Under-Development', *Social Research*, vol. 8, no. 4, Winter. Also published as 'Recent Trends in Economic Thought on Underdeveloped Countries' in Singer, 1964a, and in Spanish as 'Tendencias recientes del pensamiento economico sobre los paises sub-desarrolados', *Revista de economia latinoamericana*, vol. 1, no. 1, 1961.

1964

(k)   'Basic Problems before the Geneva Conference on Trade and Development'. Paper presented to New York University and published in the *Annual Review of United Nations Affairs, 1963–1964* (New York: New York University Press).

(l)   'International Aid for Economic Development – Problems and Tendencies'. Paper prepared for the meeting of the Society for International Development, Calcutta, India, November 1963. Subsequently published in *Revue de Science Financière*, Paris, 1964.

(m)   'The Seven Pillars of Development'. *Dean Hudson Memorial Lecture*, Long Island University, 21 April.

1965

(a)   'Social Development: Key Growth Sector', *International Development Review*, Society for International Development, vol. VII, no. 1, March.

(b)   'Comments' on H. M. A. Onitiri, 'Capital Movements, The Volume of Trade and the Terms of Trade'. Presented at the International Economic Association Round Table Conference on *Capital Movements and Economic Development*, Washington, D.C., 21–31 July.

(c)   'External Aid: For Plans of Projects', *The Economic Journal*, vol. LXXV, September, and 'Project *versus* Programme Aid: A Rejoinder', *The Economic Journal*, vol. LXXVII, December, 1967.

(d)   'Problems of Social Planning and Social Development', *Journal of Development Administration*, Khartoum, Sudan.

(e)   'Research Activities of the United Nations' (with Caroline Miles), *American Economic Association*, Annual Meeting.

(f)   'Overcoming Obstacles to Development: Midway in the Development Decade'. Statement at the Overseas Studies Committee Conference, Cambridge University.

1966

(c)   'The Notion of Human Investment', *Review of Social Economy*, vol. XXIV, no. 1, March. (See also 'El Concepto de Inversión Humana', published by Universidad del Valle.)

(d)   'Comments' on W. S. Vickrat, The *World Poverty Gap*. Presented at the Columbia University Priorities Conference, September 1966, and reprinted in *New University Thought*, special issue 66/67, vol. 5, nos 1 and 2, Detroit, USA, 1967.

1967

(d)   'Pre-Conditions for Regional Economic Integration', *International Development Review*, September.

(e)   'Over-All Development Planning and Policies', *African Institute for Economic Development and Planning*, Dakar, Senegal, 20 October.

1968

(a)   'International Aid. Targets, Commitments and Realities', *Inter Economics*, no. 2, Monthly Review of International Trade and Development, February.

(b)   'Sir John Hicks on Growth and Anti-Growth', *Oxford Economic Papers*, vol. 20, no. 1.

(c)   'Kritische Bemerkungen zur Festlegung der Ein-Prozent Klausel' ('Critical Remarks on the Determination of the 1 per cent Aid Target'), *Wirthschaftsdienst*, July.

(d)   'Debate on the Next Development Decade', FAO *Ceres*, vol. 1, no. 4, July–August.

1969

(d)   'Technical Assistance to Kenya: Some Thoughts on Flows and Programming' (with A.C. Doss), *East African Economic Review*, June. Also in *IDS Communcations*, No. 55, 1969.

(e)   'Dualism Revisited: A New Approach to the Problems of the Dual Society in Developing Countries', *Journal of Development Studies*, vol. 7, no. 1, October. Also in *IDS Communications*, No. 41, 1969. Originally prepared for a *Conference on the Dual Economy* held in Glasgow, Scotland, September 1969.

(f)   'Keynesian Models of Economic Development and their Limitations: An Analysis in the Light of Gunnar Myrdal's Asian Drama'. UN Asian Institute for Economic Development and Planning, *Occasional Papers*, December. Also in *IDS Communications*, No. 54, 1969.

(g)   'That One Percent Target', *IDS Bulletin*, vol. 2, no. 2 , December.

(h)   'Employment Problems in Developing Countries'. Paper prepared for the ILO *Human Resources Conference*, Philadelphia, USA, May 1969. Reproduced in condensed form in Cairncross and Puri, 1975.

1970

(c)   'Science and Technology', *Venture*, special issue on development, January.

(d)   'Social Implications of Aid Programs. A Contribution to Technical Assistance and Development', *Proceedings of the Truman International Conference on Technical Assistance and Development*, May. Also published by The Hebrew University of Jerusalem, Israel, 1971.

(e)   'A World Employment Programme', *Rural Life*, third quarter.

(f)   'The Foreign Company as an Exporter of Technology', *IDS Bulletin*, vol. 3 no.1, October. Also published in Spanish in *Comercio de Tecnologia y Subdesarrollo Economico*, Coordinacion de Ciencias, Mexico, 1973.

(g)   'Multinational Corporations and Technology Transfer: Some Problems and Suggestions'. Paper presented to the OECD *Conference on the Transfer of Technology*, Istanbul, Turkey, 1970. Reproduced in Cairncross and Puri, 1975.

1971

(h)   'Primary Products, Exports and Growth: The Case of Thailand', *Journal of Developing Areas*, April.

(i)   'A New Approach to the Problems of the Dual Society in Developing Countries', *UN International Social Development Review*, No. 3.

(j)   'Development Revisited' (which questions Eugene Black's 'contract approach' to development), *International Development Review*, vol. XIII, no. 3.

(k)   'Rural Unemployment as a Background to Rural/Urban Migration in Africa'. Paper presented at the *Research Conference on Urban Unemployment in Africa*, Institute of Development Studies, September. Published in special issue of *Manpower and Unemployment Research in Africa. A Newsletter*, vol. 6, no. 2, Center for Developing-Area Studies, McGill University, Montreal, Quebec, Canada in co-operation with the Institute of Development Studies, University of Sussex, November 1973.

(l)   'Unemployment in Developing Countries', *Pax et Libertas*, vol. 36, no. 4, October–December.

(m)   'The Distribution of Gains Revisited'. Paper presented to the first PAS Conference at the Institute of Development Studies, May. Reproduced in Cairncross and Puri, 1975.

1972

(h)   'The Technology Gap and the Developing Countries', *International Journal of Environmental Studies*, vol 3.

(i)   'The Riderless Horse' (article on employment and growth), *The Internationalist*, no. 7, November.

1973

(j)   'Unemployment in an African Setting: Lessons of the Employment Mission to Kenya' (with Richard Jolly), *International Labour Review*, vol. 107, no. 2, February. Also in Ndegwa and Powelson, 1973.

(k)   'The Development Outlook for Poor Countries: Technology is the Key', *Challenge*, New York, May/June. Also published in German in *Evangelische Kommentare*, no. 11, Stuttgart, November.

(l)   'The Outlook for the Poor World', *New Internationalist*, no. 5, July.

(m)   'The Commodity Boom and Developing Countries', *New Society*, vol. 25, no. 569, 30 August. Also published in German in *Evangelische Kommentare*, no. 3, Stuttgart, March.

(n)   'Trade Liberalization, Employment and Income Distribution: A First Approach' (with Richard Blackburn, Frank Ellis, Peter Hadji-Ristic, Angus Hone, Percy Selwyn, Nick Stamp, Richard Stanton and Ann Zammit), *IDS Discussion Paper*, no. 31, October.

(o)   'Cost–Benefit Analysis and the Allocation of Resources to Crime Prevention' (with David Kaplan), *IDS Mimeograph*, 1973.

1974

(b)   'Transfer of Technology in LDCs', *Inter Economics*, no. 1, Verlag Weltarchiv, Hamburg, January.

(c)   'A Mirror and a Chimera', *New Society*, vol. 27, no. 597, 14 March.

(d)   'Transfer of Technology and its Impact on Development'. Paper presented at the *Conference on Investment in Developing Countries*, organized by the Danish Industrialization Fund for Developing Countries, Hornbaek, Denmark, April.

(e)   'Global Oil Crisis will be Life or Death for the "NOPEC" Countries', *Third World*, vol. 3, no. 7, April/May.

(f)   'Aid and Donor Countries' GNP' (with Mohinder Puri), *Inter Economics*, no. 7, Verlag Weltarchiv, Hamburg, July.

(g)   'O Fracasso das Receitas do Desenvolvimento', *Novas, Utopias*, Sao Paulo, Brazil, 8 September.

(h)   'Auf dem Weg in eine Welt des Hungers – Krisenhafte Entwicklungen in der Nahrungsmittelversorgung' (German translation of 'The World Food Crisis – Part of an Interlocking Series of World Problems'), *Evangelisch Kommentare*, no. 10, Stuttgart, October.

(i)   'A Note on the Implications of the Oil Price Increases for British Aid Policy', *IDS Bulletin* (Special issue on 'Oil and Development'), vol. 6, no. 2, October.

(j)   'Labour Turnover and Employment, Some Evidence from Kenya' (with S. B. L. Nigam), *International Labour Review*, vol. 110, no. 6, December.

(k)   'La Strategia per lo Sviluppo Tecnologico e il Piano Mondiale di Azione delle N.U.' (Italian translation of 'The Strategy for Development Technology and the Least-Developed Regions of the United Nations'), *Scienza & Tecnica 74 – Annuario della EST (Enciclopedia della Scienza e della Tecnica)*, Mondadori, Milan, 1974.

(l)   'Resources and Employment', *The Economic Times Annual, 1974*, published by the *Economic Times of India*, New Delhi, India.

1975

(d)   'Postscript' to the UN World Food Conference, Rome, November 1974, *People*, vol. 2, no. 1.

(e)   'Trade Expansion, Employment and Income Distribution', *IDS Bulletin* (Special Issue on 'International Research'), vol. 6, no. 4, March.

(f)   'Für Exporte braucht man zwei – Mehr Nahrungsmittel durch Ausweitung des Handels' ('You Need Two for Exporting – More Food through Expanded Trade'), *Evangelische Kommentare*, no. 4, Stuttgart, April.

(g)   'Statistics on Particular Problem Areas – Poverty, Inequality and Income Distribution' (with George Blazyca), *IDS Communication 114* on 'Statistical Policy in Less Developed Countries'. Based on discussions at the conference on *Statistical Policy in Less Developed Countries* held at the Institute of Development Studies, May.

(h) 'Towards a Rational and Equitable New International Economic Order: A Case for Negotiated Structural Changes' (with R. H. Green), *World Development*, vol. 3, no. 6, June.

(i) 'The Distribution of Gains from Trade and Investment – Revisited', *Journal of Development Studies*, vol. 11, no. 4, July.

(j) 'Im Interesse beider Seiten. Vorstoss für eine neue Rohstoffpolitik' ('In the Mutual Interest: Initiative towards a new Raw Materials Policy'), *Evangelische Kommentare*, no. 7, July.

(k) 'Developed Country Initiatives for Forthcoming International Economic Conferences, 1975/76' (with R. H. Green and R. H. Stanton). Report of a conference at the Institute of Development Studies, 25–26 July.

(l) 'Technological Backwardness and Productivity Growth' (with Lyn Reynolds), *The Economic Journal*, vol. 85, no. 340, December.

(m) 'Food Aid: Disincentive Effects and their Policy Implications' (with Paul J. Isenman), *IDS Communication*, No. 116, December 1975. Also published as *A.I.D. Discussion Paper*, No. 31, 1975, by the US Agency for International Development, Washington, D.C., and in *Economic Development and Cultural Change*, vol. 25, no. 2, January 1977. Reprinted in, V. W. Ruttan (ed.), *Why Food Aid?* (Baltimore, MA, and London: The Johns Hopkins University Press, 1993).

1976

(d) 'Five Wasted Years', *SID Focus: Technical Cooperation*, IDR/1976/1, Society for International Development.

(e) 'Beyond Commodity Policy: Structural Changes and Financial Compensation', *IDS Bulletin* (Special issue on UNCTAD IV, Nairobi, May 1976), vol. 7, no. 4. Also published in German in *Evangelische Kommentare*, No. 5, May 1976.

(f) 'An Elusive Concept' (Article on Financial Transfers), FAO *Ceres* (Special issue on 'Development'), vol. 9, no. 4, July–August.

(g) 'Die Zukunft des Entwicklungsprogramms der Vereinten Nationen' ('The Future of the UNDP'), *Vereinte Nationen*, 5/76, Bonn, October.

(h) 'Hilfe oder Umverteilung. Enttauschende Ergebnisse der UNCTAD IV' ('Aid or Redistribution. Disappointing Results from UNCTAD IV'), *Evangelische Kommentare*, vol. 9, no. 10, October.

1977

(c) 'Food Aid: Its Potential Disincentives to Agriculture' (with Paul J. Isenman), *Development Digest*, vol. XV, no. 2, April.

(d) 'Transformation Assistance from Developed Countries to Developing Countries. An Aid to Trade Expansion' (in collaboration with S. Joekes and D. Kaplan), *The Korean Economic Journal*, vol. XVI, no. 2, June. Also published in *IDS Discussion Paper*, No. 110, May 1977.

(e) 'New Trends in Development Strategies', in *Report on the Ninth Course: Household Statistics (1 March–24 June 1977)*, Munich Centre for Advanced Training in Applied Statistics for Developing Countries.

(f)   'Reflections of Sociological Aspects of Economic Growth based on the Work of Bert Hoselitz', *Economic Development and Cultural Change*, vol. 25, supplement 977 (in honour of Bert Hoselitz).

(g)   'Appropriate Technology for a Basic Human Needs Strategy', *International Development Review*, vol. XIX, no. 2.

(h)   'Nothing is Simple' (Article on terms of trade), FAO *Ceres* (Special issue on 'Agriculture and Development'), vol. 10, no. 6, November–December.

(i)   'Poverty, Income Distribution and Levels of Living: Twenty-Five Years of Changes in Thinking about Development', *The Seoul National University Economic Review*, vol. XI, no. 1, December. (Special issue on the 30th Anniversary of Seoul National University.)

(j)   'Reflections on the Lima (25%) Target'. Paper presented at the Institute of Social Studies 25th Anniversary Conference, The Hague, The Netherlands, 16–20 December.

1978

(f)   'Technologie. Die Notwendigkeit technologischer Alternativen für die Dritte Welt' ('Technology – the Need for Technological Alternatives for the Third World') (with Walter Eigel), *Internationale Entwicklung*, 1978/IV, Vienna: OFSE.

(g)   'The Common Fund Debate. Where Do We Stand Now?', *The Round Table* (The Commonwealth Journal of International Affairs), issue 271, July. Also published in *Asian Journal*, (Journal of the Research Institute of Asian Economies, Seoul, Korea), no. 26, September, 1978.

(h)   'The New International Economic Order: An Overview' (revised version of a lecture presented to the 12th Seanza Central Banking Course, The Bank of Korea, Seoul, September 1978), *The Journal of Modern African Studies*, vol. 16, no. 4.

(i)   'Development Prospects of NICs in a Changing World', *KIEI Seminar Series*, No. 17, Korea International Economic Institute, Seoul, September.

1979

(e)   'The Crisis of Transition: A Brief Rejoinder to J. Friedmann's "The Crisis of Transition: A Critique of Strategies of Crisis Management"', *Development and Change*, vol. 10, no. 1, January.

(f)   'Food Aid to Developing Countries: A Survey' (with S. J. Maxwell), *World Development*, vol. 7, no. 3, March.

(g)   'The Role of Newly Industrialising (Middle-Income) Countries in the World Economy'. Paper presented to the International Symposium on *New Directions of Asia's Development Strategies*, Institute of Developing Economies, Tokyo, 13–16 March.

(h)   'Transfer of Technology – A One-Way Street', *Internationale Entwicklung*, 1979/III, Vienna: OFSE.

(i)   'The Price-Disincentive Effect of Food Aid Revisited: A Reply' (with Paul Isenman), *Economic Development and Cultural Changes*, vol. 27, no. 3, April.

(j)   'The Basic Needs Approach to Development Planning'. Paper prepared for the seminar on *Setting and Implementing of Statistical Priorities* held at the Munich Centre for Advanced Training, 6–25 August.

(k) 'A Generation Later: Kurt Mandelbaum's The Industrialisation of Backward Areas Revisited', *Development and Change* (a special issue entitled 'Plus ça change ... Essays in honour of Kurt Martin'), vol. 10, no. 4, October.

(l) 'Has the Korean Model a Future in a Changing World?', *KIEI Seminar Series*, No. 30, Korea International Economic Institute, Seoul, November.

1980

(h) 'The Care for Social Welfare Policy in Korea', *Asian Economies*, no. 32, Research Institute of Asian Economies, Seoul, March.

(i) 'Put the People First – World Development Report 1980', *The Economist*, August.

(j) 'The Brandt Report: A "Northwestern" Point of View', *Third World Quarterly*, vol. II, no. 4, October.

(k) 'Trade Access and Employment in Developing Countries: A Survey' (with Javed Ansari), *Canadian Journal of Development Studies*, vol. II, no. 2.

(l) 'Comments on Graham Bird's Strategy for World Economic Development', *Journal of International Studies*, Millennium vol. 9, no. 3, Winter.

1981

(f) 'Overview of Discussion and Conclusions', *Critical Issues in Development in the 80s*, Liaison Bulletin, OECD, Paris.

(g) 'The British Government and the Brandt Report', *IDS Bulletin*, vol. 12, no. 2, May.

(h) 'International Food Problems', *The Times North/South Supplement*, 2 October.

(i) 'Policies and Programs for Young Human Resource Development in Korea, 1982–86'. Published in *Child Development Policies in Korea: An Approach to Young Human Resource Development in the 1980s* (Seoul: Korea Development Institute).

(j) 'The New International Economic Order', *Economics*, The Quarterly Journal of the Economics Association, vol. XVII, part 4, no. 76, Winter.

1982

(d) 'Is There A Poverty Trap for Developing Countries? Polarisation: Reality or Myth?' (with R.A. Mahmood), *World Development*, vol. 10, no. 1.

(e) 'The Political Economy of Foreign Aid', *Lloyds Bank Review*, no. 143, January.

(f) 'North-South and South-South: The North and Intra-Third World Co-operation', *Development and Peace*, vol. 3, Spring 1982. Published by the Hungarian Peace Council and the World Peace Council, Budapest.

1983

(e) *Brandt: Mutual and Conflicting Interests in Relations with the Third World*. Third Biennial Adam Weiler Memorial Lecture, Sussex University, England, 1982. Published as *IDS Discussion Paper* No. 185, January.

(f) 'Food as Aid, Food for Thought' (with Edward Clay (eds)), *IDS Bulletin*, vol. 14, no. 2, April.

(g) 'The Role of Human Capital in Development', *Pakistan Journal of Applied Economics*, vol. 2, no. 1, Summer.

(h) 'The Ethics of Aid', *Asian Journal of Economics*, vol. 2, no. 3. Also published in *IDS Discussion Paper* No. 195, October.

(i)   'North–South Multipliers', *World Development*, vol. 11, no. 5.
(j)   'Il Secondo Rapporto Brandt. Una sola strategia per una crisicommune' ('The Second Brandt Report: a single strategy for a common crisis'), *Cooperazione* (Journal of the Italian Ministry of Foreign Affairs – Department for Development Co-operation), vol. 8, no. 34, Anno VIII, October. Also as 'The Second Brandt Report: "A Common Crisis"', *The Nonaligned World*, vol. II, no. 3, July–September 1984.

1984

(i)   'Sub-Saharan Africa in Depression: The Impact on the Welfare of Children' (with R. H. Green), *World Development*, vol. 12, no. 3, March.
(j)   'Relevance of Keynes for Developing Countries', *Estudos de Economia*, vol. IV, no. 4, July-September.
(k)   'Ideas and Policy: The Sources of UNCTAD', *IDS Bulletin*, vol. 15, no. 3, July. Special Issue entitled 'UNCTAD: The First Twenty Years'.
(l)   'Success Stories of the 1970s: Some Correlations', *World Development*, vol. 12, no. 9.
(m)   'The Concept of Development and the Ethics of Aid' (with Albert Lauterbach), Vienna Institute for Development, *Occasional Paper 84/4*.
(n)   'Modelos de Industrializacao' ('Models of Industrialization'), *Revista Critica de Ciencias Sociais*, no. 14, November.
(o)   'Aid: Time to Rationalize' (with John Wood), *Compass News Features*, 16 November.

1985

(d)   'The African Food Crisis and the Role of the African Development Bank', *Proceedings of a Symposium held in Tunis, Tunisia on 10 May 1984* (Abidjan, Cote D'Ivoire: African Development Bank).
(e)   'Una Via Complementare Al Dialogo Con Il Nord' ('Complementary Route to the North–South Dialogue'), (translated into Italian by Sergio Minucci), *Politica Internazionale*, 1985. (This volume was prepared for the 2nd National Conference on Development Co-operation organised in Rome by the Development Co-operation Department of the Italian Ministry of Foreign Affairs, 11–14 June 1985.)
(f)   'Some Problems of Emergency Food Aid for Sub-Saharan Africa' in 'Sub-Saharan Africa: Getting the Facts Straight', *IDS Bulletin*, vol. 16, no. 3, July.
(g)   'Der Beitrag zu Wirtschaftlicher Zusammenarbeit und Entwicklung' (40 years of the United Nations: Contribution to Economic Co-operation and Development), *Vereinte Nationen*, October.
(h)   'Hans Singer at 75: IDS at 20', *IDS Annual Report*, 1985.

1986

(g)   'The Roots of Industrialisation Strategy in India: 1949–56' (with S. Bhadwan Dahiya), *Asian Journal of Economics and Social Studies*, vol. 5, no. 2, April.
(h)   'Some Reflections on Past Interests and Activities', *IDS Discussion Paper* No. 217, June.
(i)   'South–South Trade Revisited in a Darkening External Environment', *Development and South–South Cooperation*, vol. II, no. 2, June. Published by

the Research Centre for Co-operation with Developing Countries, Ljubljana, Yugoslavia.

(j)   'Yuvarlack Masa: Kalkinma Iktisadi: Yasiyor Mu?' ('Future Development: Where Do We Go?') (with Paul Streeten), *Iktisat Dergisi*, 1986.

(k)   'Famines and Food Mountains', *Compass*, Special Issue on 'Perspective 87: Famines and Food Mountains', Compass News Features, 17 December.

(l)   'Import Substitution Revisited in a Darkening External Environment' (with Parvin Alizadeh), *Asian Journal of Economics and Social Studies*, vol. 5, no. 3. Also 'Strategija Supstitucike Izvoza u Sve Tezim Uvjetima' ('Import Substitution Revisited in a Darkening External Environment') (with Parvin Alizadeh),*Razvoj/Development*, vol. IV, no. 1, January–March 1987. With a Summary in English.

(m) 'Rául Prebisch and his Advocacy of Import Substitution', *Development and South–South Cooperation*, vol. 2, no. 3, December.

1987

(h)   'Food Aid: Development Tool or Obstacle to Development?', *Development Policy Review*, vol. 5, no. 4, December. Also in *Irish Studies in International Affairs*, vol. 2, no. 3, 1987.

1988

(e)   'The World Development Report 1987 on the Blessings of "Outwards Orientation": A Necessary Correction', *The Journal of Development Studies*, vol. 24, no. 2, January.

(f)   'Objectives, Strategies and Techniques: Forty Years of Changing Thought on Development Planning' (with S. Bhagwan Dahiya), *The Indian Journal of Economics*, vol. LXVIII, part III, no. 270, January.

(g)   'Food Policy, Food Aid and Economic Adjustment' (guest editor with John Shaw), Special Issue of *Food Policy*, vol. 13, no. 1, February. See 'Introduction' (with John Shaw).

(h)   'New Voices in Defence of Aid', *Development Policy Review*, vol. 6, no. 1, March.

(i)   'Trade Policy and Growth of Developing Countries: Some New Data' (with Patricia Gray), *World Development*, vol. 16, no. 3.

(j)   'Development Crisis of the North', *Mainstream*, 30 April, New Delhi. Paper presented at the Conference on *Poverty, Development and Collective Survival: Public and Private Responsibilities*, 19th World Conference of the Society for International Development (SID), New Delhi, 25–28 March. Also published in *Development*, 2/3.

(k)   'Industrial Development in Africa: What are the Options?', *Razvoj/Development-International*, vol. III, nos 1–2.

(l)   'Industrialization and World Trade: Ten Years after the Brandt Report', in 'The World Ten Years After the Brandt Report', *Vienna Institute for Development and Co-operation Report Series*, No. 2/88. Also published in *IDS Discussion Paper* no. 264, August 1989.

(m) 'Debt Pressure and the Transfer Burden of the Third World Countries, 1980–86' (with P. Sarkar), *Asian Journal of Economics and Social Studies*, vol. 7, no. 4.

(n)   'A Pioneer's Response to Food Aid Critics', FAO *Ceres*, vol. 123.

(o)   'Food Aid: Pros and Cons', *Intereconomics*, vol. 23.

1989

(e)   'When Pursuit of Surplus Ends', *India International Centre Quarterly*, Spring.

(f)   'The Relationship between Debt Pressures, Adjustment Policies and Deterioration of Terms of Trade for Developing Countries (with Special Reference to Latin America)', *Institute of Social Studies Working Papers*, The Hague, The Netherlands, July. Also published in Shaw, 2001c.

(g)   'The African Food Crisis and the Role of Food Aid', *Food Policy*, vol. 14, no. 3, August.

(h)   'A More Human Way Forward', *The Southern African Economist*, October/November.

(i)   'Manufactured Exports and Terms of Trade Movements of Less Developed Countries in Recent Years (1980–87)' (with Prabirjit Sarkar), *IDS Discussion Paper* No. 270, November.

(j)   'Pomoc un Hrani i Dugovi' ('Food Aid and Debt', in Croatian), in *Privredni Razvoj in Medunarodni Dugovi* (World Development and International Debt), published for Yugoslav Academy by the Economic Faculty, Zagreb University, Zagreb.

(k)   'The World Bank: Human Face or Facelift? Some Comments in the Light of the World Bank's Annual Report', *World Development*, vol. 17, no. 8.

(l)   'Response to James Ingram's Paper: "Sustain Refugees' Human Dignity"', *Journal of Refugee Studies*, vol. 2, no. 3.

(m)   'The Debt Issue – A Historical Perspective', *Oeconomic*, Erasmus University, Rotterdam, The Netherlands. Also in Shaw, 2001c.

1990

(h)   '"Reading between the Lines". Comment on World Bank Annual Report 1989', *Development Policy Review*, vol. 8, no. 2, June.

(i)   'The 1980s: A Lost Decade – Development in Reverse?', *Global Economic Policy*, vol. 2, no. 2, Fall.

(j)   'Third World Debt Burden Unchanged', FAO *Ceres*, vol. 22, no. 2, November-December.

1991

(k)   'Manufactured Exports of Developing Countries and Their Terms of Trade Since 1965' (with Prabirjit Sarkar), *World Development*, vol. 19, no. 4.

(l)   'Beyond the Debt Crisis', *Journal für Entwicklungspolitik*, VII JG–3/1991. Also in *Development*, 1992 and in Shaw, 2001c.

(m)   'Die aktuellen GATT-Verhandlungen im Lichte der Verschuldung der Dritten Welt und der Welthandelspolitik' ('The current GATT negotiations in the light of Third World debts and global trade policies'), in *GATT und die Dritte Welt*, Renner Institut, 13, 28 June.

(n)   'Terms of Trade: New Wine and New Bottles?', *Development Policy Review*, vol. 9, no. 4, December.

1992

(g)   'Debt Crisis, Commodity Prices, Transfer Burden and Debt Relief' (with Prabirjit Sarkar), *IDS Discussion Paper* No. 297. February.

(h)   'United Nations: Changes in Store', *Spur* (Newspaper of the World Development Movement), May/June.

(i)   'The Influence of Trends in Barter Terms of Trade and of Their Volatility on GNP Growth' (with Jerker Edström), *IDS Discussion Paper* No. 312, November.
(j)   'The Influence of Schumpeter and Keynes. On the Development of a Development Economist', *Discussion Paper* No. 68, Institut für Volkswirtschaftslehre, Universität Hohenheim.
(k)   'The Prebisch–Singer Terms of Trade Controversy Revisited' (with David Sapsford and Prabirjit Sarkar), *Journal of International Development*, vol. 4, no. 3.

1993

(g)   'International Governance – Intentions and Realities', *Development and International Cooperation*, vol. IX, no. 16, June, Centre for International Cooperation and Development, Ljubljana.
(h)   'Food Aid – An Historical Perspective', *World Food Programme Journal*, 30th Anniversary Edition, no. 25, July-September, Rome. Reprinted as 'New Orientations in Food Aid', in *Culture and Agriculture: Orientation Texts on the 1995 theme* (Paris: United Nations Educational, Scientific and Cultural Organization, 1995).
(i)   'Manufacture-Manufacture Terms of Trade Deterioration: A Reply' (with Prabirjit Sarkar), *World Development*, vol. 21, no. 10.
(j)   'The Bretton Woods System: Historical Perspectives', *Third World Economics*, no. 71, August. See also M. ul-Haq *et al.*, 1993 and Shaw, 2001c.
(k)   'Alternative Approaches to Adjustment and Stabilization', *Third World Economics*, no. 72, September. Also in Shaw, 2001c.
(l)   'Is a Genuine Partnership Possible in Western Hemisphere Free Trade Area? Some General Comments', *Development and International Cooperation*, vol. IX, no. 17, December. Centre for International Cooperation and Development, Ljubljana.

1994

(j)   'Développement: "Nous Souffrons d'un Fétichisme Financier"'. ('Development: we suffer from financial fetishism'). Interview by Jean-Marc Fontaine in *Alternatives Economiques*, no. 114, Paris/Dijon, France, February.
(k)   'La Création de la CNUCED et L'Evolution de la Pensée Contemporaine sur le Développement' ('The Creation of UNCTAD and the evolution of current development thinking'), *Revue Tiers-Monde*, tome XXXV, no. 139, Juillet–Septembre 1994.
(l)   'Ein Dollar, eine Stimme – Weltbank und Weltwährungsfonds als Teil des UN-Systems' ('One dollar, one vote – the World Bank and IMF as part of the UN system'), *Der Überblick*, 3/94, September. Also published as 'Bretton Woods and the UN System' in *Ecumenical Review,* vol. 47 no. 3, July, 1995, World Council of Churches.
(m)   'The "Golden Age" of the Tinbergen Consensus on Planning – Tinbergen's Contribution to the United Nations', *Internationale Samenwerking* (Journal of the Development Cooperation Information Department of the Dutch Ministry of Foreign Affairs), November.
(n)   'Tinbergen and International Policy Making', in P. Erthal and T. R. van Steveninck (eds), *Out of the Darkness Light!* Proceedings of the Memorial Symposium for Jan Tinbergen, 17 December 1994, Erasmus University, Rotterdam, The Netherlands.

(o)   'Aid Conditionality', *IDS Discussion Paper* No. 346, December. Also published in *ADMP Series Bulletins* No. 14, Advanced Development Management Programme, Sophia University Tokyo.

(p)   'Was Heist Schon Erfolgreich?' ('What Does Successful Mean?'), *Südwind Das Entwicklungspolitische Magazin Osterreichs*, nr. 7–8/94–Die Zeitschrift des Osterreichischen Informationsdienstes für Entwicklungspolitik, Wien.

(q)   'The Link Between Increased Trade Openness and the Terms of Trade: An Empirical Investigation' (with Matthias Lutz), *World Development*, vol. 22, no. 11, 1994.

1995

(f)   'Probleme und Zukunft der Ernährungshilfe in der Post-GATT-Ara' ('Problems and Future of Food Aid in the Post-GATT-ERA'), *Bruno Kreisky Dialogue Series* 10, Vienna.

(g)   'Austin Robinson and Keynes: Two Forecasts', *Cambridge Journal of Economics*, vol. 19.

(h)   'Bretton Woods and the UN System', *The Ecumenical Review*, vol. 47, no. 3, July.

(i)   'Fifty Years On: The UN and Economic and Social Development: An Overview' (with Richard Jolly), and 'Revitalizing the United Nations: Five Proposals', in 'Fifty Years On: The UN and Economic and Social Development', *IDS Bulletin*, vol. 26, no. 4, October. Also in *A Felicitation Volume of Reminiscences and Writings from Authors World Wide in honour of Prof. C Suriyakumaran*, 'By a Distinguished Group of Authors Worldwide', in association with KVG de Silva & Sons, Colombo, 1995, and in Shaw, 2001c.

(j)   'Propuesta para Una Moneda de Reserva Basada en Materias Primas' ('Proposal for a Reserve Currency based on primary commodities'), *Pensamiento Iberoamerican: Revista de Economica Politica*, vol. 27. Special Issue on 'El Sistema Financiero Globalización e Inestabilidad'.

(k)   'Are the Structural Adjustment Programmes Successful?', *Pakistan Journal of Applied Economics* vol XI, nos 1 and 2, and in Shaw, 2001c.

(l)   'A Future Food Aid Regime: Implications of the Final Act of the GATT Uruguay Round' (with John Shaw), *IDS Discussion Paper* No. 352, September. Different versions of this paper published in *Food Policy*, Special Issues on 'The Uruguay Round Agreement on Trade and Developing Countries', vol. 21, no. 4, August 1996; and in H. O'Neil and J. Toye (eds), *A World Without Famine? – New Approaches to Aid Development* (Basingstoke and London: Macmillan for the Development Studies Association, Basingstoke, 1998).

(m)   'Half a Century of Economic and Social Development Policies of the UN and Bretton Woods Institutions' (The Iqbal Memorial Lecture), in *The Pakistan Development Review*, vol. 34, no. 4, part 1, Winter. Papers and Proceedings (Part 1) of the Eleventh Annual General Meeting of the Pakistan Society of Development Economists.

1996

(e)   'The Future of Food Trade and Food Aid in a Liberalizing Global Economy', in E. Messer and P. Uvin (eds), *The Hunger Report: 1995* (Australia: Gordon and Breach Publishers, on behalf of Alan Shawn Feinstein World Hunger Program, Brown University, RI., USA).

(f)   'Linking Relief and Development', *ADMP Series Bulletin* No. 19, Advanced Development Management Programme, Sophia University, Tokyo.

(g)   'Heinz Arndt: Historian of Ideas', *Journal of Asian Economics*, vol. 7, no. 1.

(h)   'A Global View of Food Security'. Paper presented at the *International Symposium on Food Security and Innovations: Successes and Lessons Learned*, March 1996, University of Hohenheim. Also in *Curso de Mestrado em 'Desenvolvimento e Cooperacao Internacional'* 21, Instituto Superor de Economia e Gestao (UTL), 1995–1996, and in an abridged form in *entwicklung + ländlicher raum: beiträge zur internationalen zusammenarbeit*, 30. Jahrgang Heft 5/96.

(i)   'Kurt Martin/Mandelbaum: An appreciation', *DSA forum*, no. 51, April.

(j)   'Beyond Bretton Woods – a New Framework for International Co-operation', in *Politik und Gesellschaft*, 2/1996, Friedrich-Ebert-Stiftung, Bonn.

(k)   'Modern Relevance of Keynesianism in the Study of Development', in *Curso de Mestrado em 'Desenvolvimento e Cooperaçao Internacional'* no 21, Instituto Superior de Economia e Gestao (UTL), 1995–1996.

(l)   'The United Nations and Bretton Woods Institutions', in *Occasional Papers* No 13, *Current Issues in the Social Sciences and Humanities*, The London Office of Hosei University.

1997

(b)   'International Income Distribution and World Governance', in J. Berkouwer and K. Meylink (eds), *Rechtvaardige verdeling* (Equitable distribution) (Hodgeschool, The Netherlands: Barjesteh, Meeuwes and Co).

(c)   'The Influence of Schumpeter and Keynes. On the Development of a Development Economist', in H. Hagemann (ed.), *Zur deutschsprachigen wirtschaftswissenschaflichen Emigration nach 1933*, (Marburg: Hohenheim University, Metropolis Verlag fur Okonomie, Gesellschaft und Politik).

(d)   'Editorial: The Golden Age of Keynesian Consensus – The Pendulum Swings Back', *World Development*, vol.25, no.3.

(e)   'A Former Student's Recollections of Keynes', *Cambridge Review*, vol 118, no. 2329, May. Based on an after-dinner speech at King's College, Cambridge following a conference on October 1996 to commemorate the 50th anniversary of the death of Keynes.

(f)   'A Global View of Food Security', *Agriculture and Rural Development*, vol. 4, no. 2, Technical Centre for Agricultural and Rural Co-operation, Frankfurt, Germany.

1998

(f)   'The Terms of Trade 50 years On – Convergence and Divergence', *South Letter*, vol. 1. South Centre, Geneva, Switzerland. Also in *Zagreb International Review of Economics and Business* , vol.1, no. 1, and in *Journal of International Development*, vol. II, no. 6, 1999.

(g)   'The IMF, The World Bank, and Commodity Prices: A Case of Shifting Sands?' (with David Sapsford), *World Development*, vol. 26, no. 9.

1999

(g) 'A Tribute to Professor Amartya Sen on the Occasion of his Receiving the 1998 Nobel Prize for Economics' (with Stephen Devereux), *Food Policy*, vol. 24.

(h) 'The Origins of the Bretton Woods System: Lessons for the Future', *Current Issues in the Social Sciences and Humanities – Occasional Papers* No. 16, London Office of Hosei University (ed.), International Center of Hosei University, Japan.

Index